MEN OF LAW

IRAN: LOUVRE MUSEUM

RELIEF AT THE TOP OF THE CODE OF HAMMURABI SHOWING THE GREAT
KING OF BABYLON RECEIVING FROM THE SUN-GOD SHAMASH, THE COM-
MAND TO ESTABLISH JUST AND RIGHTEOUS LAWS.

MEN OF LAW

FROM
HAMMURABI TO HOLMES

BY WILLIAM SEAGLE

(Facsimile of the 1947 edition)

HAFNER PUBLISHING COMPANY
New York
1971

Published by
HAFNER PUBLISHING COMPANY, INC.
866 Third Avenue
New York, N.Y. 10022

Library of Congress Catalog Card Number: 78-159979

Printed in U.S.A. by
NOBLE OFFSET PRINTERS, INC.
NEW YORK 3, N. Y.

TO

THE MEMORY OF MY FRIEND

Joseph N. Ulman

A NOTABLE AMERICAN JUDGE

AND

A CHAMPION OF AN ENLIGHTENED PENOLOGY

Contents

Introduction

A SHORT HISTORY OF UG

A HUMBLE FIGURE HAS PLAYED A GREAT ROLE IN THE HISTORY of the law. English and American lawyers call him John Doe. They invoke his name whenever they are unable to think of any other. When they are unable to discover the true name of a person whom they wish to sue, they issue the summons in the name of "John Doe." When professors of law are lecturing classes of law students, they take John Doe as an example in stating their problems. John Doe is the unknown and unsung hero of legal science. There have been many great names in the annals of legal biography from Hammurabi to Holmes. But the greatest name in the history of the law has been John Doe.

Of course, John Doe did not go by the same name in all civilizations. The ancient Roman jurisconsults called him Titius. But he was always the first creative spirit of the law. Ug is as fitting a name as any other for the unknown legal hero of preliterate and archaic societies. He was conceiving many fertile legal ideas long before legal history began to be recorded.

Indeed, he had developed the few basic legal institutions long before the dawn of legal history. The great men of law whose names we celebrate today only gave new directions to these institutions. Ug dominated the pre-legal age. He devised the first methods of appeasing the injured and avoiding bloodshed. He first thought of establishing the court— the overshadowing reality of all legal systems. He even cultivated that mysterious sentiment of the rightfulness of authority which we call the state, but which perhaps was only another name for the law itself.

In laying the first foundations of the legal order, Ug certainly was not interested in refining endlessly the absorbing distinction between *meum* and *tuum*, or in drafting more and more ingenious forms of legal transactions. The law to him was not a matter of deeds and

1

mortgages, bills of sale and powers of attorney, nor was he fascinated by corporations and partnerships. He did not care for precise and complex forms of legal procedure to make it difficult to conduct a lawsuit. For him the purpose of the law was not even to be found in courts and lawyers, who, indeed, for endless centuries did not even exist. Ug was his own lawyer, and what he was after was very simple and urgent. In fact, it was precisely the same boon that we hope to attain in developing the vast and complex legal machinery of the contemporary world. Ug wanted peace.

The whole struggle for law was for him a struggle for peace, and the whole story of his efforts may be told in terms of a series of limited and precarious peaces—the peace of the kindred group, the peace of the market, the peace of God, the peace of the king. Each peace took long to achieve and was never perfect. Today we still hope for a peace of nations. Each of these peaces, except perhaps the peace of God, is now disguised as a "branch" of modern secular jurisprudence. The peace of the kindred group is family law, or the law of domestic relations. The peace of the market is the civil law, which governs property and contracts. The peace of the king has become the modern criminal law.

The law looms large in the activities of the contemporary world. It has to do with courts, judges and lawyers, sheriffs, policemen, and jailers. It brings to bear the organized force of the "government," "state," or "community" upon every individual. As civilized men we hardly seem to be able to imagine a period of human society in which law did not exist. Yet law-ways are not old in human history. Before them were the folkways. There are still primitive groups in remote corners of the world who do not possess even rudimentary organs of government, as, for instance, the Papuans of New Guinea, the Veddas of Ceylon, the Punans of Borneo, or the Tasmanians of Australia. Such "chiefs" as these people have are purely titular, and exercise no real authority.

The primitive Ug managed to get along without the luxury of law. He lived either by food-gathering or hunting or fishing. The absence of law must not, of course, be taken to imply that this was a Golden Age. Life was hard and usually miserable, but it was also simple. Ug had so few possessions that he needed no elaborate organization of public force to restrain envious members of his group. He had his spear or knife or loincloth, possibly also a boat and a rude hut, but he had no elaborate notions about an "institution of property," private or otherwise.

To be sure, he, too, had other than purely material interests. He had his own notions of right and wrong. He had his tabus: one must not eat this animal, or touch this thing, or go to this place. The gods would be angry. But the maintenance of the tabus did not necessitate an organization of public force to punish the impious violator. The breach of a tabu miraculously carried its own punishment: the violator was at once struck dead. He also had his customs, his particular ways of hunting, eating, marrying, living, and dying. Some of these customs he regarded as rather important, if not vital. Doubtless, for all his primitiveness, he was not "a slave to custom." He must have had in his make-up something of the scofflaw, and there were times when customs were broken. But apparently the situation never became serious enough to require the organization of a regular machinery for suppressing departures from the customary ways. It was not often that customs were disregarded. If they were, ridicule or reproof were deemed sufficient. In very serious cases the offender might atone by committing suicide or by going into voluntary exile. A repeated violator of tribal custom, who made a colossal nuisance of himself and seemed to threaten the very safety of his tribe, might even by common consent be suddenly set upon and put out of the way. So were treated sorcerers and bold violators of the rules of exogamy. So, much more rarely, were treated repeated killers. These were, however, spontaneous acts of retribution, and so exceptional that they did not lead to the establishment of any regular governmental mechanism. Such a mechanism might, however, be established for dealing with a particular emergency. The Plains Indians, for instance, had "buffalo police" who had authority to kill a brave who violated one of the rules of the buffalo hunt, but when the hunt was over their authority ended.

This was not the age of law. This was the age when custom was king. Whether the rules of conduct observed by Ug are to be called "law" or "custom" matters little. Jurists are in the habit of calling them "customary law." What is important, and, from our point of view, quite remarkable, is that rules of conduct were recognized as binding on the members of the community, although they were not supported by external sanctions of a repressive character as in politically organized civilized society. The community relied on natural factors of social cohesion. Doubtless some of the customs were buttressed by economic self-interest, while others took their strength from religious fears; but many customs—and sometimes the most tyrannical—were obeyed for no other reason, apparently, than that they were the customary modes of behavior. This sovereign sway of custom seems to us as mysterious as instinct. Accustomed as we are to believe that dreadful anarchy would ensue tomorrow if suddenly all the courts, police stations, and jails were closed, we are not likely to regard the sovereign reign of custom with equanimity.

Our worst fears seem to be justified by Ug's habits of retaliation. He must have been a horrible and bloodthirsty savage, for he practiced the blood-feud. When a killing occurred in his own group, punishment was rarely if ever visited upon the killer. But if a member of his own group was slain by a member of another group—whether by accident or design made no difference—he proceeded to take vengeance not only upon the killer but upon any other member of the killer's group. This disregard of personal guilt seems particularly abhorrent to our nice sense of discrimination in matters involving human life. Often the killer's group in turn retaliated upon some member of Ug's group, and so presumably the killings endlessly continued until each of the tribes was exterminated. The prevalence of the blood-feud was the foundation for the long-held belief that the state of primitive society was that of a war of all against all.

The great problem of primitive society was undoubtedly homicide. In rare cases the blood-feud might break out as the result of poaching or adultery, but the usual occasion was a homicide. There was never much to steal, and a kick or a slap was enough to deal with the petty thief. But a killing cast a shadow over the life of the group. Ug could not afford to be indifferent to manslaughter, especially since every member of his small group was such an important element of its component strength. The frequency of killings, as well as the horrors of the blood-feud, has, however, been exaggerated. Ug was far more peaceful than the average modern citizen. Food-gatherers, who have been observed by modern anthropologists, are rarely given to violence, and treat their own women and children, as well as the members of neighboring tribes, with exemplary kindness and consideration. The record of the number of our own murders, which runs to something like 13,000 a year, is nothing to boast of, and even less can we take pride in the millions who fall in the organized murder called war. Moreover, among primitive peoples, reciprocal and indiscriminate slaughter did not always follow upon a homicide. The endless chain of murders was not unknown but, particularly when the blood-feud had become well organized as a social institution, vengeance was confined to a single act of retaliation, and sometimes was visited only upon the actual murderer.

In the regulation of the blood-feud Ug first revealed his legal ingenuity. Indeed, the blood-feud may be regarded as the matrix of all law. It was a mechanism for enforcing the first peace of mankind—the peace of the kindred group—and it had a rationality all its own. Modern political society, which possesses repressive sanctions, is territorially organized, and the individual owes allegiance not to his kin but to the state. Primitive society was organized upon the basis of kinship, or blood-relationship, and an individual could obtain protection only through his group. The very absence of organized political sanctions made imperative the recognition of the absolute solidarity of the kindred group. Every man was his brother's keeper. It was a system of mutual insurance, and of collective rather than individual responsibility. Ug said: "If you slay any member of my group, I will avenge myself upon any member of your group." Responsibility could not be individualized, not only because there were no courts to conduct "trials" for the purpose of establishing individual guilt, but also because there was no adequate machinery of enforcement. The maintenance of peace was possible only on the principle of "one for all and all for one." Each kindred group was a sovereign entity, and the peace of the kindred in this respect was akin to the peace of nations, whose only real sanction has been war. The first and the last peace have had this in common.

Quite apart from its function in maintaining peace, the blood-feud was the anvil on which custom was shaped into law. In the process of retaliation the idea of the organized sanction was born. When intergroup disputes were involved, the force of a custom could no longer be ascribed to the mores of one group. It seemed now to possess an external force of its own. Law is born from the process of adjusting disputes, whether before a court or by means of a test of arms. In the ceremonialism which attends the conduct of disputes there were present the germs of later legal procedure.

Ug early discovered means of mitigating the blood-feud, which, although they did not involve a trial before a court, were nevertheless based upon a somewhat similar idea. Although the advantages of a judicial duel had not yet occurred to him, he bethought himself of various forms of the duel of arms, or other encounters. Some of his ideas are suggested by the practices of primitive tribes in modern times.

Among the Tlingit Indians it was the practice to settle quarrels by means of a duel of champions armed with daggers and protected by skin armor and wooden helmets, and the Western Eskimos were even satisfied with a boxing match as a means of appeasement. The tribes of Australia were accustomed to arrange an "expiatory encounter" in cases of homicide. The slayer submitted himself to a shower of spears hurled at him by the kin of the slain man. This continued until his blood was made to flow. It may well be that both the regulated fight and the expiatory encounter were limited to tribes that were related to each other by blood. Their future as institutions was therefore also limited.

In a later generation Ug conceived an even happier idea. He was no longer a mere food-gatherer or hunter. He was either a herdsman or had settled down to some form of primitive agriculture. He had not yet, of course, achieved an economy of abundance. But occasionally he had a surplus of domestic animals—cattle, sheep, pigs, goats, horses, camels. This pastoral wealth was as good as money; in fact, it was the money of primitive society. It occurred to him one day that the blood-feud could be prevented by buying off vengeance. So many cattle might be accepted by the victim's group in payment and satisfaction for the lost life. Thus emerged the idea of pecuniary payment for wrong, which long remained the sovereign remedy of the law. We speak of legal "damages" but, as practiced among primitive peoples, the acceptance of payment for a wrong is called "composition." It was accompanied by the making of what was, in effect, a treaty of peace, and the amount of the composition was nicely adjusted to the likelihood that the victim's kin would fly to their weapons and resort to violence. Thus there was taken into consideration in fixing the amount of a composition the victim's rank, age, and sex, and the element of accident or design.

It is probable that at first Ug accepted composition only in the case of accidental death, and also that the family of the slain remained free to choose between waging the feud and accepting the composition. Pride and notions of honor would sometimes prevent the acceptance of the "blood money," and until late in history it remained a characteristic of some races to make composition only in cases of lesser wrongs, to which the practice of composition had rapidly spread. At first, too, the amounts of the composition were fixed in each instance by agreement, but among some peoples fixed tariffs of composition became established in time for every variety of wrong. To civilized man, accustomed to the notion of the public suppression of crime and to the conviction that murder is the greatest of all crimes, composition, which permits pecuniary satisfaction even for the taking of a life, seems worse than the blood-feud itself, but Ug had no doubt of its social value, and it represented to him the greatest stride he had made in civilization.

If civilized man were not so horrified by the practice of composition, he would pay tribute to Ug for this reason alone: that he was able to bring the blood-feud under control without resorting to courts and lawyers. It certainly seems remarkable that no inquiry was necessary to determine who had been guilty of a killing. But primitive slayings were usually not done with "malice aforethought" but were open and unpremeditated, and notions of individual guilt had, in any event, little or no place in the system of collective responsibility. If, in rare instances, a slaying did seem mysterious, Ug simply resorted to some private magic or religious test, such as rubbing an all-knowing stick or animal's foot or skin.

In the absence of courts, then, the quarrel between the groups was informally arbitrated by chiefs, elders, relatives, friends, more or less professional go-betweens—the precursors of the lawyers—and even by fortuitous bystanders, who had not yet apparently learned the dolorous wisdom of the proverb that the innocent bystander always gets hurt. The composition that was made was enforced not by the process of any court but by the fear of retaliation. Nevertheless, the court was about to be created; it was the next momentous step taken by Ug. Custom was about to be dethroned; law was about to be born. Custom ceased to be king when there appeared upon the scene a king in fact. Ug proclaimed himself Ug I.

Composition already implied the existence of some surplus wealth. But as communities became more settled and increasingly prosperous, they tempted fate. In human history, the plowshare and the sword have been intimately connected. When man took to the plow, he invited the terrors of the sword. The precise nature of the origin of the state seems to be one of the great historical mysteries, but the social theorists, whether churchmen or Marxists, all agree that law and the state arose as the result of social stratification. The disagreement among them extends primarily to the question whether this stratification arose from internal rather than external causes. Doubtless the "state" could have been born when the family patriarch made himself into a petty chieftain; or when some singularly gifted individual established a personal ascendancy; or when the priest of a tribe conceived the bold idea of proclaiming himself a divine ruler; or when the elders of the tribe, taking advantage of their superior wisdom, established a ruling council. There is, however, nothing to show that any of these states were destined for great careers in human history. The states that grew into the great empires of antiquity seem to have resulted from conquest. Marauding bands of herdsmen, seeking ever greener pastures, descended upon communities of peaceful peasants and overcame them. At first, no doubt, they simply put the helpless peasants to the sword, but in time they learned that it does not pay to kill those who own the geese that lay the golden eggs.

At this point the development of social institutions ceased to be spontaneous. The element of sanctions, namely, the use of force in maintaining the social and political structure, became basic. Customs could maintain themselves only when backed by the conquerors, and the external and artificial sanctions transformed them into laws. The very commingling of peoples, which was the result of conquest, led to a struggle of competing customs, and those that survived did so because they had been given the stamp of law. But, if almost continuous bloodshed and violence was to be avoided, it was necessary that the conquered should recognize the "rightfulness" of the authority exercised over them by the conquerors. When this came to pass, the "state" was born. It was the very essence of the mystery of the state that force should be sanctified. Man's great capacity for self-delusion here came into play. To enhance their own dignity, as well as to ease their own sufferings, the conquered were ready to pretend that the conquerors had a "right" to rule over them, while the latter, to ease the burdens of rulership, began not only to protect their victims from all other external enemies but also to set some limits to the ferocity of their own bands. When the marauders finally hanged one of their own for perpetrating an especially great outrage, "justice" was established. It was the first civil sacrifice, and it had much in common with that which the priest performed on the altar. Of course, the "trial" and "execution" of the criminal were both public. But the reason for this was not merely that an effective example could be set in no other way. It was necessary that everyone should participate in the mystery of the state.

Even as theologians have assumed that God created the universe, men of law have assumed that the "state" created the "court," which is the universe of the law. But the state and the court are simply different aspects of the same reality. When the court declared "law," it was the state. The law is the rule which a court will enforce, and the sum of the rules of law constitute the state. By its "judgments," the court transmuted previously existing "customs" into "law." It was this alchemy that gave customs their etatistic stamp.

It has sometimes been supposed that the court could have evolved from the process of arbitration practiced by friends and relatives. But the processes of arbitration and judicial decision are quite unlike in their very natures. The concept of authoritativeness is missing from the proceedings of arbitral agencies, which, moreover, do not declare any law but solve only particular controversies. Conceivably arbitrators, by presuming to enforce their awards, might have converted themselves into a court. But this would have been merely another example of a form of internal social stratification which produced the state. Today arbitration is practiced at the same time that courts sit, but no one attributes the origin of the courts to the work of the arbitrators.

The true origin of the court is apparent from its very organization. Accepting the principle of the separation of powers as basic, we insist that the judicial shall be separated from the executive and legislative functions. Only when a court exists as a separate entity do we consider that it is an "independent" tribunal capable of rendering equal justice between man and man. It is true that even nowadays a blacksmith may sometimes be a justice of the peace, but a justice of the Supreme Court of the United States must devote all his time to his job. But the judicial function remained undifferentiated not only among primitive and archaic peoples but among the Babylonians, Greeks, and Hebrews. The separation of the judicial from the other functions of the state, if it had been suggested, would have been regarded as not only artificial but absurd. Judging was simply an incident of domination. The administration of justice, which meant some protection of the conquered against internal aggression, was secondary at first to their protection against external aggression. Although justice assumed ever greater importance, the conquerors insisted on holding firmly to the personal control of the court. Thus, in all early courts the judges are not professional judges but simply the nobles. The chief judge is the king, namely, the chief noble of the conquerors. Sometimes the nobles, when sitting in judgment, are assisted by a council of elders or by priests. But the council of elders is merely a survival from the days before the conquest. The priests are a later addition, indicating that religion has come to be considered a valuable adjunct in maintaining the power of the conquerors.

The chief contribution of the priests to the work of the court was to convert Ug's private magic tests for determining guilt into public religious tests performed with awesome ceremonies. These tests are called "ordeals." The deity was called upon to reveal the guilty one by his judgment. Of the protean forms of the ordeal, the most universal were the ordeals by fire and water. However, the resort to ordeals in the early history of law has been greatly exaggerated. Proof was normally by rational means, and the ordeal was usually employed in cases involving such mysterious or secret offenses as sorcery and adultery when, in the nature of things, direct evidence was usually unavailable.

It is highly significant that in the early history of the peoples of antiquity the court was always held in the open air at some public place of congregation, either at the town gate, or in the environs of the temple. Great crowds always thronged to this judgment seat. It would be a great mistake, however, to see in the location of the court merely a consideration of convenience and in the absorbing interest of the populace the curiosity-mongering which is supposed to be a characteristic of simple folk. It would be equally a mistake to perceive in the use of the temple as a court only the influence of religion in the development of early law. There was a sacrament being performed at the judgment seat, but it was a civil sacrament—the mystery of the state, which religion was merely supporting with its own mysteries. Only at the judgment seat could the submissive throng share in the covenant of the state, and it had to be sealed again and again at some place under the open sky where all men could witness its renewal.

With the creation of the court the labors of Ug were done. The universe of the law was complete, at least in the sense that its generating principle was established. But Ug was not yet prepared to rest from his labors and pronounce them good. The rule content of the law now seems to us as important as the existence of the court which applies the rules. We know that the body of these rules, which are written down in an endless number of big books, is tremendous. We can nevertheless conceive of the functioning of a court which is not bound by any pre-existing rules but fits its judgment to the facts of every particular controversy. Skeptically, we may even regard the court as the first and the last great legal invention. The availability of a forum for the determination of disputes is undoubtedly more important than the rules according to which the dispute is supposed to be decided. But we know that the observance of precedent is the very life of the law, and it is easy enough to see how this worship of precedent came to be considered essential. Ug was not ready to accept unfettered judgments, or to permit unlimited discretion to the judges. He wanted rules to bind the judges and to prevent them from exercising unlimited discretion, which he profoundly distrusted. Again, the reason is to be found in the origin of the court as a political means. Not only did conquest result in a clash of custom, which made the existence of some selective agency necessary, and not only were the conquered prepared to make every effort to preserve their own customs, but the conquered desired in general to establish procedures for restraining the conquerors in exploiting the political means. The conquered could preserve some measure of freedom for themselves only by the recognition of rules. Thus, as a result of mutual distrust, the law was fashioned as a body of rules. Each hardly won right or privilege had to be given all the compelling attributes of precedent if each battle was not to be fought over again and again. It is true that naked power could have made the judgment of the court always "right." Indeed, the power behind the judgment was what distinguished the law from custom. A rule of law was merely a custom that was enforced. But it was easier to maintain the law if it was also made to seem right, and the conquerors could maintain themselves with much less trouble by yielding to the spirit of mutual accommodation and recognizing sometimes rules which even limited their own power. After all, they had no reason to object to the maintenance of the customs of the subservient class as long as these did not impinge upon their vital interests. Their first concern was not with the administration of justice but with the exploitation of their economic privileges. The hegemony of the kindred groups, in either the dominant or the subservient class, was not destroyed all at once in the launching of the state, and the settlement of internal disputes was still left largely to the subservient class, except that the dominant class tended to lay claim to a share of the composition or peace payment. It was only when customs clashed that the dominant class revealed a vivid interest in the conflict. Not infrequently, however, the conflict was settled by allowing each class to continue to live under its own customs. A single body of custom for all members of the state, which now seems the very quintessence of justice, was everywhere a slow growth. Truly, centralized states were slow to appear.

Ug is the hero of these beginnings of the law. If the details of his work sometimes seem obscure, it is because he had not yet discovered the magic of the alphabet. He had no little letters to form big words of history. He had his customs, but neither these nor the customary law into which they were transmuted were written down in words. The customs he followed were merely exemplified and objectified in his daily life. For this very reason, however, they were tough and real and difficult to pervert. When they came to be written down in subsequent ages, they began to lead a strange new life of their own. The introduction of the written word was the first great revolution in the history of the law since the establishment of courts. In a sense, the history of law and men of law begins with the written word. In the development of the law, the written word was to prove the most fateful discovery. The history of the law not only ceased to be anonymous; it became the history of the potentialities of the written word for good and evil.

Hammurabi, King of Babylon

LAW AND THE WRITTEN WORD

ONE OF THE MOST STRIKING CHARACTERISTICS OF ANCIENT CIVI-
lizations is the prominence given in their traditions of law to myths
concerning great lawgivers. We who live in an age of the mass production of newspapers and history books know who has been responsible for
the enactment of a particular law (and are sometimes inclined to question its wisdom). We sometimes even refer to a particular law by the
name of its author or authors, as when we speak of the Sherman Act,
or the Norris-LaGuardia Act, or the Wagner Act. But the ancients were
in the habit of attributing almost all their laws to one lawgiver who,
they believed, had created their code of laws at some particular time.
Even later laws were commonly attributed to him. Invariably he was
inspired by the gods, or God, or at least by superhuman wisdom, and
not infrequently he had gone on some distant or perilous journey before
presenting the people with his inspired code.

In the Near East in ancient times there were traditions concerning
Menes and Moses and Manu—names so much alike that they raise a
suspicion of a common origin. Menes was the lawgiver of the ancient
Egyptians, and Manu of the Hindus. Moses, of course, has particularly
dominated the imagination of the West. The Book of Exodus tells us
he spoke directly to the one and only God, and, as he descended from
Mount Sinai with the holy tablets of the law, thunder and lightning
heralded his approach. But the Greeks were no less fertile in lawgiving
myths. Every little Greek city had its legendary lawgiver. There was
Lycurgus of Sparta, Charondas of Ionian Catana, Diocles of Dorian
Syracuse, Zaleucus of Achaean Locris, Aristedes of Ceos, Pittacus of
Mytilene, and above all Solon of Athens. In some Greek cities the belief
prevailed that the lawgiver had been reduced from a god to a hero. The

13

laws of Zaleucus were supposed to have been given to him in a dream by Athena while he was a poor shepherd. The Greek lawgivers in particular sought inspiration in journeys to distant lands.

It is obvious from all this mythicizing that the ancient codes were regarded by the people as highly precious possessions. This is emphasized by the fact that the laws were inscribed upon materials that were deemed extremely durable—wood, bronze, and stone—and set up in the form of pillars or tablets in public places, such as markets and temples, or were written upon temple walls. It is said that one of the hateful acts of the ill-famed Roman Emperor Caligula was that of having the laws inscribed upon a pillar so high that the people could not read them. It is significant that the emphasis was placed on the *written* law, especially in view of the fact that in ancient times the common people were illiterate.

Writing was to them something of a marvel, worthy of reverence, and it was only natural that their superstitious minds should attach a transcendent importance to the written law. Moreover, the great kingdoms of antiquity that flourished in the Near East, and the Greek and Roman states, as well, were theocracies, in which the priests encouraged belief in the myths of the divine lawgivers. But the veneration with which these ancient codes were regarded derived not only from their supernatural origins, but also from the fact that they recorded in seemingly unalterable and imperishable forms the rights and privileges that had been won only after long and bitter social struggles.

A great modern jurist once said that the motto of jurisprudence should be: "In the Beginning was the Word." The written word not only embodied the results of the first revolutions in human history, but in its applications to legal institutions was in itself revolutionary. The law may be described as the science that lives by the written word. To speak of law today is to speak of books, big and little books, of whole libraries of books, of books containing legislative acts, codes, digests, judicial decisions, forms of legal documents. Other arts and sciences have, of course, produced great libraries which, however, merely *record* their contributions to human knowledge. But in the books of the law the words themselves have magic properties—powers to loose and bind. The words themselves are the subject matter of the science, the words *are* the law. A slip in employing the wrong words may quite literally be a matter of life and death.

In even the earliest stages of society, there were already great inventions in the law. Ug had invented courts and judges to declare the law. But the judges declared only what was the immemorial custom. They were merely the depositaries of ancient usage. By their judgments they simply testified to what the community had always said and done in a case like the one before them. Customs, to be sure, were sometimes consciously altered by the action of the community. Anthropologists point out that even primitive peoples have made changes by "legislation." But this term is a misnomer, for these changes are, of course, not embodied in writing but commemorated by a colorful ceremony and proclaimed orally to the people. It is obvious that it is easy to assimilate such changes from established custom. Since they are not embodied in writing, that can lead no independent life of their own. The act of "legislation" soon becomes only another custom exemplified in the life of the community. Custom remains king—but only until the advent of the written word.

It was the written word that eventually dethroned custom. However, in primitive, as well as in archaic, communities, acts of legislation were rather infrequent, and, even when embodied in writing, they could still be integrated readily in the body of existing custom. Judges, indeed, sometimes clung to existing custom in all but contemptuous disregard of the new written law. But this game could be played only with increasing difficulty as the acts of legislation multiplied. The turning point in the history of the law was reached when the first written code was enacted. Now a code consists of many laws all enacted at one and the same time and proclaimed to the people under special solemnities. The code was the inevitable, if not the logical, result of resort to the written word, and its appearance was one of the most momentous events in legal history.

There is one myth about the origin of codes that was never invented by the ancients. It is the belief that the ancient codes were mere compilations of pre-existing custom, which thus effected no real changes in the law. This myth is entirely mechanistic. First, it is assumed, writing was invented. Writing having become known, someone with a neat sense of order thought it would be a good idea to put the existing body of custom into writing. Thus the general convenience was served, but the *status quo* remained unchanged. But in fact no code was ever proclaimed merely to take advantage of the art of writing or to enshrine existing custom. Writing was known for centuries before anyone thought of employing it for the purpose of codification, and no one would have undertaken the arduous labors of codification unless to promote some social or political end.

The first historically known lawgiver whose code has survived virtually intact is Hammurabi, King of Babylon, who reigned in the valley of the Tigris and Euphrates Rivers, called anciently the Plain of Shinar, about four thousand years ago. The discovery of the Code of Hammurabi, which greatly excited everyone interested in the origins of civilization, did not occur until almost the end of the year 1901. A French archeological expedition, excavating the great mound known as the acropolis of Susa, in Persia, unearthed a large fragment of black diorite. A few days later two similar fragments were discovered. When pieced together the three fragments proved to be parts of a single pillar in the shape of an elongated sugar loaf, on which had been inscribed in cuneiform characters a code of law promulgated by Hammurabi. The pillar, which stood almost eight feet high and was two feet in diameter, contained forty-four columns of inscription. The provisions of the Code itself were preceded by a prologue and followed by an epilogue. At the summit of the pillar was a relief showing Hammurabi and the Babylonian sun-god Shamash. Originally erected by Hammurabi in the temple at Sippara, which would be near modern Bagdad, it had remained there for a thousand years until an Elamite monarch, Shutruknahunte, who had overrun Babylon and razed Sippara, had transported it a distance of over two hundred miles, to Susa, to serve as a monument to his triumph. Five columns, or about thirty-five sections of the Code, were erased by the conqueror, doubtless to make room for a boasting inscription of his own, which for some reason was left unrecorded. However, scholars have now restored from other sources virtually all the missing sections.

Hammurabi was, however, not the first great king who reigned in the land known as the land of the Two Rivers, which was probably the seat of the oldest human civilization—even older than that of Egypt. The delta formed by the Tigris and Euphrates at the head of the Persian Gulf, which we now call Mesopotamia, is at the present time a desolate waste, but in ancient times, when it was properly drained and cultivated, it was so fruitful and lovely that it was reputed to be the site of the Garden of Eden. The rich soil, which consisted of the mud deposited by the rivers, produced abundant crops of wheat and barley, and gardens of date palms dotted the landscape. Great herds of sheep and cattle thrived. The existence of agricultural surpluses made possible a fairly flourishing caravan trade.

As early as 3500 B.C. there appeared at the head of the Persian Gulf a remarkable non-Semitic people called Sumerians, who reclaimed the marshes by means of dikes and canals, built cities and temples, and laid the foundations of the civilization of the valley. The Sumerians were not only skilled agriculturists and cattle breeders, but metalworkers as well. The sun-dried bricks from which they built their houses were made from the all-embracing mud of the valley, and the mud brick was also the basis of the art of cuneiform writing invented by the Sumerians. With sticks of bamboo, bone, or wood, they scratched rude pictographs on tablets of soft clay, and then dried them in the sun, so that they became virtually imperishable records. The pictographs evolved into more abstract wedge-shaped characters, from which was derived the name "cuneiform" (the Latin word for "wedge" is *cuneus*).

The land of Sumer was organized into independent city-kingdoms, which were united, if at all, only by the common worship of the god Enlil, whose temple was at Nippur. The great Sumerian cities were Ur, Uruk, Kish, Lagash, and Nippur. The Sumerian city-kingdoms constantly warred with one another in efforts to achieve supremacy. First one and then another gained ascendancy, which, however, never lasted very long. Very early Sumer was invaded by a Semitic people, the Akkadians, who infiltrated from the western desert into the northern portion of the land of the Two Rivers, which thus came to be known as Akkad. The Semitic Akkadians quickly absorbed the civilization of the Sumerians, but no more than the conquered were they able to achieve political unity.

The biblical tradition and some of the great historians have given Babylon its reputation as a city of sin and lust, which rests largely upon flamboyant stories of temple prostitution. The selection of the land of the Two Rivers as the site of the Garden of Eden has also created an impression that it was a land of sensual ease. But the lot of at least the common people was unusually hard. The mending of the dikes and the digging and maintenance of the canals, for which the farmers were made responsible, involved incessant labor, which was often forced. All sorts of tithes and feudal dues had to be paid, and there was a veritable army of tax-gatherers to bring them into the temple and royal treasury. As one of the inscriptions puts it, "There were inspectors down to the sea."

In the first quarter of the millennium there arose in Lagash, then ascendant in the land of Sumer, a reforming king whose name was Urukagina and who seems to have achieved power by putting himself at the head of a popular movement aiming to secure relief from the prevailing abuses. Urukagina cut down the tithes and curtailed the privileges of the priests and guilds of diviners, reduced the number of officials, and dismissed those who had been guilty of extortion. The prevailing burdens may be judged from the fact that burial charges consisted at this time of seven urns of wine, four hundred and twenty loaves of bread, one hundred and twenty measures of corn, a garment, a kid, a bed, and a seat, as well as sixty measures of corn for the priest's assistant. The nature of the feudal dues may be surmised from the fact that Urukagina had to decree that the overlord should henceforth pay for the ass born in his man's stable. Seizures of sheep, fish, and even wells were also abolished. Urukagina relieved the lot of forced laborers by compelling the overlords to supply them with drinking water, or, in the alternative, allow them to fetch it. He also crowned his reforms by a moral gesture: he ended a system under which, as the result of a payment of fees, divorce had become practically purchasable for six shekels, irrespective of grounds.

Urukagina, however, never founded an empire. The first ruler who succeeded in uniting the lands of Sumer and Akkad was the Akkadian Sargon of Agade. Legend has it that he was a cupbearer who revolted against the king of Kish and set up a new capital at Agade. After consolidating his hold on the delta, Sargon even embarked on a series of foreign conquests, inspired, no doubt, by the desire to secure the trade routes to his sources of supply. He invaded the mountainous regions of Elam to the east, and may even have driven to the Mediterranean and made contact with the lords of the Nile. But Sargon's conquests were short-lived. In less than a century and a half the empire he had founded relapsed into anarchy. When one of the scribes of the king lists wrote down the happenings of this time, he could only ask despairingly: "Who was king? Who was not king?"

The great city of the period of Sargon's hegemony was Ur, and the reputation of its splendors long survived in western Asia. But now a new city, Babylon, which in the native speech meant "The Gate of the Gods," began its rise to pre-eminence. It was ruled by another line of Semitic kings, the Amorites, who are styled the First Dynasty. The sixth of this line and the greatest of them all was Hammurabi. His father had defeated the rivals of Babylon—Ur, Nisim, and Larsam—but he had not been able to dispose of the wild Elamites who, from their mountain country, had invaded the fertile delta. This was the chief task of Hammurabi in his long reign of forty-three years, most of which, however, was spent in peaceful pursuits. It was not until his thirtieth year that he defeated the army of Elam. But in his thirty-ninth year he even moved along the Tigris and conquered Assyria, which was thus united to the empire of Babylon. The Babylonian scribes named a year after the momentous event which had occurred in its course, and it is from the date lists that we know the sequence of the great accomplishments of the reign of Hammurabi.

The date lists describe the second year of Hammurabi's reign as "the year when Hammurabi established righteousness in the midst of the land." Hammurabi was determined to establish a well-ordered kingdom. He reminds us of the benevolent despots of the Age of the Enlightenment. He regarded his domain as his patrimony and his people as a flock that had been given into his hands as a prudent shepherd. He was no wild reformer such as Urukagina had been, but he was determined to stabilize the existing order. The merchants who traveled between cities should be enabled to go their ways in peace, and one of his great concerns was the extirpation of brigandage. This was only the merchants' due from the first great merchant-king. But the cultivator of the soil must also be provided for. It was the custom of great kings to build canals, which were not only vital to the tillers of the soil (who, however, had to pay for the water they received), but were also the arteries of commerce. So, too, Hammurabi built two especially important canals. In his ninth year he built the canal Hammurabi-hegal, which means "Hammurabi is riches," and in his thirty-third year the canal Hammurabi-nuch-usch-nischi, which means "Hammurabi is the welfare of his people." Hammurabi also took thought of the morrow, and built granaries so that there should be grain in time of famine.

We get a remarkably clear picture of how the great king of Babylon administered the affairs of his kingdom from a series of letters which he sent to Sid-Idinnam, a high official of the city of Larsam in southern Babylonia, who was probably its governor. Like all cuneiform writing, the letters are in the form of clay tablets. These are oblong in shape, two to three inches in breadth, three to four inches in length, and an inch in thickness. They were dispatched by messenger, and it may be that Hammurabi even established a regular royal post for this purpose. The epistolary formula is always the same: "Unto Sid-Idinnam say: Thus saith Hammurabi." The formula is doubtless a survival from the time when oral messages only were sent. Hammurabi, like other Babylonian kings, always employed the same faithful scribe, for all his letters are in the same handwriting. And the letters, as a rule, are terse and brief, as becomes a great king writing to a subordinate official.

Hammurabi was a tireless administrator, and there was nothing too trivial to be beneath his attention. He supervised his kingdom as a careful husbandman his estate. Some of the letters relate to the inspection and care of the royal herds of cattle and flocks of sheep from which a good part of the king's revenue was derived, and others to securing adequate numbers of serfs, laborers, and public slaves for various building projects of the king. A canal had become so obstructed that the boats which had been navigating it could not proceed. The king ordered the governor to clear the canal as soon as possible. The metalworkers in one of his cities required a supply of *abba* wood. The king specified the exact sizes into which the pieces of wood were to be cut, and warned against providing dead lumber. Supplies of dates, sesame seed, and corn were needed at Babylon. The king wrote to make arrangements for their transport. In accordance with custom, it was necessary for the king to correct the lunar calendar by directing the observance of an intercalary month. "Since the year hath a deficiency," he wrote, "let the month which is now beginning be registered as a second month of Elul." But cannily he directed that the intercalary month should not be deemed to justify any deferment in the payment of taxes.

The letters show also that Hammurabi was a pious king. He saw to it that the temple shrines were beautified and the temples properly supplied. Nevertheless, the letters show also that he was shrewd enough to keep control of the collection of the temple revenues. He also received reports from the priests, and supervised the duties of the guild of soothsayers who were employed on important occasions to observe the omens. Hammurabi's superstition is illustrated by one letter written after Hammurabi's victory over Elam, which directs the transport of certain Elamite goddesses to Babylon with due and proper care. Apparently not even the enemy goddesses were to be treated with disrespect. It was not long, however, before Hammurabi was writing another letter directing the return of the Elamite goddesses to their shrines. They must have brought him some bad luck. Hammurabi once even wrote a letter to postpone the trial of a lawsuit, because the plaintiff, who was a temple baker, had to officiate at a temple feast.

But, as befits the king who was to become the great lawgiver, Hammurabi wrote most of his letters to supervise the administration of justice. Lawsuits were usually tried by local judges, who appear to have been assisted by the elders acting as a board of assessors, as in many archaic communities, but appeal ran to the king of Babylon, who apparently reserved the right to interfere with the local administration of justice. Hammurabi was constantly summoning suitors before him. When he heard of a case of bribery, he ordered the guilty officials to be brought to Babylon. He proved that he was no respecter of persons by supporting against a governor a merchant's claim for the repayment of a loan. Above all, he appears to have devoted great energy to combating the extortions of moneylenders.

There is little doubt that Hammurabi must have regarded the promulgation of his Code as the crowning achievement of his reign. As a matter of fact, posterity has not been left to guess at his motives, which are revealed in the prologue and epilogue of his Code. The prologue celebrates the glorious achievements of his reign, and the epilogue is devoted mainly to calling down curses upon those who in later years should disregard the provisions he has laid down. That the code was not promulgated until the closing years of his reign is established by the recital in the prologue of the fact that he was ruler of Assur and Nineveh, which were not subdued until his thirty-ninth year.

In the prologue Hammurabi speaks of the temples he has built, of his provision of pasture and drinking places and abundant waters, of his suppression of the bandits. But even more emphatically does he speak of his conquests and his concern for justice. "Then Anu and Bel," he proclaims, "delighted the flesh of mankind by calling me, the renowned prince, the god-fearing Hammurabi, to establish justice in the earth, to destroy the base and the wicked, and to hold back the strong from oppressing the feeble: to shine like the sun-god upon the black-headed men, and to illuminate the land." Then he goes on to describe his military prowess. He hails himself in the same vainglorious manner as "the hero king," "the invader of the Four Quarters," "the exalter of the fame of Babylon," "the grave of the foe," "the impetuous bull that overthrows the enemy," "the wrestler without rival," "the renowned potentate who has made the face of Ishtar to shine." Then again he refers to himself as "the promulgator of justice, the guider of the people."

This theme is even more marked in the epilogue, in which he declares: "The flesh of the land I have made rejoice: the resident people I have made secure; I have not suffered them to be afraid. . . . That the strong may not oppress the weak; that the orphan and the widow may be counseled . . . to proclaim the law of the land: to guide the procedure of the land, and to sustain the feeble, I have written my precious words upon my pillar, and before my image as king of justice I have placed it. . . . The oppressed who has a lawsuit shall come before my image as king of justice. He shall read the writing on my pillar, he shall perceive my precious words. The words of my pillar shall explain to him his cause, and he shall find his right." Then follow the curses upon any ruler who in after days should attempt to "alter the law of the land," or the words written upon the pillar. Such a one should have "a death with open eyes," "pour out his soul like water," fail in battle, and be destroyed by all the gods.

The mythmakers who even in modern times connect law with religion and divine inspiration rely upon the relief surmounting Hammurabi's pillar of diorite, which, they believe, represents the king as receiving his laws from the sun-god Shamash. But this would no more prove the religious origin of the Code than the divine inspiration of modern laws would be established by the fact that the sessions of legislative assemblies are still opened with prayer. The Code of Hammurabi itself is completely secular, and the relief, it is reasonable to assume, represents either a suitor for justice standing before the king, or merely the king in an attitude of adoration before the god. As a matter of fact, the prologue and epilogue tell us plainly enough that it was Hammurabi who conceived the idea of setting up a pillar containing his laws. He speaks of the laws *he* has formulated and the statutes *he* has enacted for the protection of his subjects.

The religious myth is only another aspect of the traditional disinclination to recognize the innovating character of the ancient codes. Having conquered the lands of Sumer and Akkad and united them under his rule, Hammurabi conceived the idea of giving his subjects a unified law. This must indeed have been his dominant purpose. He speaks not of the law of the city of Ur or Nisim or Larsam, or even of his own city of Babylon. He speaks of one law—"the law of the land." Certainly he was not interested merely in enshrining existing custom. Conquest brings about the mingling of peoples and the confusion of custom. Hammurabi may have selected from competing customs, but he was not overawed by any of them. His letters show that he did not scruple to interfere when necessary with the administration of justice. If the strong were oppressing the weak, it was because they were taking advantage not only of their superior wealth and power but of the prevailing confusion of custom. The redaction of existing custom is an objective of modern rather than of archaic codification and implies a greater maturity of jurisprudential technique than was known in ancient Babylon. If a systematic codification of existing custom were in question, it would have been made complete, but the incompleteness of all archaic codes is one of their most striking characteristics. The Code of Hammurabi does not treat at all two such common topics as the ordinary law of sales and murder. It provides, for instance, for the case of the seduction of a betrothed virgin but not for the case of an unbetrothed virgin. This could have been only because the law on the latter subject was well settled. Insofar as Hammurabi collected existing law, he collected not custom but pre-existing legislation. When the legislation was out of harmony with the needs of his own times, however, he did not scruple to alter and amend, and scholars have indeed demonstrated the existence of such "interpolations."

Hammurabi was not the first king in the land of the Two Rivers who conceived the idea of written law. Fragments of very ancient Sumerian and Akkadian laws still survive. Hammurabi had an important predecessor in Urukagina of Lagash, who also sought to protect the weak from the strong. There could have been no country of the ancient world where resort to writing for the purpose of consummating legal transactions was more common than in Babylonia. Almost every legal transaction was reduced to writing, and hundreds of the clay contract tablets and other business and procedural documents survived and had been discovered long before the Code of Hammurabi. The hard clay tablet seemed so final, certain, and imperishable! It is almost as if the land of cuneiform writing was destined to produce the first code. The originality of Hammurabi was to conceive the idea of an extensive popular codification of all the laws which were the prolific sources of dispute. All the laws which had been enacted before his time were written in Sumerian, which was the Latin

of the land of the Two Rivers, and were deposited in the temple archives, where they were beyond the reach of the common people. Hammurabi wrote his laws in the everyday Akkadian speech and inscribed them on a pillar which was to stand in the temple courtyard where it might be read by all men. Thus would force and oppression be prevented. Thus would justice prevail. That this was his great contribution to legal technique Hammurabi tells us in the epilogue of his Code, and it is worth repeating: "The oppressed who has a lawsuit shall come before my image as king of justice. He shall read the writing on my pillar, he shall perceive my precious words. The word of my pillar shall explain to him his cause, and he shall find his right."

The Code of Hammurabi is typical of a late archaic civilization. The realm of Hammurabi was a great one for its time, but it was no greater than modern Italy. As in early Sumerian and Akkadian days, its economy rested basically upon agriculture, although handicrafts and trade were growing in importance. The later trading prominence of the Semitic peoples, however, has led to exaggerated notions of the commerce of Babylon in the age of Hammurabi. At this time even horses and camels were unknown, and trade was carried on by donkey caravans only, or by small boats navigating the rivers. Although Hammurabi was really the first great national merchant-king, there were still survivals in his day of feudalism and rude clan justice. Although he thought of himself as the protector of the weak against the strong, he deserved the title, after all, only by the standards of archaic life. Many of the practices sanctioned by him would now be regarded as cruel and unenlightened.

The Code of Hammurabi recognized three classes: patricians, plebeians, and slaves. Status depended on birth, except that the slaves were foreigners—usually prisoners of war. The public slaves who worked on the royal domains led a miserable existence, but the private slave was regarded as a member of the family, and might even acquire wealth. A female slave who bore her master children could not be sold, and at his death she became free. The Code made no provision for the emancipation of slaves, although the practice was not uncommon.

Women occupied a relatively favored status in Babylonian life. They could even engage in trade. The paterfamilias, as in all archaic societies, was something of a petty despot, but his powers were perhaps more restricted than elsewhere. The earliest form of marriage in

Babylon was by purchase, the bridegroom or his family paying a bride price to the girl's father. But the Code also recognizes a form of marriage in which the bride received a dowry from her father. This remained her separate estate throughout her life. It is the existence of these two forms of marriage that must be the basis of Herodotus' fantastic story that once a year all the pretty girls of Babylon were brought together in the market place and sold to prospective husbands, so that with the money thus acquired the ugly ducklings could be provided with dowries and husbands. The husband by a postnuptial marriage settlement might bestow a portion on his wife, but in such case she took no share of his estate when he died. A husband had an unlimited right of divorce, except that he had to pay the wife a certain sum. Marriage was monogamous unless the wife became sick. The Code of Hammurabi also contained two provisions in the nature of Enoch Arden laws. They permitted the wives of husbands who were penniless prisoners of war, or who had run away, to remarry.

There were five classes of women who led religious lives in the temples, where they were often also engaged in important business transactions. Some of them were permitted to marry. Many of the authorities on Babylonian social life doubt that any of the temple women were sacred courtesans. The Code of Hammurabi certainly reveals that a high standard of propriety was exacted of a "holy sister," or "priestess." It decreed that such a one should be burnt alive for entering a tavern. The reason for this severity was that the taverns, which were usually operated by women, had reputations as houses of assignation and ill fame.

In the old Akkadian period, the land was owned by the clan and became concentrated in the hands of prominent families and princes. Gradually all the land came into possession of the temples and the kings, except that houses and gardens could be privately owned. In the age of Hammurabi, however, individual land tenure had reappeared, and the only surviving traces of feudalism are forms of military tenure applicable to lands that formed the king's vast estate. However, as in archaic civilizations generally, the head of the family had only a limited power of disposition over his estate. Normally the sons were his heirs, but even a rebellious son could be disinherited only after a legal proceeding before a magistrate, and the paterfamilias had no power of testation and could make no will. Indeed, a great deal of the land was in the hands of widows and other absentee owners, and for this reason was commonly farmed on shares. The agricultural provisions of Hammurabi's Code dealt primarily with this sharecropping and the maintenance of the irrigation works. The bailment of domestic animals, one of the most common subjects of archaic legislation, also received a good deal of attention in the Code.

The Code of Hammurabi itself indicates the limited scope of trading in his time. There were traders who sent agents out on the caravan routes, and these may be described most accurately as peddlers. The trader's investment appears to have been limited to a single venture, for which he supplied the funds, under an arrangement which entitled him to the return of his capital and a share of the profits. There was no long-term credit, and credit in any event was chiefly agricultural, since it was repayable at the next harvest. The provisions of the Code regulate carefully the transactions of loan and deposit. Interest was permitted, and, depending upon whether it was to be repaid in silver or corn, the maximum rate was fixed at 20 per cent and 33 per cent, respectively. There were no contractors, and any man who had work to be done himself provided the material and employed the craftsman or laborer. One of the most remarkable features of the Code of Hammurabi is said to be its extensive price-fixing. It fixed the charges of tavern-keepers, physicians, veterinarians, builders, boatmen, field-laborers, ox-drivers, shepherds, and artisans, and the fees for the hiring of threshing animals. The great Babylonian kings particularly took great pride in preventing scarcity and overreaching. However, this extremely rigid price-fixing legislation is only another indication of the modest character of the market at this time.

The Code of Hammurabi shows no disposition to pamper the debtor whose lot, as in most archaic societies, was hard. As was usually the case, he might be sold into slavery. Nevertheless, he was allowed certain privileges that were no doubt thought to ameliorate his condition. He might give his son, daughter, or wife to work off the debt, but such servitude was limited to three years. The wife, however, could stipulate against such debt slavery in her marriage contract. A penalty was imposed on the creditor if he unlawfully distrained the debtor. The debtor's obligation was canceled if he died a natural death in the house of the creditor. If the debtor who was a freeman died in the creditor's house as a result of mistreatment, the creditor's son could be slain.

The Code of Hammurabi is perhaps most typically archaic in its law of wrongs. The king had assumed the punishment of certain crimes, but these do not go beyond those offenses which are usually put down by the primitive community—sorcery, perjury, adultery, incest, and various acts of treason. The absence of any provision relating to willful homicide may be due to the fact that it was still a matter for the kindred group to be settled by blood-feud or composition. Composition was still permitted in the case of ordinary theft and other personal wrongs; and typically archaic, too, is the fact that the favorite remedy for wrongs in the Code of Hammurabi is multiple restitution either in kind or by the payment of silver or corn, the two monetary standards of the time. Hammurabi's Code contained many provisions relating to thefts, which were treated as public crimes, but they were all thefts under special or aggravating circumstances, that is, from a temple or "great house," or an ordinary house on fire, or by the practice of brigandage. Other thieves might be slain only if they were unable to pay the required composition. The most singular feature of the Code of Hammurabi, however, is the extent to which it applies the *lex talionis*, prescribing the exaction of an eye for an eye, bone for bone, tooth for tooth. If a man caused a woman to have a miscarriage as the result of which she died, his daughter was to be put to death. If a man was killed as the result of the collapse of a defectively built house, the builder was to be slain. The physician who had performed a careless operation was to have his hands cut off. But the right to demand the *lex talionis* was in Hammurabi's Code a privilege of the dominant patrician class only: the plebeian had to be content with the right of composition.

The Code of Hammurabi had little to say on the subject of procedure or on the methods of administering justice. Elaborate procedures are a luxury of mature legal systems. It is apparent from the Code, however, that Hammurabi was seeking to reduce the possibilities of dispute. As had been the case immemorially in the land of the Two Rivers, most of the important business transactions were required to be consummated before witnesses or to be put in writing. Indeed, the death penalty was imposed for purchasing goods from a child or slave without transaction witnesses or contract. Another provision was aimed at corrupt judges who, if convicted of giving a false judgment, were compelled to make twelvefold restitution and were forever banned from holding office. There are the usual instances in the Code of Hammurabi of resort to those archaic forms of procedure known as the ordeal and the oath. The ordeal by the Holy River was employed, but only in cases of sorcery and adultery, which by their very nature are secret offenses. On a few occasions an oath or purgation might also be taken. The peddler who had been robbed on the road, the shepherd who had had a beast under his care killed by a lion, might swear an oath and go free, for under such circumstances there was usually no proof. Except for these instances, the method of proof was by witnesses and was entirely rational.

The arrangement of the Code of Hammurabi shows that legal science was still rudimentary. The order of its provisions seems haphazard. They are related to each other only by external similarity of subject matter rather than by an identity of legal principles or concepts. This neglect of systematization, however, indicates quite clearly that Hammurabi was doing far more than merely compiling custom. The style of the Code is as forceful, terse, and brief as his letters. The provisions are couched in the form of a series of conditional imperatives introduced by the word "if." "If a man shall steal the minor son of a freeman, he shall be put to death." "If a man find a fugitive slave, male or female, in the open country, and bring the same to the owner, the owner of the slave shall pay that man two shekels of silver." "If a man let his field to another for a fixed rent, and has received the rent for the field, but storms come and destroy the crops, the loss falls upon the renter." It is a rather remarkable fact that every truly archaic code known is similarly couched in the conditional imperative. A code that is to be inscribed upon a pillar or a tablet in a public place must needs be terse and brief.

Hammurabi, King of Babylon, did not long survive the day when his proud pillar of black diorite was set up at the temple of Sippara, and his empire did not long survive his own death. The Kassites invaded the land of the Two Rivers from the east, and then from the northwest came the Hittites, who even captured Babylon. But the pillar of black diorite remained at the temple of Sippara for almost a thousand years before it was carried off to Susa, and men gaped at the little wedge-shaped characters that were inscribed upon it. When rulers and peoples came to devise laws of their own, they thought of the great Code of Hammurabi, and no doubt in this or that respect they sought to emulate his laws. One of the most remarkable phenomena of legal history is the tendency of the laws of empires to live on after the empires themselves have perished. The Assyrians, the Hittites, the Hebrews, all enacted written laws, and it is reasonable to assume that they copied some of them from the Code of Hammurabi.

There is embodied in the Bible an archaic code of law dating probably from the ninth century B.C. Usually called the Covenant Code, it is to be found in Exodus 21:2 to 22:19. The biblical tradition attributes it, like all the rest of the Hebrew legislation, to Moses. But the resemblances between the Code of Hammurabi and the Covenant Code are striking, particularly with reference to the extent to which the *lex talionis* dominates both codes. The Covenant Code sternly decrees "life for life, eye for eye, tooth for tooth, hand for hand, foot for foot, burning for burning, wound for wound, stripe for stripe." The civilization of Babylonia was Semitic, too, and must actually have been the source of the Mosaic legislation. Babylonian tradition also included stories of a flood and the discovery in the bulrushes of an infant destined for a great career.

Some even assert that through the Hittites some of Hammurabi's laws were passed on to the Greeks, and through the Greeks to the Romans. But what looks like imitation may just as likely be coincidence. The laws of all civilizations upon analogous levels of social and economic development are basically similar.

In his Code, Hammurabi stereotyped a corpus of archaic law. But, above all, he launched a great delusion, which continued to exercise a spell over the men of antiquity, and which still has not spent its force in modern times. It was the delusion that the weak could be protected against the force and cunning of the strong by means of the written word. Thereafter the people cried for Ten Commandments, for Tablets of the Law, for Twelve Tables, for laws engraved on wood and bronze and stone.

But written words could be bent and twisted, too, and controversies which were not governed precisely by any of the written words contained in the laws always seemed to be arising. Sometimes the written words themselves were contemptuously disregarded by the mighty. When the next generation came to examine its heritage of words, it was never quite certain what the fathers had meant. The meanings of words themselves, or the conditions to which they had to be applied, seemed to be constantly changing. The words themselves remained unaltered, but life itself was not static but dynamic—the stream of experience was in flux. The provisions of the Code of Hammurabi survive upon his stone monument, but their meaning is sometimes obscure and enigmatic, for we no longer have an entirely clear conception of the conditions which gave them life. The unhistorical age of antiquity found it impossible to guard against tampering with the laws. The scribes, who were usually priests, introduced forgeries into the written laws for their own purposes, and some such forgeries have been found in virtually every archaic code. The readiness of the common people to believe that all their laws were given by one great lawgiver only made it easier for the priests to conceal the traces of their handiwork. The written laws were not infrequently abrogated by contrary usage, which is only another way of saying that the great primary source of law was constantly reasserting its immemorial sway.

Indeed, that the written word was a better protection than custom against the encroachments of the mighty was a great delusion. Actually, custom was more vivid than the written word, for it was at least objectified daily in the lives of men: it was what men did, and said they did and thought, and it was what they remembered and imparted to their children and children's children. The written word was only what the wood, bronze, and stone declared. It was true that only the primitive community, which had no other sanction than the force of opinion, could live by custom. As soon as tribes were brought into contact by war or conquest, or split by the internal stratification of classes, there arose conflicting customs, which could be settled arbitrarily only by the application of force. The day of custom was then done. But the written word was powerless to save the weak from the oppressions of the strong.

Solon of Athens

LAW AND ADMINISTRATION

OF THE MANY LAWGIVERS WHO FOLLOWED HAMMURABI, HISTORY has little to tell. They live only in their myths. Moses looms largest in the history of Western culture, but the ancient Hebrew law is even more archaic than that of Hammurabi. The later contribution of the Hebrew people to civilization was in the realm of religion rather than law and government. If the importance of Babylonian law lies in the relation between law and the written word, the importance of Hebrew law lies in the relation between law and the word of God. It is in the Greek world, particularly in Athens, where men first thought in rational terms of human affairs, that the next original contribution in the history of law was made.

When the Athenians thought of their law, two names always came into their minds. The first was Draco, but he, too, was almost entirely a mythical figure. The later Athenians ascribed to him their first code of laws, which, however, they had never seen. The Draconian Code has been reputed to be severe and bloody, but this reputation rests upon the statement of the orator Demades, who had said that Draco's laws "were written not with ink but with blood." It has also been part of the tradition that when Draco was once asked why he had made death the punishment for most offenses, he had replied: "Small ones deserve that, and I have no higher for the greater crimes." But it is not even certain that Draco enacted any code. He may have legislated only on the subject of homicide, or his reputation as a legislator may have rested on the determined manner in which he enforced the law of his time.

The second name that would occur to an Athenian would be Solon. It was Solon who was really regarded as the lawgiver of Athens,

31

and, in common with other ancient peoples, the Athenians of later generations had a habit of attributing to him a great many more laws than he ever enacted, as well as the whole wisdom of their polity. The Greeks of later generations also spoke of Seven Wise Men, but, although they did not always agree on the seven to be included in the list, they always included Solon. Aristotle said of Solon that "he was the first to come forward as a champion of the people," and he was indeed commonly regarded as the founder of Greek democracy. He was also the first Athenian poet, and wrote some five thousand poems—elegies, iambics, and trochees.

As is to be expected from a people who populated Olympus with gods and heroes, many of the stories the Athenians told about Solon had only a spiritual foundation in fact. Essentially the traditions were true, for Solon is a historical character, and the basic facts of his life and career are known. Indeed, many fragments of his poems are extant, and in them he speaks of his labors for the welfare of the Athenian people. But the traditions were full of exaggerations and anachronisms. Many steps had still to be taken after Solon's life before democracy, even in the sense in which the term applies to the ancient world, could be said to exist in Athens. But the reforms which Solon introduced did mark the beginning of a new order in Athenian society, and when his work was done he had accomplished what was perhaps the first bloodless revolution in human society. There are signs that in his own time the people were dissatisfied with their champion and that Solon was in the usual position of a prophet without much honor in his own time, but the later Athenians venerated his name, because they enjoyed the blessings which, they believed, he had first inaugurated.

In modern times the name Solon is a synonym for legislator, and some, in both ancient and modern times, have regarded him as great by virtue of the fact that he gave the Athenians their first known code of written laws. Solon did indeed give the Athenians written laws. The copies of the laws employed by the magistrates were called "axones," and were inscribed on revolving wooden tablets, while those set up publicly were called "kyrbeis," and were inscribed on tapering stone pillars shaped like a Persian hat. But the giving of written laws could hardly have been regarded any longer as a new legal device, nor could there have been much faith in their efficacy as a protection to the weak against the strong. It is true that the laws of Solon were not the decrees of a benevolent king or god, but were enacted—perhaps for the first time—upon the demand of the people themselves. But this novelty can hardly be regarded as a sufficient foundation for Solon's fame. His originality is to be discovered rather in the nature of his laws. From the point of view of legal technique, Solon's originality was to shift the emphasis from the written word of the legislator to the method of the law's administration; from the texts themselves to the men who would interpret the texts. From the point of view of substance, the significance of Solon was bound up with the first dissolution in legal history of an archaic society and an archaic legal order. Solon initiated this process of dissolution, and hence came to be regarded, not unnaturally, as the architect of the completed order. The sophistication of legal technique only reflected a new sophistication of society and the impact of social change.

The first Greek civilization in Asia Minor and the Aegean Islands had been stimulated by contact with Egypt and the land of the Two Rivers. But in the age of Homer the civilization of the Greek tribes was still archaic. One of the most famous of legal monuments is the Homeric trial scene depicted on the shield of Achilles. The disputants have come before the elders in a case involving a homicide. From the scene it is not entirely clear whether the family of the slain man must accept a composition; it may be that the blood-feud is still permitted. The enigmatic nature of Homer's passage has been an endless subject of dispute among scholars, for they have perceived in it the possible origin of the Greek court. But it is clear, in any event, that the administration of criminal justice is still in its beginnings.

The first Greeks, like the first Hebrews, were nomads who had settled down and turned to agriculture. Like other archaic peoples, the Greeks, when they began to live in settled communities, came to be ruled by kings and many magistrates. Unlike the peoples of the Near East, however, the Greeks were able to get rid of their kings, and at a comparatively early date. The duties of the kings were transferred to members of the nobility who were called "archons." The members of the King's Council, which the Greeks called the "Areopagus," continued to function as the most important magistrates. But the destruction of the power of the kings meant the severe and unchecked rule of the nobles, who engaged in piracy on the seas and despoiled the peasantry at home. The whole land of Attica groaned under their exactions. The misery of the Greek peasant may be judged from the description of his lot in the poems of Hesiod, who was himself a tiller of the soil in Boeotia.

Thus far wealth had existed only in the form of lands and flocks. But in the sixth century there dawned the era of Athens' commercial greatness and prosperity. Other Greek cities were already founding colonies and were engaging in a lively trade with the Near East and the islands of the Aegean, but Athens rapidly outstripped them. An extensive pottery industry, which relied largely on slave labor, was established in Athens, but there was a considerable export, too, of agricultural products, particularly olive oil. Along about this time coined money came into use in Attica, by way of Lydia. The new money economy, however, although it benefited the new class of mercantile capitalists, only made harder the lot of the tillers of the soil. There appears to have been a class of serfs, called hektemors, who were bound to the soil and received one-sixth of its produce as a share of their labor. As long as they paid their rent in kind, they were little affected by the conditions of the market, but when they paid their rent or made purchases in money, they rapidly fell into debt, which ultimately led to slavery. The lands of the free peasant proprietors were mortgaged to the rich nobles, and when the peasants were unable to pay their debts, they lost their lands, and the estates of the nobles grew larger and larger. The terms of the mortgages were inscribed on small stone pillars, which were called "horoi" by the Athenians. They were erected on the mortgaged farms themselves, and the Attic countryside was dotted with these melancholy monuments. As so often, prosperity made the rich richer and the poor poorer.

Aristotle tells us, by way of summarizing the conditions of these times, that "the poor were in a state of bondage to the rich, both themselves, their wives, and their children." The antagonism between the classes was so great that violent revolt threatened. Not only were the debtors demanding to be released from their chains, but the landless were demanding a division of the large estates. But civil war never broke out. That fact alone would not be remarkable, for discontent has often been repressed, nor is it remarkable that the oppressed classes were able to get something done. By themselves they would not have succeeded, but they found powerful allies in the new mercantile capitalists, who hated the nobles because they were despised by them and were determined to break their hold upon the machinery of the state. At this time, moreover, the nobles themselves were engaged in violent feuds, and were thus weakening their position against the rival classes. What does seem strange is the method chosen to resolve the conflict and restore social peace, and perhaps no less so the terms of the settlement, if the reigning tradition is believed.

The method of appeasement chosen was not only to select Solon as archon, which in itself was a normal governmental event, since an archon had to be chosen every year, but to appoint him also as an arbitrator with plenary powers to revise the constitution and introduce whatever reforms were necessary, all parties agreeing to abide by his decisions and decrees. This handling of a revolutionary situation by arbitration probably did not seem extraordinary to the Attic community of the time. When we speak of a commercial revolution in Athens in the sixth century, the term must not be taken to imply what it would mean in modern times. The Athens of that day could not have had a population of much more than twenty-five thousand, and, while commerce and industry were growing rapidly, Athenian life still showed survivals of tribal simplicity in its political and social organization. At the present day, in some primitive communities a wise man or chief who has established a great reputation in one community will sometimes be called in by another to act as judge. While Athens was far from primitive, it was, like a great many archaic communities of antiquity, disposed to honor and venerate the sage. His advice was sought as well as that of the oracle at Delphi.

But how did it come about that Solon was chosen as archon and mediator? How did his wisdom and disinterestedness come to the attention of the people of Athens? How did he secure his reputation as a sage, so that all parties were ready to entrust their fates to him? It seems that the ancients themselves were somewhat puzzled by these questions, for the traditions were various and conflicting. Some of them contain obviously legendary elements.

Little is known of Solon's life before he assumed the archonship. His father was Exekestides, who was said to be descended from Codrus, the early king of Athens. Solon was thus of noble birth. When he was born is uncertain, although it can be said that it was after the middle of the seventh century. The tradition was that Solon's father had almost ruined the family by his excessive generosity, and that it was for this reason that Solon entered a life of trade, which took him to many foreign countries. He is said to have done well as a trader, although the wealth he amassed was only moderate. In his early youth he is said to have written erotic poetry, but the dissipation of the family fortune no doubt had caused him to settle down to an industrious and gainful life.

By virtue of his birth and early activity, Solon was peculiarly suited to undertake the role of mediator. Since he was of noble birth, he would have the confidence of the upper class. On the other hand, his fortune having been amassed in trade, he could understand the aspirations of the new moneyed class. His character was such that he abhorred violence and extremes. He was fitted to be a statesman because he shared the common opinions and feelings of his times. In his religious and philosophical views, he was an average man of the sixth century. He was a poet, it is true, but his surviving poems contain no heresies or even brilliant images or flashes of inspiration. They exhibit no bold spirit of innovation and experiment. On the contrary, they strike a note of sadness and quiet resignation. In one of his poems he wrote: "No mortal is blest with happiness; wretched are all human souls on whom the sun looks down." Solon was indeed the born moderator even though he was not the born poet. Antiquity attributed a proverb to Solon: "Overdo nothing."

Solon was not the poet and philosopher who remained aloof from the pressing political problems of his day. His didactic verses deal with contemporary issues. There are indications that he was skillful as a practical politician, that he knew how to talk in vague and glittering generalities and to make promises that were not too definite in their terms. He had the gift of making each of the contending parties believe that he was on its side. He coined the slogan, "Equality breeds no war," and obviously every man could have his own ideas concerning the requirements of equality. That there was a campaign before Solon was elevated to the archonship, and that Solon himself made campaign pledges, appears from the fragments of one of his poems, in which, defending himself against subsequent attacks, he emphatically asserted: "That which I promised I have fulfilled by heaven's aid."

But neither generous words nor fine traits of character suffice, without deeds, to explain Solon's choice as the savior of Athens. He appears to have achieved some fame by intervening to help settle a feud which had long been raging between two of the noble Athenian families, the Kylonians and the Alkmaionids. But, by the almost unanimous opinion of antiquity, Solon had found favor in the eyes of his fellow Athenians by his share in the conquest of the island of

Salamis, which was then in the possession of Megara. It was inevitable that the island should have become a subject of bitter contention between Athens and Megara, both enterprising commercial cities and old rivals. Salamis lay in the Aegean midway between them, and its possession by one of the rivals threatened the trade routes of the other. Solon was undoubtedly connected with the struggle over Salamis, although his exact role is uncertain, for he wrote a poem of one hundred lines on the subject, of which one of the extant fragments shows that he sought to rouse the Athenians to take the island.

> Onward to Salamis, beloved isle!
> For her we'll fight, repulsing bitter shame.

The legend was that the Athenians, weary of the contest over Salamis, had enacted a law threatening the death penalty for agitating for the recovery of the island. Solon wrote his poem and, pretending to be mad, ran out to the market place with a cap upon his head and recited his verses to the people, as if he were a herald just arrived from Salamis. The poem, indeed, begins:

> I am a herald come from Salamis the fair,
> My news from thence my verses shall declare.

According to this tale, the Athenians were so roused that an expedition was organized at once to wipe out the shame of Salamis, and Solon himself not only participated in the venture but also devised the ruse that made possible the taking of the island. He is said to have lured the Megarians to Colias, another island, by dispatching an Athenian to pretend that he was a renegade and to spread the news that the Athenian women were at Colias, where they could be seized.

According to still another tale, Solon was told to go to Salamis by the oracle of Delphi. He then went there with five hundred volunteers, who had been induced to come forward by the enactment of a law that those who took the island should be the highest in the government. The fighting proving inconclusive, the Spartans were chosen as arbitrators, and Solon won the case by showing that the sons of Ajax had given Salamis to the Athenians, who once inhabited the island. This Solon proved by opening the tombs, in order to show that the bodies were buried in Athenian fashion facing the west.

In any event, Solon was the hero of Salamis, and he was chosen archon and mediator, probably in the year 594 B.C., according to the best reckoning. The people, no longer distracted, no doubt, by the turmoil over Salamis, bethought themselves again of their woes, and renewed their outcries for relief. Solon responded by introducing a series of reforms. The nature of some of them is not open to question, but concerning some of the others there has been endless dispute. If the most radical version is accepted, it was the most remarkable blood-less revolution in history. But even if it is rejected, the lower classes among the Athenians had a good deal to be thankful for.

As soon as he took office, Solon proceeded to attack the problem of debt. Some assert that he canceled all debts owed by one Athenian to another. Others maintain that he canceled only the debts which were secured by the person or the land of the debtor. This would still leave in effect a large number of commercial debts secured by personal property, such as cattle, slaves, ships, and their cargoes. Did he cancel debts for which the debtor had already served a good many years? Or did he, as one ancient writer expressly asserts, cancel no debts, but lighten their burden by reducing the rate of interest and by inflating the currency?

The latter is undoubtedly a minority view, but the reduction of interest rates and the inflation of the currency is an expedient that in times of crisis has appealed to legislators of all countries and climes. That the "cancellation" of personal debts may have amounted only to this is a strong possibility in view of the fact that tradition ascribed to Solon not only the revision of the Attic system of weights and measures but also the revaluation of Attic currency.

But it is highly probable that Solon decreed a general release of Athenians from debtor slavery. This accords entirely with the treat-ment of debtor slaves in antiquity. Among the Babylonians a debtor was released after three years, and among the Hebrews after six. It was only one step forward to release all debtor slaves at one time. But it is improbable that in an expanding commercial economy all debts should have been canceled, even those that resulted from the ordinary course of commercial investment, and that such action should have been taken by a lawgiver who was himself a man of commerce and owed his power to the new moneyed class. There is, however, one step Solon took in reforming the law of debt about which there can be no doubt at all. He prohibited enslavement for debt in the future. This act certainly did not trespass upon vested rights. At the same time he prohibited a practice which was all too common in Athens, as in other countries in antiquity—the selling of children into slavery.

On the other hand, it is improbable that Solon really canceled all debts secured by a mortgage on land. In one of his iambic tetrameters, a good portion of which has survived, Solon himself made his claim to the remembrance of posterity in these terms: "A witness I have who will support this claim full well in the tribunal of time—the mighty mother of the Olympian deities, Black Earth, from whose bosom once I drew out the pillars everywhere implanted; and she who is formerly enslaved is now free." But the passage is enigmatic. These pillars were the mortgage pillars, but they could, metaphorically speaking, have been drawn out merely by making it possible for the owners of the land to pay off the mortgages themselves without resorting to outright cancellation of the debts. Solon undoubtedly undertook some revision of the debt structure, which could have produced the happy result indirectly. Solon does not say explicitly that he abrogated the mortgage debts. Such a drastic step would have been quite unprecedented and unparalleled, and the measures of Solon were always moderate. The landless Athenians doubtless made the demand that the great estates be broken up, and that the land be redivided. But Solon probably gave no heed to this demand. He may have limited the size of estates which might be held in the future, and such a measure alone might in the long run have resulted in freeing the "black earth" from its bondage. He also did something for the lowly hektemors, but he did not make them free proprietors. He may have modified some of the incidents of their servile status, but beyond this he probably did not go. After all, was not his motto, "Overdo nothing"? Solon also helped to keep agrarian prices down and indirectly struck at the power of the nobles by prohibiting the export of all agricultural products except oil.

Solon's moderation was even more marked in his expedients for constitutional reform. He left undisturbed the vast powers of the ancient Areopagus, which was the guardian of the laws and the safety of the state, and did not disturb the archons and the other magistrates in the exercise of their traditional functions. At that time political rights in Athens depended upon the possession of property, and the Athenians were divided into property classes, based upon agricultural holding, for the rights of the members of each class depended on the size of their income in terms of measures of corn. At least three of these classes must have been in existence in the time of Solon, but he may have added a fourth class, the "thetes" or day laborers. In any event, Solon did not alter this aspect of the timocratic scheme, although he may have modified the property qualifications and liberalized the standards of eligibility for office. While the nobles were left in control of the high offices of state, Solon gave the thetes a voice in the ecclesia, or assembly, and allowed an appeal from the decisions of the magistrates to a popular court, the Helaea, in which the thetes could also sit. Solon must, however, have been apprehensive even about the share of the common people in the assembly, for he also created a new council or "boule" of four hundred, which he charged with the duty of preparing the measures that were to be submitted to the assembly.

Solon also enacted some laws which were not of a constitutional nature, apart from those related to debt. Of the innumerable laws attributed by the Athenians to him in later times, it is extremely doubtful that he enacted more than a few. These laws are either too archaic to have originated in the time of Solon, or represent the sumptuary type of legislation which derived from the conditions of later Athenian society, or appear so odd that it seems hard to believe that they ever existed. A genuine law of Solon is one permitting a husband to slay an adulterer taken *flagrante delicto,* a law suited to the conditions of archaic societies which generally permit summary treatment of wrongdoers taken in the act. On the other hand, Solon is credited with laws prohibiting idleness, drunkenness, and excessive mourning, or regulating the dress and behavior of women in public—types of laws that are very suggestive of those enacted by meddlesome or Puritanical commonwealths in later times.

Solon undoubtedly enacted other laws which proved extremely important for the development of the ordinary civil and criminal law of Athens. Two of them attacked in different ways the hegemony of the kindred group. As in other archaic societies, the family had paramount property rights. Thus, the head of the family had no right to make a will which would give the family estate to strangers on his death. Solon laid the foundation of freedom of testation by enacting that the head of a family who had no male heirs could make a will leaving his estate to whomsoever he pleased. Previously, by the law of intestate succession, the collateral kindred had inherited.

Solon made an even greater departure from archaic tradition when he broke up the monopoly of the family in prosecuting wrongs against its members. Solon enacted that every Athenian could initiate proceedings, even in the case of offenses which had hitherto been regarded only as attacks upon the security and safety of individuals and their families rather than upon the state. However, even in this respect he compromised, for he did not disturb the law tradition has attributed to Draco, which permitted only the relatives to take action in the case of homicide. The Athenians emphasized the novelty of Solon's enactment by a familiar story: Solon is supposed to have been asked how men could most effectively be deterred from committing injustice. He is said to have replied: "If those who are not injured feel as much indignation as those who are."

Such were the labors of Solon as a lawgiver. But apparently he did not receive the thanks and plaudits of a grateful people. The people were angry because he had not divided the land. The nobles were incensed that the people had been given new privileges and that the burden of their debts had been lightened. Indeed, scandalous stories were circulated about the lawgiver. The poor even said that Solon had told some of his wealthy friends that he was going to abolish all debts so that they could go and buy up large tracts of land by obtaining loans which they would not have to pay. The wealthy said that Solon himself had taken advantage of the situation to make a profit.

According to later tradition, which obviously owed its origin to the days of Athens' greatness and prosperity, the people soon realized their folly and displayed their gratitude to Solon by giving a great feast to celebrate their liberation. There is no doubt, however, that bitter feelings persisted into later generations, for the dissatisfaction of the people is recorded in many of Solon's own poems, which he wrote in later years in order to defend himself. "To the people," wrote Solon, "I have given just as much power as suffices, neither taking away from their due nor offering more; while for those who had power and were honored for wealth, I have taken thought likewise, that they should suffer nothing unseemly. I stand with strong shield flung around both parties, and have allowed neither to win an unjust victory." In another poem Solon wrote that if anyone else had had his task, "he would not have checked the people, nor stopped before he had stirred up the milk, and extracted its fatness"; but that he had taken his stand "like a boundary stone in the debatable land between the two parties." Again the moderator complains: "Those who came as pillagers had lavish hopes; every man of them believed he would light on a great fortune, and that I, though I coaxed so smoothly, would soon reveal a lavish purpose. Vain were their imaginings then, and now in their anger against me they all eye me askance as if I were an enemy." Even more plaintively he says: "I stood at bay, defending myself on every side, like a wolf among a pack of hounds."

The traditions concerning Solon as the lawgiver of Athens also perpetuate the disappointment of the people. They were disillusioned with the efficacy of written laws even before Solon began his work, for otherwise they would not have demanded economic reforms so loudly. Solon himself, as well as the people, was apparently skeptical about law and the written word. He did not believe that his laws realized abstract justice or even approached perfection. In one of his poems he said that he had fashioned "that blend of force and justice that is law," and legend, in commemoration of this wonderful characterization, perhaps, includes the story that when Solon was asked whether "he had left the Athenians the best laws that could be given," he had replied: "The best they could receive." To Solon, as well as to one of the other of the Seven Wise Men of Greece, was attributed the saying that "laws are like cobwebs in that if any little thing fell into them, they held it fast, but if a thing of any size fell into them, it broke the meshes and escaped." All traditions agreed that Solon had not regarded his laws as eternal. One tradition was that he had instituted them for a hundred years, another for only ten years. But even for this brief period it was apparently feared that they might be disregarded, for it was believed that the archons were accustomed to take an oath that they would cause a gold statue to be erected if they transgressed any of Solon's laws. The most remarkable belief of all emphasized the greater importance of the administration of Solon's laws. Some said that Solon had purposely made his laws uncertain in order that the people might be able to control the magistrates!

After the completion of his legislative labors, Solon left Athens to travel abroad. The accounts differed about the reason. Some said that it was because too many Athenians questioned him about the meaning and application of his laws. But this interpretation of his departure could only have reflected the discovery that many of his laws were uncertain—as laws invariably prove to be. Others said that Solon decided to go abroad because, after his laws were published, he was subjected to such hostile criticism. This would seem to be by far the more likely reason, but it is also possible that Solon merely decided to resume the life of trade which had been interrupted when he was called to end the civil dissensions of Athens.

Little that can be accepted as historical is known of Solon's travels. From a fragment of one of his poems it is known that he went to Egypt. While there he is supposed to have studied with the Egyptian priests at Saïs and to have learned from them the story of the lost continent of Atlantis. It is also said that from Egypt he proceeded to the island of Cyprus, whose ruler founded a city in his honor named Soli. The most famous legend concerning Solon's travels is the story of his interview with Croesus, King of Lydia. The king asks Solon to tell him whom he would regard as the happiest man on earth, expecting, of course, that Solon would say, "Croesus, King of Lydia." But Solon mentions some obscure Athenians who were then dead and of whom Croesus had never heard. Then the king demands angrily: "Am I not the happiest man on earth?" But Solon replies: "No man can be called happy until his whole life has run its course, for no man can know what the fates have in store for him." Later Croesus is conquered by Cyrus, King of Persia, who condemns him to the pyre. As he mounts its steps Croesus calls three times bitterly upon the name of Solon. Cyrus asks to know the reason, and when Croesus tells him, he is so moved and impressed by the wisdom of Solon that he spares the life of the vanquished king.

The work that Solon had begun was to be carried further by the men whom we call the tyrants of Athens. "Tyranny" has become an evil word, but it was not so regarded by the people of Athens. The so-called "tyrants" were members of the new moneyed class, who were able to seize power only because they had the support of the common people, and their historic mission was to destroy finally the noble class, and so liberate the Athenian peasantry. They thus completed the social revolution, and made possible the later Athenian democracy. Solon tells us in one of his poems that he could have made himself, if he wished, tyrant of Athens, but that instead he resisted the blandishments of the people. It was left, therefore, for another to do so. Thirty years after the archonship of Solon, Pisistratus, who some say was a cousin of Solon, seized power.

It is said that Solon returned to Athens when he heard of the trouble that was brewing, but he was already too late. Pisistratus had seized power by pretending to have been wounded by his enemies and by asking the people to give him a guard, which he employed to establish himself as tyrant. The people succumbed despite the warning of Solon that the ruse was only a bad copy of Homer's Ulysses. When they gave Pisistratus the guard, Solon remarked of himself that "he was wiser than some and braver than others." He meant by this that he was wiser than those who did not see through the plot, and braver than those who did but were afraid to come out in opposition. When, supported by his guard, Pisistratus seized the Acropolis, Solon proceeded to the market place, where he urged the people to rise. When he perceived that his appeal was falling on deaf ears, he brought out his arms and laid them in the portico before his door, as a sign that he was resigned to the inevitable. Solon's boldness caused people to ask him why he stayed in Athens and to what he trusted for his protection. He replied: "To my old age."

Solon must then have been a very old man. He certainly could not have long survived the establishment of the tyranny of Pisistratus. It is probable that the tyrant was a great admirer of Solon, and that he did not abrogate any of his laws. In fact, Pisistratus owed his power to the same social revolution that had brought about the Solonian reforms. Exactly when Solon died is not known. The legend is that Solon's ashes were scattered to the wind over his beloved island of Salamis. Statues to him were erected, which in the fourth century still stood in public places in Athens and, of course, in Salamis.

An acute agrarian question no longer existed a half century after Solon's death. Pisistratus was bolder than Solon, and divided some of the large estates among the peasantry. Although the number of slaves in Athens increased enormously, they were no longer debtor slaves but were recruited by war and conquest or supplied by a flourishing slave trade. The democratic revolution in Athens was completed by Cleisthenes, who converted the popular court of appeal into a court of first instance. Thereafter the magistrates held only preliminary hearings in order to prepare cases for trial before the people. The power of the noble families was further undermined when Cleisthenes abolished the old tribal divisions and reorganized the Athenian state upon the basis of new geographic divisions. An important survival of the archaic order of society was thus also destroyed. Upon the basis of the new geographic divisions, Cleisthenes converted the old Solonian Council of Four Hundred into a Council of Five Hundred, which rapidly assumed a dominant role in the government of Athens. In order to prevent the recurrence of tyranny, Cleisthenes also introduced a political device called "ostracism." Once a year the people by vote could declare a citizen dangerous to the safety of the state, whereupon he was banished for ten years.

In the latter part of the fifth century the ancient Areopagus was finally shorn of its power. It was restricted entirely to the trial of homicide cases and to the disposition of questions of state religion. The right to hold office was greatly extended, and all the higher officers of state, except the military leaders, were chosen entirely by lot. Finally the step of providing pay for citizens who were called to serve in the popular court was taken. Thus, even the poorest Athenians could participate in the administration of justice.

The Athenian judicial system was the very foundation of Athenian democracy, and it realized in full the potentialities of the reforms of Solon. Since the whole body of Athenian citizens could not, of course, sit in the popular court, it was divided into panels or "dicasteries." The citizens who thus sat as "dicasts" were supreme judges of the law and facts, and not only brought in the verdict but imposed sentence. Normally a public or criminal case was tried by a panel of five hundred and one citizens, while civil suits were heard before panels of two hundred and one. Despite the popular nature of the courts, procedure was elaborate and highly developed. There was a preliminary hearing; the complaint and the answer had to be in writing; the art of pleading was highly developed; and not only could special pleas be interposed but objections taken in point of law. Only a few archaic survivals existed in this precocious procedure: the taking of decisory oaths, which stemmed from an earlier practice of compurgation; and the necessity for co-operation by the plaintiff in executing a judgment, a reminiscence of the ancient resort to self-help. The average Athenian citizen was quite capable of conducting a lawsuit and was expected to do so. But while there were no lawyers in the modern sense of the term, litigants often employed speech-writers to compose the orations which they would deliver before the dicasts. Greek orators thus wrote many a speech for tongue-tied Athenians caught in the toils of the law. Not infrequently a hard-pressed orator would insert a reference to a law of Solon.

The evils of the Athenian system of administering justice have long been a favorite theme. It is said that many an Athenian practically made a living by serving as a dicast. The dicasts themselves, like all "jurors," are said to have paid little heed to precedent, and Athenian law was thus volatile and arbitrary. Solon's innovation of allowing any citizen to initiate a prosecution is said to have led many an Athenian to become a professional prosecutor in order to blackmail citizens or to collect the fines and forfeitures which were allowed to the prosecutor under many of the laws. These evil prosecutors have been called "sycophants"—a term, however, that does not mean "flatterer," but is merely a transliteration of the Greek word. But the picture of the litigious Athenian rests largely on the comedies of Aristophanes, and satirists are always allowed some latitude. There is no way of measuring the litigiousness of the Athenian in comparison with other peoples; professional judges have disregarded precedent, too, or the law could not have changed or developed; later civilizations were to produce official public prosecutors, but this system of enforcing the criminal law led to evils of its own. The public prosecutor represented a more practical and efficient method of guarding the safety of individuals as well as that of the state. What is everybody's business proves all too often nobody's business. On the other hand, the system of official prosecution often tipped the scales of justice too much in favor of the state, and thus endangered individual liberty. In no civilization have litigation and law enforcement proved wholly satisfactory.

The inherent limitation of the law as a system of social appeasement is, indeed, the ultimate measure of Solon's labors on behalf of the people of Athens. In some respects he made a direct attack upon the archaic foundations of Athenian society. In the imagination of the people of Athens he made his deepest impression undoubtedly by the steps he took to free them from the burden of debt. There was even a word current in Athens to express this phase of his activity— "seisachtheia," which may be translated as "disburdenment." Solon's reform of the law of debt was an assault upon one of the basic foundations of archaic law. Whatever changes Solon made in the system of landholding could have been no less deeply felt and appreciated. The very tendency of modern historians to magnify the extent of Solon's economic reforms is itself deeply significant. Laws that directly introduce radical changes in the economic order are so rare that historians generally tend to magnify their significance. To think that Solon really launched a bloodless revolution, which was accomplished at once by his fiats, is an exhilarating thought. All too often is reform legal reform rather than economic reform. The law is a method of dealing with social conflicts rather than a method of removing their causes, and ordinarily legal reformers content themselves with assuring merely equality before the law, and with tinkering with this or that cog in the machinery of justice. They hope that by changing the administration of the law they will be able to shift the balance of power. They change the procedure for enforcing rights rather than make any alterations in the rights themselves. Solon's effort to solve the social conflict of his day was made primarily in this way. He hoped that by giving the people a share in the administration of justice they would be able to help themselves. The right of appeal from the magistrates to the people, which he instituted, probably did not seem at first such a great concession, nor did the right conferred upon every Athenian to prosecute wrongdoers, although actually it was a momentous and even revolutionary step. But in the end they accomplished all that legal and political reforms can accomplish. They created the Athenian democracy of the great age of Pericles, which regarded Solon as its founder, but this democracy, limited as it was to the small circle of Athenian citizens, was unable to solve its social and economic problems. Undermined in the conflicts with the Persians, it perished as the result of the shocks of the Peloponnesian Wars and the imperialism of Alexander. It fell finally under the sway of Rome, which was to build the greatest legal system of the ancient world.

Gaius

THE BEGINNINGS OF JURISPRUDENCE

Each of the three great peoples of antiquity who have most influenced the modern world has been selected by historians for a special vocation. It is a well-worn historical platitude that the Hebrews excelled in moral theology, the Greeks in philosophy, the Romans in law and government. In histories of law it is customary to contrast the Roman genius for "practicality" with the imaginative fancy of the Greeks, and to point out that the latter, despite their rich mental endowment, were unable to create stable and enduring legal institutions such as were in existence in ancient Rome. Now the greater stability and fecundity of Roman law is an undoubted historical fact. The Roman law was, it is true, the only legal system of antiquity that achieved maturity, and there are few legal devices even in modern law which do not have their Roman counterparts or whose origins may not be traced back to the Romans. However, the reason for this does not lie in any mysterious genius of the Roman people or in the incapacity of other peoples. On the contrary the artfulness of Solon's reforms bears witness to the Attic genius for legal invention, and, indeed, historians attribute many of the most striking features of Roman law to the influence of Greek ideas. The evidence would seem to substantiate this view. That the Greeks failed in legal administration is commonly attributed to the unbridled power of the Athenian jury system, which is supposed to have prevented the orderly development of precedent, the very foundation of any legal system worthy of the name, as any lawyer will tell you. Unfortunately for this theory, however, we shall see that an enormous amount of discretion existed also in the Roman legal system. But it was entrusted to magistrates rather than to juries.

Apart from its intrinsic merits, the ascendancy of Roman law in the ancient world has a very simple explanation. The vocation of the Roman was war; law was his avocation. Law and arms have been inseparable; the great lawgiving peoples have always been the great empire-builders; and ancient Rome, which began as a village on the Tiber, succeeded in building the universal empire of the ancient world. To be sure, every one of the great peoples of antiquity built an empire, but none endured for long. Babylonians, Assyrians, Hittites, Persians, Greeks, Phoenicians, and Carthaginians all had their day in the sun, but invariably vanished into the darkness. Only the Roman Empire endured long enough for its archaic legal institutions to develop into maturity. The continuity of empire is a necessary condition for the unfolding of legal "genius."

The early laws of the Romans reveal much the same features as those of other archaic civilizations. Like the Greeks, the Romans rid themselves of their kings at an early date, and a struggle ensued between the nobles, who were called "patricians," and the common people, who were called "plebeians." As in the ancient Near East, the administration of justice was for a long time dominated by a priestly class, called the "pontiffs," who alone professed to know the ancient law and the necessary forms of legal remedies, which they kept secret as a cherished monopoly of their class. The plebeians struggled to break the strangle hold of the patricians upon all the important offices of the state, and to invade the sacred precincts of pontifical jurisprudence.

As among the Greeks, the victory of the Roman plebeians was marked by the unwilling grant to them by the patricians of a written code of laws, which was drafted in 451–449 B.C. by special commissioners, or "decemvirs," appointed for the purpose. This code, inscribed upon bronze tablets, was called by the Romans the Twelve Tables, and they resembled the laws of Solon so much that the legend arose that a commission had been sent to Greece to study Solon's work before the Twelve Tables were drafted. The Twelve Tables were long venerated by the Romans as the *fons omnis publici privatque iuris* (the fountain of all public and private law), and Cicero, who lived from 106–43 B.C., relates that even in his own youth they had to be learned by heart by boys in school. Although a rather late archaic code, they betray very primitive legal institutions. The procedure for commencing a legal action is still very simple, that is, by oral summons of the defendant who, it is laid down, may demand a cushioned carriage if he is sick or an old man. The law of debt is still savage, for it seems to be expressly provided that creditors may cut up the body of a defaulting debtor in proportion to their debts, although there is no proof that the rule was actually enforced in historical times. The power of the father over his children is absolute and endures for his whole lifetime, but this *patria potestas,* as the Romans called it, was unique among ancient peoples only in its lifetime duration. The law of wrongs is still based upon composition, and there are survivals of both self-help and the *lex talionis.* A nocturnal thief, as well as a daytime thief caught in the act, may be slain; and retaliation is permitted in the case of the breaking of a limb if composition is not made. The Twelve Tables apparently envisage the possibility of making a will, but it was to be made before a public assembly, which probably could have refused its consent, and there may have been limitations upon the property to be willed. In case of intestacy, in the absence of adult sons, the rule of agnatic succession prevailed, that is, inheritance by those who traced their descent in the male line.

This simple system of barbarian usage was converted in the course of some six centuries into the highly subtle and complex system of jurisprudence which ever since has been so much admired. The Roman law became an integral part of the grandeur that was Rome. The process of the dissolution of the ancient law began after the First Punic War, which was the beginning of the end for Rome's only great rival, Carthage, and inaugurated the unparalleled period of Rome's commercial expansion. As Rome became the trading center of the world, foreigners flocked there in ever increasing numbers. Consequently the ancient Roman law had to be remade to take care of the interests of Roman citizen and foreigner alike. In the last century of the Republic, the Roman law was already in its classical period, although its greater glories were still to be achieved in the first two centuries of the Empire, when the economy of Rome developed into a system of capitalism based upon large-scale production by slave labor.

The early phase of the transformation of the Roman law was accomplished by an official magistrate. After the expulsion of the kings, their judicial functions were taken over by the consuls. But about a century after the adoption of the Twelve Tables, the Roman Senate transferred the judicial functions of the consuls to a new magistrate called the *praetor urbanus,* or urban praetor. The political motive for this change appears to have been the fact that at this time the plebeians had been admitted to the consulship; its ultimate effect upon the mode of development of the Roman law was far-reaching. The urban praetor, who, like the other Roman magistrates, possessed a large discretionary authority, was able gradually to undermine the old law. There grew up the practice of having the praetor, when he entered upon his office, issue an edict in which he would lay down what rules he intended to follow and what remedies he would allow during his annual term. At first, however, the praetor could affect the traditional law to a limited extent only by means of his edict, because the ancient forms of legal remedies, called *leges actiones,* were very rigid. Every action had to be fitted to some set form of words and a pantomime enacted before the praetor. If the necessary forms were followed, the praetor had to allow the trial of the action.

During the whole period of the classical Roman law, however, the trial of a civil suit was not before the praetor himself but before a jury of one Roman citizen, called a *iudex,* who was chosen by lot from a list of men of substance, usually of the patrician class. The single Roman *iudex* has been much extolled in contrast to the huge Greek dicasteries, but the system did not prevent vast changes from taking place in the Roman law. Some scholars argue that the *iudex* was originally a voluntary arbitrator, but this is pure surmise.

In Roman law we encounter for the first time the curious phenomenon of two seemingly parallel but actually conflicting legal systems within the same state. The one the Romans called *ius civile,* which literally translated means the civil law, and the other the *ius gentium,* which may be described as "the law common to all nations." Now the *ius civile* was simply the ancient Roman law whose archaic forms and ceremonies were the exclusive privilege of the Roman citizens. Like most archaic peoples, the Romans regarded their law as very personal and sacred to themselves. When, however, foreigners continued to flock to Rome in ever increasing numbers and to engage in business transactions, their legal interest had to be afforded protection. Thus, in 247 B.C. a *praetor peregrinus,* or praetor for foreigners, was created, and he began to apply, first in controversies between foreigners, but soon in controversies between foreigners and Roman citizens, new legal rules which had no counterpart in the traditional *ius civile,* and which were, indeed, free of its ancient formalisms. Doubtless the peregrine praetors thought that the new rules were derived from the practices common to all nations, but actually they represented their own ideas of expediency and right conduct. This was the law called the *ius gentium.*

The *ius gentium* developed with particularly great rapidity, because the peregrine praetor, unlike the urban praetor, who had jurisdiction over Roman citizens only, was not bound to adhere to the forms of the ancient *leges actiones*. In all probability the peregrine praetor originated the "formulary" procedure of classical Roman law. It was so called because it allowed the praetor to frame a formula that was adapted to the facts of a particular case. After about a century of development, the formulary procedure was, by a special *lex,* or law, called the *lex Aebutia,* made applicable to proceedings before the urban praetor, whose annual edict now became a book of flexible formulas and rules for coping with contemporary legal problems. When the praetor thought that the old *ius civile* was no longer desirable in particular circumstances, he could insert an *exceptio,* or exception, in the formula, which would permit the *iudex* to disregard it. Thus the *ius gentium,* which originally had been only for foreigners, became virtually the whole system of Roman law, which even Roman citizens were only too happy to claim for their own.

The two chief sources of law under the Republic seem to have been the Twelve Tables and the praetorian edict. The first was the work of legislators, and the second was officially the work of magistrates. The early magistrates, with the help of the pontiffs, no doubt had a great deal to do with the invention of the *leges actiones*. Even officials can invent a certain amount of procedural formalism. But the gradual abolition of this formalism and the very adroitness immanent in the conceptions of the *ius civile* and the *ius gentium* betray the activity of lawyers. Here are present for the first time fictions, evasions, duplicities, and subtleties that are not to be found among any other people of antiquity. Ancient forms were observed, but they were now almost completely devoid of substance. However, this dubious miracle was not wrought by the praetors. The edicts were published in their names but were actually the work of a rising legal profession. The praetors were simply the mouthpieces for new creators of the law. For the first time in the history of civilization the beginnings of jurisprudence were to be perceived.

All archaic peoples produced the institution of the court. Also they all produced more or less elaborate officialdoms. But only the Romans remained long enough on the scene of history to produce lawyers—the creative architects of mature legal systems, the indispensable midwives of a thriving commerce. The Babylonians produced professional scribes, who may even have composed some books of legal forms. The Hebrew priests, like the early Roman pontiffs, dabbled a little in the law. The Athenian orators, who wrote the speeches for litigants and even accepted fees, approached the creation of a legal profession. But only the Romans produced jurisconsults and advocates whose kinship with the modern legal profession is exceedingly close. Thus was born the Roman vocation for law.

Lawyers are such an established part of our civilization that it seems remarkable that great civilizations could have flourished in antiquity without them. But archaic societies were hostile toward interference on the part of mere private individuals with the enforcement of rights enshrined by immemorial custom. They were dominated not by a businesslike approach to contracts and other transactions, but by a desire to avenge injuries. Even the man who did not pay a debt was regarded as something of a thief. When the cry of the litigant is for vengeance, the interference of others, especially for hire, is likely to be regarded as immoral. Moreover, in archaic societies, in which the trial of some especially grievous offenses, such as sorcery and adultery, is usually by such irrational means as the ordeal, the chief role is bound to be played by the priests rather than by any interloping layman.

But in late archaic societies exceptions gradually began to be made. These were, however, more apparent than real. When the master defended his slave, the guardian his ward, the great lord his vassal, servant, or client, he was really defending himself by honoring the ancient relations of kinship solidarity or status. While the general representation of one man by another in litigation was still not permitted, the prohibition might be relaxed in emergencies, as when the litigant was too old or too sick to speak for himself. This artful excuse seems indeed to have been universally the origin of forensic oratory and the profession of the advocate. But the early advocate was regarded strictly as the mere mouthpiece of the litigant on whose behalf he spoke. The litigant might, however, quietly seek advice, especially from some notable sage, the lay oracles of archaic societies.

This would appear to have been the origin of the legal profession in ancient Rome, although it is perhaps not quite accurate to use the word "profession." There were in the beginning no professional law schools or even organized modes of teaching. As soon as the giving of such assistance became permissible, any Roman could set himself up as an advocate or as the giver of legal advice, without previous training or license. It is safe to suppose that the source of this practice was the duty of protection owed by the patron to his clients, of whom there were many in ancient Rome. In Republican times the law was never practiced exclusively as a profession, and no Roman devoted all his time or energies to it. It was not a mode of livelihood at all, but a means whereby the wealthy patrician who had a gift either for oratory or legal ingenuity sought to secure influence and fame in the state. Whatever services he rendered, either as advocate or juristic adviser, were gratuitous, and when in later days fees began to be taken surreptitiously, the practice was forbidden by the so-called Cincian law. Until late in Roman history the general procedural representation of one Roman by another was possible only under very cumbersome conditions, and then only by making the representative the nominal party in the suit.

The two commodities lawyers have always offered their clients are eloquence and learning, although the same lawyer has not always possessed both. In general the possessor of eloquence has been the advocate, the possessor of learning the legal adviser, the jurist. In Republican Rome there were jurists, but the important figures were the advocates, and it was for them that the plaudits of the multitude were reserved, as the heroes of the judicial duel. The name of one of these has become virtually synonymous with advocacy, Hortensius. Cicero, another great orator, declared that forensic oratory was the first and jurisprudence the second art in Rome. Sometimes the advocate and jurist was one and the same person, but this was unusual. The jurists did not put on a great show. The custom was for clients to consult them as they strolled about in the forum. The answers they gave to legal questions were called the *responsa prudentum,* answers of the sages, a characterization that still betrays an archaic cast of thought. The jurist, however, functioned somewhat differently from the legal adviser in modern times. He gave his legal opinion not only to the private client but also to the *iudex,* who, however, was at first not bound by it.

The early jurists were men high in the Roman state, who gave only a small part of their time to the law. They were consuls, praetors, aediles, censors, augurs, and pontiffs. Appius Claudius, who was victorious over the armies of the Sabines and the Tuscans and achieved his chief fame by paving the Appian road from Rome to Capua, composed forms of action. Sextus Aelius, who was successively aedile, consul, and censor, wrote the first juristic work of any real importance in the history of the Roman law, the *Tripertita,* which was regarded as containing the "cradle of the law" because it dealt with the Twelve Tables. Cato the Censor is far more famed as a farmer, trader, soldier, and statesman, than as a jurist. Manilius, who commenced the siege of Carthage, was frequently consulted as a jurist, and so, too, was Rutilius who was deep in the political machinations of his times, as a result of which he was unjustly convicted of extortion and compelled to go into exile. There is a story that when someone sought to comfort Rutilius with the news that he would soon be able to return to Rome because of a civil war, he observed: "What ill have I done that you should wish me a return worse than my departure. I would sooner that my country should blush at my banishment than mourn at my return."

For the science of jurisprudence to flourish it is not enough that legal opinions should be given. It is necessary first that legal treatises should be written, and among the jurists of Cicero's time a growing literary activity was noticeable. Quintus Mucius Scaevola, who wrote the first systematic treatise on the civil law, may be regarded as the founder of Roman jurisprudence. In the estimation of later Roman jurists, the greatest jurisconsult of Republican times was Servius Sulpicius, who is said to have written not less than one hundred and eighty law books. He had practiced as an advocate but turned to jurisprudence when reproached with his ignorance of the law. But he became even more than a jurist; he dabbled in literature and dialectic, and his work shows significantly the influence of Greek philosophy.

The Augustan Age saw the fulfillment of still another condition for a robust jurisprudence. Famous jurists had long attracted not only clients but also pupils who were eager to be initiated into the mysteries of jurisprudence. Now there arose two opposing schools or sects of lawyers, known respectively as the Proculians and Sabinians. The two schools took their names from later followers; the founder of the Proculians was actually Labeo; the founder of the Sabinians was Capito. Both were very learned jurists—indeed, Labeo retired to the country for six months every year to write legal treatises. Labeo was devoted to the old Republican constitution, while Capito championed the new imperial order. Despite his constitutional conversatism, Labeo was a liberal constructionist in matters of private law, while Capito had a tendency to cling to the letter. It is a rather ironic commentary on juristic disputes that we do not know precisely by what legal principles the schools which they founded were divided in the later course of their history.

The whole complexion of Roman juristic activity changed during the imperial period. Augustus, who founded the Principate, took the first step towards integrating the jurists in his bureaucracy. Distrusting the established jurists, whom he regarded as a menace to his claims of power, he proceeded to create a new class of patented jurists. Thereafter only certain jurists, who were not necessarily the most eminent, were to have the right of giving legal opinions, a right known as the *ius respondendi*. With the decline of political liberty, which discouraged advocacy, especially in political causes, there began an intense preoccupation with the technical aspects of jurisprudence. In addition to the sects of lawyers, professional law schools arose in Rome and in the provinces. The heyday of the classical Roman law was reached under the Antonines, whose reigns marked the Golden Age of the Empire.

All this may sound like a pretty lengthy introduction to Gaius. But the work of Gaius, who lived in this Golden Age and who was the first of the line of the great classical Roman jurists, cannot be approached without some initiation into the mysteries of jurisprudence. A great jurist cannot be approached with the suddenness which may be appropriate in the case of mere lawgivers. There are subtleties to be understood and institutional complexities to be unraveled. If it be asked why Gaius was selected, and not Scaevola, or Servius Sulpicius, or Labeo, or Capito, or one of Gaius' successors, the answer must be the rather melancholy one that one of the works of Gaius has survived in its original form in something like its entirety, and that he is the only classical Roman jurist whom this good fortune befell. Of the works of the others we have at best only generous fragments. It is a disturbing thought, considering the supposed glories of Roman jurisprudence, that the Romans themselves did not better preserve the works of its masters. But, after all, to practical men there is really nothing more useless than a hopelessly antiquated law book.

Gaius wrote many works—thirteen at least. Among them is a commentary on the Twelve Tables and on the Provincial Edict, for the governors of provinces issued edicts, too. A very popular work of his, which was called *Res cottidianae*, discussed common legal truths, and was referred to as the *Aurea*, the "Golden Book." But the work for which Gaius was best known in his own time, and for many following centuries, was his *Institutes*. This was an elementary textbook of Roman law written for the benefit of students. Previous jurists had written commentaries, digests, or books of responses, or legal opinions. Gaius was the first to write a book of Institutes.

But the *Institutes* too was lost and was not rediscovered until the year 1816. It was one of the great discoveries in legal history, comparable to the unearthing of the Code of Hammurabi. In 1816 it happened that Barthold Georg Niebuhr, the great German historian of ancient Rome, was traveling to modern Rome as Prussian Minister to the Apostolic See. In the course of his journey he arrived at Verona, where he decided to spend several days at the Chapter Library at the Palazzo dei Canonici. Among the parchments which he examined was a palimpsest upon which in the early Middle Ages some pious scribe had written the epistles of St. Jerome. If the scribe knew that he was erasing a great classic of Roman law, the knowledge apparently was not sufficient to stay his hand. Niebuhr, suspecting that the manuscript had some writing of special interest, obtained permission to apply an infusion of nutgalls to the ninety-seventh leaf, which proved to contain juristic writing. Upon communicating with Friedrich Karl von Savigny, the most eminent Romanist of the time, the latter expressed the opinion that the manuscript was that of a work of Gaius. It proved, indeed, to be the long-lost *Institutes*. There began then the difficult task of recovering and deciphering the obscure and mutilated text, a task which was completed by 1820, owing largely to the energy and devotion of the Royal Prussian Academy of Sciences. It was a miracle of patience, learning, and chemistry.

Although the *Institutes* of Gaius has been rediscovered, the story of the life of its author remains an unsolved mystery. Sometimes it is said that we know nothing about him. At other times it is said that we know more about him than about any other classical jurist. As one historian of the Roman law puts it: "Of Gaius we know at the same time more and less than of any other classical jurist." Certainly it cannot be said that we know nothing of a man when we possess one of his works. In any event, speculation about Gaius has been rife. To men of law he is what Shakespeare has been to men of letters.

We do know the precise period of Gaius' activity. He was born in the reign of Hadrian and lived through the reigns of Hadrian, Antoninus Pius, and Marcus Aurelius. This much may be deduced from the legislative references in the *Institutes*. Apparently, he was engaged in writing at least a part of the *Institutes* in A.D. 161. Gaius regularly employs the word "divus" to characterize a deceased emperor, and it is applied to Antoninus Pius, who died in A.D. 161, after he is first mentioned by Gaius without any reference to the Emperor's divinity.

But we do not know even the full name of the jurist who is known to us as Gaius. Gaius was only a praenomen, and Romans generally were not known by a praenomen only. Various nomens and cognomens have been invented for Gaius, and he has been named Gaius Bassus, Gaius Noster, Gaius Laelius Felix. The theory of one historian is that there were two jurists bearing the same nomen and cognomen, but differing in their praenomen. So it became customary to call our Gaius by his praenomen. But who was this mysterious namesake? Another theory is that Gaius was a popular nickname.

Just as there is a theory that Shakespeare was really Sir Francis Bacon, there is a theory that Gaius was really C. Cassius Longinus, a famous jurist who followed Masurius Sabinus in the leadership of the Sabinian school, which for this reason was also known as the Cassian school. This theory is based upon the fact that C. Cassius Longinus is sometimes cited simply as Gaius in surviving passages from the works of the later jurists. But Cassius was consul in A.D. 30, and our Gaius was not even to be born until the next century. Moreover, there is another reason why no one who has read the *Institutes* and understood the character of Gaius could confuse the two jurists. It was the Roman law that when a man was murdered all his slaves who were under the same roof and were not shown to have come to his aid, should be put to death. When, in A.D. 61, the city prefect, Pedanius Secundus, who possessed four hundred slaves, was murdered by one of them, public opinion was opposed to the holocaust of so large a number of human beings. But Cassius took the position that the relaxation of the law would endanger the safety of every master, and the slaves were executed.

There can be little doubt of the vocation of Gaius. He has been properly described as "the law-coach Gaius." He achieved his fame and popularity as a teacher of law. It seems reasonable to suppose that only a law teacher would have hit upon the idea of writing an elementary textbook for students. From the very fact that it held undisputed sway as a manual of instruction in the schools for over three hundred years, it would also seem obvious that it was written by a jurist with long experience as a teacher. It is possible, in fact, that the *Institutes* constituted a course of written lectures. They are, however, too well written and organized to have been no more than notes for lectures, as some have supposed. That Gaius was not a practicing lawyer seems quite clear from the fact that he did not leave books of responses and collections of cases, as, with his literary gifts and reputation, he would have done if he had been in active consultation. An even better indication of his academic standing is the virtual certainty that he was not a jurist who possessed the *ius respondendi*. A jurist of his fame and eminence would have been a patented jurist if he made a practice of giving legal opinions.

The only reason Gaius could have been excluded from the *ius respondendi* would have to be sought in his political position. But we know definitely from the *Institutes* that Gaius was an adherent of the Sabinian school, which in its origin was connected with support of the imperial authority. Gaius frequently speaks of "the opinions of the opposite school," and takes many a sly opportunity to discredit them. This opposite school was, of course, the Proculian. But nowhere in attacking a Proculian view does he reveal any taint of political heresy. Gaius was indeed the last jurist in whom the conflict of the schools was reflected. After him there was only one stream of Roman jurisprudence.

The most celebrated theory about Gaius seeks to account at the same time for his name, origin, and scene of activity. This theory is based upon the assumption that Gaius was a person of humble origin and station. The vocation of pedagogue is humble enough, but even his personal station must have been lowly. Just as we should assume that a man who was universally known as "Bill" could hardly be an aristocrat, it has been conjectured that Gaius must have been a freedman, or at least a provincial. The celebrated theory in question is that Gaius was by birth a Greek who taught law at the little town of Troas in the distant province of Asia.

There is some proof offered for this deduction. Troas is one of three towns, Troas, Berytus, and Dyrrachium, which are mentioned by Gaius himself in a fragment surviving from one of his works; and Troas, which was one of the most important towns in the province of Asia, employed Latin as its official language. Only in Greek districts could a man have been called by his praenomen alone. Gaius wrote an extensive treatise on the Provincial Edict. The *Institutes* shows that Gaius was familiar with Greek and with Greek literature and legal history. He quotes Homer and Xenophon, and shows himself to be familiar with the laws of Solon. He compares provisions of Roman law with corresponding provisions of the law of the Galatians and the Bithynians, both of them peoples of Asia Minor. The fact that he was a provincial may also help to explain the singular circumstance that he did not possess the *ius respondendi*. There is, moreover, an even more astounding fact that becomes explicable upon the assumption that Gaius taught not at Rome, but in the provinces: for two and a half centuries after his death there is not a single mention of his name by any jurist or historian, whether contemporary or otherwise! While this certainly makes Gaius a man of mystery, the suggested solution presents too many difficulties.

The selection of Troas is obviously based upon a guess. Why not one of the other towns, Berytus or Dyrrachium, which are also mentioned by Gaius? As a matter of fact, there is nothing to show that there was a law school at Troas. In a revision of the original theory, it has therefore been suggested that it should be assumed that Gaius mentioned Troas first because he was born there and Berytus second because he taught there. To this a French jurist has replied with typical Gallic wit that it should be assumed that the reason Gaius mentioned Dyrrachium last was that he died there. As for Gaius' composition of a work on the Provincial Edict, it is not clear whether it dealt with the edict of a particular province, or with a general provincial edict. Considering the extent of the influence of Greek literature and philosophy, any educated Roman could have displayed Gaius' familiarity with Greek sources. Gaius wrote excellent Latin, and the *Institutes* itself makes it very doubtful that he was a foreigner. He says "we" whenever he speaks of the Romans, although it is true that he is very fond of the editorial "we," and it is not always possible to tell when he is employing one form rather than the other. There is, too, the fact that Gaius is an obvious partisan of the Sabinian school, and there is nothing to show that the rivalry of Sabinians and Proculians extended beyond the Roman capital. It is ironic that the very cosmopolitanism of Gaius should be employed to make a provincial of him.

It has been said of the Roman jurists that they may be regarded as "fungible personalities." This brilliant characterization expresses a partial truth. The Roman jurists and all jurists since them have displayed a tendency toward abstraction in formulating their thought. Consequently, it is difficult to detect the qualities of their own personalities in their works. But this may also be the result of the very meager knowledge that has survived concerning their personal lives. Even

jurists are human, however. Certainly a good many clues to the character of Gaius may be discerned in his *Institutes*.

It is easy to imagine that Gaius was one of those handsome Romans,
that he made an impressive appearance in the classroom, and that he
was a very popular teacher with his students. If later generations lov-
ingly called him Gaius Noster—Our Gaius—certainly the students who
listened to his lectures must have responded even more readily to his
personal influence. The success of the *Institutes* must have been due
to more than its mere quality as a book. Such success could have been
due only to the great personal appeal of the author. A great German
jurist, struggling amidst dense clouds of cigar smoke with a difficult
problem of Roman law, once summoned before him the shade of
Gaius. The shade turned out to be that of a tall, lanky, bowlegged
man with freckles on his forehead. There could have been no baser
libel—even as a joke.

It is obvious also that Gaius knew all the tricks of a born school-
master. The man who composed the *Institutes* must have known how
to hold a class spellbound. He enlivened the technicalities of jurisprudence by means of the personal touch. He is always employing personal pronouns—"you" and "I," as well as the editorial "we." He has a
stock hero to talk about. His name is Lucius Titius, the John Doe of
Roman jurisprudence. Titius is invaluable in the classroom. It is always:
Suppose Titius does this, or Titius does that. The examples Gaius
chooses to illustrate a point of law are always striking or dramatic, or
are characterized by a sly humor. Speaking of the circumstances under
which a man can be summoned to court, he says: "There is no doubt
that a man can be lawfully summoned from his vineyard, the bath, or
the theater." An agreement to deliver a nonexistent thing is void, "for
instance, a centaur." Even a eunuch may adopt a child. To illustrate
the rule that a legacy to an uncertain person is void, he chooses this
example: "Let my heir give ten thousand sesterces to him who first
comes to my funeral." He knows when he has reached the point at
which too many legal technicalities will begin to bore his listeners.
Thus, he abandons a discussion of the different varieties of guardianship because "the discussion will be tedious." He knows that the interest of a class is stimulated by references to controversial questions.
It is for this reason, perhaps, as well as to defend Sabinian views, that
he is always referring to authorities "of the opposite school."

The examples of Gaius indicate that the jurists did not debate tremendous questions all the time. Some of their controversies remind us of theologians disputing about the angels. When did a boy arrive at the age of puberty? The Sabinians said it should depend upon his actual physical development, but the Proculians were in favor of one age for all, fourteen. To whom did a ship belong that had been made out of somebody else's planks? The Sabinians declared that it would belong to the owner of the planks, but the Proculians supported the enterprising builder. The Sabinians thought an exchange could constitute a sale, but not the Proculians, who ridiculed the idea that each of the articles exchanged could constitute the price of the other. When a goldsmith was hired to make a ring with his own gold, the Sabinians regarded it as a sale of the material, and a letting and hiring of the workmanship; but most other jurists held the view that the transaction was merely a sale. The jurists also disagreed when it came to the question whether a partnership could be said to exist when it was agreed that one of the partners was to have a larger share of the gain and pay a smaller share of the loss; some of the jurists thought that such an arrangement was irreconcilable with the very nature of partnership. And so on, and so forth.

Gaius reveals a genial and humanitarian temper, which would be particularly popular with youth. He protests, for instance, against cruelty towards slaves, saying, "We ought not to make a bad use of our right, and on this principle, too, the management of their property is forbidden to prodigals." He can see scarcely any reason of value for the rule of Roman law which kept women of full age under perpetual guardianship. Of rules which he disapproves he speaks his mind much more strongly, perhaps, than is customary among jurists. He speaks of particular rules not only as "anomalous," but as "absurd," or as existing for "no good reason." For example, it was a rule of Roman law that a legacy to take effect after the death of an heir was invalid. Nevertheless, it was held that a legacy could be validly bequeathed in the words: "When my heir shall be dying." But it was also held that a legacy could not be left thus: "The day before my heir shall die." Gaius observes that the rule seems adopted "for no good reason."

It has been mentioned that the cosmopolitanism of Gaius is shown by his familiarity with Greek authors. But his cosmopolitanism, as well as his humanitarianism, is even better illustrated by his frequent references to natural law, for which the Roman term was *ius naturale*. The Greek philosophers had speculated much on man in a state of nature and on the dictates of natural law. As the influences of Greek philosophy grew, the conception of a *ius naturale* became current among the Roman jurists, but it had small practical importance in the development of Roman law. It was to play an important role only later, in creating the foundations of the modern world. In Gaius the *ius naturale* is virtually identified with the *ius gentium*. Whatever is in effect among all foreign nations seems to him established by natural reason rather than by the artificial requirements of the distinctively Roman *ius civile*. But, as so understood, the *ius naturale* plays an important part in the thinking of Gaius, when he is considering incidents of the status of slaves, minors, or women, or some of the burdensome technical formalities connected with the consummation of legal transactions.

The mind of Gaius is distinguished particularly by a love of legal antiquarianism. He was not only the last jurist to write a commentary on the Twelve Tables, but he also imported his familiarity with the legal past into the classroom and the *Institutes*. That he did so is fortunate, for a large part of our knowledge of the ancient Roman law is derived from Gaius' interest in history. It might be supposed, however, that it was not suited to the practical requirements of teaching and that it was a contradiction in the cosmopolitan outlook of Gaius. But the antiquarianism of Gaius was only a foil to his cosmopolitanism. It is true that most students are primarily interested in the law as it is, and have little patience for a professor's discourses on legal history. But Gaius does not indulge in antiquarianism for its own sake. As a rule, he relates some incident of the ancient law merely to point out its absurdity and to imply that his own age was far more enlightened. Such an attitude is bound to make for popularity. Thus, Gaius relates that the Twelve Tables provided that the owner of stolen property who insisted on making a search for it in another's house should enter naked except for a girdle about his middle, and should carry a dish in his hands. The purpose of these rather bizarre requirements was possibly to prevent the planting of the "stolen" object. Gaius thinks the whole law "absurd." He asks what conceivable purpose the law could have served when the stolen object was so large "that it can neither be introduced by stealth nor placed on the dish." He concludes his remarks by observing slyly: "On this point, at any rate, there is no dispute, that the law is satisfied whatever the material of which the dish is made."

Gaius possessed the supreme gifts of the jurist. He had a mind that loved order, system, and clarity. He tells us now and then of his distaste for excessive refinement. Of the endless disputations over *meum* and *tuum* he attempts to make something of an art. The excellent organization of the *Institutes* is matched by the elegance and lucidity of its style. Even as he always knew how to select a striking example, he could appreciate a nice turn of phrase—whether his or somebody else's. "Not even freedom," he tells us, "can be given by way of penalty," and, "Whatever one has written on my paper or parchment, though it be in golden letters, is mine." His pages are also sprinkled with the quaint legal maxims in which the Roman jurists excelled: "That is regarded as added by alluvion which is added so gradually that it cheats our eyes"; "Nothing can be acquired for us through a stranger except possession"; "An inheritance can be left by way of trust even by a nod."

Since the *Institutes* constitutes an elementary textbook of Roman law, its primary value lies in what it tells us, not about Gaius, but about the state of classical Roman jurisprudence. The art of legal classification and analysis has made vast progress since the days of the Twelve Tables, which, like all even late archaic codes, is arranged by the similarities of subject matter. The basic classification of Gaius is famous. "The whole body of our law," he writes, "relates either to persons, or to things, or to actions." The first of the four books into which the *Institutes* is divided deals with the law of persons, the second and third books with the law of things, and the fourth book with the law of actions. It has remained a characteristic of jurisprudence ever since to concern itself less with the law of persons than with the law of things. Indeed, the law of persons has been only another aspect of the law of things. It is primarily as the possessors of property that persons have aroused the interest of the jurist.

The subject of the law of persons is the status of individuals—of the heads of households, wives, children, slaves, and freedmen, of Roman citizens and foreigners. Perhaps the most remarkable feature of the law of persons was the survival of the absolute character of the *patria potestas*. The head of the household was still a domestic despot, but there were some ways by which sons were enabled to secure their freedom or to hold property to a limited extent. The Twelve Tables had provided that if the father had sold the son for a third time, he should be free. Such repeated sales were possible because, if the purchaser emancipated the son, he reverted to the *potestas* of his father. One of the very early juristic discoveries had been to take advantage of this provision to emancipate sons by a thrice-repeated fictitious sale to a friend. Moreover, daughters and grandchildren, who were also under the *patria potestas,* could be emancipated by a single sale, for it was held that the word "sons" should be strictly construed. The absolute power exercised by the husband over the wife was known as *manus*; the wife, in one of the most striking expressions in Roman jurisprudence, became the daughter of her husband. But marriage with *manus,* accomplished by means of the archaic ceremonies of eating a rice cake or going through the forms of a sale, had become highly exceptional in the classical Roman law, in which it was based upon customary cohabitation for a year. Again advantage had been taken of a provision of the Twelve Tables, which permitted the wife, in cases in which the basis of the marriage was mere cohabitation, to avoid subjection to her husband by absenting herself from his house for three nights each year. The prescriptive rights of the husband were thus broken. It is interesting that a conception derived from the law of property, that is, prescription, which the Romans called *usucapio,* should have been employed to liberalize an aspect of the law of persons, and that the severity of the old law should have driven the Romans to practice a *de facto* form of marriage, entirely free of ceremony, which in other civilizations has been regarded as only legalized concubinage.

In the classical law of property there still survived an ancient form of classification, which was that property was either *res mancipi* or *res nec mancipi. Res mancipi* comprised the most important forms of archaic property, principally land, cattle, and slaves, which could be transferred only by a special ceremony, while other forms of property, which were transferable by simple delivery, were *res nec mancipi.* But in Gaius is to be found a principle of classification which, though not entirely abstract, is far more advanced. He speaks of a distinction between corporeal and incorporeal property. There is also to be perceived a distinction between possession and ownership, which is conceived as the quality of absolute dominion.

The second book of Gaius' *Institutes* is devoted primarily to wills and intestate succession, and it is obvious that he is especially fond of discussing varieties of legacies. The better part of the third book is, however, devoted to the law of obligations, and here Gaius lays down another important principle of classification: "Every obligation arises either from contract or delict," that is, from voluntary undertakings or as the result of the commission of a wrong. Gaius supplies also a famous classification of contracts, which he separates into four groups: real, verbal, literal, or consensual. A "real" contract arose from the actual transfer of property in certain cases; a "verbal" contract arose from the exchange of a question and answer in a certain form, which thus constituted a "stipulation," destined to become the most general form of contract in Roman law; the "literal" contract was based upon a statement of indebtedness by the creditor in a cash book; and the "consensual" contracts—sale, hire, partnership, and agency—were those based upon mere consent, irrespective of the observance of forms. The two most important Roman delicts were called *iniuria* (outrage), and *dolus* (fraud). They deserve to be called the most important, because by the ingenuity of the jurists they were converted into remedies for an ever increasing variety of wrongs. In the fourth book of the *Institutes,* which deals with the law of actions and is primarily devoted to a history of the *leges actiones* and a description of the classical formulary system, Gaius makes a distinction between actions *in personam,* intended to enforce a personal liability, and actions *in rem,* directed toward specific property.

A remarkable feature of the *Institutes* is that it is not only a textbook of Roman law but a fascinating kind of formbook. A modern formbook, which is a collection of written documents, is perhaps the dullest kind of lawbook. But Gaius' forms, which are not part of an appendix but are integrated in his text, are, rather, colorful and even dramatic ceremonies. They are, indeed, little plays. Gaius describes a great many of these forms—those that are necessary for transferring property, making wills, bequeathing legacies, making contracts of various kinds, and bringing actions. Gaius, the antiquarian, must have had a special love for these ceremonies, considering that he describes some that were already obsolete or were falling into disuse. The most famous ceremony in the Roman law was called mancipation, from which was derived the name of the most important form of Roman property, *res mancipi.* It was an ancient ceremony which consisted of weighing copper in a scale before a required number of witnesses and of setting forth the terms of the transaction in certain forms. The ceremony was also employed in consummating the Roman form of marriage by purchase. Such ceremonies were survivals from the days when writing was either unknown or employed but little, and the memory of legal transactions had to be preserved by other symbolical means before living witnesses. The influence of jurisprudence did not necessarily abrogate such ceremonies, for jurists love forms, whether written or acted, and it must have been only in later times that the inconveniences suffered by the laymen drove the jurists to simplify the requirements of legal transactions.

In the classical law the ceremonies of the ancient *ius civile* were not abolished, but the holding and transfer of property, as well as the making of wills, were simplified in accordance with assumed conceptions of *ius gentium,* which were introduced by the praetorian edict. It is significant that in the very first sentence of the *Institutes* Gaius sets forth the distinction between *ius civile* and *ius gentium.* An increased emphasis upon good faith in legal transactions, a greater tendency toward abstraction in the formulation of rights, and an increased use of writing, all combined to make the law less rigid and more flexible. The praetorian law, nominally created by the praetor but actually formulated by the jurists, not only reduced the emphasis upon formalism, however, but brought into existence altogether new substantive rights by creating new remedies. Possession was protected regardless of formal defects, and the law of contract was liberalized in response to the needs of commerce by giving effect to the intentions of the parties and by nullifying frauds. The whole of the old law of inheritance, which was based upon the artificial agnatic family, was undermined by protecting the possession of the cognates.

Thus, the classical law of the time of Gaius was still a dual system. The new legal system had been superimposed upon the old without formally abrogating the latter. The Roman genius for "practicality" thus expressed itself rather strangely by clinging to meaningless historical survivals. It is significant that we find in the pages of Gaius a discussion of the role of legal fictions by which jurists from time immemorial have been accustomed to change the law, insisting at the same time, nevertheless, that the letter is still honored. Fiction, however, is only a grosser form of "interpretation," the whole sum and substance of the juristic art, of which Gaius has also much to tell us. He declares boldly that a rule may be "gathered by construction as surely as if it had been set down in the words of the law."

A modern reader would expect to find in an elementary textbook describing a mature system of law an account not only of its civil but also of its criminal law. But he will search for such an account in vain in the *Institutes* of Gaius. He will find, to be sure, a discussion of theft and violence, but these are treated as private delicts to be redressed by a civil action brought by the injured person! This survival of an archaic conception is, however, not inexplicable. The classical Roman law was a mature legal system, but the Roman economy rested on slavery. In view of the powers of chastisement which masters could exercise over their slaves, it was not urgent for the state to interfere. Homicide, however, had been a public crime since an early date, possibly because the imposing status of the Roman citizen made his person almost sacred. Treason, too, was a serious crime, and was suppressed even by primitive societies. Throughout the Republic the Roman criminal law had something of an *ad hoc* and emergency character, and at first was more or less arbitrarily administered by the magistrates or the popular assemblies. The only check upon the arbitrariness of the magistrates was a right of appeal to the popular assembly in capital cases. This right, which the Romans called *provocatio,* is strongly reminiscent of the celebrated device of Solon. Indeed, it is possible that Greek influence was responsible for the method of administering criminal law in the last century of the Republic. Permanent jury panels, called *quaestiones perpetuae,* were created, each of which dealt with separate crimes. These panels were not, however, popular courts or commissions as in Athens, for the jurors who sat in the *quaestiones* were always men of substance. They were either *equites,* which is to say representative of the middle class of bankers and traders, or senators, who were great landowners. Significantly, most of the *quaestiones* were created by the Roman dictator Sulla in a period of violent civil war, and Sulla was particularly careful to pack them with senators.

Gaius stands midway in the stream of classical Roman jurisprudence. He was followed by a triad of illustrious jurists—Aemilius Papinianus, Domitius Ulpianus, and Julius Paulus, all of whom lived and worked in the third century. The originality of Ulpian and Paul was not great, but Papinian has been regarded as a far more creative figure than Gaius. Still, it is hardly fair to judge Gaius by a textbook of Roman law written for students. On the other hand, it must be considered that the successors of Gaius worked not in a peaceful but in a chaotic age, which witnessed the death throes of the Roman Empire. The praetorian guard was making and unmaking emperors, and Papinian and Ulpian, both of whom were high in the imperial councils, ultimately met their deaths at the hands of the soldiers. One of the reasons given for the murder of Papinian was his refusal to justify Caracalla's murder of his own brother, and the tradition is that Papinian showed both his wit and his courage by remarking: "It is not so easy to justify murder as to commit it." It is customary to picture the late classical jurists as nobly serving the law in a period of turmoil, but the purity of their characters and motives is certainly open to question. After all, Papinian was the lifelong friend of Emperor Septimius Severus, who is said to have waded through slaughter to the throne. It is probable that Ulpian had a part in the machinations which put Alexander Severus on the throne in place of the bizarre and obscene Heliogabalus, the high priest of the Syrian sun-god who had made himself a Roman Emperor. It is rather curious, too, that so many of the great lights of the classical Roman law should have been men of oriental extraction. While the origins of Gaius and Paul cannot be established, we know that Papinian was born in Syria and Ulpian probably at Tyre. The extent to which they imported alien ideas into the Roman law has been a common subject of dispute.

Since Roman law owed its achievements to the security of the Roman state, it was inevitable that the decline of the Empire should lead to a deterioration of Roman jurisprudence. The line of great jurists closes, and men could do no more than attempt to preserve the legacy of the past. In A.D. 426 the Emperors Theodosius II and Valentinian III took a step which had been foreshadowed when Augustus created the *ius respondendi* but which now ended the spontaneous development of Roman jurisprudence. They enacted in desperation the Law of Citations, by which they confirmed and gave the force of law to the juristic writings of Papinian, Paul, Ulpian, and his pupil Modestinus, and last but not least our Gaius. When these jurists disagreed, the majority ruled, but if they were equally divided, the view of Papinian was to prevail. Considering the fact that Gaius had never even had the *ius respondendi* and had never even been quoted by his successors, it was indeed a great posthumous triumph, despite the decisive role accorded to Papinian. Moreover, as we shall see, Gaius was to achieve still more remarkable recognition.

The glories of Roman law have been celebrated for over two thousand years. One of the most striking expressions of this admiration has been the assertion that modern jurists have had to invent only one legal institution—the free-labor contract. Among the Roman jurists the influence of slavery was such that they conceived of a labor contract as a lease of labor. The Roman jurists, to be sure, had conceived and developed all the ordinary legal transactions, such as sale, agency, partnership, and the like, which have been serviceable in modern times. Still to be invented, however, were forms of doing business by means of great corporate institutions and forms of documents embodying immaterial rights, of which the Roman jurists, for all their ingenuity, never dreamed. Moreover, many of the conceptions which they had begun to analyze, and which were familiar to them, were yet to be refined into juristic concepts of a general and abstract nature.

The classical Roman jurists were tied to concrete modes of thought. They dealt with individual cases, and proceeded only from precedent to precedent. Gaius especially hated definitions, but in this he was typical of all the classical Roman jurists. They were all suspicious of philosophy and generalization. Although they were familiar with the conception of the *ius naturale*, which they had borrowed from the Greek philosophers, they did not employ it as a tool of civil jurisprudence. Although they worked out with infinite patience and understanding the nature and incidents of each of the principal forms of obligation and delict, they never achieved any general theory of contract or wrong. Although they had invented any number of formulas for bringing specific forms of action, they had no general conception of abstract rights and thought of rights only in terms of the available remedies.

Gaius' distinction between corporeal and incorporeal things is a first timid approach to an abstract conception of rights. But the purer and more sophisticated jurist of modern times perceives that all rights are incorporeal, although they may have corporeal objects. The *right* to a horse or a cow is precisely the same as the right to a bond or a certificate of stock. To the pure jurist the physical objects with which he deals are but the visible manifestations of invisible rights, the evidences of things not seen. A mortgage on a kennel is as worthy of his attention as a mortgage on a star. In juristic contemplation the rich do not have automobiles and country houses, stocks and bonds, but abstract rights, privileges, powers, and immunities. Even the poor have something, although, alas, only no-rights, duties, disabilities, and liabilities.

Jurisprudence has always been beset by a fateful dilemma. The concrete approach produces a complex technology of individual rights and remedies, while the abstract approach may lead to an abandonment of reality—the reign of a jurisprudence of logical conceptions. Each has its separate attractions for the jurist. Formalism is a valuable stock in trade, which makes the layman helpless and entirely dependent on the jurist's aid. General conceptions are, in a way, less difficult for the layman to understand, but professionally they are more satisfying to the jurist, although, to be sure, even individual transactions can be worked out with a great deal of refinement and abstraction. The jurist is never so happy as when he can think in purely abstract terms and manipulate juristic conceptions which remain always the same irrespective of the change of social and economic conditions, the variations in the needs and status of individuals, and the conflicts of classes.

For these reasons the greatest triumphs of jurisprudence, from the classical Roman jurists to the present day, have always been in the field of civil law. This has been even more happily known as "private law." The term expresses the success of the jurists in creating a private preserve in which they can think their problems out almost free from the turmoils which may rage in the outside world. The civil, or private, law deals with the relations of proprietors among themselves, and these, after all, have proved the most constant, the least affected by the passing of dynasties, nations, and classes. Sale, partnership, agency —their basic incidents remain eternal, at least so long as there is a system of private property. After all, the only difference between the economic systems of slavery and capitalism is that in the former there is one more form of property: the slaves and the cattle are both *res mancipi*. But to the credit of the Roman jurists be it said that they had no liking for the institution of slavery. This is sufficiently shown by their opinions that it was against the *ius naturale*. Gaius shows a distaste for the disabilities of women, and modern jurists were finally to sweep away almost in their entirety all the incidents of status. For jurists need an abstract counter in working out their schemes of jural relations, and a status-ridden society is a constant reminder of the real differences between individuals. The Roman jurists had no conception of a human being as an abstract juristic person assumed to be the subject of rights and duties. Perhaps the greatest triumph of jurisprudence, this was still to be achieved in subsequent ages. On the other hand, the indifference of Gaius and the other classical Roman jurists to the problems of the criminal law has remained a characteristic of jurisprudence to this very day. Not only is there little profit in the criminal law, but it is too full of the tribulations of society and the war of classes to be a congenial subject to the jurist. Gaius was certainly wise to pay no attention to it and to devote the *Institutes* to the civil law. They made him an immortal in the history of jurisprudence.

Justinian, Emperor of the East

THE LAW AND THE BOOK

ABOUT THE MIDDLE OF THE FIFTH CENTURY OF OUR ERA, THERE was born to a peasant family of Latin stock living in the town of Tauresium, in that part of the Balkan Peninsula now known as Macedonia, a boy who was duly christened Justin. He grew up tall and strong, but he had no taste for farming, or perhaps there was no land for him to cultivate. He heard stories of a golden city which was called Constantinople, where good pay could be earned by enlisting in the imperial guard and where pleasure and amusement could be had by going to the circus in the Hippodrome. With a bundle or a knapsack slung over his shoulder, he set forth one day with two companions to walk, if necessary, the four hundred miles or so that separated the town of Tauresium from the metropolis of Constantinople. Perhaps the youths got a lift; at any rate they arrived at Constantinople in due course. What happened thereafter to Justin's two companions we do not know, and it does not matter. Justin, we know, was accepted and inducted into the imperial guard. While the event was to be of no great consequence for military history, it was to prove momentous so far as the history of Roman law was concerned.

The peasant youth Justin must have had a genuine taste for soldiering, for decades later we find him as Commander of the Imperial Guard, with the rank of count and senator. But apparently he had never taken the trouble to acquire any kind of education, for, despite his honors and dignities, he remained illiterate. He did, however, have high regard for learning, and regretted not having children to whom he could give the advantages of an education. His wife, Euphemia, whom he had rescued from being sold into slavery as a prisoner of war, had not rewarded Justin's fancy by presenting him with an heir. He therefore did the next best thing: he decided to adopt one. In his native village lived his sister Vigilantia, who had given birth to a

73

daughter and to a son named Peter, or, to give him his full Latin name, Petrus Sabbatius. Justin adopted this boy, who in honor of his uncle and benefactor took his name and called himself thereafter Petrus Sabbatius Justinianus. He took the same road Justin had taken from Tauresium to Constantinople, but, more impressionable than his uncle, he must have paid more attention to the glories of the Eastern Roman Empire. He always remained a person who was easily dazzled. Arriving in Constantinople, he was sent off to school, where he received the best education the times could provide, which included some knowledge of Roman law. Justinian, the nephew of Justin, applied himself assiduously to his studies, and did not shrink from cramming during the late hours of the night. A sustained capacity for hard work remained his most valuable character asset throughout his long life. After he had risen to the throne of Byzantium, an admiring subordinate dubbed him "the Emperor who never sleeps."

Another family, no less obscure, but less reputable, was destined to influence the history of the Roman law. There was a bear-keeper named Acacius, in the Hippodrome of Constantinople, who had been blessed with three daughters, Comito, Theodora, and Anastasia. Acacius had died when they were little girls, but their mother had remarried, and had secured for her new husband the succession to the post of bear-keeper. She accomplished this by thrusting her little daughters into the arena crowned with garlands, to stretch forth beseeching hands to the two circus factions, known as the Blues and the Greens. The little girls thus grew up in the theatrical atmosphere of the Hippodrome, but it was Theodora who learned how to exploit the situation best. The bear-keeper's second daughter was destined to become the spouse of Justinian and Empress of the East.

Theodora made her way in the theatrical world of the capital. She had charm and wit. She was a brunette with large eyes, long lashes, and a delicate complexion. Her wit was of the impish style, and she attracted men without the least effort. In her professional career she devoted herself neither to dancing nor straight acting. She specialized in mimicry and what the French now call *tableaux vivants,* in which she readily displayed the glories of her undraped beauty. Naturally she did not lack for lovers, and there was quite a succession of them. She finally ran off with a gentleman by the name of Hecebolius, who was governor of Pentapolis. She lived with him for a while in Egypt, but not for long. Either Hecebolius wearied of his mistress or, as is more likely, Theodora wearied of him. Theodora made for Alexandria, and after a while she managed to return to Constantinople.

This trip must have been a fairly profitable one, or else some of Hecebolius' gold still clung to her fingers. At any rate she had enough to get a house and set herself up in the nontheatrical and respectable business of working a loom. She sat at the loom waiting demurely, and before long an admirer showed up. He was none other than Petrus Sabbatius, the future Emperor Justinian. Brunettes were apparently his type, and Theodora was no ordinary brunette. It was a case of infatuation at first sight, and before long the ardent suitor, who was then already approaching forty, quite dazzled by his beloved's beauty and charm, resolved to offer his hand in honorable marriage. Naturally, considering Theodora's premarital career, which could hardly have been a secret in Constantinople, Justinian's mother wept, and his aunt Euphemia interposed a veto.

The problem was rather a ticklish one, for by now Euphemia had become no less than the Empress of the East! Yes, Justin, the peasant youth who had come to seek his fortune in the golden city, had, at the age of almost three score years and ten, become the acknowledged ruler of the whole Byzantine Empire. The feeble old man, who still could not sign his name, had been called to the imperial purple in the year A.D. 518. He had been placed on the throne as a result of an obscure palace intrigue, which, there is every reason to suppose, was carefully stage-managed by his nephew Justinian, who thus furnished the first proof of his adroitness as a politician. The party of Justinian took advantage of the religious and political situation, of the opportunity offered by dynastic failure and the stupidity of the deceased Emperor Anastasius' palace eunuch. Anastasius had supported Monophysitism, one of the early Christian heresies, which threatened early Catholic orthodoxy; and four years before his death his throne had been shaken by the revolt of the champion of Catholic orthodoxy, Count Vitalian. Although the revolt was crushed, its leader was not, and the issue was left undecided. When Anastasius died, he left no sons but three nephews, Hypatius, Probus, and Pompeius, who seem to have been rather feeble characters. The palace eunuch, Amantius, had a candidate of his own in one Theocritus, and he entrusted to Justin a large sum of money to sway the votes of the right people in the imperial election. Justin took the money, but Justinian showed him how to use it for their own advantage.

Although Justin reigned from A.D. 518 to 527, he was never more than a figurehead. From the beginning of his reign the real ruler of the Byzantine Empire was Justinian, who took advantage of these years to secure his own succession to the throne upon the death of his uncle. He took over the policy of Vitalian and courted the orthodox Catholics and the Bishop of Rome by persecuting the Monophysites, and he heaped favors upon the Blues, supporting them in their internecine struggle with the Greens, who had been the party of Anastasius. These two circus factions had been organized as a city militia, but survived as political parties by a perversion of democratic municipal institutions tolerated by the imperial power which sought for its own ends to take advantage of their fierce antagonisms. One by one most of the supporters of Anastasius were liquidated. Not long after the commencement of Justin's reign, Amantius and Theocritus were executed, and Vitalian, after being courted and flattered and raised to the consulship, fell, after seven months, a victim to an assassin's dagger at a banquet in the palace. Whether Justinian instigated the murder directly or not, he certainly regarded the deed with equanimity.

While these great events were transpiring, Theodora, already practically assured of everything that money and power could bring her (and she liked them both), was waiting for her Justinian. The Empress Euphemia conveniently died a year before old Justin, and the chief obstacle to their marriage was thus removed. A minor obstacle was a law which prohibited the marriage of anyone of at least senatorial rank with a woman of servile origin who had been an actress. This law Justin obligingly repealed by the simple exercise of his supreme legislative authority, and the way was clear for the nuptials of Justinian and Theodora, which now were celebrated. Justinian arranged a marriage settlement for Theodora with a prodigal hand. He gave her wealth and, consequently, independence, as befitted her exalted station, and set her up in the great house of Hormisdas on the seacoast, from which for over two decades she helped Justinian rule the Byzantine Empire. Justinian, who always spoke of her as his "sweetest charmer," was ever ready to listen to her advice. She made and unmade prelates, generals, and great officers of state; and, tainted with Monophysitism herself, she at times confused Justinian's ecclesiastical policy. In her new-found respectability, she supported piety and virtue—unless, indeed, the encouragement of immorality was necessary for high reasons of state.

As if to atone for her own misspent youth, she even founded a home for wayward girls.

During Justin's last illness in A.D. 527, he had associated Justinian with him in the imperial purple and had placed the crown of the Caesars upon his nephew's head. When the old man died, there was no one to question Justinian's claim to the sole succession. During his long reign of thirty-eight years, Justinian was dominated by a single passion. Even as he was dazzled by Theodora, so were his eyes blinded by the grandeur that had been Rome.

It will be remembered that the Roman Empire had been split in twain by Constantine, the first Christian emperor. In order to find a better center from which to repel the barbarians in the West and the Persians in the East, and to remove himself from the influence of paganism, in A.D. 330 Constantine had set up his capital in the town of Byzantium, on the very edge of the European continent, and had renamed it Constantinople in his own honor. When, toward the end of the fourth century, Theodosius the Great had died, leaving two sons, these two shared the Roman Empire between them, and before another century had passed the Western Empire was no more. The Goths now reigned in Italy and the Vandals in Africa, and they paid no more than lip service to the emperor at Constantinople. Justinian now resolved on nothing less than to restore the Roman Empire in all its former glory. He vowed, to use his own words, "to reconquer the countries possessed by the ancient Romans, to the limits of the two oceans."

Justinian was a man of great ability, expert in the devious ways of statecraft. He had, no doubt, many reasons for desiring the restoration of the Roman Empire to its greatest territorial extent. For one, there was the religious motive for the reconquest of North Africa, where Monophysitism was especially strong. Only thus could the heresy be extirpated successfully. A universal Church and a universal empire are naturally complementary, especially when the head of the state and the head of the Church are one and the same, as was the case under Justinian, whose policy has been aptly described as "Caesaropapism." Justinian considered it only natural and proper that the city of Rome should be ruled from the city of Constantine, the first Christian emperor.

There were also economic motives for conquest. Constantinople, the link between East and West, was a great trading metropolis that could brook no rivals. Its corn came from Egypt. In a crowded factory quarter of the city silk was manufactured on a large scale. But Persia, which Justinian fought throughout his long reign with various degrees of success, straddled the trade routes by which the raw material was brought from China. The economic importance of conquering Persia was no secret in Byzantine society. However, in the reign of Justinian two monks were persuaded to smuggle silkworms out of China in a hollow cane, and the production of raw silk was established in Syria.

There is no doubt that to Justinian the restoration of the glories of Rome was a shining ideal and a spiritual necessity. Blinded by the brilliance of the Roman world, the boy from Tauresium felt impelled to appoint himself the guardian of this splendor, a mission that seemed capable of realization when the imperial diadem was placed upon his head. He thought how wonderful it would be to be called savior and restorer. Vanity was one of the basic ingredients of Justinian's character, and it was carried to excess precisely because of his humble origin. How vain he was is demonstrated by a change which he made in court etiquette (doubtless with the advice of Theodora). In previous reigns patricians entering the presence of the emperor were accustomed only to bend the knee. Justinian insisted they throw themselves upon their faces and kiss his feet and those of his "sweetest charmer."

It is ironic that the civilization of patrician Rome was restored by a group of men who, like the master whom they served, were almost invariably of very humble origin. Justinian was either a shrewd judge of men or extremely fortunate in selecting the instruments for the execution of his grand design. In Belisarius he found a great general who could not only conduct his ambitious campaigns but who could also be kept in line through Theodora's questionable moral influence over his wife. In John the Cappadocian, an obscure clerk in the war office, he found one of the most efficient, conscienceless, and ferocious taxgatherers of all times, who spent his days in solving the financial problems of the great military campaigns and his nights, it is said, in drunken revelry. In Anthemius of Tralles he had an inspired architect who built one of the great wonders of the world, the church of Saint Sophia. In Tribonian he had a chancellor who, whatever might be said of his sense of justice, was the most learned jurist of his day. And last, but not necessarily least, in Procopius of Caesarea he had an observant historian who has given us a record of Justinian's ways and accomplishments and the *Secret Anecdota,* containing the scandalous rumors of his reign.

We need not concern ourselves with Justinian's conquests. Suffice it to say that he did succeed in reconquering Italy from the Goths and Africa from the Vandals, and even in re-establishing once more a Roman province in Spain. He brought the islands of the western Mediterranean under his sway and made this historic inland waterway a Roman lake again. Belisarius deserved his reputation as a military genius and Justinian his fame as the emperor who never sleeps. A series of mighty fortresses were constructed around the far-flung boundaries of the empire to keep out the wild barbarian tribes, and these the Emperor insisted on calling, with his usual childish vanity, "Justinians." Nevertheless, the conquered provinces fell away again soon after Justinian's death.

One phase of Justinian's efforts to restore the grandeur of the Roman Empire, however, proved far more enduring and of tremendous importance in the history of law. Almost as soon as he was proclaimed emperor, and indeed before he embarked upon his military conquests, Justinian initiated a vast project which had for its object the restoration of the Roman law. There had been no creative jurists in the centuries of disorder that followed the close of the classical period. But law never ceases to develop even when jurisprudence declines, although such development may be retrogressive, as had been the case during these years when much of the classical Roman law had become obsolete in practice. The authorities were indeed in a state of indescribable confusion, and this had been recognized in the famous Law of Citations, which had sought to provide a rule of thumb for the perplexed judges. However, the confusion had become worse in the century or so since the enactment of the Law of Citations. The treasure house of jurisprudence was now cluttered with works of only antiquarian interest, or with the works of many inferior intellects who doubtless had not hesitated to tamper with the writings of even the most illustrious of the classical jurists. Justinian, who conveniently wrote down his motives for posterity in a series of prefaces to his work, speaks of the "immense volumes of ancient jurisprudence," and declares that the task of examining them had been like wading "through the depths of the ocean," a task, moreover, that could be successfully completed "only with the favor of heaven." Again he declares: "We have found the entire arrangement of the law which has come down to us from the foundation of the city of Rome and the times of Romulus to be so confused that it is extended to an infinite length and is not within the grasp of human capacity."

Justinian undertook, therefore, to provide an authoritative compilation of the sources of the Roman law that should eliminate what was obsolete and restore what had been perverted by the jurists of lesser understanding. "There is nothing to be found in all things so worthy of attention," he said, "as the authority of the law, which properly regulates all affairs divine and human, and expels all injustice." The direction of the Herculean labor of reforming the law was entrusted to Tribonian, who stood high in Justinian's favor despite numerous complaints against him. Tribonian was unpopular with Justinian's subjects for two reasons. He was, first, suspected of a love of paganism and Hellenism, and indeed he seems to have made little effort to conceal his leanings. But what was even worse, so far as life in this world is concerned, he was corrupt in the administration of his judicial office. His impartiality as a judge consisted simply of his readiness to take bribes from either side; and his venality was such that where a legislative provision stood in the way of his making a decision in favor of the party who had bribed him, he did not hesitate to use his influence and the advantages of his office to secure an amendment to the existing law.

The labors of Justinian's commission, which, in addition to Tribonian, included law professors from Beirut and Constantinople and some practicing advocates, covered the seven years from A.D. 528 to 534. But in the month of January, 532, there occurred a great revolt in Constantinople which shook the very foundations of Justinian's throne. It has been named by historians the "Nika Sedition," from the battle cry of the insurgents, which means "Victory." Indeed, they came very close to victory, and if they had succeeded, Justinian's compilation never would have been completed, and the development of the law of modern Europe would doubtless have been vastly different. The person who saved the day was none other than the consort of Justinian —the Empress Theodora.

The basic cause of the revolt was the unpopularity of Justinian's impending campaign to reconquer Africa and the exactions it made necessary. The Greens, too, were incensed at Justinian's toleration of the violence of the Blues. From the fact that one of the demands of the rioters was the removal of Tribonian, which was partly met by depriving him temporarily of the office of quaestor, it may be surmised that Tribonian's irreligion and judicial misconduct were contributing factors. The great landlords, whose bugaboo was John the Cappadocian, may be suspected of having conspired to instigate the revolt. In fact, Belisarius himself, who organized the military force and directed the strategy that finally suppressed the revolt, had no particular relish for leaving his bones to whiten on the sands of Africa.

The first episode of the insurrection was a rather remarkable dialogue which took place during an interval between two races at the Hippodrome. A man rose among the Greens and began to shout for justice against a powerful oppressor and to call upon the name of Justinian. Justinian's official speaker demanded to know who the oppressor was, and the Green named someone close to the imperial circle. From this point on the exchange became very heated. The Greens chimed in in a body and shouted that their lives were not safe because of their party loyalty. The tumult grew, violent epithets were hurled across the Hippodrome, and Justinian, the emperor who aspired to rule the East and West, withdrew in haste to the palace.

The revolt, nevertheless, might not have gathered such force but for an unfortunate accident which had the result of uniting the Blues and the Greens. Seven rioters were condemned to death, but the hangman in executing the sentence bungled the job. Two of the condemned men were found to be alive, one a Green, the other a Blue. Both sought sanctuary in a church, which was forthwith surrounded by soldiers dispatched by the prefect. When Justinian refused to pardon the two condemned men, the revolt flared up. Fighting began in earnest and spread through the streets of Constantinople. Even Belisarius could not gain the upper hand over the rioters. A large part of the city went up in flames, including a hospital full of helpless patients. Hypatius, one of the nephews of Anastasius, was proclaimed emperor by the rebels. The news spread that Justinian had fled from Constantinople, and the crowds surged into the Hippodrome to cheer Hypatius.

The rumor was not true, although it had some foundation. Justinian, fearing for his life, had all but resolved on flight by sea, the way to which was still open. A council was being held in the palace to go through the motions of considering the question. Both John the Cappadocian and Belisarius advised flight. But at this point Theodora rose to her full height and declared: "If safety only remains in flight, still I will not flee. Those who have worn the crown should not survive its loss. I will never live to see the day when I am no longer hailed as

Empress. Flee if you wish, Caesar; you have money, the ships await you, the sea is open. As for me, I stay. I hold with the old proverb which says that the purple is the best winding sheet."

Justinian's courage revived as he listened to his "sweetest charmer." He put away all thoughts of flight. Emissaries plentifully supplied with money were sent to win back the allegiance of the Blues and to get them away from the Hippodrome. There Belisarius and his steel-clad men surprised the mob that was cheering for Hypatius. Ruthlessly the rebel subjects of Justinian were put to the sword. The most conservative estimate of the number of those who lost their lives that day is thirty thousand. Some say that as many as fifty thousand were slain. Many years were still to elapse before the imperial purple should have to be used as a winding sheet. Theodora went back to her intrigues and the incessant care of her charms in the great house of Hormisdas. Justinian went ahead with his rebuilding of the imperial city and his plans for the African campaign. Tribonian and his colleagues, who must have been as frightened as their master, dusted off some of the parchments in their libraries and resumed their communion with the sages of Roman law. Or had the scholars in contempt of the mob never so much as interrupted their labors?

The first task of Justinian's commission was to collect the legislative sources of the Roman law. During the first years of their labors they edited and assembled the constitutions of the previous emperors. This first code, which appeared in 529, rapidly became obsolete, however, principally because, in order to harmonize it with the juristic law which was being examined in the following years, Justinian had been compelled to promulgate the so-called Fifty Decisions settling conflicting views. The code therefore had to be replaced by a second more inclusive and permanent collection which, published in 534, has been known since then as the Codex. The supplementary legislation of the subsequent years of Justinian's reign has been known as the Novels.

By far the more important phase of the work of Justinian's compilers was the collection they made of the juristic law. The Roman private law had been developed primarily by juristic means rather than by legislative changes, and any collection based on the works of the jurists was bound to constitute a veritable thesaurus of the practical problems of jurisprudence. Justinian's order to the commission was "to collect from the work of the ancient sages," who possessed the *ius respondendi*, but, abandoning the principle of the Law of Citations, neither the view of the majority nor that of Papinian was to have any greater authority. The commission was to read and make extracts from the works of the jurists, assembling them into a single work divided into fifty books and further subdivided into titles according to subject matter. The orders of Justinian were so strictly obeyed that virtually no Republican or postclassical jurists were included. The commission read with praiseworthy diligence and extraordinary patience no less than two thousand volumes containing three million lines. It reduced this mass of juristic literature to fifty thousand lines. About two-thirds of the nine thousand one hundred and forty-two extracts was taken from the works of Gaius, Papinian, Ulpian, Paul, and Modestinus. Each extract was identified by placing at its head the name of the jurist from whose work it was taken. The arrangement of the collection appears rather haphazard, but this was due to the fact that the commission had divided itself into three subcommittes, each of which worked independently: one concentrated on the *ius civile*, a second on edictal commentaries, and a third on casuistical works, principally Papinian's. It had also been Justinian's desire that all obsolete or superfluous as well as contradictory or repetitious matter should be eliminated. But the commission met his wishes not only in the selection of the extracts but also by tampering with the extracts themselves. The search for these "interpolations," as they are called, has occupied much of the energy of modern scholars of Roman law. The whole collection of extracts from the juristic writings, which constitutes the bulkiest as well as the most important part of Justinian's compilation, has been known as the Digest, or the Pandects. Justinian looked upon the finished work and saw that it was good. He declared, indeed, that it would be eternal, and forbade all further commentaries under pain of prosecution for forgery.

Of all the Roman jurists who figure in the compilation, Gaius achieved the most singular triumph. It appears that Justinian was interested not only in the administration of justice but also in the reform of legal education, and he sought to rearrange the course of study in the law schools. The freshmen, who went by the mysterious name of "two-pounders," still studied the *Institutes* of Gaius. But this long-lived textbook was rather out of date. Justinian, therefore, ordered Tribonian and two of the law professors to prepare a new one, which was issued on the same day as the Digest. But the "new" textbook, entitled *Imperatoris Justiniani Institutiones*, was really only a revised edition of the *Institutes* of Gaius. For the first time in the history of law, a legal textbook was officialized and given the force of law by legislative enactment. Justinian also decreed that the "two-pounders" were thereafter to be called "Justinian's freshmen," and forbade, incidentally, the hazing of freshmen.

In the pages of Justinian's compilation is reflected the last phase of the maturity of the Roman law. It was the classical Roman civil law unified and rationalized as the result of the elimination of archaic procedures and concepts. A cosmopolitan system, it was peculiarly fitted to enter upon the great career which awaited it in the future. Despite the shattering political changes which had occurred, the economic system of the Roman Empire still functioned, and the practicing lawyers, less patient of doctrinal subtleties than the classical jurists, had generalized the basic results of the latter. Greek and oriental philosophy and example no doubt worked in the same direction. The unity of the Roman Empire had once been a reality, but the unity of its law had been to a great extent a fiction. The provinces had preserved divergent institutions, and these had made their influence felt. The very cruelties of autocracy, which had established an absolutistic public law, brought about a softening of the rigors of the private law. As more and more ruined men clamored for relief against an ever increasing burden of debt and other exactions, the autocratic government with its summary methods could more readily grant them relief. It was particularly easy to dispense with technicalities which had been originally designed for the protection of the individual. The decisive step which made possible the wholesale destruction of post-archaic survivals was taken by Emperor Caracalla, when in A.D. 212, in order to broaden the tax base, he had extended Roman citizenship to all the subjects of the Empire.

When the distinction between citizen and foreigner disappeared and the formulary procedure, based upon particular forms of action and the division of proceedings between *praetor* and *index* was abolished, there was no longer any point in distinguishing between *ius civile* and *ius gentium*. The later and more equitable rules triumphed completely, and there was now only one system of Roman law, which united dual conceptions of ownership and succession. The old ceremonies, which had been preserved primarily in the *ius civile*, also lost their meaning, and the copper and scales were only a quaint remembrance. With the continuing decline in formalism, there was also some approach to general conceptions of obligation and delictual liability, with a consequent tendency to magnify the intention of the parties above the observance of mere forms. The stipulation, which significantly was the most general form among the old Roman contracts, still survived, but the oral technicalities of question and answer were no longer of any importance.

With the disappearance of the formulary system of procedure, justice was now administered in the court of the prefect, who had replaced the old city praetor. Since he was endowed with all the vast and uncontrolled administrative powers of his imperial master, he saw no difficulty in establishing a unified magisterial procedure, which was completed in all its stages before him. The plaintiff now merely set forth his claim in a document called a "libel," and in this "libellary" procedure, as it has been called, it was the substantive law governing the claim and not the procedural excrescences that counted.

In this system of substantive law the post-archaic survivals had either disappeared altogether or had been so undermined as to be only shadows of their former robust selves. The *patria potestas* no longer brought to the head of the family absolute property rights over wife and children. The wife was assured of control of her dotal property, and the children of their own acquisitions. The guardianship of mature women, which had been criticized by Gaius, was a thing of the past, and in general the ward was protected against the guardian. Sons and children now inherited irrespective of whether they had been in the *potestas* of the father, and the principle of agnatic succession was no more. In theory, the heir may still have been a universal successor, but he no longer incurred the danger of bankruptcy in accepting the heirship, for he was allowed the "benefit of inventory," which meant that he was liable only to the extent of the assets of the estate. Finally, the debtor was now actually protected against the creditor—possibly so that he might more readily meet his obligations to the imperial treasury and to the Church.

The imperial despotism and the influence of the Church made themselves manifest, although in different ways, also in the criminal law. The old *quaestiones*, and with them the right of popular appeal, were gradually destroyed. The prefects and the governors of the provinces became responsible for the suppression of crime, and in the absence of private accusers they might proceed inquisitorially upon their own initiative. The Senate tried political crimes. Torture was introduced in the examination of suspects, and penalties became increasingly severe, including death and forced labor in the mines. The lower classes were subjected to particularly harsh differential treatment. There was a great expansion in the category of crimes, but they were ill defined and the criminal law was arbitrary. The influence of the Church accounts for the punishment of such new crimes as heresy, adultery, and the seduction of women.

Most of these changes had been accomplished before the days of Justinian. In his own legislation Justinian revealed both his piety and ' uxoriousness. Justinian forbade divorce by mutual consent—a reform which proved to be highly unpopular. He permitted a wife to be repudiated by her husband if she went in bathing with other men. None other than Theodora could have inspired the famous pronouncement of Justinian on adultery: "We have set up magistrates to punish robbers and thieves; are we not even more straitly bound to prosecute the robbers of honor and the thieves of chastity?" He betrayed his uxoriousness even in his legislation on debt. In giving a wife a mortgage against all of her husband's property, including antenuptial property, in order to secure her dotal claims, he, as a witty Frenchman has said, "destroyed the credit of bachelors after having already ruined that of married men." Yet, when he did not yield to his fanaticism or avarice or the advice of his "sweetest charmer," he could be even a wise and provident legislator. He decreed, for instance, that a slave who was abandoned and cast out should go free, but he was harsh toward the *coloni*, the agricultural serfs who were bound to the soil which they tilled. It was Justinian, no doubt, who inspired Justin's famous prohibition against impounding the corpse of a debtor with the object of compelling the payment of a debt.

In modern times the compilation of Justinian has become known as the *Corpus iuris civilis*. It is commonly spoken of as a "codification" —indeed, as the most famous of all codifications. But a codification, even when it introduces no changes, implies at least a systematic restatement of all the sources of law that are codified. Justinian's "codification" is really only an anthology of the writings of the classical jurists. Whatever adaptations were made to contemporary practice were accomplished by means of the interpolations, which is to say, by stealth. It is rather ironic to think that the first major codification of a mature legal system was actually far less creative than any archaic code had been. For the first time in legal history a "codification" was made that even in form presumed to be no more than a collection of case law. However, when jurists dominate a legal system, the legislator must necessarily play second fiddle. Justinian made his selections from jurists who had been dead for several hundred years, and one of the most debated questions among scholars is the extent to which the Digest represented existing law. One modern Romanist has expressed this paradoxical situation by saying: "The most influential codification of all time represented at no time the actual law in force." It is suspected that Justinian himself was less interested in legal practice than in creating a literary monument which should perpetuate his glory for all time. He was the first—and last—anthologist in the history of legal systems. In legal history there are many instances of great conquerors who have attempted to cement their conquests by assuming the role of lawgiver. But Justinian reversed this process, and proceeded to inaugurate his "codification" even before he had reconquered the Western Empire by the force of arms. He attempted to create a law for a unified empire before the Empire itself had been reunited. The whole enterprise reflected from the beginning the bizarre unrealities of the Byzantine world.

The whole legislative power of the Byzantine Empire was Justinian's. With a stroke of his pen, the constitutions of former emperors, as well as the *responsa* of the classical jurists, would have been only so much debris. But, like the eunuchs in the royal palace at Byzantium, Justinian was impotent as a legislator. All he could do was to order his minister "to collect from the works of the ancient sages." He could not even be as bold as Hammurabi, King of Babylon. If the idea of a true codification occurred to Justinian at all, it must have been rejected at once as sacrilege.

For, after all, who was Justinian but the fortunate peasant from the Macedonian mountains, who had risen by a series of accidents to the imperial purple? From the day he trod the road from Tauresium to Byzantium, he remained dazzled by the glories of Roman culture. As a peasant by birth, he had a superstitious regard for the written word and a veneration for book learning. He had been taught to believe that the greatest glory of Rome was its jurisprudence. It was for him to preserve what the great Roman jurists had created.

Even his "interpolations," actually made necessary by the base demands of practice, were conceived only in a spirit of restoration. It is not sufficient to say that the state of contemporary legal science did not favor a creative codification. Justinian, the first literate member of an illiterate family, could not have transcended his origins.

Thus it came about that Justinian assembled the law in one big book, and his deed was to have great consequences for the history of law on the continent of Europe, as well as for the history of law in general. The law in a book is even worse than the law engraved on a stone monument or inscribed on bronze or wooden tablets, for it can much more easily lead a life of its own; the law in a library is more like a secret vice. Moreover, much more can be written in a big book than can conveniently be inscribed upon stone, bronze, or wood. The big book is better suited to express the subtleties and complexities of the maturity of law. It affords the jurists who can retire with it to the quiet of a library or consultation chamber a better opportunity to play with each and every word.

Now, it is true that a body of case law has at least the merit of retaining the context of the realities from which it arises. Each case is more limited in its reach than a legislative text. But, unfortunately, the Digest of cases was to be treated in the latter Middle Ages with all the veneration of a legislative text, and law was to be regarded as legislative in form and origin, always looked for in a book. Moreover, although the cases were to be found only in extracts which had been lifted from their own contexts, every word of every extract was regarded as precious. Legal science was to become ultimately the art of discovering the logical limits of every word. It was to become a science of the book rather than of life. The law was shaped by the words in the book rather than by the needs of life.

Justinian reigned for three decades after the completion of the *Corpus iuris*, until A.D. 565, when he died at the age of eighty-three. In these decades he carried on his wars in the West against the Persians. Historians are inclined to think that his destruction of the Gothic kingdom in Italy did more harm than good, for it destroyed the last power that could have preserved order in the West and prevented the anarchy that followed. In A.D. 542–43, one of the great bubonic plagues of all time raged in Constantinople, and Justinian himself was stricken, but recovered. Theodora escaped the plague but died of cancer in A.D. 548. Her influence over the destinies of Justinian was attested by an abortive conspiracy against the throne shortly after her death. After Justinian's death it is doubtful that his subjects regarded his *Corpus iuris* as a great and glorious accomplishment. In less than a century after his death it was completely forgotten in the West, while in the East it was discovered to be so unsuited to the needs of practice that it was continually revised and abridged. Despite Justinian's stern prohibitions, there were produced, as someone has said, "epitomes of epitomes of epitomes."

After the lapse of six centuries, however, the big book that had been projected by the peasant who became Emperor and saved by the courage of a fascinating whore who became Empress of the East, was brought back to life in the West. With the revival of commerce in the cities of Italy in the twelfth century, the need arose for a more highly developed body of law than that of the Goths and the Vandals. The compilation of Justinian happened to be rediscovered, and a class of new jurists arose who sought to master its treasured texts. There occurred the strange phenomenon of a dead law awakening to new life. This "lesser Renaissance," which was a phase of the contemporary diffusion of Roman culture, has been described by jurists as the "Reception." The greatest center of the revived Roman jurisprudence was established in the famous law school of Bologna, and the reputation of the Bolognese doctors spread all over the continent of Europe. The first school of the new learning has been known as that of the "glossators." They dared to do no more than to gloss the sacred text of Justinian in the margin, a method typical of the barren scholarship of the Middle Ages, and they reasoned, as it has been aptly said, "as if the Lord Justinian was still holding sway over Italy." His words were to them *ratio scripta*, or "written reason." The next great school was that of the "commentators," whose great leader was Bartolus of Sassoferrato, but even his pious commentaries were not written until the fourteenth century. From Italy the Justinian compilation traveled to France and was received in almost all of the countries of continental Europe. However, even in France, the northern provinces, known as the region of unwritten law, lived under Germanic customary law. In the sixteenth century France produced the great humanist and jurist Jacques Cujas, who worked indefatigably to recover the texts of the classical Roman law unadulterated by the adaptations of the practitioners. A general reception of the Roman law occurred in Germany as late as the fifteenth century, where it became known as "the law of the pandects." The lateness of the German reception has been responsible for an endless amount of speculation concerning its causes. Doubtless the rise of the German towns, the growth of commerce, and the development of a money economy required a more highly developed legal system. The decisive cause of the Reception lay, however, in the political disunity of the country which prevented the appearance of strong central courts capable of acting as law-creating organs. Insular England, which did produce strong central courts, was the only country of importance that remained relatively immune to the influence of the Reception. It was destined to be the home of the common law, the great rival legal system of the modern world.

The continental countries, which thus inherited the Roman law through the devotion of Justinian, to this day live under its influence. Although the reception of the Roman law accelerated the legal development of the continental countries and facilitated the more rapid growth of commerce, these benefits were obtained only at a considerable price. While the doctors of the civil law, as the new masters of the *Corpus iuris civilis* were called, undoubtedly made adaptations to contemporary needs in their practice—and the evils of the Reception have been exaggerated—such changes were often very slow and usually were unacknowledged, even as Justinian's own interpolations had been. Merchants were sometimes hampered in their enterprises, and poor wretches were tortured and hanged from the gibbet, upon the turn of a phrase in one of the extracts from a long-dead Roman jurist, whose words were enshrined and preserved in the compilation of Justinian. But, quite apart from any specific miscarriages of justice, this sacred text gave a scholastic bent to the thinking of the doctors of the civil law which endured for centuries. Only in theology did a book exercise a comparable influence. Indeed, the compilation of Justinian was the secular Bible of Christendom.

Hugo Grotius

THE LAW OF NATURE AND OF NATIONS

W HILE THE REPUTATIONS OF THE TRULY GREAT MEN OF SCIENCE and art tend to be universal, those of even the greatest men of law are generally limited to the spheres of their own national cultures. It is true that the law deals with universal problems and values, but these tend to be obscured by the peculiarities of parochial practice and are perceived in true perspective only by the philosophers of law. The influence of a jurist is likely to be particularly small if he belongs to a people that has not loomed large on the scene of history, for the fortunes of a legal system are closely bound up with the fortunes of the state which nurtures it. Yet, toward the close of the sixteenth century there was born in Holland a man of law whose international significance must be obvious, for he founded the science of international law. His name was Huig de Groot, but he is better known by the Latin name Hugo Grotius, and he has been traditionally acclaimed the father of international law. With him begins the history of the law of the modern world, both national and international.

This may sound like something of a paradox. The modernity of international law will be readily admitted. It seems as modern as the radio and the automobile and perhaps no less indispensable. A law governing the relations of nations would seem to be the greatest triumph of the reign of law, and should, indeed, form the climax of its story. But, for that very reason, it would seem strange that the history of modern law should begin with it. To attempt to create a law of nations before establishing the foundations of domestic law would seem to put the cart before the horse. Moreover, if there is one fixed idea which the average man has about international law, it is that it is so frequently honored in the breach that it hardly deserves the name of law at all. The man in the street thinks of law in terms of the policeman on the beat, and he knows that there has never been an international police force to execute the decrees of the law of nations. The two kinds of law seem to him, therefore, to be derived from totally different sources —the one resting on the apparent power of the state and the other on no more than vague international sentiment. But in the world in which the law of nations was born there were as yet no nation-states, and the stream of law was one. In a world in which Justinian's books of Roman law were accepted as obligatory, there was less interest in the more obvious national sanctions of legal rules. Paradoxically, the state of international anarchy was such that the authority of any body of law was less likely to be based upon the availability of political sanctions.

Of the triad of Renaissance, Reformation, and Reception, the second had yet to make its influence felt upon the growth of European law. The Reception had recovered the lawbooks of Justinian, and the glossators and commentators had attempted to adapt them to the needs of their own times. The humanists of the Renaissance, who had recovered the classical Roman law, prepared the way for the building of the national legal systems which accompanied the Reformation. While the Reformation was a religious movement, it was part of the political and economic revolution which led to the economy of modern capitalism. The era of discoveries, which had been inaugurated by Columbus, had opened up new worlds for commercial exploitation. But, while Catholicism was not uninterested in the acquisition of wealth, its otherworldliness and its opposition to such practices as interest-taking impeded the drive of business enterprise. Protestantism, on the other hand, with its emphasis upon individualism, encouraged thrift and enterprise. The division of Europeans into Catholics and Protestants encouraged separatist tendencies which destroyed the universal character of the medieval papacy and empire. In the place of the universal Church and the Holy Roman Empire, there arose the national states characteristic of modern Europe, and these competed with each other for commercial supremacy. The new merchant class which had been formed needed, in the first place, a more simple civil law, shorn of the anachronistic trappings of the medieval Roman law, which had to be restated in terms of the new individualism and nationalism. In the second place, it needed a law to govern the relations of the individual members of the new world of nation-states—a law to mitigate the horrors and ferocity brought about by intolerance and the wars of religion, in comparison with which the wars of succession and feudal ascendancy had been merciful and humane, and also to create the conditions necessary for the conduct and expansion of international trade.

It was no mere accident that the legal apostle of the Reformation should be Hugo Grotius, a Hollander. The northern provinces of the Netherlands were at the time of the birth of Grotius engaged in a life and death struggle with Spain, as the result of which they were to emerge as one of the strong Protestant states. At the same time Dutch merchants and mariners were busy in all the seas, establishing colonies and making a bid for commercial supremacy. The newly discovered world had been divided by Pope Alexander VI in 1493 between the Portuguese and the Spaniards, but the Dutch ignored the papal disposition. There is little cause for wonder, therefore, that Philip II of Spain had sworn to extirpate the inhabitants of the Netherlands as heretics, and had sent his armies to besiege and ravage their cities. It was in this stirring but unhappy world that an unhappy man created the unhappy science of international law, whose contradictions were accurately reflected in the very life of its own founder.

By a fitting coincidence, Hugo Grotius, who was to attempt to bring peace to men, was born at Delft on Easter Sunday, the tenth of April 1583. Delft was then not only an important commercial town but a political capital, for it was the seat of residence of William the Silent, whom the Dutch regard as the father of their country. Because of the valiant struggle he carried on against the armies of Spain, he was assassinated at the instigation of Philip II little more than a year after the birth of Grotius. William died with this prayer upon his lips: "Lord, have pity on this poor land." He might have added, "And all Europe."

The family of Grotius belonged to the ruling commercial oligarchy. His father, Jan de Groot, was himself a learned man. He was one of the curators of the University of Leyden, and also served four times as burgomaster of Delft. He married Alida van Overschie, of an illustrious family, which was to become interested chiefly in the affairs of the Dutch East India Company, and Hugo was the first child born of this union. In the circle in which the father of Grotius moved were to be found Prince Maurice of Nassau and Jan van Olden Barneveldt, who were to become rivals for the domination of the Dutch provinces, and such famous scholars or divines as Lipsius, Scaliger, Francis Junius, and Casaubon. Grotius himself became an intimate friend of Frederick Henry of Nassau, who was to become *stadholder* after the death of

Prince Maurice; of Van der Myle, who was to become Dutch ambassador to France; and of Daniel Heinsius, who was to achieve fame as a poet and philologist.

The family of Grotius seems to have been determined to give a famous man to the world. From the moment of his birth it seemed that they would succeed with Hugo, who turned out to be one of those troublesome creatures, a child prodigy. A strong, eager, blue-eyed boy, he possessed a phenomenal capacity and zeal for acquiring learning. Legend has it that when his mother, who did not want him to study at night, refused to give him candles, he hoarded his Sunday money so that he might buy them secretly. Before he was seven years of age, he had commenced the study of Latin and Greek, and in his eighth year he was writing Latin verses, in one of which he comforted his bereaved father upon the death of his brother.

At the age of eleven he entered the University of Leyden, where, as one of his biographers puts it, he "exercised himself in all sorts of knowledge," learning Greek and Roman history, philosophy, astronomy, mathematics, theology, and law. During his university days he was a frequent visitor at the home of the famed Scaliger, and had the advantage of boarding at the home of Francis Junius. In his twelfth year Grotius performed the feat of converting his mother from Catholicism to the Protestant faith, but it is questionable whether his success is to be attributed to the persuasiveness of his theological arguments or to the mother's love of the young theologian. In his fourteenth year the young Grotius was so far advanced intellectually that he was able to participate in two public debates upon philosophical questions and to take his degree at the University of Leyden.

On the whole, his parents had handled the wonderfully endowed youth intelligently, and he was growing into tall and vigorous manhood. In spite of the fact that children of that time devoted themselves to serious study at a far younger age than those of today, the accomplishments of the young Grotius must be considered amazing. It was appropriate enough, however, that the prodigious science of international law should be ushered into the world by a prodigy.

With his university career behind him, Grotius at the age of fifteen had the unparalleled opportunity of securing an introduction to the world of diplomacy and international politics. The Dutch received word that Henry IV of France, whose war against Spain had proved a great boon to them, was planning to make peace with their common enemy. To prevent the consummation of the plan, the Dutch decided to send a mission to the French Court. It consisted of Count Justin of Nassau, the natural son of William the Silent, and Jan van Olden Barneveldt, the Grand Pensionary of Holland. The young Grotius was taken along on this mission as a protégé of Barneveldt, who wanted a companion for his son.

It is said that such was the fame of the young Grotius that when he was presented to Henry IV, the king exclaimed in the presence of all his courtiers: "Behold the miracle of Holland! Look you upon the marvel of Holland!" Grotius stayed behind in France when the mission, unable to prevent the approaching peace, quit the country. He remained in France for about a year, making many friends, among them the young Prince of Condé, and attending the University of Orléans, which conferred upon him the degree of Doctor of Laws, presumably an honorary one, since his attendance at the University had been brief.

Before his departure from Holland, Grotius had completed work on an edition of *Martianus Capella,* the dismal but extraordinarily long-lived medieval encyclopedia of the seven liberal arts cast in the form of an allegory representing the marriage of Philologia and Mercury. Upon his return the learned young editor hastened to arrange for its publication, and solemnly dedicated the work to the Prince of Condé, who was himself then only eleven years old. Within two years he also published his first tragedy in verse, *Adamus Exul,* from which it is said Milton borrowed in writing *Paradise Lost.* Later in life Grotius wrote other tragedies. While still a youth he was made official historiographer of Holland. His maturity was occupied with theological works, among which the greatest celebrity was achieved by *The Truths of the Christian Religion,* a book singularly free of the spirit of bigotry so characteristic of the times.

Nevertheless, the main business of the life of Grotius was the profession of the law. It was not only the source of his enduring fame; the fact that he was a practicing lawyer proved fateful for the development of the science which he founded. On the thirteenth of December, 1599, although then not quite seventeen years of age, Grotius was sworn in as a lawyer before the Court of Holland. It is worth pointing out that, while Grotius had devoted many years to the acquisition of an immense store of learning, relatively little of this could have been spent in the study of jurisprudence, for he had not specialized in law at the University of Leyden, and his stay at the University of Orléans had been very brief. Grotius must therefore have been initiated into the mysteries of jurisprudence in the course of his practice. Despite his excellent family connections, this was at first very light, probably because it was felt, even by those who were sponsoring his career, that he was not yet prepared to handle important matters, and certainly because his literary activities were then so extensive that he could have had but little time for the infinite details of practice. There is evidence that at this time he regarded the idea of devoting his whole life to the drudgery of legal practice with considerable distaste. In a letter dated July 21, 1603, he wrote to his friend Daniel Heinsius that the profession filled him with disgust. But this feeling, almost inevitable in a young man of Grotius' scholarly temper and manifold interests, was rapidly overcome as his practice grew in importance. It was not long before he had Prince Maurice himself as a client and was being consulted by the Dutch East India Company. He was rapidly becoming a real everyday lawyer, as is shown by the fact that one of the cases he handled was a breach of promise suit brought by a servant girl against a pious but lecherous friend of his, Dominicus Baudius, Professor of Rhetoric at the University of Leyden. That he learned all of the tricks of the lawyer's trade is apparent from some advice he later gave to his son concerning his method of pleading. "Put in place," he said, "all that can be said by both sides, keeping it strongly in your memory, and whatever your adversary says, refer to it not under his, but under your classification."

Still, the concern with petty cases "about dripping eaves or party walls" (to refer to some examples of his own) rankled in the mind of the youthful lawyer. When Grotius was not quite twenty-two, he began work on a book, which was undoubtedly the prototype and original of the masterpiece of his mature years on the law of nations. It was called *De jure praedae* (The Law of Prize). Although it was probably written with the encouragement, if not at the instigation, of the Dutch East India Company, it was never published by Grotius in his lifetime, and the manuscript was discovered at The Hague only in 1864. However, a portion of the work, which dealt with the question of the freedom of the seas, was published by Grotius. The rediscovery of the lost work on the law of prize excited scholars, because it helped to clear up the mystery of the evolution of Grotius' ideas. It certainly is significant that the attention of Grotius was turned first to the issues of immediate

commercial importance in the law of nations rather than to an amelioration of the horrors of contemporary warfare.

The work on the law of prize was a piece of juristic journalism
which had its source in the competition of Dutch and Portuguese
merchants in the waters of the Far East. When the Dutch were barred
by Philip III from commerce with the Spanish mainland, they turned
to the Indies, but there they found the Portuguese, who had preceded
them by more than a century. In the resulting conflict the Dutch cap-
tains began to seize Portuguese ships as prizes, and the immediate
occasion of the *De jure praedae* was the capture of a richly laden
Portuguese galleon by a Dutch admiral in the Straits of Malacca. Not
all the shareholders of the Dutch East India Company, however, approved of the taking of prizes, partly because of religious scruples but
also because they doubtless feared that it would prove a ruinous policy
in the long run. Grotius argued that the warfare against the Portuguese
was justified and that prizes might lawfully be taken from them because they had wrongfully attempted to exclude the Dutch merchants
from the Indian trade.

The plea of Grotius for the freedom of the seas and the freedom
of trade is very eloquent. He assumes also a highly moral attitude. The
freedom of the seas and of trade is a "law of nature," an "unimpeach-
able axiom of the law of nations," a "decree of divine justice." "For,"
asks Grotius, "do not the oceans, navigable in every direction, with
which God has encompassed all the earth, and the regular and occasional winds which blow, now from one quarter and now from another, offer sufficient proof that nature has given to all peoples a right
of access to all other peoples?" Grotius held, too, that the principle of
the freedom of the seas extends even to the right of fisheries, for did
not the Dutch fish off the English coast? He ended with an apostrophe
to his countrymen: "Arise, O nation, unconquered on the sea, and
fight boldly, not only for your own liberty, but for that of the human
race." In modern times the principle of the freedom of the seas has been
regarded as axiomatic, but in ancient and medieval times it seems that
the security of persons and property was better served by the closing of
the known seas. Such was the extent of piracy that a sea became safe
only when it came to be completely dominated by a single power,
which occupied its shores and could control its waters. The Romans
brought peace to the Mediterranean only by making it a Roman lake,

and the medieval trading cities on the Italian littoral continued the policy of *mare nostrum*. The argument of Grotius came, therefore, as something of a bombshell, and he had, indeed, to pervert ancient authority to make his point.

Now the opportunity arose which permitted Grotius to shake off the trammels of private practice and to devote himself entirely to public affairs. Toward the end of the year 1607 the influence of his family secured for him the appointment to the post of Fiscal General of the provinces of Holland, Zeeland, and Friesland. The office, which combined functions of police, public prosecution, and supervision of revenues, was so important that the Fiscal General was said to be "the eye and arm of the prince." But the attainment to public office was to prove only the first of a series of events which were to sweep Grotius in an irresistible tide to ruin and exile.

First, however, there was a quiet and happy interlude. Settled in not only an important but a remunerative office, it was time for Grotius, who had passed his twenty-fifth birthday, to marry. He took as a bride Maria van Reigersberg, who came of one of the first families of Zeeland, and whose father had been burgomaster of Veer. It was not a romantic marriage, for the bride had been selected for the groom by his father, but it proved nevertheless very happy and successful, although four of the six children of the marriage died prematurely. Maria was not only a devoted and understanding wife, but, when the occasion arose, she showed herself to be a woman of heroic mold whose courage and resourcefulness stood her husband in good stead in the supreme crisis of his life. It was fit that the founder of international law, which was destined to emphasize reason and good will in international relations rather than the tempestuous virtues of blood and honor, should have taken as a wife a woman who was a helpmeet rather than a glamorous mistress won only after a dramatic and romantic courtship.

Grotius seemed destined for a great career when early in 1613, upon the death of Elias van Barneveldt, the brother of Jan van Olden Barneveldt, the Grand Pensionary, he was appointed to the office of Pensionary of Rotterdam, one of the chief cities of the Dutch state. Not only did the new office carry twice the emolument of the fiscal generalship, which he now resigned, but it was a steppingstone to the still greater and more influential office of Grand Pensionary. The Pensionary was the representative and negotiator of the city, and ex officio had a seat in the States of Holland, the provincial assembly. Later Grotius also secured a seat in the States-General, the general assembly of the Netherlands.

One of the first duties of Grotius as Pensionary was to accompany a Dutch commercial and diplomatic mission to England to settle a controversy of some years' standing which had arisen as the result of the rivalry of the Dutch and English merchants in the Far East. The situation had reached an acute stage, for the Dutch had been violently ejecting the English from some of their ports and had seized English cargoes and mistreated English seamen. Now it was the English who were championing the principle of freedom of the seas and demanding the right of free trade, while the Dutch stood forth as the champions of monopoly! And who should be their advocate but Hugo Grotius, the future founder of international law and the author already of *Mare liberum,* that eloquent little work on the freedom of the seas. To be sure, he argued now as the paid lawyer and representative official of the States of Holland; but here, already before the science of international law was full-blown, was an example of that shifty expediency which was to be the curse of its maturity. There is even reason to think that Grotius attempted to use his influence with King James to persuade him to oust the Spaniards from the Philippines while the Dutch drove them out of the West Indies, and that he was also on a secret mission on behalf of the Dutch Arminians, who sought to secure the support of the English king for their cause.

Grotius hastened back to Holland to plunge into this Arminian controversy, which in a few years was to bring him to disaster. The Dutch Reformed Church had split into two sects, the Arminians, or Remonstrants, led by Jacob Arminius, and the Calvinists or Contra-Remonstrants, who acknowledged Franciscus Gomarus as their leader. Theologically, the controversy revolved about the doctrine of predestination, but its bitterness was intensified by political and economic differences between the disputants, and these were the factors that made its peaceful solution impossible. In 1609 the Dutch provinces had made a truce with their Spanish enemy but, having achieved at least temporary peace, they were now in danger of being rent asunder by their own political jealousies. If they were to survive, it was essential that they should achieve political unification. The United Provinces were a loose aggregate of independent sovereignties which had delegated a very limited power to the States-General. The cities, such as Amsterdam and Rotterdam, were suspicious of the power and influence of the state governments and the states themselves were suspicious of the province of Holland, which because of its great wealth, tended to occupy a paramount position. Although Jan van Barneveldt was only the chief representative of the province of Holland, his power seemed as great as that of Prince Maurice, who was the *stadholder*. In this struggle over states' rights, the Arminians supported the claims of the provinces and the ruling oligarchies of the cities, which were composed of the great merchants, while the Calvinists championed greater power for the central government and popular sovereignty. Although the Arminians had a majority in Holland, the most important province, they did not have full control of Amsterdam, the most important city of the province, and in the seven provinces as a whole they were distinctly in the minority.

It was not Arminius but Jan van Barneveldt who determined the lines of the conflict, while the forces of national unity were represented by Prince Maurice. The Grand Pensionary and the *stadholder* were old rivals. Barneveldt had championed the Twelve Years' Truce which had been made with Spain on April 9, 1609, precisely because he had feared that a continuance of the war, which would be waged under the leadership of Prince Maurice, would increase the latter's ascendancy in the Dutch state. But not even the truce had been able to prevent this, for the Prince's power was based not only upon his control of the military but upon his support by a majority of the people. The result of the ensuing struggle was a foregone conclusion.

Who should be Barneveldt's right-hand man but Grotius? The father of international law was the champion of states' rights. It was Grotius who was entrusted by the States of Holland with the task of preparing an edict which should formulate the terms of settlement for ending the conflict between them, but his inability to secure its acceptance by the city of Amsterdam stultified the whole effort. Barneveldt then began preparations for the inevitable hostilities by attempting to induce the states to raise militia, ostensibly to suppress the riots which broke out when the edict failed of its purpose. The failure to get the city of Utrecht to raise an armed force was particularly fatal to this plan. Maurice, perceiving what was in the offing, forestalled the threatening civil war by arresting the leaders of the opposition, a move that proved easy of execution because of the failure of the provinces to call forth their militia while Maurice was proceeding against them at the head of his own army.

Barneveldt, Grotius, and Hogerbeets, the Pensionary of Leyden, were arrested on August 29, 1618, and confined in the Binnenhof, a castle at The Hague, where they were tried in the spring of the following year by twenty-four commissioners nominated by the States-General from among the nobility and magistrates of the seven provinces. During his confinement Grotius had written a long letter to Maurice, in which he had attempted to win back the Prince's favor by attempting to put the whole blame upon Barneveldt. This he did by pleading that he had only been carrying out orders from his superiors, and that actually his object had always been to mediate between the contending parties. This letter, which is rather discreditable to Grotius' character, may perhaps be excused on the grounds that the young man of thirty-five was faced with the most dire prospects for his whole future career, but it failed of its purpose. It did not move the Prince, and the trial proceeded. Barneveldt, the archconspirator, was condemned to death, while Grotius and Hogerbeets were sentenced to perpetual imprisonment. While the other prisoners were still confined there, Barneveldt was beheaded in the beautiful courtyard of the Binnenhof.

It is doubtful that the special court had any jurisdiction to try the prisoners, but nations are not infrequently born in illegality, and it is certainly ironic that the founder of the law of nations was tried and condemned unjustly at The Hague, the very city which some centuries later was to be the seat of the first Court of International Justice. It was discovered a year after Grotius was sentenced that the commissioners had neglected to find him formally guilty of treason, but this technical oversight was now corrected so that his estate might be duly confiscated as that of a traitor.

Shortly before midnight on June 5, 1619, Grotius, together with Hogerbeets, each seated upon a separate wagon, began their journey to the formidable fortress of Louvestein situated upon a narrow point of land where the Meuse and Waal Rivers meet to flow on together to the sea. Said to have been built by the Normans in the ninth century, the fortress was surrounded by water on three sides. Outside the walls, which were two yards in thickness, ran an outer moat, a wide, deep ditch, which could be crossed by means of a bridge. Within these massive walls the prisoners were to spend the rest of their natural lives. It seemed hardly possible that they should ever escape.

Yet Grotius found the path to freedom in his devotion to study and in the courage and cleverness of his wife. The States-General at least allowed her to share her husband's imprisonment, and she joined him with their children in the fortress, where they were assigned two rooms. At periodic intervals Maria was even permitted to go to the neighboring town of Gorcum, where she did her shopping. There she formed an intimate friendship with a Madame Daatselaer, the wife of a ribbon-and-thread merchant whose house was used as a distribution center for the books borrowed by Grotius from his friends.

For over two years Grotius remained a prisoner at Louvestein. He kept physically fit by whipping a huge top, and exercised his mind with various literary and juristic projects. He composed a catechism for his son and daughter, and wrote a dialogue between a father and son on the virtues of taciturnity. He wrote the first version in verse of his work *The Truth of the Christian Religion,* and completed a valuable work of jurisprudence, *An Introduction to the Jurisprudence of Holland.* All these efforts required a constant stream of books, and these were brought to the learned political prisoner periodically in a good-sized trunk or chest, which Madame de Groot accompanied in and out of the fortress. At first the chest was regularly opened by the vigilant commandant of the fortress, but in time his caution relaxed, and it was permitted to pass unexamined. The wife of Grotius saw in this carelessness her husband's opportunity to escape, which she now proceeded to plan with great care. The plan was, of course, that Grotius should be substituted for his books, but its successful execution involved many risks and perils, as events indeed proved.

The escape required many rehearsals. Grotius practiced doubling himself up in the none too roomy chest. It would arouse suspicion to bore holes in the chest. Hence, it had to be determined how long Grotius would be able to breathe with air coming in only through the lock. The wife of Grotius visited her friend Madame Daatselaer in Gorcum, and began to drop dark hints that she might have an unexpected visitor. The maid of the Grotius family, Elsje van Houuvening, had to be taken into the plot, and instructed in the role she was to play. Elsje was only twenty years old, but despite her youth and inexperience she was very clever and possessed great presence of mind and courage. Finally, the wife of the commandant had to be put in a good humor with a present of venison and other dainties.

It happened that on Sunday, March 21, 1621, the commandant of the fortress, Lieutenant Deventer, who was of a much more suspicious nature than his wife, having just been promoted to a captaincy, left the fortress to receive his new regiment. Madame de Groot at once hastened to his wife. "I should like very much," she requested, "to send away a trunk of Arminian books. My husband exhausts himself so with study that I can bear it no longer." The commandant's wife offered no objections.

Early Monday morning, March 22, 1621, Grotius entered the chest, dressed only in his underclothes and silk stockings. He had to be so tightly wedged that he could not take along even a pair of shoes. His head, however, rested upon a copy of the New Testament, which was his pillow. To avert suspicion and to make it appear that he was still asleep in bed, his outer garments had been placed ostentatiously upon a chair, and his slippers before the bed, while Madame de Groot herself entered the bed before summoning the servant to get the soldiers who would carry out the chest.

The soldiers were more suspicious than the commandant's wife. As one of them lifted the chest, he remarked: "How is it that this chest is so heavy? The Arminian might well be in it." But Madame de Groot remarked readily from within the bed: "They are Arminian books." Examining the chest for air holes but finding none, the soldiers thereupon proceeded to carry it out. They carried it through no less than thirteen doors, each securely bolted, and during their progress one or another of them remarked several times that Grotius himself must be in the chest. But when, having grumbled their way out of the fortress, they asked the commandant's wife whether they should open the chest in order to examine its contents, she inquired what the practice had been in the past, and, when told that it had been to let the chest pass unopened, she ordered: "Madame de Groot has told me that Arminian books are in it; carry it to the vessel."

It was due to the vigilance and presence of mind of Elsje, who was accompanying the chest, that it arrived with its human contents at its destination in Gorcum. As it was about to be loaded on the vessel, Elsje noticed that the plank connecting it with the dock was too thin, and, explaining that the weight of the books was too great, she had it replaced with a heavier one. During the journey a stiff breeze caused the boat to keel considerably, whereupon Elsje explained to the captain: "Lash the chest fast else it may slide overboard, and then the books would not only be ruined but lost." After this was done, an officer who was one of the passengers took it into his head to sit down on the chest, and to drum on its side with his heels. Elsje politely asked him to sit elsewhere, explaining that the chest contained not only books but delicate porcelain. When the boat reached Gorcum, Elsje first had to dissuade the captain from landing other cargo first, in which case Grotius might have suffocated, and then to persuade him to carry the chest with his son upon an ale-porter's yoke rather than a wheelbarrow. As they proceeded, the son exclaimed: "Father, something living is within the chest," but Elsje was ready as usual. "Yes," she observed, "books have both life and spirit."

Thus did Elsje and the chest arrive at the house of the Daatselaers. Madame Daatselaer, when informed who was in the chest, turned white with fear but soon recovered her poise. The two women hastened to the rear of the shop where the chest had been left. "Master," cried the maid before she opened the chest, but no answer came. "Your mistress has not done wisely," wailed Madame Daatselaer. "Before she had a living husband, now she has a dead one." But Grotius, who had been listening to the conversation, knocked on the cover of the chest, saying: "No, I am not dead. I did not recognize the voice."

Madame Daatselaer hastened to the house of her brother-in-law, Cornelis van der Veen, a clothier by trade and a Baptist. The clothier called to his assistance Jan Lambertszoon, a mason who was a Lutheran and whom he trusted. The latter supplied a mason's outfit, in which Grotius dressed. It did not, of course, fit him very well. The telltale hands of the scholar also had to be touched up with bits of plaster. Attired in this absurd costume and accompanied by the genuine mason, Grotius crossed by ferry to Waalwyks, where he would be able to get a carriage to take him to Antwerp. To quiet the suspicion of the driver, Grotius had Lambertszoon tell him that his passenger was really a bankrupt who was fleeing the country. Nearing Antwerp, Grotius thought that all was lost when he encountered a detail of soldiers, who stopped the carriage, but they turned out to be men of the sheriff of Antwerp, who was friendly to the Arminian cause.

Grotius was safe and free. But the real heroine of the escape was the wife who had stayed behind to avert suspicion. Madame de Groot had prayed when she fastened the chest and kissed the lock: "Go on, my husband, and may I never see you again unless in freedom." Now, when the flight of Grotius was discovered, she showed no contrition. She exclaimed happily to the furious commandant, "The cage is still here but the bird has flown." For weeks she was kept in confinement, and her fate hung in the balance. But the States-General finally decided not to be vindictive and set her free. She hastened to join her husband, who had in the meantime arrived in Paris.

Although his greatest work was still to be done, for the remainder of his life Grotius was to lead the unhappy life of an exile. Shortly after his arrival in Paris, influential friends induced that gracious monarch, Louis XIII, to grant the great scholar Grotius a handsome pension of 3000 livres per annum. But, alas, Grotius was able only rarely to collect the installments of this pension, and soon it became apparent that it had been granted so readily only because there had never been much prospect that it would be regularly paid. Grotius' only sources of income were the limited separate estate of his wife, which had escaped confiscation, and such funds as he was able to obtain from his father.

Restless and distraught, Grotius was nevertheless able to write. It was in Paris that he completed *The Truth of the Christian Religion,* upon which his fame as a theologian rests, and it was in Paris, too, that he undertook that most pathetic of all endeavors, the writing of an apology for his acts. But, above all, it was in Paris that Grotius, appalled by the horrors of the Thirty Years' War, which was then raging in all its fury, and to bring to consummation a project that he must have cherished ever since he had written his little book on the law of prize, now composed his magnum opus, which is called *De jure belli ac pacis* (The Law of War and Peace), the work that has earned for him the title of father of international law.

Grotius no doubt hoped that the publication of *The Law of War and Peace,* which occurred in June, 1625, would somehow be instrumental in opening for him a new career. He hoped, too, that it might help to make it possible for him to return to his native land. The book brought him international fame but unfortunately did not improve his immediate prospects. Prince Maurice had died on April 23, 1625, but his successor as *stadholder,* Frederick Henry of Nassau, turned a deaf ear to the appeal of Grotius, although he was an old friend and had been a fellow student at the University of Leyden. In 1626, upon the accession of Richelieu to power, the payment of Grotius' pension stopped altogether, because he would not accommodate himself to the scheming Cardinal's plans, and, after struggling for a number of years, Grotius resolved to return to Holland. He stayed there for about six months, attempting to establish himself in Amsterdam and Delft, but he was forced to flee when the States-General offered a reward of 2000 florins for his delivery. He thereupon made his way to Hamburg, which he found unbearably dull after the brilliance of Paris. As a result of his stay there, however, he was able to meet Oxenstiern, the great Chancellor of Sweden, who offered him the post of ambassador to France.

Grotius thus returned to Paris in the new role of Swedish ambassador, a position he held from 1635 to 1645. The chief purpose of his mission was to keep up an active alliance between Sweden and France, and toward the end of his embassy he secured the renewal of the treaty between the two countries upon advantageous terms. But Grotius was not cut out to be a diplomat, and he was never very popular with his colleagues. He was too much the scholar, and the formalities and frivolities of the Court irked him. His fellow diplomats were annoyed by a man who, while waiting in the anteroom for an audience, would sit apart studying his Greek testament. When war broke out between Sweden and Denmark, Queen Christina of Sweden sent an agent to Paris to act as coadjutor in the embassy. Grotius correctly evaluated the significance of this step and requested his own recall. He proceeded to Sweden to see the Queen in the hope that some other post would be offered to him. But, although he was lavishly entertained and loaded with presents, none was forthcoming.

Grotius left Stockholm for Lübeck, but no one has ever discovered what his ultimate destination was. In fact, he never reached Lübeck. The vessel which carried him was shipwrecked in a storm at sea, and though he survived this disaster, his end was near. He arrived in Rostock in an open, shaky cart, and, as the result of his exposure at sea, he was a very sick man. After a short illness the celebrated exile died among strangers, attended only by a Lutheran pastor, John Quistorpius. According to one story, his last words were, "By undertaking many things I have accomplished nothing."

Posterity has not accepted this harsh judgment. Grotius was a poet, scholar, historian, theologian, and moralist; but, above all, he was a jurist, and his fame rests upon his reputation as the father of international law. *The Law of War and Peace,* a vast and monumental work, which achieved no less than six editions before the death of its author, and which arrested the attention of all learned men, must be pronounced at least an enormous literary success. It is more difficult to say to what extent it had an immediate influence upon practice. The international morals of monarchs and statesmen, even in the seventeenth and eighteenth centuries, were not remarkably high, if the keeping of faith be the test, although possibly a greater degree of humanity was introduced into the actual conduct of hostilities. There is a pretty story that when Gustavus Adolphus fell on the field of battle in the course of the Thirty Years' War, a copy of Grotius' book was found in his tent, but there is no proof that the embattled and hard-pressed monarch had found much time to peruse its pages.

The low estate into which international law has recurrently fallen has indeed reacted upon the fame of Grotius, and there has been an increasing tendency of late to minimize the originality of his contribution and even to question the justice of his claim to be regarded as the father of international law. It has been pointed out almost as a discovery that Grotius was not the first writer on the law of nations but had many precursors, although Grotius himself mentions them by name and acknowledges his indebtedness to them. Even more curiously, Grotius himself bemoaned the disregard of the law of nations in his own day. He commented that it was viewed "with contempt as having no reality outside of an empty name." Obviously, therefore, he could have invented neither the general conception nor the particular rules of the law of nations. The explanation of this seeming paradox is that Grotius was the founder of international law as a *juristic science*.

Even primitive peoples, whom we like to regard as utterly savage, observe some rules in conducting warfare and making peace. Sometimes women and children may not be slaughtered, or poisoned arrows may be forbidden. Indeed, many a primitive tribe has been far less bloodthirsty than the mighty conquering states of remote antiquity, such as those of the Babylonians, Assyrians, Hebrews, or Phoenicians, who had developed the ideas of tribal exclusiveness and righteousness to such a marked extent that they could not bring themselves to spare their enemies. Although there are occasional examples of the making of treaties in very ancient times, the lack of adequate means of communication made the regular conduct of international relations impossible. In the successive clash of empires is to be perceived only the attempt of each of them to achieve mastery over the whole known world. The Greeks were the first people of antiquity to approach the conception of a system of international relations, but this was because they were derived from a common stock and were united in confederacies for their mutual protection. They had, therefore, really a sort of intermunicipal rather than international law. Yet one encounters in Thucydides' *Peloponnesian War* the melancholy refrain: "And so they put the women and children to the sword." Although the Romans were the greatest law-creating people of antiquity, they, too, created no system of international law. The reason is obvious. They had actually succeeded in conquering the whole known world and in imposing the *pax romana* on all other peoples. They might recognize certain rules of making war, but there could be no system of international law in a universal empire. In theory the medieval Holy Roman Empire maintained the same claim to universal dominion. But in practice it struggled against an ever increasing degree of political anarchy. There was, however, the reality of the universal Church, which sought to curb the prevailing violence by such devices as the Truce of God, which limited fighting to certain times and seasons. The medieval trading cities, especially in Italy, and the medieval Hanse sought, too, to nurture rules of international intercourse, but with no remarkable degree of success. It was only when the Catholic Church was rent in twain by the rise of Protestantism and the national states emerged to compete with each other for possession of a newly discovered world that a system of international law became both a possibility and a necessity.

But classical antiquity and its heir, the medieval Empire, while they did not develop a system of international law, did develop an idea which was to become the foundation of the law of nations. This was the conception of a law of nature. It has never meant the same thing in all ages and to all its votaries, but as a historical phenomenon its chief significance has been to provide a means of protesting against the existing law and constitution of society. As Benedetto Croce, the Italian historian, has remarked: "Natural rights are nothing but new historical rights in the struggle of their becoming." For this reason the protean idea of natural law has loomed large in every age of transition and social change. From the positive law under which men lived they appealed to the superior validity of the law of nature.

The idea of the law of nature appeared first among the Greek Sophists, who lived in an age of crashing orthodoxies following the expansion of Greek trade and the rise of the Athenian Empire. Like the apostles of the Enlightenment which preceded the French Revolution, the Sophists speculated on what man was like in a state of nature and protested against social inequality. The popular organization of Greek justice made appeals to a law of nature an easy means of argument. While Plato and Aristotle tended to identify natural law with the established order, the Stoics, who flourished in the age of imperialism inaugurated by the conquests of Alexander the Great, regarded it as a universal law, cosmopolitan and equalitarian. From the Stoics the idea of natural law passed to the Roman jurists, who, however, made little of it as a practical component of jurisprudence. There was little opportunity for the application of *ius naturale* in the well-developed system of the classical Roman law, which was supported by a strong and absolute political system. The great achievement of the Roman jurists was rather with *ius gentium*. Although this was not at all a "law of nations" but an integral part of Roman law applied to individuals, such was its universal character that it was easy to identify it with *ius naturale,* and it became, indeed, the equivalent of natural reason. The foundation was thus laid for regarding the *ius gentium* as the law of nations itself. The idea of the law of nature, however, played a great role in medieval times. It has been said that appeals to the law of nature grow more frequent as times grow darker, and this was the condition in medieval society. The Church identified the law of nature with the law of God, of which, however, it claimed to be the exclusive guardian, and employed the law of nature as a potent weapon in the struggle between empire and papacy. When both fell, the idea of the law of nature, divorced from theology and restored to secular possession, was ready to be launched upon a new career—and perhaps its most important—as the basis of a law of nations. The internal law of states rested upon the availability of law-declaring and law-creating organs and upon the use of physical force for the execution of their decrees. The law of nations, which was to govern sovereign states, could rest only upon the law of nature.

It was out of the practice of nations and the law of nature that the law of nations was compounded. In a sense, all men who in past centuries had been dismayed by the horrors of war and had dreamed of ending them were the precursors of Grotius. Canonists and church fathers had been preoccupied with the subject; but the most important of the forerunners of Grotius had been the Spanish jurist-theologians of the sixteenth century, among whom the most notable was Francisco de Vitoria, and Alberico Gentili, an Italian Protestant who had fled to England to escape the persecution of the Inquisition. While Vitoria had a conception of a world community, it rested upon the assumptions of Catholic theology, and his work, *De Indis,* was primarily concerned with the question of the justice of expropriating the aborigines of the New World. Gentili, a practical lawyer and a Protestant, came closer to meeting the needs and spirit of the new age, but his work, *De jure belli*, was limited in scope, dealing only with the law of war. The age needed also a law of peace.

Grotius approached his task with the fullness of a reformer's zeal. A lonely exile, now free of the exigencies of practical politics, regretting no doubt the equivocations and inconsistencies of his own career, he raised his voice in protest against the barbarities of a belligerent world, and pleaded the cause of humanity with all the powers of his maturity. In a passage that has become famous, he indicted the nations of his day. "Throughout the Christian world," he wrote, "I observed a lack of restraint in relation to war, such as even barbarous races should be ashamed of; I observed that men rush to arms for slight causes, or no cause at all, and that when arms have once been taken up there is no longer any respect for law, divine or human; it is as if, in accordance with a general decree, frenzy had been openly let loose for the committing of all crimes." In a society of nations torn by religious and political antagonisms, which were being resolved only in accordance with the Machiavellian conception of reasons of state, he sought to introduce and establish the idea of the reign of law.

But Grotius did not confine himself to mere moral indignation. He was not only a Protestant moral reformer and theologian but also a practical jurist. There had been many, he observes in his very first paragraph, who had written commentaries or digests on the municipal law of Rome. His task was to write a systematic treatise on the body of law "concerned with the mutual relations among states," and, whatever may be thought of the originality of its particular ingredients, it cannot be gainsaid that it was the first systematic treatment of the law of nations. None of his predecessors could be compared with him with respect to the fullness of argument and exposition, the extent of the marshaling of precedent, the grandiosity of conception and scope. Others had written on the law of war; he would write on the law of war and peace. Of the three books into which the work of Grotius is divided, the first and third deal with the law of war, while the second, which is longer than the other two combined, deals with the law of peace. This is indeed the most original feature of the work.

The laws of both war and peace rest upon the law of nature, which is, however, now divorced from the preconceptions of theology and rooted firmly in the social nature of man. Man is a social animal, and "the maintenance of the social order" is the source of law. To be sure, the laws of nature can be attributed to God in the sense that He has created the human traits from which they derive, but they would have validity "even if we should concede that which cannot be conceded without the utmost wickedness, that there is no God, or that the affairs of men are of no concern to Him." Sometimes, too, Grotius seems to say that the law of nations rests upon consent, which is shown by the usages and customs of nations, but this is because as a practical jurist he wants to rely upon precedent as well as upon natural reason. After all, the dictates of the law of nature can be proved *a posteriori* as well as *a priori*. What is in force among many nations must presumptively at least accord with the law of nature; this is only another example of the identification of the *ius naturale* with the *ius gentium*. Grotius indeed employed the principle of consent as the basis of the law of nature as well as of the law of nations. This reliance upon agreement was to be an ever more marked characteristic of his successors. It was an idea alien to the status-ridden society of the Middle Ages, but the new forms of business enterprise made it a cardinal article of faith. In the form of the Social Contract, it was to become in the Age of the Enlightenment the theoretical foundation of all law and government.

When it is said, however, that the work of Grotius deals with the law of peace as well as of war, it must not be understood merely that he treated the problem of international relations in times of peace as well as of war. He developed also that law of nature which should govern the conduct of individuals in their relations with one another. The scope of this law of nature he summed up as "the restoration of anything belonging to another, the obligation to fulfill promises, making good losses caused by fault, and the infliction of penalties." Indeed, his book might well have been entitled "The Law of Nature and of Nations," and there is reason to think that he would have written it from this point of view and under this title if the urgency of the times had not counseled an emphasis upon the problems of war and peace. The natural law of private rights and duties had therefore to be smuggled into his treatise and be subordinated to the law of war and peace.

The reason that Grotius was able to combine the law of nature with the law of nations, the law of individuals with the law of states, is that his mind was dominated by a breath-taking conception. Incredible as it may seem to us, the founder of the law of nations really based his system upon the assumption that nations were subject to the same principles of law as individuals. The system of Grotius is entirely modern in recognizing the principles of the equality, independence, and sovereignty of states, which became the basic axioms of the international law of succeeding centuries. Nevertheless, the mightiest of states should govern their conduct by the rules applicable to the torts and contracts of individuals. A state should not go to war unless it had first attempted to secure the peaceful settlement of its grievance, and a wrongdoing nation should submit to arbitration. War, which was conceived as a form of action at law, was permissible only because there were no tribunals for the adjudication of disputes between nations. But, for a nation to go to war, its cause had to be just, and only just war was allowable by the law of nations. This notion of "just war" (*iustum bellum*), which went back to antiquity, is the most prominent characteristic of the Grotian system. The word "neutrality" is not to be found in the pages of Grotius. He tells us that "it is the duty of those who keep out of war to do nothing whereby he who supports a wicked cause may be rendered more powerful, or whereby the movements of him who wages a just war may be hampered."

The Law of War and Peace was not only a bigger but a better book than had been written by any of Grotius' predecessors. But the secret of its success lies not only in its scientific merits. It appeared at just the right time. The Thirty Years' War was at its height in 1625 when the book was published, and Europeans needed to be told as never before that there were laws of war. The Thirty Years' War was ended by the Peace of Westphalia in 1648, and Europeans needed to give heed to a law of peace. The Peace of Westphalia created the modern European system of national states and thus recognized the basic axioms of the new law of nations—the equality, independence, and sovereignty of states. Grotius' book became the international Bible of Protestant Christendom, although, as is not unusual in the case of Bibles, in practice the believers fell far short of all the exacting demands of piety. The system of the law of nature and of nations was, indeed, nothing less than legal protestantism, and Hugo Grotius was its prophet. The Catholic and Apostolic Church estimated the situation with its usual shrewdness, for it immediately put *The Law of War and Peace* on the papal Index and did not remove the ban until 1901.

It is another of the paradoxes of the career of the founder of the law of nations that he should have exercised even greater influence as the apostle of natural law. The rules derived from the immutable prescriptions of the law of nature simply embodied the program of the rising *bourgeoisie* in law and politics. The rules of the classical Roman law, which was a mature system dealing with all the subtleties of contract and tort, were not really unsuited to the needs of the new bourgeois society, but they had to be stripped of their historical excrescences and Roman dress and restated in abstract and general terms. In the absence of central law-creating organs capable of formulating new national law, this task was entrusted to the jurists who were the teachers of natural law. In continental Europe, therefore, natural law became a technical phase of jurisprudence, and not only the foundation but the substance of the civil law that determined the rights of individuals. The two basic axioms of the system were those already enunciated by Grotius—that a promise as such is binding, and that liability follows from fault. The program of natural law was realized more fully by the French Revolution. It was embodied in the form of positive legislation in the Code Napoleon, which was proclaimed in 1804 and carried by conquests, as well as by its intrinsic merits, across the continent of Europe. The Code Napoleon was thus not only a French civil code but a new common law.

The influence of Grotius was perpetuated by his great disciple, Samuel von Pufendorf, the son of a Lutheran pastor, who rebelled against theology and embraced the fashionable philosophy of rationalism. In his political writing Pufendorf blasted with ridicule the tottering structure of the Holy Roman Empire, and in his juristic work he propagated the claims of natural law. He wrote the book which Grotius was prevented from writing only by his reformist zeal. The title of Pufendorf's greatest work was significantly *De jure naturae et gentium* (The Law of Nature and of Nations). It set forth a homogeneous system applicable to the law of individuals as well as of states. It is based entirely on the principles of natural law, rejecting treaty as well as custom as sources of the law of nations. Pufendorf, for whom there was established at the University of Heidelberg the first professorship of the law of nature and of nations, only carried to their logical conclusions some of the basic doctrines of Grotius. He still subscribed to the doctrine of just war, but he argued against the recognition of any laws of war, because to wage war humanely was only to prolong hostilities and postpone the restoration of the natural state of peace!

Like Grotius, the real influence of Pufendorf, which endured for a century, was in shaping the civil law. Pufendorf's rejection of the laws of war was only a rationalization of the very unsatisfactory practice of the times. By the middle of the eighteenth century the natural law of nations was cast into the discard, at least in the books. Positivism reigned in its stead, and treaty and custom were now the primary sources of the law which soon came to be known as international law. It was in this way only that sovereign states could be bound, if at all. International jurists no longer subscribed to the doctrine of just war. International law now recognized war as perfectly legal and sought only to limit its effects by means of laws of war. International law became, indeed, a system of international quarantine. Belligerent nations were left to fight it out, while the nonbelligerent nations refrained from interference. Thus the doctrine of neutrality assumed central importance in the application of international law. In other words, the stupendous private-law analogy of Grotius was no longer even a literary theory in international law.

In the nineteenth century diplomats held one international conference after another, and vied with each other in arranging innumerable treaties, which were duly deposited in the national archives of the world. The anarchic doctrine of sovereignty prevented the formation of any true international society. Yet, surprisingly enough, the positive system of international law worked far better in practice than anyone would have expected from the theory, and certainly better than the natural law of nations. This was probably due less to the superiority of the one system over the other than to the steady improvement in cultural standards, the increasing interdependence of nations in international trade and all other activities, and particularly to the golden opportunities for imperialism that still remained.

It is now a familiar story how the whole system of international law collapsed in the First World War and how the attempt to build a new international society was made. The nations who made the Peace of Versailles seemed to behave as if the hour of Grotius had struck. They accepted in effect his doctrine of just war and carried out his audacious analogy by creating the League of Nations and the World Court as the organs of an imitation superstate. They seemed, indeed, to be proceeding to implement the vision of Grotius.

But it is an equally familiar story how all these well-intentioned efforts failed. After what had really been only a long armistice the

Second World War broke out. It became easier than ever before to sneer at the law of nations. But in a world engulfed by the greatest war of all time—by a total war—the rights of individuals, too, were at their lowest ebb, and the internal law of states became another phase of international anarchy. All law—the law of nature as well as the law of nations—was threatened with extinction.

However, the small regard in which international law has been held has been basically due to the over-evaluation of the legal systems for protecting the individual. Murder may not be legal as war is, but its suppression is still everywhere a serious problem. At least, Grotius perceived that the law of individuals and the law of states rest upon the same foundations. He had a vision of the unity of all law: international justice could rest upon no higher plane than national justice. When the states which were brought into existence by the grand competition for international markets inaugurated in the sixteenth century have solved their internal social problems, they may suddenly discover that they have solved the international problem. Only then will it be possible to resolve the contradictions manifest in Grotius' own career and in the law of nations from the very beginning. It was a magnificent folly of Grotius to suppose that the tremendous interests of nations could be subjected to the forms of action at law, because in his day as in ours justice was the handmaiden of power politics.

Edward Plantagenet

THE SCHEME, MOLD, AND MODEL
OF
THE COMMON LAW

THE BLACK-GOWNED DOCTORS OF THE ROMAN LAW FASHIONED THE civil law of modern continental Europe, a system that has also become the law of a large part of the modern world. But there was one island in the sea of Romanism—an island in the geographical as well as in the metaphorical sense—which, although constantly drenched with its spray, nevertheless resisted its overwhelming waves. That island was England. In England there grew up a rival legal system called the "common law," with which the civil law was destined ultimately to share its hegemony. The common law was the law of the first modern state, the first state to make the transition from medieval European feudalism to the economy of the modern world. It was the law of the first national kingdom that was not a part of the Holy Roman Empire. It came to be called the common law because it struggled to become the law common to all Englishmen as such, rather than the law of churchmen, or merchants, or burghers, or lords—the law of one land rather than the law of a benefice, or fief, or town.

That the English common law became the great rival of the civil law is not surprising. As always, arms and the law go together, and the fortunes of the legal system are bound up with those of the political state. The Roman law was the law of the greatest of the ancient empires, and was perpetuated in its shadowy successor, the Holy Roman Empire. The common law was destined to spread to a large part of the modern world as the law of the colonies which made up the British Empire, the greatest Empire of modern times.

In the early history of the common law, two kings stand out as important influences in its development. Creative kings fashion legal

systems as gods fashion solar systems and other wonders of the universe. In fact, it is surprising that more men of law have not worn
the royal purple. The king tended to wield whatever central political
power there was, and the king's law had a great advantage in ousting
and replacing the law of the clan or fief. Even when his political position was weak, the king usually had personal privileges and special
prerogatives. It was deemed a particularly grievous offense to fight in
the king's palace, for instance, or to strike or affront one of his servants,
or to rob on the king's highway. Traces of these ideas are to be found
in the ancient codes, and they still prevail in the practices of some
primitive peoples among whom chiefs exercise marked political power.
But a well-formulated idea of a special king's peace made its appearance in the early history of English law and became the general test of
the jurisdiction of the king's courts, so that to this day it is necessary
to allege, in order to make out that an act is a public crime, that it was
committed "against the peace of our Lord the King, his Crown and
Dignity." When this had happened, the special king's peace had become the general justification of all the king's law. Yet the king had
to strive mightily before this concept was extended to the whole realm
and the king's law was made the prevailing system of public justice.
Indeed, the king had to be so vigilant and fierce that the king's peace
sometimes looked more like the king's violence. Naturally the ruler
was concerned mainly with his own interests rather than with the
blessings of peace for his subjects; he was thinking of the gains to the
royal treasury that would accrue from the administration of justice. An
English constitutional historian has said of the Norman kings that "it
was mainly for the sake of the profits that justice was administered
at all."

Of all the early English kings, the greatest was undoubtedly Edward I, and his importance in the legal and political history of England
was so great that he has been flattered with the title of the English
Justinian. The comparison, however, is a little absurd. The work of
Edward Plantagenet had nothing in common with that of Justinian,
although there is some slight similarity in the events or circumstances
attending their reigns. What Justinian did was to stereotype a highly
developed but decaying legal system, while Edward laid the foundations of a rising legal system. As a great English legal historian has said,
to compare Edward with Justinian was "something like a comparison
between childhood and second childhood." There is far more truth,

however, in another celebrated characterization of the reign of Edward I. It has been said that at the end of his reign was to be perceived "the scheme, mould and model of the common law," and indeed of the modern English state—the country known as Great Britain.

Edward was born at Westminster on June 17, 1239, the son of Henry III and Eleanor of Provence. He was the grandson of King John, who had been compelled to sign Magna Charta. His parents piously named the royal infant after Edward the Confessor—a happy choice, for the youth who was to prove the first really national English king. Edward was delicate in his very early years, but he grew into a tall, strong, and handsome boy with flaxen locks, which turned tawny as he grew older and deepened into black in his manhood. His skin was bronze-toned, and his eyes dark and smoldering. From his father he inherited a drooping lid of the left eye. The King's son was easily moved to anger and, particularly as a youth, his manner was domineering.

Edward was taught French and acquired some Latin. He was also trained in a knowledge of the law. But he was not the sort of youth who loved books or was given to introspection. He could hardly have been devoted to the spoken word, because he was a stammerer. All his life he loved action. He devoted himself to all the manly and martial sports of the day and became extremely proficient as a swordsman, hawker, and hunter. His great passion was for tournaments, a passion that remained with him throughout his long and busy life. The tournament was his way of relaxing from the heavy cares and burdens of state, and it was also a substitute for the excitements of battle in the intervals of peace.

Edward's youth was wild and unbridled. With a troop of horsemen and some boon companions, notably Henry of Almaine and the four young Montforts, all of whom were his cousins, he rode about the countryside engaging in mad escapades and even cruel and wanton deeds. The progresses of Edward and his band have been described as "the movements of a desolating plague." It is said that he once ordered the cutting off of an ear and the plucking out of an eye of a harmless youth whose only crime was that he had crossed the Prince's path. Such was the violence of at least a prince's peace.

When Edward was still in his teens he was betrothed to Eleanor, a half sister of Alfonso X, King of Castile, in whose reign was compiled the famous Spanish code of law known as the *Siete Partidas,* or Code of the Seven Parts. It happened in 1254 that Edward's royal parents were on the Continent, and Edward, who had been taken along, took advantage of the opportunity, it seems, to go off by himself to have a look at his bride. He was well pleased with what he saw, and before the year was done he had been married to his Eleanor. The marriage took place at the monastery of Las Huelgas, whence the pair went on a long honeymoon to Bordeaux, and before long arrived in England. The marriage of Edward and Eleanor, which endured for thirty-five years, has come down the centuries as an idyll of royal wedded love. They had many children, most of whom, however, never reached maturity and were mourned by their grief-stricken parents. The devotion of Edward and Eleanor to each other was singular in the royal families of the Middle Ages. It is a temptation to say that it anticipated Victorianism, and certainly it was appropriate in a king who founded the greatest of all middle-class states. There is evidence that Eleanor was accused of mistreating and even despoiling the tenants of her own estates, but the fault may have been that of her bailiffs. Certainly these charges did not make her husband love her any less.

During the period of his preparation for the throne, Edward was endowed by his father with a vast domain, not only in order to supply him with an independent source of income, but also in order to prepare him for the business of government. But the domains customarily received by the heir to the throne were those outlying portions of the kingdom which were none too firmly under the royal scepter. The reigning king thus generously endowed his lineal successor with his troubles. Edward received nothing less than the whole of Ireland, the earldom of Chester, the king's lands in Wales, the islands of Jersey and Guernsey, and the whole of Gascony, which was at that time the only fief still held by the English Crown in France.

The only subjects of Edward who appear to have expressed any satisfaction with their new ruler were the merchants of Gascony. England was the chief market for their famous wines, and they no doubt hoped that Edward, as an absentee lord, would interfere with them as little as possible. Dynastic and feudal rivalries between England and France were already complicated by economic motives, namely, the desire to control the wine trade of Gascony and the wool trade of Flanders, where the weavers were dependent upon the English wool supply.

Edward now began to serve an apprenticeship as king in good earnest. He overcame the wildness of his youth and took to the responsibilities of power. His career resembles that of Justinian at least in that, while he never intrigued against his father, he rapidly became king in all but name. This was most fortunate for England, which then, as never before, needed a strong king. The Conquest had disrupted the homogeneity of English life and institutions and had brought only turmoil and confusion. William the Conqueror had, it is true, avoided the worst mistakes of Norman feudalism in setting up the government of his English kingdom, but the bloody strife that followed his death, in which royal fathers contended against sons, and brothers against brothers, had a devastating effect upon the lives of the common people and gave the ever rebellious feudal baronage one opportunity after another to escape from the yoke of royal rule. Following the anarchy of Stephen's reign came the more orderly times of Henry II, the first of the Angevins and the first of the English kings after the Conquest to leave a permanent mark upon the legal and political institutions of England. But Henry had to engage in a bitter war against his rebellious sons, and the governmental reforms he introduced into England were only the fitful measures of a king who was more preoccupied with his vast possessions in France than with the domestic concerns of his English subjects.

Henry II was followed by Richard the Lionhearted, who is known in English history only for his crusading efforts to wrest the Holy Sepulcher from the infidel; and by King John, whose chief claim to fame is that his misgovernment precipitated the revolt of the barons which led to Magna Charta, that grant of baronial privileges and exemptions which in the course of the centuries was to be transformed into a glorious charter of national liberties.

The reign of Henry III and Eleanor of Provence only deepened the dismay of the common people. The King was weak and irresolute, and the Queen greedy and rapacious. Their personal extravagances led them continually to extort money from their subjects, which, however, was squandered on favorites, most of whom were foreigners. These Poitevin and Savoyard relatives, chiefly Peter de Roches, who was made Bishop of Winchester, and Peter of Savoy, who was endowed with great domains, were extremely unpopular with the long-suffering people, who were welded into some sort of national solidarity by the very outrages to which they were subjected by these foreigners. It was long enough after the Conquest for a growing consciousness of Englishry to begin to make itself felt. Henry was foolish enough, too, to get himself embroiled in the quarrels of the shadowy Holy Roman Empire by accepting the crown of Sicily for his second son, Edmund, in opposition to the Emperor Conrad's son, and by allowing his brother Richard of Cornwall to be elected king of the Romans and emperor in prospect. This put Henry in a position to be mulcted by the Pope for the support of the Holy Father's war against the Hohenstaufens. Moreover, the King conceived a violent dislike of the citizenry of London, who had taken advantage of Richard the Lionhearted's need of money for his crusade by obtaining the right to elect their own mayor and sheriffs. Henry was always quarreling with the citizens of London instead of attempting to enlist their resources for national ends, the most important of which was the control of the feudal baronage.

The result of Henry's misrule was a revival of the feudal reaction which had set in at Runnymede. For once the rebellious barons found an extraordinary and resourceful leader in Simon de Montfort, the brilliant but tempestuous Earl of Leicester. He had been unpopular as seneschal of Gascony, probably because of his energy and determination, and he had returned to England. In 1238 he married the King's younger sister, Eleanor. It would be incorrect to say that the Earl was a champion of the people, but he did have the imagination to perceive that times were changing and that the barons could hope to win only by enlisting the aid of the lesser gentry and by giving them some voice in the government of the country.

The first phase of the struggle between the King and the barons ended in 1258, when they succeeded in exacting from Henry the so-called Provisions of Oxford. Under these arrangements, the powers of the Crown were virtually to be administered by a committee of fifteen barons. Both King Henry and his son Edward solemnly agreed to observe the Provisions. The King, however, was only playing for time. The knights and squires were far from being satisfied with the baronial ascendancy, and they appealed to Edward. The Prince seems to have sided with them, as did Simon de Montfort, who had more sympathy for the smaller gentry than Richard of Claire, the Earl of Gloucester. The latter shared with Simon the leadership of the barons, but he died in 1262 in the midst of these events. For a time suspicion and bad feeling existed between Henry and his son, who went off to France to attend a tournament.

Henry and Edward, however, were soon reconciled. Edward appears to have decided to embrace the ideas of Simon de Montfort, who had always exercised great influence over him, but to make use of these ideas in insuring the triumph of the royal cause. Henry, having obtained papal absolution from observing the Provisions of Oxford, repudiated them, and by Whitsuntide, 1263, the civil war broke out again. As Simon took the field, Edward withdrew to Windsor Castle, while the King and Queen took refuge in the Tower of London. Finally it was agreed to submit the dispute to St. Louis, King of France. St. Louis was married to a sister of Queen Eleanor, and whatever may have been his piety and his feelings as a feudal rival of King Henry, his decision could not but favor his brother-in-law. Simon and his party not unnaturally refused to accept the verdict, and took up arms again. On May 14, 1264, the King's forces were decisively defeated at the Battle of Lewes. By a ruse of Simon, Edward was induced to pursue across the river the Londoners whom he, too, hated, because they had humiliated his mother in 1263 by pelting her as she passed under London Bridge to join the King. The result was that Edward lost the battle. He was imprisoned at Kenilworth, and the Provisions of Oxford were restored.

In 1265 Simon de Montfort sought to secure the results of his victory by calling a Parliament which has become famous in English history because it was the first time that knights and burgesses sat side by side with the greater lords in such an assemblage. The proceedings were not lost upon the prisoner at Kenilworth, who, when he became king, was to make the summoning of periodical parliaments one of the cardinal maxims of his policy.

Simon's victory, however, was short-lived. The Pope fulminated against him, and he was charged with associating with the lower classes. The union of the great barons with the knights and burgesses was unstable, and the contradictions of the popular party rent it asunder. Gilbert, the new Earl of Gloucester, sulked and retired to his estates, while Simon marched off to the East, taking Edward with him as a valuable hostage. Edward, however, soon escaped from Simon's hands through the connivance of a brother of the Earl of Gloucester. Edward pretended to be trying out various horses and suddenly rode off upon the fleetest. He made terms with the Earl of Gloucester and raised a new army in Wales. By the Treaty of Ludlow he swore to observe the laws of the land and to do away with all evil customs. Having learned his lesson at Lewes, Edward defeated Simon at the battle of Evesham on August 4, 1265. The great Earl, together with many of the baronial leaders, died on the field of battle, and the revolt of the baronage was ended. Henry III was set free, but henceforth he was no more than a puppet in the hands of his son, who now took over the program of Simon de Montfort and the popular party and stood forth as the champion of the national cause.

The defeat of the barons prepared the way for the transition from a feudal to a more modern economy. When the thirteenth century opened, the English villages were almost completely isolated from one another. A famine in one county brought no relief from the next. Nearly the whole population lived and worked on the soil, which yielded not more than a threefold harvest. Almost the only articles imported were salt and iron, which were carried by peddlers on pack horses. Yet before the end of the century this simple feudal economy was undergoing marked changes. Agriculture was becoming not only a means of subsistence but a source of profit. A new class of farmers was coming into existence that preferred to render its dues, not in kind, but in money. A class of laborers was also making its appearance, and by the end of the century the wool and the wine trades were fundamental factors in English politics, as well as in English economy.

After his victory over feudal reaction, Edward, who was now King of England in all but name, turned his energies toward a crusade! The heyday of this sort of expedition had been over two centuries; the hosts of Islam had long since been united; and it was no longer possible for a Western monarch to win a fair Eastern province in this manner. The growing complications of Western politics kept the princes at home, making impossible any united effort of Christendom against the infidel. The new mendicant orders who succored the poor, and hence had a grasp of social realities, no longer had any crusading ardor. But the military orders still supplied recruits, and if there was no longer any profit in such an enterprise, there was still opportunity for personal glory and pious satisfaction. Edward was far from superstitious, and he was to prove no respecter of the Church when it interfered with the royal interests; but the cultural values he held dear were still medieval. Certainly he could not see that a crusade in the second half of the thirteenth century was *opéra bouffe*. Perhaps he had in mind to atone for some of the violences of his youth. At any rate, when St. Louis of France decided to consecrate his old age with a second crusade, Edward determined to join him, although he had to mortgage Gascony to the pious king to obtain the funds. He took the crusader's vow in June, 1268, but it was two years before he was able to embark for the Holy Land in the company of his dear wife, Eleanor. By then St. Louis had died of fever, and his son and successor, Philip the Hardy, his army devastated by sickness, had decided to conclude a truce with the infidel and sail for home. Edward raised his voice against this surrender, but he had to join the French ships when they sailed for Sicily. A storm arising in the harbor of Trapani almost wrecked the whole French fleet, but not a single ship of Edward's little squadron went down. Naturally the pilgrims pointed to the hand of God.

The following spring, Edward was back in the Holy Land, besieging the great trading city of Acre. But the English died off because of their intemperate use of fruits, grapes, and honey, and when Charles of Anjou concluded a truce with the Sultan, Edward could do no more than sulk in his tent at Acre. Moreover, he nearly lost his life there. When the Sultan learned that Edward was refusing to depart, he sent the Emir of Jaffa to assassinate him. Pretending to want to become a Christian, the Emir gained admittance to Edward's tent and attacked him with a dagger. He succeeded only in stabbing his victim in the arm, but the dagger was poisoned, and for days Edward lay between life and death. The legend is that his life was saved by the devotion of his beloved Eleanor, who, when all seemed hopeless, sucked the poison from his wound with her own fair lips.

Edward now received news that his father, the King, was sinking fast, and in the middle of August, 1272, he sailed from Acre for Sicily. When he arrived at Trapani, he received the news of Henry's death. A revolutionary step was now taken by the King's Council in England. The king's peace had always been regarded as so personal that it was conceived to die with him and to be revived again only by the proclamation of his successor. But the Council now proclaimed the peace of Edward I during his absence. This established the precedent whereby the king's peace was deemed unaffected by the reigning monarch's death.

His succession thus assured, Edward made a most leisurely journey home, taking almost two years to return to England to be crowned. On the way, the good doctors of law of the University of Padua made Edward an honorary member of their faculty. He lingered also in Gascony and Paris. During his stay, the Count of Châlon challenged him to a passage of arms in a great tournament. Edward joyously accepted, but he narrowly escaped with his life. It is said that the Count deliberately plotted to slay him, and the encounter has gone down in history as the Little Battle of Châlon.

Finally Edward returned to England and was crowned king. He never wore his crown after the coronation, however, and he felt that he could be every inch a king without regal robes. He wore a simple tunic and spent his days in hard work. The outlines of his domestic and foreign policy he had already laid down during his apprenticeship. He was determined, above all, to secure the upper hand over the feudal forces of disruption and to build a strong national state. But this state would not be confined to the isle of England. He would revive the policy of the strong Anglo-Saxon kings of effecting a union of England, Scotland, Ireland, and Wales. Upon the European continent he would seek to maintain a political equilibrium to prevent French domination and maintain English interests in the wool trade of Flanders and the wines of Gascony.

The subjugation of the principality of Wales occupied a good deal of Edward's energies in the first decade of his reign. Earlier attempts by King Henry and his son to subdue Wales had been without success. The border earldom of Chester had been the base of operations for these attempts. Beyond the earldom lay the feudal fiefs known as the Marches, ruled over by Norman lords; the Lords Marcher were the buffers supposed to protect the English shires against the incursions of the Welsh clans. However, with the Welsh national revival, Llewellyn ab Iorwerth had extended the territory of Wales almost to the walls of Chester, and before his death in 1240 he was able to call himself Prince of Wales. While his weak son, David, lost many of these gains in the few years of his rule, Welsh power revived when Llewellyn ab Gruffydd succeeded him. Simon de Montfort had shrewdly allied himself with Llewellyn in his revolt against Edward's father, but Llewellyn had later made peace with the English king. Now, upon the accession of Edward, however, Llewllyn refused to appear and pay homage. It had been the one ominous note in Edward's coronation ceremonies.

Edward at once took up the challenge. He was fortunate enough before beginning the campaign to capture Llewellyn's bride off the Welsh coast as she was sailing to join him. She was none other than Eleanor de Montfort, the daughter of Earl Simon. Llewellyn himself, who could have regarded his bride's misfortune only as an evil omen, was defeated by Edward in 1276 and compelled at Rhuddlan to do homage and surrender the eastern portion of his lands. But in 1282 the Welsh rose again, and another campaign became necessary. This time Edward was greatly assisted by the betrayal of Llewellyn by his own brother, David, and when Llewellyn was taken, Edward did not make the mistake of sparing his life. His head, crowned with ivy, was fixed upon the walls of the Tower of London. The Welsh, who were still a primitive people living in kindred groups, had never really had a chance against the superior numbers, armaments, and resources of the English king. The hereditary domains of Llewellyn were made into "shire ground," and when, shortly thereafter, a son was born to Edward, the King presented the infant to the Welsh as their prince. The King could say with literal truth that he was giving them a prince who could not speak a word of English. The death of Edward's eldest son not long thereafter made the infant prince, who was also called Edward, the heir apparent to the throne, and thus was established the custom of calling the heir to the throne the Prince of Wales.

The period of the conquest of Wales was by far the happiest and most successful of Edward's reign. It was also the most constructive, for it was the period during which Edward was busy ordering the affairs of his kingdom. It was during this decade and a half that he earned the title of the English Justinian. Inappropriate as the title is, it at least expresses the wide scope of Edward's legislation. Two great statutes of many chapters, that were really little codes attempting to bring order into the disorderly growth of the medieval common law, frame the momentous decade. The first, enacted in 1275, is known as the Statute of Westminster the First, and the second, enacted in 1285, is known as the Statute of Westminster the Second. Westminster was a name that was to loom large in the history of the common law, for it became the place where the courts of the common law found their permanent abode. But to understand Edward's legislation it is necessary to know something of the growth of English law before his time.

The dominant role of English civilization in the modern world has created a cult of the common law, which has been glorified beyond all other legal systems, including even the Roman law. The unique character of every element of the common law has been exaggerated to such an extent that every peculiarity of form and phraseology has been interpreted as a profound difference of function and substance. Apart from exaggerating the institutional originality of the common law, the patriotic English·legal historian has represented it as "common" to the whole of England long before it became so in fact. England never stood completely apart from the Continental development, and it even absorbed a good deal of the Roman law, although only in homeopathic doses. It, too, experienced the great movements of the Reception, the Renaissance, and the Reformation. England was indeed the first modern state, but the pace of its development was only somewhat more rapid than on the Continent, which more than caught up with it after the French Revolution. Indeed, the age of Edward was on the Continent also one of intense legislative activity, which betrayed the first stirrings of nationalism. St. Louis, Edward's brother-in-law in France, Alfonso X, Edward's father-in-law in Castile, Frederick II in Sicily, and Magnus VII in Norway were all busy attempting to reform the customary law of their kingdoms in harmony with contemporary needs. Edward, in his travels in France, Italy, and the East, undoubtedly became acquainted with the legislative monuments of the age. Edward only succeeded better than the other kings, and his success was more permanent.

The beginnings of the common law are typically primitive. In the Anglo-Saxon period, English law knew blood-feud and composition and the archaic modes of trial including compurgation and the ordeal. The Normans when they came brought with them trial by battle. The primary local court was the court of the hundred, and for greater and more general matters there was available the shire court, the court of the county, presided over by the sheriff. There were neither professional judges nor lawyers, and the freemen themselves, as the "suitors" of the court, gave judgment by acclamation. The transition from the age of arbitration and self-help is marked by the practice of putting pressure upon the defendant to appear and plead. The enforcement of any judgment was left to the successful litigant himself. This simple legal machinery sufficed in an age in which there was little foreign or domestic trade, no large-scale industry, no credit, and when payment was still in kind. Most of the suits arose from manslaying, wounding, and cattle stealing. Contracts, which have always been the most prolific source of civil litigation, were represented primarily by contracts of marriage and by contracts to pay composition. Writing was not employed in the making of legal obligations, and so the presence of the witnesses who could swear to the nature of a transaction was still all important.

The Conquest, which brought with it the highly developed system of Norman feudalism, profoundly disturbed the scheme of things. There was a confusion of custom, as well as a babel of tongues, that resulted from the mingling of the races. Men no longer knew what their rights were when they went to the court of the hundred or of the county, and no peril was so great as the peril of a lawsuit. The unsettled conditions of the times, moreover, made the journey to the shire court difficult and dangerous. In fact, the lowest orders of the peasant class could seek justice only in the court of the manor, which was held by their lords. This private jurisdiction, which may have antedated the Conquest, was one of the dominant aspects of feudalism, confusing the right to hold a fief, which was property, with the right to administer justice, which was a public function. A powerful lord was needed to make headway against this confusion and disorder and to solve the problems that were no longer purely local in nature. Who could it be but a king?

Edward had a great predecessor in Henry II, in whose reign the common law of England may be said to have really been founded. Henry imitated the great Charlemagne and the splendid but short-lived Frankish Empire. The fundamental device he adopted was a universal means of making effective the claims of central power. He sent itinerant justices out to administer royal justice, even as Charlemagne had set forth his *missi*. In his Council the English king had a reservoir of administrative energy from which he could draw in order to create new royal courts, and the three great courts of the common law undoubtedly grew as offshoots of the Royal Council. Henry, by ordaining justices to sit at Westminster, created a permanent central court long known simply as the Bench, which was probably the origin of the Court of Common Pleas, whose function was to hear cases between subject and subject. The Barons of the Exchequer, who supervised the administration of the King's revenues, began in Henry's reign to become a court of justice by taking over suits involving claims of the royal treasury. They were soon asserting a more general jurisdiction by means of the ingenious fiction that the plaintiff would not be able to pay his debt to the King if he could not collect from the defendant. This court became known as the Court of the Exchequer, taking its name from the checkered cloth upon the table around which the Barons of the Exchequer sat. The third and last court of the common law, the Court of King's Bench, did not begin to take definite shape until Edward's own day. In its origin it was simply a method by which the King in person, with the assistance of his councillors, heard particularly important cases, but gradually it developed into the chief of the common law courts. It heard pleas of the crown, exercising original jurisdiction in both civil and criminal cases and controlling most of the important judicial business of the kingdom. The royal courts were at first ambulatory, following the person of the king, for in those days, when every distance was long, the king had to bring his justice to the litigants; but in time the royal courts became fixed at Westminster.

Another Frankish device had been introduced into England by the Conquest. This was the sworn inquest, the procedure that enabled the visiting Frankish official to compel the prominent men of the neighborhood to reveal under oath what crimes had been committed there, including any acts of malfeasance by royal officials. Vanishing on the Continent with the decay of royal power, it entered upon a new career in England as the most celebrated institution of the common law—the jury. In its evolution in England, the Frankish inquest became not only a system of neighborhood accusation but also a method of trying disputed issues of fact by men of the neighborhood. Arriving at their verdicts at first on the basis of their own knowledge, the jury gradually came to decide on the basis of the testimony of witnesses whose stories they heard for the first time in court. Henry II shrewdly realized the importance of the jury as a means of attracting litigants to the royal court, and extended its use in trying the right to the possession of land. Eviction and disherison were, alas, the great evils of these unquiet times, and by means of the possessory "assizes," as they were called, Henry sought to employ the jury as a means of coping with them. By the Grand Assize, any man whose right to a freehold was questioned did not need to incur the risks of trial by battle, but could get an order from the King's Council to stay proceedings in the local courts until, by the "recognition" of twelve chosen men of the neighborhood, it had been decided who, according to the common knowledge, was the true and rightful owner. By the Assize of Clarendon, Henry also introduced the grand jury for the purpose of indicting suspected criminals. "Assize" was to be a word of frequent occurrence in the common law. It signified originally a session or sitting, and came to be applied to the sessions of courts, so that Englishmen spoke of circuit judges as "justices of assize." But it also referred to especially noteworthy royal edicts, which were promulgated by the King in his Council, the ultimate source of royal justice.

The more rational method of trial by jury—and undoubtedly it was more rational than trial by ordeal or compurgation or trial by battle—is usually offered as the primary explanation of the success of the king's courts in competing for jurisdiction with the local tribunals. But far more important was the fact that a judgment of the king's court was more likely to be respected when it was obtained by a hard-pressed litigant. The measures of Henry II were undoubtedly ambitious, but they were far from always realized in practice. The truly great lords were not always frightened by the king, and continued in their evil ways. The activities of the itinerant justices, and the ambulatory courts of the king, could at best be no more than fitful. During the almost anarchic reigns following that of Henry II, the great feudal lords had seized the opportunity of usurping jurisdiction. They claimed franchises to hold their own courts. But in Edward these claims of private jurisdiction found a determined and resourceful enemy.

During his whole legislative activity Edward was forced to carry on a more or less covert war with the feudal lords and great ecclesiastics. At times his strokes were bold, but at other times he had to compromise and proceed by indirection. In order to determine the lines of demarcation between feudal and royal jurisdiction, Edward's very first act of domestic policy was to initiate a great inquiry into the rights to feudal franchises. Commissioners were sent forth to take an inquest, and their labors produced a franchise book known as the Hundred Rolls, which is almost as famous in English history as Domesday Book. When Edward pored over the Hundred Rolls, he found a sorry picture of feudal usurpation, and his mind was soon made up. He took the next step of ordering an inquiry to determine "by what warrant" each feudal lord was exercising the rights which should appertain to the Crown. No franchise was to be recognized unless it could be established by an express royal grant.

But few indeed were the lords who could produce any charters. It had been an age during which the sword was mightier than the pen. There were rumblings of revolt. The Earl of Warenne summed up the feelings of the feudal lords when, unable to produce any parchment, he unsheathed a rusty sword and thundered: "Here is my warrant. My ancestors came with William the Bastard and won their lands with the sword. With my sword will I defend them against all usurpers." Edward, who was never disposed to push matters to extremes, took the hint and agreed to a middle course. Any lord who could establish

the exercise of his franchises as of right since the accession of Richard I
should be in as good a position as if he had been able to produce a
royal charter. Thus it is to this day in English law that the "commencement of legal memory" is the beginning of the reign of Richard
the Lionhearted. It is "the time whereof the memory of man runneth
not to the contrary."

Edward did much to settle the jurisdiction of the courts of the
common law. The inquiry into the franchises had fixed the spheres of
the courts which were held under feudal grants. By the Statute of
Gloucester, Edward undertook to establish the jurisdiction of the com-
munal courts—the courts of the shires and the hundreds. Among other
things the statute provided that no action of trespass, which was to
prove the most fertile of the forms of action in the common law,
should be brought unless the plaintiff should "swear by his faith that
the goods taken were worth forty shillings at the least." This provision
was actually intended to favor the local tribunals, but the judges at
Westminster perverted its purpose by holding that no action of any
kind should be brought in a local court for more than forty shillings.
Edward also put the system of itinerant justices upon a new basis, by
conferring upon them comprehensive civil as well as criminal jurisdiction and by regulating the frequency of their visitations. They were
too prone to levy fines and forfeitures for the benefit of the royal treasury
for them to be welcomed at every season.

A great deal of Edward's legislation had to do with procedure. The
King had an infinite capacity for taking pains with small details, and
loved to define precisely the spheres of rights and duties. In his predilection for procedural change, he may have been motivated also by a
desire to avoid actions that would look like direct attacks upon established rights and privileges. Perhaps the most celebrated of Edward's
procedural reforms, which was contained in a clause of the twenty-
fourth chapter of the Statute of Westminster the Second, related to the
issuance of royal writs by the officials of the Chancery. The writ was
the very fulcrum of royal procedure and was of basic importance in the
development of the sphere of the common law. Like the Frankish ban,
the English writ was a written order from the king to one of his
officials. Before any action could be brought, a writ had to be obtained
authorizing the king's judges to take jurisdiction. Each writ thus became
connected with a particular form of action in the royal courts, and it
became an established method of filching jurisdiction from the local

courts. The use of the writs had become common in the twelfth century, and each writ, as it was invented, came to be carefully recorded and was as highly prized by the royal officials as each formula of the praetor's edict had been in Rome. Edward, however, took a bold, if not a revolutionary, step. He enacted that henceforth writs might be issued not only in cases for which there was a precedent but *consimilis casus*, that is, in like cases. By thus providing for the issuance of writs in analogous cases, Edward was really laying claim to a general jurisdiction for the royal courts, which would have rapidly destroyed the courts of the feudal lords, the Church, the chartered boroughs, and the merchant guilds. But the king's judges were more conservative than the king, and refused to issue writs which represented radical departures from existing forms. The common law was thus foredoomed to remain, far longer than might otherwise have been the case, a system of special forms of action (rather than a system of general principles) and to advance only slowly and painfully from case to case, from precedent to precedent.

The details of the Statutes of Westminster the First and Second were many. But the two chief objects of the statutes were to correct the abuses of royal administration and to curb feudal excesses and pretensions. The first object was accomplished by carefully regulating the conduct of the royal officials. The king was ceasing to be merely the military leader of an army of feudal barons, and a host of officials was growing up around the royal Exchequer and Chancery. They must therefore be brought within bounds and made to respect the rights of subjects. It was to become a maxim of the common law that "the King can do no wrong," but the steps Edward took to require wrongdoing officials to pay damages to their victims prevented the extension of the same maxim to the king's officers. Thus was established one of the basic principles of English liberty, which was that even the servants of the state were not immune from the reach of the common law. The only drawback to the application of this principle was that the king's servants were often too poor to pay for the damages they had caused, and the supremacy of the common law was thus assured only in theory. The accomplishment of Edward's second object was necessary to the successful achievement of the first. It would have been useless to curb the royal officers if the feudal lords were to remain unrestrained. It was provided, for example, that landlords were not to exercise self-help in distraining for services; that travelers were not to be stopped by feudal lords through whose domains they passed; that outrageous tolls were not to be levied in the markets.

In the very year of the enactment of the Statute of Westminster the Second, Edward promulgated another of his celebrated statutes, the Statute of Winchester. This sought to enlist the local freemen in the suppression of crime and the performance of other public duties. They were to report felons known to them, and assist in pursuing them. They were to serve in the watch, and help keep the highways clear; they were to maintain themselves in arms in accordance with their means, and appear biannually at the view of armor in their hundreds, so that the king might keep in touch with the state of his forces. These measures represented a return to ancient methods of preserving and keeping the peace; but by seeking to revive the obligations of service which the old English law had imposed upon the freeman, Edward's purpose was only to undermine in another way the political influence and position of the feudal lords. In subsequent years Edward sought to implement the statute further by appointing special "Conservators of the Peace" to aid in its enforcement. These seem to have been the forerunners of the celebrated Justices of the Peace, the landed gentry who by the end of the fourteenth century had begun to preempt almost the whole sphere of English local administration.

But Edward was not content with mere procedural and administrative changes. A king of the thirteenth century who was bent on curbing feudal pretensions had to make a frontal assault on the land law. In fact, the law that was then common to the whole realm was primarily the land law. In this sphere particularly the king had to tread warily, for any fundamental change was bound to arouse fierce opposition. In his first step, however, Edward had at least the tacit support of the feudal lords. By the Statute of Mortmain he prohibited the grant of lands to ecclesiastical corporations, from whose "dead hand" they could never be retrieved. Enjoying perpetual succession as juristic personalities, the ecclesiastical grantees escaped all feudal forfeitures and all feudal dues or incidents such as relief, wardship, and marriage. By prohibiting the evasion of these feudal burdens, Edward seemed to be doing something for the feudal lords, but actually he strengthened the position of the Crown in dealing with the Church, which was a powerful rival of the nascent state. Edward's next step, however, was a deadly blow at the feudal lords, although ostensibly it was not aimed at them. The merchants were growing in importance, as trade expanded, but, since they were often foreigners and were engaged in a mean activity from any feudal point of view, they were a despised class needing the special protection of the king. By the Statute of Merchants, Edward provided them with an easier way of recovering their debts. When a debt was evidenced by a special document sealed before the mayor of a chartered borough, it was to be enforced thereafter even against the lands of the debtor, although real property had theretofore been immune from such seizure. The formalities and restrictions helped only to sugar-coat the bitter pill. The barons grumbled, but doubtless they reflected that the merchants would not go on lending forever without some assurance of repayment, and each hoped, too, no doubt, that he would be able to escape the clutches of his creditors. But, alas, a little experience with the working of the statute must have soon taught them that they were flirting with ruin. When they discovered that they were losing their lands, tenements, and hereditaments, they exacted from Edward a concession which the King could hardly have relished. By a provision of the Statute of Westminster the Second they were permitted to entail their estates, so that they could not be made liable for debt and would descend in unbroken succession from father to son as long as the family line should last. But even in this defeat Edward gained something. If the family line failed, the estate reverted to the original grantor, and, after all, Edward was a feudal lord, too, and the greatest of all. In his final struggle with the feudal lords over the land question, moreover, Edward managed very adroitly to further the free alienation of land, although here, too, it was at a price. It had long been a disputed question whether a feudal tenant could transfer only part of his holdings to another. The lords were opposed to such a multiplication of undertenants, for, as the chain of feudal obligation became longer and longer, it became difficult for the capital lord to collect feudal dues. They therefore sought from the King an enactment which would arrest this process of subinfeudation, as it has been called, by prohibiting any alienation of land. Edward promulgated the Statute of Westminster the Third, which did forbid subinfeudation; but it expressly permitted the alienation of land, provided only that all purchasers, whether of a part or of the whole of an estate, should stand in the same relation to the seller's lord as the seller himself. Thus was land made in fact a more ready article of commerce.

By the end of 1285 the best part of Edward's legislative labors had been accomplished. The king's peace was spread over the land. In

1286 the King himself felt that his kingdom was secure enough for him to go abroad, and from 1286 to 1289 he lingered in the pleasant vales of Gascony. There, in 1288, he was able to prove, as he had already often proved in battle, that he bore a charmed life. A stroke of lightning passed between him and Queen Eleanor as they were sitting with their backs to a window, and killed two ladies in waiting who were standing before them. Nevertheless, misfortune was approaching. The next summer ugly rumors began to reach Edward of trouble at home. A violent quarrel was brewing between the Earls of Gloucester and Hereford on the always uneasy Welsh border. But when he landed in England his ears were assailed by the rumblings of an even worse storm.

Despite all his efforts to reform the abuses of royal administration, Edward's judges had fallen into the most frightful corruption. Their crimes had become notorious and intolerable. Edward appointed a commission of inquiry, which brought the most ghastly aspects of the prevalent corruption to light. Adam of Stratton, a baron of the Exchequer, had engaged, for instance, in a systematic campaign of spoliation; Thomas of Weyland, the Chief Justice of the Common Pleas, who was even accused of being accessory to murder, had to take sanctuary and abjure the realm; and Ralph de Hengham, the Chief Justice of the King's Bench, was found to have been guilty of the vilest perversions of justice. The miscreant judges were, of course, driven from office, but the King was merciful, and, while he made them disgorge by paying enormous fines, he did not send them to the gallows or the headsman's block. While the story has not been glossed over by English legal historians, they have attempted to explain it at least in part by Edward's absence abroad. To be sure, while the cat's away, the mice will play. But there was a good deal more to the episode than that. It was in part symptomatic of the dissolving feudal society, which, still harboring proprietarian conceptions of jurisdiction, quite frankly regarded public office as an opportunity for private plunder. With government still far from free of this curse, it is scarcely to be wondered at that it plagued the first of modern states. The royal judges, too, had become corrupted by the very severity of the justice they lawfully administered in the name of the king. They could not continually levy enormous fines and forfeitures in the name of the king without being tempted to victimize the king's subjects on their own accounts. According to the tale of a thirteenth-century chronicler, when the approaching visit of the king's itinerant justices was proclaimed in Cornwall, the terrified inhabitants all fled to the woods, and who could blame them? The king's peace was bought at a heavy price, but such is the way kingdoms are fashioned.

The corruption of Edward's judges has been called England's "one great judicial scandal." That it never recurred on any comparable scale was due in some measure at least to the fact that in Edward's reign a legal profession was coming into existence. The lawyers watched the judges, if for no other reason than that the interests of their clients were at stake. The profession began to be organized when the practitioners took up quarters in various inns in the neighborhood of Westminster. The professional organizations of English lawyers have thus long been known by the rather peculiar name of "Inns of Court."

The rest of the tale may be quickly told. In 1290 Edward not only purged the royal judiciary, but, after finally listening to his debt-ridden barons and the clergy, expelled the Jews from the realm of England. (The Jews, however, were promptly replaced by Christian usurers from Gascony and northern Italy.) The year 1290 may, indeed, be said to mark the end of the happier and more successful period of Edward's reign. After 1290 none of his affairs seemed to prosper.

In November of 1290 occurred the death of Edward's beloved Queen Eleanor. She died of a fever at Harby, near Lincoln in Nottinghamshire. To the dying queen, who urged him to remarry, Edward had whispered, "I shall never take another mistress," and he was inconsolable. With great pomp and circumstance the body of Eleanor was borne from Lincoln Cathedral to Westminster Abbey, its final resting place. At each of the twelve places where her mortal remains had rested on the melancholy journey, the stricken king caused a great cross to be erected. Charing Cross in the city of London is one of the places that still commemorates the last journey of Queen Eleanor.

But a king cannot mourn too long. Edward's energies were soon absorbed by a dispute over the Scottish succession and by the attempt of Philip the Fair of France to seize Gascony. A brawl in a tavern in Normandy between French and English sailors furnished the French king with an appropriate pretext. As Edward's feudal suzerain, he summoned the proud English king to justify the depredations of his mariners, and, when Edward temporized, Philip declared forfeited the province he had long coveted. The war dragged on from 1293 to 1298, at a great cost of blood and treasure to both sides, but with no decisive result. Edward and Philip finally consented to submit the quarrel to the mediation of Benedict of Gaeta, who sat on the papal throne as Boniface VIII. One of the terms of the bargain was that Edward should marry the French king's sister, Margaret, which he did, despite his declaration to the dying Eleanor. The French war represented an attempt on the part of Edward to maintain a feudal position vis-à-vis the king of France, which he would never have conceded in his own kingdom and certainly did not concede with regard to Scotland.

The growing menace of the situation in Scotland was a principal reason for inducing Edward to make peace with Philip. The English king had long claimed a vague feudal suzerainty over the king of Scotland, but he had had no good opportunity to intervene in Scottish affairs until the sudden death of Alexander III, in 1286. Alexander's daughter Margaret had married Eric, King of Norway; she had died leaving an infant daughter, also named Margaret, who was now heiress of the crowns of both Norway and Scotland. At first it seemed that the vexing problem of the Scottish succession would be happily settled by the marriage of the little "Maid of Norway," as she has been known in history, to Edward's son. But, alas for the success of this scheme, the little Maid of Norway most inconveniently died almost immediately after the betrothal. The uncertainties of feudal law now produced two rivals for the crown of Scotland, Robert Bruce and John Balliol. Edward, claiming as suzerain of Scotland the right to decide as between the competitors, chose Balliol. The new Scottish king was grateful and for a while was submissive enough to his English over-lord, but Edward's claims became more and more highhanded. When Edward finally had the effrontery to summon the Scottish king to Westminster "for defect of justice," even the meek Balliol was driven to revolt. Edward was compelled to invade Scotland in 1296, and, after the Scottish forces were defeated at the Battle of Dunbar, Balliol was deposed and Edward personally assumed the crown of Scotland. As a sign of his victory Edward carried off the famous coronation stone at Scone. The Norman nobility readily swore fealty to Edward, but the Scottish burghs and lesser gentry would have none of him. Scotland was to prove a far tougher conquest than Wales. The national spirit of the Scots was aroused, and Edward never succeeded in subduing Scotland permanently. His stubbornness only produced two great national heroes, William Wallace and Robert Bruce, the grandson of Balliol's competitor. The power of Wallace was broken at Falkirk, and, captured soon thereafter, he was hanged, drawn, and quartered with all the cruelty and barbarity of the English law of treason. In his place Bruce arose as the national deliverer and ultimately gained a brilliant victory at Bannockburn. Every schoolboy is familiar with the poet's lines:

> Scots, wha hae wi' Wallace bled,
> Scots, wham Bruce has aften led . . .

Wars have always been costly, and Edward's wars in France and Scotland were no exception. Edward was in need of money as never before, and he constantly had to call on his subjects to replenish the royal exchequer. Edward doubtless thought that since he was not spending the money on personal extravagances, his subjects should not grumble. But even the most appreciative subjects will complain when heavy taxes are levied upon them, and in this period of his reign Edward was always quarreling with all classes of his subjects. He particularly loved to annoy the city of London, but the lesser towns also received his attentions. A particularly heavy tax on wool, known as the maletolt, aroused the displeasure and opposition of the merchants. There were even occasional rumblings of revolt among the baronage, although they never were very serious. In 1299, however, while Edward was in Flanders, his ministers were compelled to issue a Confirmation of the Charters in his name.

Edward's greatest quarrel was with the Church. It was a quarrel of long standing, which went back to the Council of Reading, at which John Peckham, the austere but scheming Archbishop of Canterbury, had ordered a copy of Magna Charta to be hung in every church. Edward's Statute of Mortmain had in part been a reply to the Canons of Reading. When Peckham died in 1292, he was succeeded by Robert Winchelsea, who became Edward's implacable enemy. The King was particularly annoyed with the Pope—and hence with his appointees— because on each of the occasions when the see of Canterbury had become vacant the Pope had rejected Edward's candidate, who was none other than his chief minister and faithful friend, Robert Burnell. Edward succeeded in having him made Bishop of Bath and Wells, but the profligacy of Burnell's private life was too great for even the most practical Pope to consent to his becoming Archbishop of Canterbury. Under Winchelsea the relations between Edward and the clergy rapidly reached a crisis. When the primate inspired a bull which, under pain of excommunication, forbade the clergy to contribute so much as a farthing to the royal treasury, the King responded with the temporal counterpart of excommunication, which was outlawry. The clergy were denied access to the king's courts, and all protection was withdrawn from their property. Edward with sly humor decreed that if any one of his subjects met an ecclesiastic upon the highway riding a horse which he deemed better than his own, he might appropriate it for his own use. In the end the clergy had to yield and consent to a levy like the rest of the king's subjects. For all of his crusading piety, Edward never allowed the Church to stand in the way of his material interests. In this, however, he was no different from other monarchs of his time; the struggle between the temporal and the spiritual powers was general in the thirteenth century.

But out of all this travail, out of all these mistakes of Edward, is said to have come perhaps the greatest glory of his reign. The King could not gather taxes and hope to allay discontent unless he took his subjects into some sort of partnership. He had, moreover, an instinct for the theatrical, and the story goes that at one public assembly the King gained his way by suddenly bursting into tears and demanding of his listeners to know if what he was asking was for himself or for the good of the realm. Doubtless he remembered, too, the great example of his cousin Simon de Montfort, the mentor of his youth. And so, as he got into difficulties, the King began to add to his Council representatives of the estates of his realm, the knights and burgesses as well as the barons and the clergy. Out of the King's Council grew Parliament, and while neither the composition nor the functions of this body were what they are today (for its primary purpose was to air grievances and perhaps to grant money), by the end of Edward's reign the foundations had been laid for the creation of the most celebrated legislature of the modern world. Edward could not only boast that he had shaped the three courts of the common law, whose function was to declare the law, but he could also lay claim to the creation of a body whose function was to be to make the law. The greatest of Edward's parliaments was that of 1295, which has been known in English history as the Model Parliament. In the summons issued for this Parliament, Edward laid down the pregnant maxim: "That which concerns all should be discussed of all."

Edward died at the age of sixty-eight, on July 7, 1307, in the little village of Burgh-on-Sands, as he was on his way to put down another revolt in Scotland. His body was brought back to Westminster, but without the pomp that had been lavished on Eleanor's last journey. He was put to rest under a plain marble monument which bears an inscription in Latin. The inscription does not describe him as the English Justinian, or as the founder of the common law and the first modern state, or as the creator of Parliament. The writers of inscriptions for the tombs of kings were in those days primarily interested in their martial glory. So the inscription reads: EDWARDUS PRIMUS SCOTORUM MALLEUS HIC EST. PACTUM SERVA. (Here lies Edward the First, the Hammer of the Scots. Keep troth.)

Thomas Egerton, Baron Ellesmere and Viscount Brackley

THE KEEPING OF THE KING'S CONSCIENCE

O N THE THIRD OF MAY IN THE YEAR 1596, QUEEN ELIZABETH summoned to the Court at Greenwich a man by the name of Thomas Egerton, who had been born a commoner and upon whom a few years earlier she had conferred the honor of knighthood. He was received by Lord Cobham, Lord Buckhurst, and Sir Robert Cecil, who conducted him to the Virgin Queen's antechamber, where she was standing upon an embroidered carpet attended by Lord Burghley, the Lord Treasurer. There, as Egerton knelt down on his right knee, Her Majesty delivered into his hands a precious royal possession known as the Great Seal, which, since the death of its last Keeper, had rested in the privacy of her own bedroom. Placing her hands upon his shoulders, Her Majesty raised the kneeling Egerton from the floor. She thus elevated him to the great office of Keeper of the Great Seal, and made him in effect her Lord Chancellor. Egerton, having been sworn of the Privy Council, performed the ceremony of sealing a writ in the Queen's presence, after which the new Lord Keeper gave the Great Seal to his purse-bearer, who bore it solemnly and proudly before him.

If the shade of Edward I had been hovering in the wings of the Queen's antechamber, he would not have been entirely mystified by the scene he had just witnessed, even if he had not understood all its implications. Almost three hundred years had elapsed since he sat on the throne, and England had become a great European power. English ships were in every port, and her busy merchants were buying and selling in every market and outdistancing all their competitors. Protestantism and the spirit of business enterprise were making a new world. The mold of the common law was still recognizable, but it had been reshaped by many hands. Apart from legislation, the change had not, however, been accomplished primarily by the courts of the common law which were already in existence in Edward's reign, but by a new court called the Court of Chancery, which had become an independent tribunal during the second half of the fifteenth century. The dignitary presiding over its functions was the Lord Chancellor, who was, by virtue of his office, the Keeper of the Great Seal. There had been a Lord Chancellor in England as early as the reign of Edward the Confessor, and although he was then already the keeper of the royal seal, his position was relatively modest. Invariably a learned ecclesiastic, he was the king's secretary and the head of the king's chaplains. At that time the chancellorship was valued chiefly as an avenue of preferment leading to a bishopric. The Lord Chancellor ranked only sixth among the Crown's great officers, coming after the Chief Justiciar, the Constable, the Mareschal, the Steward, and the Chamberlain. In the reign of Edward I, it will be remembered, the Chancellor was discharging a judicial duty of a purely ministerial nature by issuing from the Chancery those potent writs bearing the imprint of the Great Seal which were the necessary preliminary of instituting any action in the courts of the common law. But not long after Edward's death the Chancellor began to become the greatest of the king's ministers and the most important of his judges, whose destiny it was to transform the law of the kingdom. He had always been a member of the King's Council, but by virtue of the fact that he was a learned ecclesiastic and the Keeper of the Great Seal, he was able to become the chief instrument of the king's justice.

The story of the rise of the Lord Chancellor and the Court of Chancery is the story of the royal talisman known as the Great Seal and the wonders that were accomplished in transforming English law by its use. The story is appropriately somewhat Gilbertian. It illustrates that peculiar genius of the English people for preserving ancient forms long after they have ceased to serve any real function—a characteristic which to this day makes the Lord Mayor of London ride in a coach and four upon great ceremonial occasions. The manipulation of the Great Seal produced that part of English law which is known as "equity," in contradistinction to "common law."

As a form of law, English equity was not unique. Toward the close of the first quarter of the sixteenth century, an English barrister by the name of Christopher St. Germain, who was well versed in the canon as well as the common law, wrote a dialogue called *The Doctor and Student,* in which he attributed the growth of equity to the generality of rules of law which, since they sometimes worked hardship in individual cases, had to be rectified by considerations of higher justice, which were regarded as "equitable." But even if the first application of equity in a given case is to be explained in terms of dispensing power, it is apparent that if equity is to become a settled part of the legal system, it must itself be formulated in rules of a general and universal character, which in turn will work hardship in individual cases. Equity, in the sense of a moderating legal force, was familiar to the Babylonians, as well as to the Greeks and Romans. But only the Romans and the English, who achieved analogous levels of social and economic development, ever made equity a technical component of their legal systems.

English "equity" repeated the history of the Roman *ius gentium,* and the Lord Chancellor, particularly as a result of the acquaintance-ship of the early ecclesiastics who held the office with the Romanized canon law, followed in the footsteps of the Roman praetor. To be sure, the points of origin of Roman and English equity were superficially different. The excuse of the Roman praetor was that there had to be some law for foreigners, while the English Chancellor worked in the interest of foreigners and Englishmen alike, in order to prevent the lives of both from becoming intolerable. But the true significance of the activity of both praetor and Chancellor was that they were engaged in transforming outworn legal systems. Both the Roman *ius gentium* and the English equity were supplementary bodies of law existing by the side of an earlier legal system, which technically remained in force, but in actuality was superseded. The English method of renovating the law, however, was far more involved and cumbersome, as well as far more ludicrous, than the Roman. The Roman praetor administered both kinds of law, and in a sense his new law was legislative in character, although technically the legislation was good only for his term of office. The new law of the English Chancellor was executive in character, dispensed to the king's subjects as a matter of grace, at least at first.

This was done by creating a new court, the Court of Chancery, to remake the old law of the courts of the common law. To us who are accustomed to change our laws by enacting new ones rather freely, it may seem remarkable that such a circuitous method of approach as a

separate Court of Chancery should have been necessary. It was remarkable without a doubt, for the Chancellor always virtuously pretended that he was not disturbing the hallowed rules of the common
law! In the heyday of their development of equity, both Rome and
England had adequate legislative bodies which could, and in some
respects did, modify the law. But the principal reason for their failure
to make use of the legislative machinery was simply that the law of
private property and contract in all its infinite variety and subtlety
could not be adapted to the needs of a rapidly expanding commerce,
except by the day-to-day activity of lawyers, who, in Rome as well as
in England, found in the official judge only a convenient sanction for
their inventions. Even today the statutes enacted by legislatures are
often less important than what the lawyers do to them.

Edward Plantagenet, who was a straightforward king, would have
been contemptuous of the devices of the Chancellor and his Court of
Chancery. He had pursued a more direct method. Had he not secured
the enactment of a statute ordering the clerks of the Chancery to issue
writs "in like cases"? In his day the judges of the courts of common
law were still sufficiently close to his person and influence to do a
little equity themselves in a pinch. But after his death the common-law
judges, although they still held office only during the royal pleasure
and were on the same plane as others of the king's servants, began to get
strange notions of judicial independence, and to yield to the force of
professional tradition. They would no longer be complaisant when the
king ordered a new writ, like a new pair of shoes, and actually began
to quash the writs issued out of the Chancery "in like cases." The
common law, therefore, began to become rigid and stereotyped. But
even worse, there were troubled times after Edward's death, when the
king's subjects could not always get even this meager and unsatisfactory justice. They were threatened with the force and violence of still
tempestuous barons who did not always fear the king's peace. They
began to cry for relief against both the inadequacies of the common
law and the oppressions of the mighty. More and more petitions for
justice were presented to the king, who referred them to his Council,
that inexhaustible reservoir of justice and new courts. The members of
the Council got more and more into the habit of referring them to their
colleague, the learned ecclesiastic who, as Chancellor, was Keeper of the
Great Seal and therefore able to dispense justice in the king's name.

The early Lord Chancellor, who was always an ecclesiastic, worked very adroitly. He made no frontal attacks upon the well-entrenched courts of the common law. He did not presume to say that the defendant's rights were not good at common law. He even made of a pious pretense that "equity follows the law" a basic maxim. But if he thought that the defendant in good conscience should not exercise a right at common law, he put pressure upon him to renounce it, and thus the right "good" at common law became "bad" in equity. The Lord Chancellor, moreover, unlike the common-law judges, did not at first award the plaintiff any judgment for damages which the sheriff could directly levy either on his lands or chattels. He simply ordered the defendant personally to do what conscience dictated, and it was only when he obstinately refused that the Lord Chancellor put him in jail, to remain there until such time as he could hear the still, small voice of conscience. The great and potent weapon of the Chancellor was the Writ of Injunction, by which he ordered litigants to do his bidding or to refrain from doing what conscience forbade. Thus did the Lord Chancellor act as the keeper of the king's conscience, as well as the Keeper of the Great Seal, and the Court of Chancery began to be called a court of conscience. The whole procedure of the Chancellor's court was strongly suggestive of the methods of the Church in dealing with heretics. There was no such luxury as trial by jury allowed in the Court of Chancery. When the rascally defendant was summoned, he could not choose to stand mute. He was compelled to answer under oath a series of written interrogatories designed to test the truth of the plaintiff's bill of complaint.

It must not be supposed that everybody was deceived by the Chancellor's pretended regard for the common law. The net effect of his interventions was only too apparent. While, as time went on, the equity enforced by him came to be governed more and more by precedent, as in the case of all new tribunals, the precise relation of the Court of Chancery to the courts of the common law remained unsettled. Whenever the standards of good conscience were set too high, there must have been some murmurs among the lawyers and judges who practiced in the courts of the common law. But there were times when even they must have needed the help of the Chancellor, and open and public conflict was avoided. The first of the lay chancellors was Sir Thomas More, from whose celebrated *Utopia* lawyers were barred altogether, and he followed the very sensible practice, whenever the common-law judges demurred at steps he proposed to take, of inviting them to dinner, at which, over a glass of good port, he would convince them with little difficulty that he had the greatest respect for the common law. But in the year of our Lord 1616, the relations between the Chancellor and one of the courts of the common law did become strained. The Chancellor emerged the victor from this struggle, and historians are agreed that thereafter the position of the Court of Chancery as an independent court was never again questioned. The hero of this affray was the Sir Thomas Egerton whom we left kneeling in Queen Elizabeth's antechamber. By 1616 he had risen to the baronage, and bore the name and title of Lord Ellesmere. No one could have been better cast for the role of defender of the royal prerogative.

Thomas Egerton was born sometime in the year 1540. The exact date of his birth is not known. The vindicator of the upstart Court of Chancery was a bastard, and there was even less likelihood than usual that a birth record would be kept for an infant of such lineage. The father of the future Lord Chancellor was Sir Richard Egerton of Ridley in Cheshire, and his mother a lady by the name of Alice Sparke. The tradition is that the infant Thomas was nursed by a farmer's wife at Lower Kinnerton, which was in the neighborhood of his father's estate. He was acknowledged by his father, and to the tender regard which was responsible for this acknowledgment of paternity, he owed also the advantage of a good education.

Thomas is supposed to have been entered in his sixteenth year at Brasenose College, Oxford, although his name does not appear upon the official register of the college as a student. But it is certain that he entered Lincoln's Inn in 1559 and that he was called to the bar in 1572. He had been a diligent student, and his handsome appearance, which included a singular gravity of countenance, his keenness of mind, and his great gifts of speech quickly brought him a large practice, particularly in the Court of Chancery.

As so often in the case of men who have risen to great eminence, there is a tale which, although quite certainly apocryphal, is nevertheless worth telling as a tribute to Thomas's professional capacities. It is related that while yet a student he saved from ruin a good lady who kept a public house in Smithfield. It seems that three graziers who had stopped there had deposited a considerable sum of money with her, with instructions to keep it until they should return and claim it. Later one of the graziers had returned, and, fraudulently representing that he had been authorized by the others to call for the money, he had induced the gullible lady to give it to him. After he had absconded, the other two graziers sued her for the money, and the judge was about to award judgment to them when the young student craved permission, as a friend of the court, to call its attention to a fatal objection to the suit which had thus far escaped the lady's counsel as well as the judge. Permission having been granted, the fledgling advocate spoke as follows: "This money, by the contract, was to be returned to *three*, but *two* only sue; where is the *third*? Let him appear with the others; till then the money cannot be demanded from her." The judge saw the point, and from that day, it is said, the young lawyer's fortune was made.

Egerton was fortunate enough early in his career to attract the attention of Queen Elizabeth herself. The Queen, who followed closely cases in which her revenues were concerned, happened to be present in court one day when Egerton was pleading a case against the Crown. After listening to him, Her Majesty is said to have exclaimed: "On my troth, he shall never plead against me again!" She was as good as her word, too, for she immediately made him one of her counsel. Having thus become entitled to wear a silk gown, it was not long before he had ascended the second rung in the ladder that led to high judicial or ministerial office. In 1581 he became Solicitor General, and during the twelve years that he held this office, he took a leading part in conducting the prosecutions for treason which were such a marked feature of the times. The Solicitor General was expected to show his hatred of the victims of the Queen's anger by a suitable degree of venom and vituperation in the conduct of the case. It is said that by the standards of the time the behavior of Solicitor General Egerton was mild. Yet in his prosecution of the Earl of Arundel he argued that the Earl's guilt was established by the fact that he had said that he would be ruled by Cardinal Allen in anything that should concern the Catholic cause. "My Lord," he exclaimed, "must needs be culpable for all the treasons Allen hath practiced or procured." He also prosecuted Sir John Perrot for treason, although he had done no more than speak disrespectfully of the Queen.

Egerton was suitably rewarded on the second of June, 1592, when the Queen made him Attorney General; and on the tenth of April, 1594, he was made Master of the Rolls. The Master was the Lord Chancellor's chief assistant, and everybody expected that the Great

Seal would be his as soon as the greater office should be vacated. The general expectation was substantially fulfilled, as already related, on the third of May, 1596. The Queen made him only Lord Keeper of the Great Seal, but it was established that whoever held the Great Seal exercised all the powers of the Lord Chancellor. The new Lord Keeper did not, as usually, surrender the office of Master of the Rolls, but continued to fill both offices until 1603. He clung to the office, with its considerable profits, like the proverbial leech, against desperate attempts to obtain it by one of the Queen's sergeants by the name of John Heele. The Lord Keeper encouraged the hopes of the sergeant by borrowing £400 from him, but he privately denounced him to the Queen as a "gryping usurer, ambodexter, drunkard and brawler."

It is said that the Lord Keeper proved to be an able judge. He made a handsome and impressive figure on the woolsack, and the Court of Chancery became a place of interest visited by idle ladies and gentlemen in search of entertainment, if not instruction. "Happy were they," observes one commentator, "who had no other business there." The Lord Keeper's judgments were usually characterized by great learning and precision of doctrine, but better still they were prompt. He labored to eliminate vexatious delay, and did a good deal to check the tendency toward procedural complexity becoming manifest in the Court of Chancery, which was then already manned by a small army of clerks hungry for fees. Sitting on the woolsack, the Lord Keeper listened attentively to counsel, and was usually grave of mien and sober of speech. But sometimes he could not help giving vent to sly humor. Once when he read a petition which aroused his ire, he asked the petitioner: "What, you would have my hand to this now?" Receiving an affirmative answer, he exclaimed, "Well, so you shall; nay, you shall have both my hands to it," and with both his hands tore the petition to pieces. Once when Richard Mylward, a litigant, caused to be filed a replication to a plea which ran to sixscore sheets when sixteen would have been sufficient, the Lord Keeper took a step which alone deserves to enshrine his name in the judicial annals of all time. He ordered that

. . . the Warden of the Fleet shall take the said Richard Mylward into his custody, and shall bring him into Westminster Hall on Saturday about ten of the clock in the forenoon, and then and there shall cut in a hole in the myddest of the same engrossed Replication, which is delivered unto him for that purpose, and put the said Richard's head through the same hole, and so let the same Replication hang about his shoulders with the written side outward, and then, the same so hanging, shall lead the same Richard, bareheaded and barefaced, round about Westminster Hall whilst the Courts are sitting, and show him at the bar of every of the three Courts within the Hall, and then shall take him back again to the Fleet and keep him prisoner until he shall have paid £10 to her Majesty for a fine, and 20 nobles to the defendant for his costs in respect of the aforesaid abuse, which fine and costs are now adjudged and imposed upon him by this Court for the abuse aforesaid.

The Lord Keeper, however, had many more duties than presiding in the Court of Chancery. He was much more than a judge. To understand the secret of the power of the Keeper of the Great Seal, it must be realized that he stood closer to the throne than any other of the ministers. He was one of the Queen's chief advisers. It was the custom for him to open Parliament with an address which constituted a message from the throne, and to perform other nonjudicial functions. The relations between Egerton and Elizabeth seem to have been particularly close. Although, after the death of the mighty Lord Burghley, his son, Sir Robert Cecil, became her chief councillor, she leaned a good deal on Egerton. She employed him to negotiate a treaty with the Dutch, who came to London for the purpose, and he played the diplomat again in concluding a treaty with Denmark. These treaties not only saved the economically minded Queen a great deal of money, but secured for her valuable allies.

But the best illustration of the nature of the Lord Keeper's position in the royal court is the part he played in the celebrated quarrel between Elizabeth and her favorite, Robert Devereaux, the Earl of Essex. The Lord Keeper was one of the few who were present when the Queen gave her favorite that awful box on the ears, the sound of which has reverberated down the centuries. Lytton Strachey, in his *Elizabeth and Essex,* has amusingly pictured the incident as in a sense the last revolt of the baronage. We must take it as an instance of the responsibilities that went with the keeping of the queen's conscience. In the handling of this delicate affair, the Lord Keeper was the intermediary between the Queen and her outraged Earl. Egerton had met Essex at court and, despite the disparity in their ages, a warm friendship had sprung up between them. The Lord Keeper was not a romantic himself, but he admired the quality in others. Yet for him the Queen could do no wrong. In a long letter he argued with the unreconcilable and rebellious Earl. "Let policy, duty and religion, enforce you to yield," he pleaded, "and submit to your sovereign, between whom and you there can be no proportion of duty." After the quarrel had been finally patched up, Essex was sent to Ireland to suppress a rebellion, but he suddenly returned to court without permission. The irate Queen once more made use of the Lord Keeper by committing her incorrigible Earl to his custody. The paternal jailer then had to head a commission of judges to try the culprit. When at this mock affair Essex attempted to defend himself, the Lord Keeper hinted benignly that "all extenuation of his offence was but the lessening of Her Majesty's mercy in pardoning," and when the Earl cited the example of his predecessor, Egerton observed with his usual command of the neat phrase: "If the Earl of Leicester did evil in coming over contrary to the Queen's commandment, the Earl of Essex did more in imitating the Earl of Leicester, and was so much more to be punished for it." Nevertheless, the Queen pardoned her favorite again, remitting the punishment of her judges. When in the end the unhappy Earl rose in revolt and attempted to rouse the city of London, the Lord Keeper headed a group of notables who went to his house to persuade him to keep the peace. The Lord Keeper and the others almost lost their lives on this dangerous mission. The mob cried: "Kill them, keep them for pledges, throw the Great Seal out of the window."

Such, however, was not the daily life of the Queen's judge and minister. The Lord Keeper Egerton, upon whom fortune had smiled from the very beginning, had become a person of great wealth and lived placidly in a fine house at Harefield in Middlesex. He was a marrying man, and he was uncomfortable except in the blessed state of matrimony. When his first wife, Elizabeth, daughter of Thomas Ravenscroft, Esquire, of Bretton in Flintshire, had died, he had married another Elizabeth, the sister of Sir George Moore of Loseby and the widow of both John Polstead of Abury and of Sir John Wolley. Then, when the second Elizabeth had died, he had married Alice, the daughter of Sir John Spencer of Althorpe and the widow of Ferdinando, the fifth Earl of Derby. His third wife was celebrated in youth under the name of Amaryllis by the poet Edmund Spenser, whom the Lord Keeper had befriended.

The great man of law loved to play the part of patron of art and letters. He particularly patronized Ben Jonson, who wrote epigrams in his praise. Of his eloquence Ben Jonson said: "The fear of every man that heard him was lest he should make an end." John Milton, when a small boy, was taken to Harefield to see the venerable Lord Keeper, who doubtless patted him kindly on the head. Many years later the immortal poet was to produce his *Arcades* at Harefield.

Yet long before this, Harefield had been the scene of a great event. As a special mark of her favor, Queen Elizabeth paid a visit in state to the house of her Lord Keeper. She stayed there for three days, from July 31 to August 3, 1602, and she was lavishly entertained at enormous expense by her faithful Lord Keeper. The weather being inclement, hunting and falconry were ruled out, but the indoor amusements more than made up for them. That fellow Shakespeare had recently written his *Othello*, and Burbage's company was sent for, to perform the play. There was dancing and vaulting and a lottery, for which, it is probable, Ben Jonson wrote the quaint devices. Her Majesty's departure was marked by a pageant, which must have been the inspiration of the Lord Keeper himself. Harefield, personified as a disconsolate widow attired in rich sables, bade the Virgin Queen farewell.

It was in truth farewell for the Queen, who did not live long after her visit to Harefield. With Sir Robert Cecil and the Lord Admiral, the Lord Keeper was present at Richmond during her last illness, to await the hour of the Queen's dissolution. When she had breathed her last, in the dark, early hours of March 24, 1603, Egerton joined in proclaiming King James, and waited with some anxiety to discover whether the new sovereign would continue him in office. He hastened to write a letter to Sir Thomas Chaloner, who, he knew, had gained the King's confidence. He had heard that one of his enemies had described him to King James as "haughty, insolent, and proud." The letter pleaded the innocence and clearness of his own conscience, which the Lord Keeper declared to be better than a thousand witnesses. "I have learned no waye," he declared, "but the King's highe waye . . ." To King James, on his way from Scotland with his dreams of royal absolutism, these were honeyed words. On the third of May, 1603, King James restored the Great Seal to the Lord Keeper, and on the nineteenth of July, having caused a new seal to be made, the King gave it into his hands with the title of Lord Chancellor of England and at the same time created him a peer with the title of Baron Ellesmere.

In gratitude the new Lord Ellesmere now surrendered the office of Master of the Rolls to a needy favorite of King James, one Edward

Bruce, Lord Kinlosse, who, since he was interested only in the emoluments of the office, in no way attempted to interfere in the business of the Court of Chancery. But James himself proved an exacting master, and he frequently called upon his Lord Chancellor to give the stamp of legality to measures of doubtful constitutional import. The whole of Lord Ellesmere's life and activities were now bathed in prerogative as in an enveloping atmosphere. The keeper of the king's conscience now had not infrequently to wrestle with his own. He proved more than equal to the task.

During the first five years of his chancellorship, the energies of Lord Ellesmere were consumed in assisting King James to bring about a legislative union of the Crowns of England and Scotland. The project was coldly received by both the English and the Scotch. The former feared that England would be overrun with Scotsmen, while the latter, as someone put it, though they had taken the English king, refused to be governed by any English laws. The Lord Chancellor headed the commission that treated with the Scotch, but although the legislative union failed, what would have been one of its important benefits was accomplished by judge-made law. A case was rigged up in the Court of Chancery, as well as in the Court of King's Bench, to test the right of subjects born in Scotland after James's accession to the Crown of England to hold land in England and to secure its protection in English courts. These cases have been known as the "Post-nati," or "afterborn." On account of their importance, they were adjourned into the Exchequer Chamber and argued before the Lord Chancellor and all the judges. Francis Bacon, of evil and glorious memory, who was a protégé of Lord Ellesmere, and who was to be his successor as Lord Chancellor, was deputed to present the case for the Crown. Bacon, in legal terms, stated "the depth of the question" to be: "Was naturalization accessory to sovereignty, which in this case was joint, or to the Legislature, which was several?" The Lord Chancellor, of course, held that "naturalization was accessory to sovereignty," and all the judges but two agreed with him. Upon the two dissenting judges the Lord Chancellor poured out the vials of his scorn. "They did not amount," he observed, "to the plural number in Greek."

Lord Ellesmere virtually closed the Court of Chancery to arguments against the royal prerogative. He adopted James's hostile attitude toward the Puritans, and after the Hampton Court Conference in 1604 he declared that the King's speech then made him first realize the full import of the saying, *Rex est mixta persona cum sacredote* (The King as a person is both human and divine). The Lord Chancellor even attempted to interfere with the right of the House of Commons to judge of the validity of the elections and qualifications of its own members. He also made an effort to prevent Parliament from discussing the power of the King to levy impositions, and supported him when he took upon himself the power not merely to enforce, but to alter, the law by issuing proclamations. The Lord Chancellor argued that

. . . every precedent must have a first commencement, and that he would advise the judges to maintain the power and prerogative of the King; and in cases in which there is no authority and precedent to leave it to the King to order it according to his wisdom and the good of his subjects, for otherwise the King would be no more than the Duke of Venice.

All these attempts were unsuccessful, but they show the extent to which Lord Ellesmere was willing to go to support James's claims to arbitrary power, which were sowing the seeds of civil war. Perhaps the most ignominious act of Lord Ellesmere was to seal the pardon of the Earl and Countess of Somerset for their atrocious murder of Sir Thomas Overbury. This step was taken because King James wished to have buried in oblivion some secret which was in the possession of the Somersets. The depths to which Lord Ellesmere sank on this occasion in serving King James may be judged from the fact that he would not seal the pardon unless the King should first pardon him for sealing it. Perhaps it should be said in defense of the Lord Chancellor that these were the days of arbitrary power, and that it was widely held that even an Act of Parliament to abolish the dispensing power would be inoperative, since the king could first dispense with the abolishing act, and then with the act to be dispensed with.

It was not until almost the close of Lord Ellesmere's life and career that the struggle occurred that vindicated the position of the Court of Chancery in the judicial system of England. His opponent in this struggle was Sir Edward Coke, the Chief Justice of the King's Bench, who was a greater man than he—indeed, one of the greatest figures in English legal history. Ellesmere, at the time of his quarrel with Coke, was an ailing old man hardly able to attend to his duties, but the doughty champion of the common law was no respecter of persons or conditions. Their differences are said by Lord Campbell, the biographer of the Lord Chancellors, at last to have "produced an explosion which shook Westminster Hall to its centre," and a similar opinion has been commonly expressed by English legal historians. It is true that the battles of the law are no sham conflicts; usually great interests are at stake when individuals clash over the administration of justice. Nevertheless, the conflict between Ellesmere and Coke was far from titanic. It was one of the great sham battles of legal history. The mere fact that it was won by the ailing old man, by the lesser man, by the man who had been defeated in every other attempt to assert arbitrary power, should make this apparent. The contest may have been the opening gun in the Puritan Rebellion but, if so, it was not much more than a popgun. It is very much to be doubted that it would ever have occurred but for the quarrelsome temper of Coke, who was no doubt encouraged by his victory, not long before, in the matter of the king's proclamations. Francis Bacon, who stood far closer to the disputants than any other contemporary, attributed the affair to no more than personal rivalry and jealousy. "The former discords," he observed, "were but flesh and blood; and now that the men were gone the matter was gone."

The controversy originated in a type of action by the Chancellor that was especially calculated to strain the relations between his court and the courts of the common law. Whenever the Chancellor issued an injunction to restrain proceedings which had already been begun by a litigant in one of the common-law courts, or, worse still, to prevent the execution of a judgment which had already been obtained from one of the common-law courts, it was particularly difficult to pretend that the Chancellor was not interfering with the course of the common law. Moreover, to disturb the judgment of any court violated one of the basic premises of all settled legal procedure, denominated by the lawyers the doctrine of *res adjudicata,* which assumes that at some predetermined point there must be an end to litigation. The perils and costs of a lawsuit are too dreadful to be permitted to continue forever.

In the *Earl of Oxford's Case,* and in several other cases, Lord Ellesmere granted a perpetual injunction against the execution of judgments which had been obtained by the grossest fraud in the Court of King's Bench. In one action for debt, the plaintiff had secured the judgment by decoying away the defendant's witness, who could have proved its payment. The witness had been plied with drink at a near-by tavern, but the plaintiff had made the judge believe that

he was in a dying condition by having his accomplice swear that
"delay would be vain, for that he had just left the witness in such a
state, that if he were to continue in it a quarter of an hour longer, he
would be a dead man."

In one of these cases, Coke sent for the attorney for the plaintiff in
the Court of King's Bench, and advised him to seek an indictment
against the party who had obtained the injunction in the Court of
Chancery, on the ground that he had violated the dreadful Statutes of
Praemunire which, Coke must have known, were aimed at attempts
by the papal courts to interfere with the jurisdiction of the common-law
courts. At the same time, Coke instigated Justice Crook, one of his
colleagues in the King's Bench, to charge the Grand Jury "to inquire of
all such persons as questioned judgments at law, by bill or petition,
in the Court of Chancery." The particular weapon selected by Coke
from those available in the legal armory was a poor one, for the penalties
under the Statutes of Praemunire were too severe and their applicability
too doubtful. When the jury would not find any indictments, Coke
bullied them, and it is believed that Lord Ellesmere himself even accused Coke of telling the jury that they need fear nothing because
the Lord Chancellor was dead. The Chancellor, however, unexpectedly
recovered, and proceeded to lay the matter before James, who in turn
referred the question to Bacon and other law officers of the Crown,
who without hesitation informed him that "according to reason and
many precedents" the Statutes of Praemunire did not apply to the
issuance by the Chancellor of injunctions against the enforcement of
fraudulent judgments at common law. The precedents, indeed, went
back to the reign of Henry VIII at least, and there had even been
occasions when the common-law judges themselves had advised parties
to seek relief against such fraud in equity. King James ended the controversy by upholding Lord Ellesmere, but he confused future historians
by failing to mention the precedents and by resting his decision entirely
on the royal prerogative. "It appertained only to his princely office,"
he said, "to judge over all the judges, and to discern and determine
such differences as at any time might arise between his several courts
touching their jurisdictions." Coke, soon after his defeat, was dismissed
as Chief Justice of the King's Bench—much to the joy and satisfaction
of Lord Ellesmere—but his fall must not be interpreted as proof of the
importance and reality of the injunction controversy. His dismissal
may have been due to a quarrel over the filling of the office of chief

clerk of his court, a lucrative position desired by Lord Buckingham, the King's favorite.

It is no great feat to win when the cards are stacked. The triumph of Lord Ellesmere was a foregone conclusion. Equity had become too vital a part of English law for the position of the Court of Chancery to be undermined. There was some grumbling at the Chancellor's court during the course of the Puritan Rebellion, but no one seriously thought of abolishing it, or even of curtailing its activities. Its justice was, to be sure, considered somewhat unpredictable. There was a saying of Selden that was much quoted. "Equity," he said, "is a roguish thing," and he added that its measure was "the length of the Chancellor's foot." But the foot nevertheless continued to dangle from the woolsack.

In truth, the Court of Chancery had the support of every great landowner and wealthy merchant. The whole system of landholding depended on its existence. The legislative efforts of Edward I to undermine the system of feudalism had not been enough, but the solution had been provided by the ingenuity of the lawyers. They invented, in the second half of the fourteenth century, the device known as the "use," which enabled them to evade all feudal dues and burdens. The legal title to land was conveyed by the great landowners to groups of friends or kinsmen under an agreement to hold it to certain "uses" of the grantor. These groups were known as the "feoffees to uses," and since the group itself could be continuously reconstituted, it was possible to avoid the feudal burdens which attached only on death. The common-law courts recognized only the legal title, and would not intervene if the feoffees betrayed their trust, but the Chancellor, who enforced the dictates of conscience, held them vigorously to the obligations of the use. The device of the use was transparent enough but, when it was threatened in the sixteenth century, the Chancellor saved it by a still more transparent device. A rather reluctant Parliament was induced by Henry VIII in 1535 to enact a statute known as the Statute of Uses, which was intended to end them. But estates were now simply conveyed upon a double use, namely to the use of John Smith for the use of John Doe. The Chancellor now held, in obedience to the command of the Statute of Uses, which provided that, when one held land to the use of another, the feoffee should be deemed the legal owner, that the statute executed the first use but not the second! As it has been said, "by this means a statute made upon great consideration, introduced in a solemn and pompous manner, has had no other effect than to add at most three words to a conveyance." The double use was called a trust, and the protection of the beneficiary of the trust, known as the *cestui que trust,* became the most important aspect of the jurisdiction of the Chancellor.

Another great head of equitable jurisdiction was the protection of the hard-pressed landowner who had to mortgage his land. The common-law courts held that the legal title passed to the mortgagee subject to revesting in the mortgagor upon the payment of the bond on the appointed day, but if the mortgagor then failed to pay, he lost his land even though it may have been mortgaged for a fraction of its value. The Chancellor, however, with his higher ethical standards, recognized an "equity of redemption," which permitted the mortgagor to get the difference between the value of his land and the amount of the loan.

The Chancellor was also a mainstay of the merchant class. He helped commerce by recognizing the free assignability of debts and contracts, and enforced some simple types of contracts that did not square with the formalities required to uphold their validity in the common-law courts. He not only granted a remedy of specific performance in the case of executory contracts for the sale of land, so that the merchant who had set his heart on the estate of Blackacre could get not merely damages but precisely what he had bargained for, but also ordered the specific performance of other types of contracts for the breach of which an award of damages would have been inadequate.

Moreover, the Chancellor, who did not need to struggle with the dull understanding of a middle-class jury, was better able, with the assistance of a considerable retinue of clerks, to take accountings and to manage partnerships and testamentary estates, particularly when the guardianship of infants was involved. The trust was also the basis of an arrangement known as "the marriage settlement." Immediately upon marriage the common law vested the wife's property in her husband. Long before the emancipation of women in the country of the common law, the marriage settlement made it possible for the rich merchant who married his daughter to a great but impecunious lord to protect her dot from the clutch of her grasping husband. The breadth of the Chancellor's jurisdiction inspired this sixteenth-century rhyme:

> These three give place in court of conscience,
> Fraud, accident, and breach of confidence.

No one knew better than Lord Ellesmere that the business of the Court of Chancery was to serve the convenience of the propertied classes, consisting of the landed aristocracy and the rising merchant class. One of the most significant of all his acts was an order he once made that paupers who sued in the Court of Chancery without adequate cause should be whipped. This is usually attributed to the fact that he was a strict disciplinarian. But the real reason was that it interfered with the important business of the Court of Chancery and wasted the time of the Chancellor without supplying an adequate return. Already in the time of Lord Ellesmere the costs of a suit in the Court of Chancery were growing to bankrupting proportions. There were fees and still more fees—those of the Chancellor, the Master of the Rolls, twelve other masters, and the six clerks, each of whom had eight other clerks under him. The clerks were supposed in theory to be the solicitors of the parties, but all they did was to compel suitors to take useless copies of papers and pleadings at extortionate rates. Somebody called the Court of Chancery "a mere monoply to cozen the subjects of their moneys." Obviously, under such circumstances a pauper plaintiff could not be permitted to waste the Chancellor's time.

It is instructive to compare the survival of the Court of Chancery with the extinction of two courts that were still in existence at that time but which were soon destined to disappear. The first, now remembered only by legal antiquarians, was called the Court of Requests. A minor offshoot of the King's Council held before the Lord Privy Seal, it was designed to administer equity to poor men. Toward the close of Elizabeth's reign, however, its practical usefulness was destroyed by a decision of the Court of Queen's Bench that it had no contentious jurisdiction. It was after this that poor litigants were allowed to sue at their peril as paupers in the Court of Chancery without paying its onerous fees.

The second court was the celebrated Court of Star Chamber, of evil memory. It, too, was an outgrowth of the inexhaustible reservoir of justice, the King's Council. It took its name from the ceiling decoration of the room in the royal palace at Westminster. Held by members of the Privy Council and some of the judges ex officio, it dealt with offenders too powerful to be reached by the process of the ordinary courts. Although sentence of death could never be pronounced in the Court of Star Chamber, the enormous fines and imprisonments it could impose proved more than an adequate substitute, and procedurally it had the enormous advantages of being able to dispense with the jury and of employing torture, when necessary, to secure confessions.

The Chancellor sat in the Star Chamber, and Ellesmere particularly took a great interest in its work and played a leading part in its deliberations. He once concurred, for instance, in a sentence imposed upon a Catholic subject nearly eighty years old, whose only offense was that he had presented a respectful petition to the king, praying for an investigation of the conduct of a judge in condemning to death a neighbor for entertaining a Jesuit. For this he was sentenced to the loss of his ears, exposure in the pillory, a fine of £1000, and perpetual imprisonment.

The Star Chamber was certainly a dread tribunal, but it performed a historic function, which was nothing less than to liquidate what was left of the power of the baronage. This mission fulfilled, it was abolished in 1641 by an act which ended the jurisdiction of the Council in England and thus destroyed this ancient reservoir of justice. The abolition of the Star Chamber was the first great triumph of the Puritan Rebellion; it had perforce to tolerate its civil analogue, the Court of Chancery, which a great English legal historian has called "the Star Chamber's twin sister."

In his last days Lord Ellesmere was made Viscount Brackley, a title which, to annoy the ailing old man, the wits of the time chose to pronounce as Viscount Break-Law. Lord Ellesmere, who had risen from a sickbed to defend the Court of Chancery against Coke, did not long survive his triumph or his added honors. On the third of March, 1617, when he had become bedridden and incapable of discharging his duties, he was the recipient for the second time of a royal visit. But this time there were no festivities. King James came to York House, where the Chancellor lay, in order to accept his resignation in person. Lord Ellesmere died only a few days after the surrender of his office, on the fifteenth of March, 1617. He was buried under a flagstone in the chancel of the parish church at Doddelstone in Chester. The natural son of Sir Richard Egerton left an estate created entirely by his own efforts, which was valued at £8000 a year and represented the average wealth of the high hereditary nobility of the time. His wife, Alice, survived him by seventeen years, and no doubt enjoyed to their full extent the fruits of equity.

It is the traditional view of English legal historians that in the two centuries following the death of Lord Ellesmere, particularly in the important chancellorships of Nottingham, Hardwicke, and Eldon, who rank as the great names in the history of English equity, equity was gradually shorn of its discretionary elements and transformed into a system as rigid and precedent-bound as the common law. It is very probable, however, that this view is only another form of the misunderstanding of the significance of the quarrel between Ellesmere and Coke, and of the seventeenth-century belief that the measure of equity was the length of the chancellor's foot. Doubtless Lord Ellesmere was much freer than his successors in manipulating the principles of equity, but this must have been due to the fact that precedents were fewer then than in later times rather than to the fact that the binding character of precedent was not recognized. This is apparent from the mere fact that Lord Ellesmere and his defenders relied upon precedent in resisting the designs of Coke. There were, in fact, very few reports of cases in the Court of Chancery in Lord Ellesmere's time. But the failure to preserve reports does not necessarily argue a disregard of precedent, any more than the publication of reports argues a strict observance of precedent, and, in any event, in the absence of reports, it must be obvious that there is great risk in comparing one period with another. The assumption that equity in Lord Ellesmere's time was a loose jade ready to give her favors to all comers also casts too exclusive an emphasis upon the hidebound character of the common-law courts. This view in turn is based upon the immemorial failure to see that in all courts, whether legal or equitable, precedent has always been a good deal of a snare and a delusion. It is true that in the formative period of equity the common-law courts failed to respond to many pressing needs of the time, but the common law did grow and change to some extent in relation to social needs, and the measure of this growth was also the common-law judge's foot. Indeed, in their early history, the common-law courts afforded many remedies which were equitable in nature, and in the century after Ellesmere's death they began again to give some heed to equitable considerations. This process of change was aided by legislation, upon which, rather than upon Chancery miracles, chief reliance was now placed.

In the final phase of its development in the nineteenth century, the Court of Chancery became a court of bad conscience, a byword for delay, precedent-worship, and the denial of justice. The substantive principles of equity jurisprudence were now refined beyond belief, but the procedure of the Court of Chancery had become a public scandal. The written interrogatories by which evidence was taken had become endless in number; so, too, had the number of parties who had to be joined in a complicated equity suit, so that the Chancellor, plagued by his highly refined conscience, might not overlook the interests of anybody; and endless indeed had become the number of fees that had to be paid to the swarm of Chancery clerks for services they now hardly ever performed. Dickens's satire of the Court of Chancery in *Bleak House* may be taken to be an almost sober picture. His representation of the Chancellor in the opening scene of the book, in which he sits on the woolsack while a thick fog envelops the city, is highly symbolic. The system of pleading in the courts of common law also came to be a public scandal, and it, too, produced a classic—Charles Warren's *Ten Thousand a Year*.

After an incredibly long period of agitation, which at first led only to piecemeal reforms, the English judicial system was reorganized on modern lines by the so-called Judicature Acts of 1873–75. All the English courts were consolidated into one High Court of Justice, the two component elements of the English legal system were fused, and all the judges of the High Court were made competent to administer both law and equity. The traditional courts survived only as the names of various divisions of the High Court of Justice. Thus there was a Chancery Division, but it represented only a convenient distribution of the business of the court subject to change at any time by action of the judges. In 1903, Lord Justice Buckley, sitting in the Chancery Division of the High Court of Justice, pronounced the obituary of equity as a growing system of law when he declared: "This court is not a court of conscience." It is not recorded whether, when this dictum was uttered, Thomas Egerton, Baron Ellesmere and Viscount Brackley, turned in his grave.

Sir Edward Coke

AND

HIS LADY OF THE COMMON LAW

SIR EDWARD COKE IS THE GREATEST NAME IN THE HISTORY OF the common law. He has traditionally been regarded as its oracle. The stirring period in which he lived has been characterized by one historian of the common law as that in which "that wonderful Edward Coke was loose." Unquestionably he was the dominating figure of the Elizabethan legal world, and his significance looms even larger (than that of other great Elizabethans) in the embattled and precarious world of today. Yet his personal character and the nature of his achievements are such that he has always been as much the despair of the biographer and historian as a challenge to them.

Sir Edward Coke was nothing less than the legal mouthpiece of the Puritan Rebellion. He was the great legal hero of the constitutional struggles which were fought in England in the sixteenth and seventeenth centuries. The fruits of these struggles were those basic English civil liberties which have everywhere become the foundations of democracy. Having served so long as models for the whole democratic world, these civil liberties have come to be regarded as a peculiarly English heritage, as a national expression of the very "genius" of the common law. It has been said that "if there is any virtue in the common law . . . it is that freedom is her sister." In legal parlance English liberty is said to derive from the central dogma of the common law, which is "the rule of law" or "the supremacy of law." As a technical doctrine of the common law, the supremacy of law means simply that all the king's servants and all the king's men are to be treated in courts of justice in the same way as all others of the king's subjects. It means, in other words, that no royal officer may plead as a special justification of an action claimed to be illegal that it was done at the king's command; the king himself can do no wrong, but every one of the king's servants may be held liable for wrongdoing if he has violated the law; there are no rules of liability that apply to the king's subjects but not to the king's officials. The supremacy of law, stated in more general terms, is thus a limitation upon the unlawful exercise of executive power, which particularly needs to be kept in leash. In the political theory and the constitutional practice of the modern democratic world, however, the doctrine of the supremacy of law has come to have a far more sweeping meaning. It signifies nothing less than the subjection of the state itself to law; law and the state are identified, and law is commonly conceived to exist only when it is a limitation upon power.

In the era of the French Revolution the great slogan was natural rights. But the natural rights of the eighteenth century were only the common-law rights of the embattled Englishmen of the seventeenth. The Tudor kings had built a strong centralized English state, but unlike the French kings and other continental rulers, they did not succeed in making good their claims to absolute monarchy. They encountered a stronger and more resistant middle class, whose need for the security of capitalist accumulation and enterprise did not permit them to brook the constant interferences of personal royal government. But the English middle class in the first phases of its opposition to royal absolutism did not rely upon such a vague generality as the law of nature. They spoke of "reason" rather than nature, and persuaded themselves that reason was embodied in the common law. Shrewdly they appealed to the common law and the common-law courts. The judges of the common-law courts were still the king's servants and held office only at his pleasure, but centuries of uninterrupted legal development had created a strong professional tradition and sanctified the position of the common law. The custom of the realm was the common law, and Englishmen revealed a greater attachment to its precepts than even the most archaic peoples have felt for their ancient and immemorial customs.

It is true that in its origin the common law was the king's law, but nevertheless the king's law was to be set against himself. Englishmen had been in the habit, for a long time, of getting their kings to affirm the ancient customs of the realm whenever trouble brewed. They had extracted such promises from the first two Henrys and from the first Edward. But, above all, they had Magna Charta, which the determined barons had compelled the reluctant King John to sign as early as 1215. Magna Charta, although it was in its origin only a grant of feudal privileges, did contain in its thirty-ninth chapter a provision that was to have a magnificent career in creating the intoxicating ideology of the supremacy of law. "No freeman," it set forth, "shall be taken, or imprisoned, or disseized, or exiled, or in any way destroyed, nor shall we go upon him, nor send upon him, except by the lawful judgment of his peers, or by the law of the land." Were the Tudors and the Stuarts to be permitted to override what earlier and no less illustrious kings had granted?

The "law of the land" was the common law, and its guardianship was entrusted to the courts of the common law. Hence it is usually said that the English constitutional struggle of the sixteenth and seventeenth centuries assumed the form of a contest between the courts and the Crown. It would be more exact to say, however, that the issue was Coke's common law, and that it was fought out between the courts over which Coke presided and the Crown. Yet in the very legalistic basis of the controversy lies the first embarrassment of the biographer. Coke was the great master of the medieval common law, whose learning he had absorbed and was restating for the lawyers of his and subsequent generations. The common law had become a complex and recondite science of writs and forms of action utterly beyond the comprehension of the layman. Nevertheless, it was precisely this science that furnished the armory of weapons that assured the triumph of the supremacy of law. The layman can understand the victory and its importance, but he will never understand entirely the means by which it was won. He must take Coke and his precedents largely on faith.

Unfortunately, Sir Edward Coke was not the sort of man who could always be taken on faith. He has been charged with an even greater degree of inconsistency than is usually allowed to great men, and with stretching a precedent now and then when it suited his purpose. He had the happy faculty of being able to persuade himself that what he was doing was legal, and all that ever interested him was the legal aspect of things. From this very narrow point of view his inconsistencies seem to grow less. There were three almost distinct phases in his career. In the first he was a law officer of the Crown, in which capacity he seems to appear as the defender of the royal prerogative; in the second he was undoubtedly the stalwart and courageous champion of the common law, defending popular liberties; and in the third he was one of the leading exponents of the sovereignty of Parliament. He seems almost to have been three men rather than one. Yet he had one great and overmastering passion. He was in love with the Lady of the Common Law. The story of his life is the story of the love of a man for an abstraction. Undoubtedly, in his own mind, at least, he could always think that he had been faithful to the lady in his fashion. His own unhappy domestic life was only to lend piquancy to his devotion to his lifelong mistress. His character has long been regarded as something of a psychological enigma, but if it can be explained at all, it must be in terms of the harsh compromises life imposed upon   him in serving the Lady of the Common Law.

Sir Edward Coke is one of the great heroes of the cause of human freedom, and the great champion of civil liberty. It would be pleasing to be able to say that his character was noble; that as a man he was generous, kind, considerate, patient, and unassuming; and that as a public servant there were no stains upon his career. But to say all this would be more pleasing than true. In fact, Sir Edward Coke was one of the most arrogant and avaricious of men. While he never betrayed (or perhaps never had the opportunity to betray) a friend, he could exhibit an unparalleled cruelty to his enemies. The English historian Trevelyan has described Coke as "one of the most disagreeable figures in our history," as well as "one of the most important champions of our liberty." He was in this respect like a later champion of liberty, John Wilkes. But it is not a paradox to say that both characterizations of Coke went well together. The great civil liberties were not made for a perfect world of brotherly love and understanding. They were made as rules to insure a minimum of decency in the conduct of social struggle in a world of bitter and unending competition. They would not be needed, any more than law itself would be needed, if men were like angels. But their appearance and recognition coincided with the emergence of the system of ruthless competition. The great freedoms in their origin were coupled with the need for the freedom to buy and sell.

Edward Coke showed push and enterprise in the very act of his birth. When he was born, on February 1, 1552, it was at the fireplace in the parlor, before his mother could be taken to her bed. He was born into a substantial middle-class family. His father, Robert Coke, was a well-to-do lawyer who lived on the Manor of Burghwood, in Mileham and Tittleshall, Norfolk. He had married Winifred Knightley, the daughter and heiress of William Knightley, who was also a lawyer.

In a sense, therefore, Edward Coke was born to the common law. He was an only son but not an only child. The marriage of his parents was also blessed with seven daughters named Winifred, Dorothy, Elizabeth, Ursula, Anna, Margaret, and Ethelreda. Every one of them was successfully married off, and, since in those days this could not have been done without providing each of them with a suitable portion, the enterprise of their mother and the industry and resources of their father can well be imagined, even if it be assumed that the girls were not married merely for their money. Edward we know grew into a strong handsome man, and it is reasonable to suppose that his sisters had good looks, too. Nevertheless, there must have been a good deal of competition to overcome. All the scheming and plotting of the matrimonial campaigns could not have failed to leave their mark on the male child of the family. This environment was certainly not calculated to nurture nobility of character. Doubtless it bred in him, however, a good deal of respect for pounds and shillings, and taught him the shrewd lessons of self-interest which he subsequently took advantage of in getting on in the world. Also, a household of seven marriagable daughters could hardly have been a quiet place. The life of Edward Coke was to be frenzied enough.

Coke's mother was his first teacher, and she not only taught him how to read but also instilled in him the habits of industry and application. When he was ten years old, he was sent to the free grammar school at Norfolk, which was then something of a provincial capital. The town had suffered from the general decline of English woolen manufacture, but this, however, was soon to be revived to such an extent that the economic history of the times seems one of sheep-raising and inclosures. Coke remained at the Norfolk Grammar School for seven years, but he had not been there very long when his busy father died in his chambers at Lincoln's Inn, on November 15, 1561. The young orphan's mother soon remarried, and his education was left largely to the headmaster of the school.

On October 25, 1567, Coke entered Trinity College, Cambridge. Whitgift, later to become Archbishop of Canterbury, is said to have been his tutor. Little is told of Coke's days at Cambridge that is not pure surmise, but he certainly could have shown no interest in philosophy, history, art, or science. He believed all sorts of historical legends and was convinced, for instance, that the ancient Britons had talked Greek. Like most of his contemporaries, he regarded actors as no better than vagrants; but, unlike them, during his long life he never once went to the theater to see a play of Shakespeare or of any other dramatist. His ignorance of science was abysmal, even for his time. "The metals," he once said, "are six—gold, silver, copper, tin, lead and iron; and they all proceed originally from sulphur and quicksilver as from their father and mother." Coke was not endowed greatly with gifts of the imagination, but he did show that he had a phenomenal memory. He was to become the supreme embodiment of the truth of Burke's future dictum that the law sharpens the mind by narrowing it. He stayed at Cambridge four years but, for reasons not precisely known, he left the university without taking his degree.

He did not, however, return to the country to become a squire and a justice of the peace. No doubt the necessity of providing portions for seven daughters had depleted the family fortune. But the charms of the Lady of the Common Law also attracted him for their own sake. The lady beckoned to him alluringly, and he hastened to London to enter the Inns of Court. After a year at Clifford's Inn, he transferred to the Inner Temple. After six years of absorbing application—a year less than was usual—he was called to the bar on April 20, 1578.

Coke's great love for the Lady of the Common Law was conceived during his years at the Inns of Court. He communed with his mistress during the last hours of the night and the early hours of the morning. He followed a strange and inexorable regimen, which he maintained during the whole of his long life. He would always retire at 9:00 P.M., and rise regularly at 3:00 A.M. He had a strong constitution, and boasted in his old age that he had never been ill a day and never taken physic. While a student at the Inner Temple, Coke devoted the time from 3:00 A.M. to 8:00 A.M. to legal study. He would light his own fire, and then pore over the treasures of the common law. These were the Yearbooks, in which were reported decisions of cases. In the days of his maturity, he was himself to become the most painstaking and original reporter in the history of the common law, publishing eleven volumes of reports, in which he resurveyed and analyzed all the doctrines of the common law, making each case serve as a point of departure for a little essay on some question of law. But there were also the precious lawbooks produced by the worthies who had loved the common law before him. These were the authors known as Fleta, Britton, Bracton, and Littleton. He was absorbed especially by a book of Littleton on all the numerous and baffling varieties of land tenure

known to the history of the common law. Littleton certainly was the
man for Coke! He gave it as his considered opinion that Littleton's book
was "the most perfect and absolute work that ever was written in any
human science." A man needed such an opinion to sustain him in
the lonely hours. Coke himself quoted a Latin couplet which he
thought described his regimen, and it has been translated thus:

> Six hours in sleep, in law's grave study six,
> Four spent in prayer, the rest on nature fix.

Coke's rise in his profession was rapid. It was not then an over-
crowded profession. When he was called to the bar, there were less than
two hundred barristers in all England. There were probably more
wenches than lawyers frequenting the environs of Westminster Hall;
the former went under the name of "termers." Part of the explanation
of Coke's success was the fact that he had the patronage and support
of the great Lord Treasurer, Burghley, but he owed it also to his own
deep knowledge of the law. Those lonely nights were to bring dividends. Coke was no great master of eloquence, but he excelled in the
intellectually much more difficult art of special pleading. The procedure of the common law had become something fearful to contem-
plate, and the layman caught in the toils of the law stood in desperate
need of a fellow like Coke.

Coke won fame in his very first case, which enabled him to make
use of his cleverness at pleading. It was an action under the statute
De scandalis magnatum, which was aimed against the defamation of
the great of the realm. We should call it a libel action. When Lord
Cromwell, the leader of the Puritans, imported into his parish church
two unlicensed Genevese preachers who spoke unkindly of the *Book
of Common Prayer,* his vicar, the Reverend Denny, remonstrated with
him, whereupon Lord Cromwell said to him, "Thou art a false varlet,
and I like not of thee." The vicar, however, had the impudence to
reply, "It is no marvel that you like not of me, for you like of men who
maintain sedition against the Queen's proceedings." This reply caused
Lord Cromwell to bring his action. Coke, who appeared for the unfortunate vicar, first pleaded truth as a defense but, when the plea
was rejected by the judges, he moved in arrest of judgment on the
ground of a technical flaw in the declaration under the statute, and his
motion was sustained. In disgust, Lord Cromwell, mulcted of costs,

abandoned all thoughts of vengeance against the vicar. Coke has been much criticized for the use he made of the statute *De scandalis magnatum* when he was a law officer of the Crown. No doubt the statute, which did not allow truth to be pleaded as a defense, was inimical to freedom. But had not the judges themselves, when Coke was a neophyte at the bar, told him that truth was no defense?

The twenty-seven-year-old lawyer won even greater fame in the most celebrated case in the history of real-property law in England. It is known as *Shelley's Case*, and its doctrine as the "Rule in *Shelley's Case*," which established a basic method of construing words of conveyance in a grant. By his ingenuity in this case Coke enabled a posthumous nephew to take the estate away from his uncle.

When Coke was thirty years old, he was well enough established to think of marriage. There lived at Norwich, William Paston, Esquire, a wealthy lawyer who had a family of twelve children, among whom was a daughter, Bridget, then eighteen years of age. Coke asked for her hand, and her father showed his confidence in the bridegroom by settling £30,000 on his daughter when she was married, on August 13, 1582. There is nothing, however, to show that Coke, for all the avarice he was to show in later years, married Bridget solely for her money. She was a lovely girl, with gentle eyes and blonde hair. She had, too, an amiable disposition, which made it possible for her to soothe her husband's irascible temper. Coke may have known her from her childhood. On the other hand, it is very doubtful that Bridget represented so romantic a passion that she was likely to alienate Coke from the Lady of the Common Law. Coke could not have loved her in anything but a hurried and absent-minded way, for all that he had ten children by her in the sixteen years of their marriage. Within six months of his marriage, Coke's father-in-law conveniently departed this world, and doubtless left him a further increment of worldly goods, at least by way of added opportunities for legal fees.

In fact, Coke's reputation as a master of the mysteries of the common law grew so great that the municipalities of England competed with each other to secure his legal services. The town of Coventry in 1585, the town of Norwich in 1586, and finally the great city of London in 1592, elected him Recorder. At the same time he was appointed Reader at the Inner Temple, and lectured to goodly numbers of eager law students with great success. When the plague caused the

suspension of his lectures, Coke fled to the country, and to do him
honor a throng of benchers and barristers accompanied him part of the
way to his house at Huntingfield in Suffolk. As Coke completed his
fortieth year, Queen Elizabeth, prompted no doubt by Burghley, recognized his importance by making him her Solicitor General.

Phase (1)

Thus began Coke's career as a servant of the Crown. In this phase
of his career, he certainly never opposed or questioned the royal prerogative. In 1593, not long after he became Solicitor General, he even
served the Queen when he was supposed to be a representative of the
people. Elected a member of Parliament from Norfolk, and selected
by the House of Commons as its Speaker, he engaged in a nice bit of
duplicity to defeat a bill to reform the abuses of the ecclesiastical courts.
When the bill was introduced, he pretended that it was too long for
him to consider it then, and hastened to acquaint Queen Elizabeth
with its contents. Its unfortunate author found himself in the Tower
not long thereafter.

Both in his speech to the throne upon the assembling of Parliament,
and in his speech upon its dissolution, he showed an attitude of profound abasement before the royal will and pleasure. When presented
to Her Majesty by the House as its Speaker, Coke humbly declared:
"As in the heavens a star is but *opacum corpus* until it hath received
light from the sun, so stand I *corpus opacum,* a mute body, until Your
Highness's bright shining wisdom hath looked upon me and allowed
me." After the Queen had "allowed" her submissive servant, and he,
in accordance with custom, had prayed for liberty of speech and other
privileges of the Commons, Queen Elizabeth gave utterance, haughtily,
to the Tudor conception of these privileges. "Liberty of speech," she
said, "is granted you, but you must know what privilege you have;
not to speak everyone what he listeth, or what cometh in his
brain to utter, but your privilege is *aye* or *no.*" When the Parliament
was dissolved on April 16, 1593, after granting an appropriate supply,
Coke made a curious speech comparing Her Majesty's realm to a bee-
hive.

The little bees [he said sweetly] have but one governor, whom they
all serve. . . . Your Majesty is that princely governor and noble
Queen whom we all serve. Being protected under the shadow of your
wings, we live. Under your happy government, we live upon honey,
we suck every sweet flower; but where the bee sucketh honey, there
also the spider draweth poison. But such drones we will expel from the

hive. We will serve Your Majesty, and withstand any enemy that shall assault you. Our lands, our goods, our lives, are prostrate at your feet to be commanded.

Is it any wonder then that almost a year to the day after the closing of the Parliament of 1593 Coke was advanced to the position of Attorney General? In fact, he would have obtained the appointment even sooner if a scheming and persistent rival had not appeared in the person of Francis Bacon, the "wisest, brightest, meanest of mankind." Francis Bacon, the son of Sir Nicholas Bacon, Keeper of the Great Seal, was ultimately to become eminent in the law himself as Lord Chancellor of England, and, with the publication of his *Novum Organum,* to achieve immortal fame as a philosopher. But at this time he was only a young man of thirty-two, with neither fame nor fortune. He had, to be sure, been to the Inns of Court, and was presumably learned in the law, but he had never yet pleaded a case! For such a one to aspire to be Attorney General was presumptuous indeed, and Coke undoubtedly so regarded it. But if Bacon had no fortune, he had a powerful friend and supporter in the Earl of Essex, Elizabeth's favorite. The generous and passionate Earl for the better part of a year pleaded, stormed cajoled, and brought himself to the point of distraction, but his royal mistre s never let her feelings get the better of her judgment. Bacon had made a sad mistake in the Parliament of 1593: he had not only questioned the amount of the supply desired by Her Majesty, but had also given free rein to his wit by remarking that gentlemen would have to sell their plate and farmers their brass pots. Bacon did not then even get the lesser post of Solicitor General, ror Coke preferred to carry the office until a more suitable incumbent could be chosen.

Thus began—but did not end—the great competition between these two celebrated men. Coke never forgave Bacon for aspiring to the favors of his mistress of the common law, and he conceived for his rival an implacable enmity. The temper of the two men may be judged from an altercation between them in the Court of the Exchequer after Bacon had begun to obtain some practice. "Mr. Bacon," said Coke to his despised opponent, "if you have any tooth against me, pluck it out; for it will do you more hurt than all the teeth in your head will do you good." Whereupon Mr. Bacon replied: "Mr. Attorney, I respect you; I fear you not; and the less you speak of your own greatness, the more I will think of it." To which Coke rejoined with his usual arrogance: "I think it scorn to stand upon terms of greatness towards you, who

are less than little—less than the least." Coke, who had no use for
philosophy, could never understand the more subtle Bacon, but the
latter, with his greater imagination and understanding of human
foibles, could appreciate the merits of his rival—even when he was
seeking with every means in his power to undo him. Bacon once even
said that if it had not been for Coke's reports, "the law by this time
had almost been like a ship without ballast." But Coke, when Bacon
presented him with a copy of his immortal *Novum Organum,* wrote on
the title page, which showed a ship in full sail passing through the
Pillars of Hercules:

> It deserves not to be read in schooles,
> But to be freighted in the Ship of Fools.

The rivalry between Coke and Bacon flared anew not long after
the former had become Attorney General; this time the cause was not
a striving for political preferment, but for the hand of a fair lady.
Coke's wife, Bridget, died on June 27, 1598, and was buried with
appropriate regrets and ceremony in the parish church of the town
where Coke had been born; but the desolate husband was practical.
Sir William Hatton, a nephew of Sir Christopher Hatton, who had
been Lord Chancellor, had died on March 12, 1597, and left a dazzling
young widow of twenty, Lady Elizabeth Hatton, who belonged to the
powerful Cecil family. She had wealth and position at Court, as well
as beauty. Both Coke and Bacon sued for her hand. Lady Hatton decided to be practical and marry her older suitor of forty-six, who had
superior wealth and position to offer, rather than the much younger
but impecunious Bacon. But Lady Hatton was not going to make
a laughingstock of herself by going through an elaborate church wedding. She and Coke were married in a private house without a license
or the publication of banns, which was illegal. Coke was, therefore,
threatened with ecclesiastical punishment, and had to make due sub-
mission. The oracle of the common law had to plead ignorance of
ecclesiastical requirements, which may or may not have been a truthful
plea. In any event, the marriage itself proved one of the most tempestuous, ridiculous, and unhappy in history—a lifelong quarrel rather than
a lifelong partnership. Lady Hatton would not even take her husband's
name, which, to annoy him, she persisted in spelling as Cook. The
result was foreordained. It was entirely a marriage of convenience; no
husband and wife could have had less in common. Lady Hatton was

young and gay and enamored of all the pleasures of the Court and the
city of London. Coke was already married to the Lady of the Common
Law.

As long as Bridget had lived, Coke's activity as Attorney General,
whose duty it was to prosecute the enemies of the Crown, particularly
traitors, under conditions that left the unfortunate victims small chance
of escape, must have furnished a strange contrast to his domestic
felicity. He would go home from the rack to a good dinner and the
arms of a loving and amiable wife. But now Coke's domestic infelicity
conformed more fittingly with his days of public ferocity. He now
conducted a series of prosecutions for treason which have never been
praised by any of his biographers. His chief victims were Elizabeth's
favorite, Robert Devereux, the Earl of Essex, who had befriended his
rival; Sir Walter Raleigh; and the conspirators of the Gunpowder Plot.
He represented Essex as the most depraved of men, and continually
taunted him at his trial. "But now," he said, "in God's most just judgment, he of his Earldom shall be 'Robert the Last,' that of the kingdom
thought to be 'Robert the First.'" Although he must have had some
doubt that Sir Walter Raleigh was guilty, he accused him as a "monster" with an English face but a Spanish heart, and behaved toward
the prisoner with such venom that he had to be admonished by one of
the judges: "Good Mr. Attorney, be not so impatient. Give him leave
to speak." Raleigh made such an adroit and appealing defense that
popular opinion turned in his favor, and he escaped the axe for thirteen
years.

Certainly Coke's conduct as a prosecutor can hardly constitute the
basis of his claim to the remembrance of humanity. But his ferocity
can be easily exaggerated. There is no such stain upon his character
as upon Bacon's, who joined in the prosecution of Essex, although the
Earl had generously befriended him and even settled an estate upon
him so that he might pursue the pleasures of philosophy. The fact that
Essex had done his utmost to prevent Coke's appointment as Attorney
General could hardly have been calculated to soften his attack, especially since he had at the same time championed the cause of his hated
rival.

The duties of a prosecutor often leave little room for humanity or
decency, and this was particularly true at the end of the sixteenth
century, when a man on trial for his life was neither allowed counsel
nor permitted to cross-examine the witnesses against him. Even torture

was allowed in the Star Chamber. Coke could justifiably plead that the fault was not his but that of the law of his time. He did what the law allowed, and as a lawyer he served the interests of his client, who, in this phase of his career, happened to be the Crown. To be sure, he gave the Crown the benefit of the doubt when it came to interpreting the commandments of the common law, but sometimes the common law did not speak in clear and unequivocal terms to her servant. After all, it was for the judges, as her oracles, to decide. As a law officer of the Crown, he tolerated, if he did not approve, the infliction of torture, commitments to prison by the Council, and the creation of monopolies, all of which he opposed after he had left the service of the Crown. Coke was all for legality, but is it always easy to say what is lawful and what is unlawful? If a man would attain to the highest favors of his mistress, he must sometimes do discreditable things, and perhaps this is how Coke justified what must have seemed to him the minor inconsistencies of his conduct.

A new and far more satisfying life began for Coke when in 1606 King James finally rewarded him for his services by making him Lord Chief Justice of the Common Pleas. His contemporaries would certainly not have predicted that the Chief Justice would become a faithful servant of the Lady of the Common Law. A judge held office then only at the king's good will and pleasure. He was only a little better than others of the king's servants. It was said at this time that the judges should be like lions—but lions under the throne. This must have seemed the lot of a judge under such a king as James I, who had been called to the throne only a few years before. Coke became a judge when James was bent on putting into effect his ideas of absolutism. He encountered, however, an unflinching opponent in Coke, who proceeded to uphold the integrity and independence of the judicial office even at the cost of his own ultimate ruin. The arrogant servant of the Crown proved quite incorruptible as a judge. There had never been a stranger reversal of character. He wished perhaps to atone for his career as a law officer of the Crown. Perhaps he felt that he had become so wealthy and powerful that he could afford to play an independent hand in the service of his lady. Perhaps, also, the fact that his scheming rival, Bacon, had at last become Solicitor General helped to make Coke incorruptible. He was bound to oppose every wish of James when one of the King's closest advisers was Francis Bacon. Coke, who was no fool, could not but have known that the course on which he had embarked would lead to his fall, but he refused to betray the Lady of the Common Law. Might God preserve him, but he could do no other. *Fiat justitia ruat coelum* (Let justice be done although the heavens fall).

The struggle of Coke as a judge was to vindicate and preserve the jurisdiction of the courts of the common law against the encroachments, as he regarded them, of all those special tribunals that were such a marked feature of the Tudor and Stuart reigns. As has been already related, he was defeated in his attack on the Court of Chancery, and he tolerated the Court of Star Chamber as an extraordinary tribunal. But he had far greater success against the Court of Requests—the minor court of equity—and against the Court of High Commission—that instrument of ecclesiastical "tyranny" so hated by the Puritans—which did not proceed "according to the course of the common law." Having largely fulfilled their historic roles, the Courts of Star Chamber and High Commission had become engines of Stuart tyranny destined for extinction. In Chief Justice Coke the common lawyers found the judge who had the courage of his convictions. The fight with Ellesmere was only an anticlimax of the drama.

In seeking to curb the Crown, Coke employed two ancient weapons in the arsenal of the common law far more effective than the Statutes of Praemunire, which he had caused to be invoked against the Court of Chancery. These were the writ of prohibition and the writ of habeas corpus. The writ of prohibition had always been issued by the common-law courts to inferior tribunals to determine whether they had exceeded their jurisdiction, and had been particularly useful in the campaign of the royal courts to limit the jurisdiction of the feudal and popular courts. The writ of habeas corpus, perhaps the most celebrated writ in the history of English law, since it became the guarantee of the liberty of the subject, was in its origin a method whereby the king put a subject into his jail rather than helped him to get out of it. But the common lawyers in the course of the sixteenth century had begun to convert it into a procedure for testing the unlawfulness of an imprisonment, although much remained to be done to determine the scope of the return under the writ and to assure its issuance by the judges when the courts were not in session. Thus the means of establishing the hegemony of the king's courts were employed in resisting the king himself.

It was by means of writs of prohibition that the Court of Requests had been laid low. An endless number of prohibitions were also issued against the ecclesiastical courts, especially in cases involving the payments of tithes. The common-law courts claimed jurisdiction by virtue of the fact that the tithes were no longer paid in kind but had been commuted by agreement into money payments. Even though, as a result of the fall in the value of money, the tithes were no longer a heavy burden, they were still unpopular with the farmers, who had been taught by the Reformation to rely for salvation upon inward grace rather than upon payments to the clergy. The parsons, who were becoming impoverished, desired, however, a return to payment in kind or commutation in terms of the current value of money. Naturally, they preferred to have such issues tried in the ecclesiastical courts. The common-law courts, however, would issue prohibitions when the ecclesiastical courts sought to assert their jurisdiction.

The assault of Coke was directed particularly against the greatest of the eccelesiastical tribunals, the Court of High Commission, against which were leveled the writs both of prohibition and habeas corpus. The High Commission, in relation to the other ecclesiastical courts, acted in somewhat the same way as the Court of Chancery did in relation to the common-law courts. It had been established as an instrument for consolidating the Elizabethan religious settlement, but now it was attempting to exercise jurisdiction over temporal offenses and interests, and was coming to be thoroughly hated by the Puritans. Since, as a court, the High Commission's rules were fluid and its judgments were not subject to appeal, it was an ideal tool for royal tyranny. Despite James's special love for the Court of High Commission, Coke constantly interfered with its proceedings, and when the King sought to stop his opposition by naming him also a judge of the High Commission, he resolutely refused to sit. Thus, as was said at the time, "the principal feather was plucked from the High Commissioners." After Coke's dismissal the court revived, but it made itself so odious that it was abolished by one of the first acts of the Long Parliament.

Coke displayed his greatest courage, however, in resisting James's attempts to establish his claims to personal government. In all the annals of the common law, there is no more famous story than Coke's own account of a memorable Sunday morning conference between King James and his judges. It occurred probably on November 13, 1608, when, upon the suggestion of Bancroft, His Grace the Archbishop of Canterbury, the judges were summoned before the King. The Archbishop, who was anxious to put an end to their interference with the Court of High Commission, suggested that the King himself could take over any case he pleased. "The judges," he argued, "are but the delegates of Your Majesty and administer the law in your name. What may be done by the agent may be done by the principal." All the judges except Coke assented to this proposition, which would practically have destroyed the supremacy of the common law. But Coke, although he fell upon his knees, declared: "By the law of England, the King in his own person cannot adjudge any case, either criminal, as treason, felony, etc., or betwixt party and party concerning his inheritance or goods; but this ought to be determined and adjudged in some court of justice, according to the law and custom of England." But James shrewdly turned against him Coke's own glorification of the common law as the perfection of reason. "My lords," said the King, "I always thought, and by my soul I have often heard the boast, that your English law was founded upon reason. If that be so, why have not I and others reason as well as you, the judges?" But Coke was not daunted.

May it please Your Majesty [he said] true it is that God has endowed Your Majesty with excellent science, and great endowments of nature; but Your Majesty is not learned in the laws of this your realm of England, and causes which concern the life, or inheritance, or goods, or fortunes of your subjects, are not to be decided by natural reason, but by the artificial reason and judgment of law, which law is an art which requires long study and experience before that a man can attain to the cognizance of it. The law is the golden met-wand and measure to try the causes of Your Majesty's subjects, and it is by the law that Your Majesty is protected in safety and peace.

Whereupon King James fell into a great rage, and exclaimed: "Then I am to be *under* the law—which it is treason to affirm." But Coke replied: "Thus wrote Bracton, *Rex non debet esse sub homine, sed sub Deo et lege.*" (The king ought not to be under any man but under God and the law.)

Coke continued to defend the Lady of the Common Law against every attempt at royal exceptionalism which would have compromised her honor and integrity. He would brook no denial of the supremacy of the common law. He resisted no less vigorously James's attempts to modify the common law by issuing proclamations. To concede the

King's power in this respect would have rapidly led to government by decree. King James was getting more and more impatient with his judicial servant, and when in 1613 the Chief Justice of the Court of King's Bench died, Coke was "promoted" to the vacant office on October 28. It was a "promotion" in the sense that the Chief Justice of the King's Bench took precedence over the Chief Justice of the Common Pleas, but the emoluments of the new post were much less. The change was made at the suggestion of the wily Bacon, who desired to become Attorney General but could achieve his object only by getting the incumbent of the office of Attorney General promoted to Chief Justice of the Common Pleas. Bacon persuaded James that the promotion to a place of lesser profit but greater honor would constitute a warning to Coke and make him turn obsequious.

Little did the King and his adviser know Coke. He became more arrogant than ever. He began to call himself Lord Chief Justice of England although his official title was only Chief Justice of the Court of King's Bench. What was worse, he persisted in refusing to compromise with his conceptions of judicial independence. Bacon, as Attorney General, wished to prosecute for treason a Puritan clergyman by the name of Edmund Peacham, in whose house, when it was raided, was discovered an undelivered and unpublished sermon inveighing against tyrannical rule. The Attorney General, who was not certain that he could get a conviction, sought to get the judges to commit themselves in advance. Two of the judges agreed to give their opinions, but when Bacon consulted Coke, the Chief Justice told him that "such particular and auricular taking of opinions is not according to the custom of this realm," that it was unfair to the accused, and that "the judges ought not to deliver their opinions beforehand in any criminal case that may come before them judicially."

The King's anger was even more boldly disregarded by Coke in the *Case of Commendams,* so called because it involved the right of the King to appoint a clergyman to a benefice *in commendam,* that is, with the right to have its duties performed by deputy. Fearing that his prerogative of appointing to plural benefices might be denied or brought into question, James instructed Bacon to write to the judges to command them not to proceed further until they had consulted with him. Upon the instigation of Coke, however, the judges wrote to His Majesty to tell him that by their oaths they were bound to disregard a private letter from the King in any suit between party and party. James was furious and summoned the judges before the council, where all but one of them fell upon their knees, and, acknowledging their error, begged the King's forgiveness. The obstinate one, of course, was Coke, and his obstinacy was strengthened by the fact that Bacon supported the King in the course of the argument. Coke witheringly told the Attorney General that it was his duty to plead before the judges, not to dispute with them. The King now put this question to the judges: "In a case where the King believes his prerogative or interest concerned, and requires the judges to attend him for their advice, ought they not to stay proceedings till His Majesty has consulted them?" All the judges except Coke cried: "Yes, yes, yes!" But Coke said firmly: "When the case happens, I shall do that which shall be fit for a judge to do."

The relations of James with his Chief Justice of the King's Bench were becoming very strained. Ironically, Coke's last act of defiance had nothing to do with the supremacy of the common law. The immediate occasion of his fall was probably his refusal to hand over the chief clerkship of his court, which was a sinecure paying £4000 a year, to the candidate of Sir George Villiers, who had already become the King's favorite and was to wield power as the Duke of Buckingham. It was the last straw. On June 26, 1616, Coke was suspended from the Privy Council, forbidden to go on circuit, and, like an offending schoolboy, commanded to spend the leisure of this enforced vacation in correcting the "errors" of his *Reports*. On November 14, 1616, he was finally dismissed as Chief Justice of the King's Bench. A contemporary letter-writer thus reported the causes of Coke's downfall: "The common speech is that four P's have overthrown and put him down; that is, Pride, Prohibitions, Praemunire, and Prerogative." It was all the harder for Coke to bear the blow, because only a few months earlier Francis Bacon, the lawyer-philosopher, had achieved the summit of his ambition. He had become Lord Keeper of the Great Seal.

The four years that followed were the most miserable and distracted of Coke's whole life. Some regard them as also the least creditable. It would be easy to describe them as four years of sycophancy. It looks as if Coke, hoping to be restored to royal favor and to resume his place among the mighty of the realm, was ready to stoop to anything to achieve his purpose. Surely there was nothing evil in Coke's attempt to return to power. That he thought he could succeed reflects only upon his judgment. But in those years he was like a man who had been struck by a thunderbolt. In the excitement of the fray, he had perhaps never paused to think of the consequences of his conduct. Perhaps his arrogance had prevented him from conceiving that the King could ever dispense with his services as a judge. Despite some of his acts as a law officer of the Crown, however, he had proved by his career as a judge that he was no mere opportunist, and, to convict him of sycophancy now, it is necessary to assume that he was actuated entirely by opportunist motives. Certainly there is nothing to show that Coke, if forgiven by James, would at last have turned "obsequious." Since the King remained obdurate, Coke's probable repentance can be only pure surmise. Above all, the character of the times in which Coke lived must be taken into consideration before he can be called names. Everybody was a sycophant, more or less, in the days of Stuart absolutism. To be deprived of office and disgraced was too often only the first step toward a charge of treason and the loss of life and estate. It was merely prudent of Coke to behave as if he were no outlaw, as if in fact the royal countenance were not absolutely turned from him.

There was something disgraceful, to be sure, in the means chosen by Coke in seeking restoration to royal favor. But in this almost incredible episode of his life he was at least as much sinned against as sinning. It seems as though Coke, in order to mend his fortunes, plotted to marry his fourteen-year-old daughter, Frances, his only daughter by Lady Hatton, to Sir John Villiers, the dissolute and impecunious brother of the very man who had been at least the immediate occasion of his downfall. Actually the idea was that of the family of the King's favorite. Buckingham must have known perfectly well that Coke's hopes of real political preferment were vain, but the former Chief Justice of the King's Bench was a man of vast wealth, capable of providing his daughter with a handsome marriage settlement. The Villiers family demanded for their precious scion no less than £10,000, and the folly of Coke was simply to consent to this abominable match between a child and a broken, middle-aged nobleman. But Lady Hatton refused to be a party to this disposition of her daughter's hand. Upon Coke's dismissal she had rallied to the support of her husband. But now she issued a declaration of war again, and embarked upon a determined campaign. Taking advantage of her husband's habit of retiring early to bed, she spirited Frances away and hid her at the house of Lord Argyle near Hampton Court. When Coke discovered her whereabouts, he provided himself with a search warrant and, putting himself at the head of a band of retainers armed with pistols, galloped off to recover possession of his daughter. Refused admittance to Lord Argyle's house, he battered his way through the gate and several doors and tore Frances from her mother's arms.

Bacon tried to help Lady Hatton get her daughter back, not in order to be of service to an old flame, but in order to forestall the realization of Coke's ambitions; but he soon discovered that it was a mistake to oppose the wishes of the Villiers family. Frances was duly delivered to her intended spouse, and married off as planned. She subsequently ran off with a more congenial companion. Lady Hatton, of course, now permanently separated from Sir Edward. All that Coke's £10,000 and his lovely daughter brought him was the lifting of his suspension from the Privy Council. When Sir Henry Montagu, Coke's successor as Chief Justice of the King's Bench, was made Lord Treasurer and the vacant place which he had once occupied went to another, it must have become apparent to Coke that he could not expect very much from the King—if he did indeed expect anything.

It may well be that Coke's four years of idleness were not merely an interlude of waiting to test his chances of political preferment. He may have been communing long and ardently with the Lady of the Common Law to determine in what way he could serve her best. It had been his hope and his dream to enthrone her above all other rivals in the state. The courts of the common law were not only to mediate between the king and Parliament but perhaps even to stand above them. The common law was to be a "fundamental" law supreme over both king and Parliament. It was an intoxicating idea and, as the Puritan revolt gained momentum, more and more was heard of "fundamental" law. It must have been in Coke's thoughts quite early in his career as a judge, for in *Dr. Bonham's Case,* which Coke reported, he had gone so far as to declare:

And it appears in our books, that in many cases, the common law will controul acts of Parliament, and sometimes adjudge them to be utterly void: for when an act of Parliament is against common right or reason, or repugnant, or impossible to be performed, the common law will controul it, and adjudge such act to be void.

This dictum was to assume enormous importance in the subsequent history of constitutionalism, but in the period when it was uttered it was regarded as one of the "errors" of Coke's *Reports.* Very well, then,

if the common law was not to be supreme, it was at least to be preserved from violation by the king. To work for the supremacy of
Parliament was to renounce, as a matter of form, the supremacy of
the common law. But at least Parliament, which represented the people, would not ride roughshod over the common law. In theory the
supremacy of Parliament would mean an unlimited power to change
the common law, but in practice it would be left virtually untouched.
If Parliament was to be allowed to change the common law, there must
be a common law for Parliament to change.

The end of the year 1620 coincided not only with the disposition
by James of the position of Lord Treasurer, but with arrangements to
call a new Parliament. There had been no Parliament since 1614, but
James could no longer get along without one. Coke decided to join the
parliamentary opposition. The die at length was cast. James had undoubtedly made a bad mistake by driving such a redoubtable figure
into the camp of the enemy. Coke was then approaching seventy, but
in full command of all his powers as a politician and a lawyer. He had
never really been an enemy of the royal prerogative, but he had always
been determined to check its excesses.

Coke, the Parliamentarian, now took his place in the galaxy of
leaders who had declared war on Stuart absolutism. With Hampden,
Eliot, and Pym, Coke took his place among the architects of the
Glorious Revolution of 1688. He sat in the stirring Parliaments of 1621,
1624, 1625, and 1628. He was again in the midst of great events. In
the Parliament of 1621 he had his revenge on Bacon. He who laughs
last laughs best. The lawyer-philosopher was discovered to be a taker
of bribes and was driven from office as Lord Chancellor of England.
The Parliament of 1621 also made the famous protestation of its rights
and liberties, the entry of which James with his own hands tore from
its journal. It had been moved by Coke. Yet, in this very same Parliament, Coke led the prayer for the King with tears in his eyes. Was it as
a father who weeps for a wayward son? On March 27, 1625, James
died, but the struggle continued against his son Charles.

Many a philippic was thundered in those Parliaments against the
evils of monopolies. The days of mercantilism were numbered, and an
emerging middle class was beginning to talk of the advantages of free
trade. "Freedom of trade," declared Coke, "is the life of trade; and all
monopolies and restriction of trade do overflow trade." There was to
be freedom to buy and sell. But there was also to be freedom from

arbitrary search and seizure and freedom from arrest except for a lawful cause. There could be no security of property without security of the person. The writ of habeas corpus was to be given new life. Again Coke struck the keynote: "No restraint," he said, "be it ever so little, but is imprisonment." There must be an end to arbitrary power: "That power, which is above the law, is not fit for a king to ask, or the people to yield." Who was to be the guardian of all law? Coke proclaimed: "The liberties and privileges of Parliament are the mother and life of all laws." But was there not also a fundamental law? Surely, if it was not the common law itself, Magna Charta was such a law. Under the ministrations of Coke, the feudal document was transformed into a charter of national liberties. "Magna Charta," he thundered in the Parliament of 1628, "is such a fellow that he will have no sovereign."

The Parliament of 1628 was the climax of Coke's career as a member of the House of Commons. It was in this Parliament that Coke moved the adoption of the famous Petition of Right as another article of the fundamental law, second only to Magna Charta. This guaranteed the people against those abuses which had become the most baneful aspects of Stuart tyranny. These were the levying of forced loans and benevolences, unlawful imprisonments in the name of the king and the Privy Council, and the billeting of soldiers in time of peace. After a stubborn fight, King Charles was forced to give the royal assent to the momentous document. That night there were bonfires all over London. The results of the Glorious Revolution of 1688 were ultimately to be embodied in another constitutional document known as the Bill of Rights. Magna Charta, the Petition of Right, and the Bill of Rights constitute the English political trinity of fundamental law.

During his career as a parliamentarian, the royal party supplied many proofs of its appreciation of Coke's importance to the popular cause. On December 27, 1621, Coke was lodged in the Tower and was imprisoned for almost seven months, until the King and Buckingham decided that it would be impolitic to keep him there any longer. In 1624, the King, in order to keep him out of Parliament, informed Coke, now an old man of seventy-two who had never been out of England and had never been on a sea voyage, that he intended to send him on a commission to Ireland, but at the last moment decided that the step would be unwise. In 1625, however, again in order to prevent him from sitting in Parliament, Coke was made Sheriff of Buckinghamshire, and he who had issued writs to all the sheriffs of the realm was actually reduced to the necessity of receiving them. What was worse, it cost Coke money, for the sheriff had to supply lavish entertainment.

The Parliament of 1628 was Coke's last appearance in public life. The cantankerous old lawyer, who had become a champion of the people, now retired to his house at Stoke Poges. He still had six years of life before him. He had no close and intimate friends, for his was a nature that had no need for the warmth of friendship. He had lived through exciting times, but he had no ambitions to write an auto-biography. There was for him only one solace. She was not Lady Hatton, from whom he had been long separated, and from whom he could hardly have expected contributions to his repose. She was, of course, the Lady of the Common Law. He was now free at last to commune with her and to communicate to the world her true teachings, uninfluenced by the hopes of gain or political preferment. So he sat down to work again on his *Reports* and on his *Institutes of the Laws of England.* The first and most famous part, known as *Coke upon Little-ton,* was published in 1628, but its other three parts were not published until long after his death. Coke may have been thinking of these labors when he wrote that "as out of the old fields must come the new corn, so do our old books excellently expound and express the matter, as the laws holden at this day."

Coke, as a writer, was technical, pedantic, and crabbed. The *Institutes* cannot be recommended as exhilarating reading. But Coke was an Elizabethan, too, and every now and then he broke forth into the magnificence of Elizabethan speech. Some of his phrases and sentences have been enshrined in Bartlett, and the familiar quotations are repeated in daily speech by many who are unaware of their origin. When you say that "corporations have no souls," or that "every man's house is his castle," you are echoing Coke. When you speak, perhaps ironically, of "those two great pronouns, *meum* and *tuum,*" you are surprisingly enough quoting Coke. The ruling passion of Coke's life is revealed in such a musing as this: "The knowledge of the law is like a deep well, out of which each man draweth according to the strength of his understanding." He spoke, too, of "the gladsome light of jurisprudence." The law officer of the Crown had at least a glim-mering of the claims of humanity when he spoke of "that cursed tree of the gallows." Of special interest are those sentences that are ob-viously inspired by the incidents of Coke's own tempestuous career.

The rallying cries of the defenders of the common law are implicit in such sentences as "Nothing that is contrary to reason is consonant to law"; or, "Reason is the life of the law"; and, "The common law is the perfection of reason." The great stake of the constitutional struggle is apparent in his dictum: "Certainty is the mother of quiet and repose." Coke, the judge, spoke from experience when he said, "The law is the rule, but it is mute: the King judgeth by his judges and they are the speaking law." He left no doubt, too, as to which one of the courts of the common law was the most important to the king's subjects. It was only the Court of Common Pleas that he called "the lock and key of the common law." There is a delectable irony in Coke's observation: "The King can never be poor when his subjects are rich." Finally Coke, the parliamentarian, speaks in one of the quaintest of his dicta: "The Parliament being, as hath been said, *commune concilium,* every member of the house being a counsellor, should have three properties of the elephant: first, that he hath no gall; secondly, that he is inflexible and cannot bow; thirdly, that he is of a most ripe and perfect memory." There is one reference in the *Institutes* that is unexpected. He speaks of James as a king "of famous and ever blessed memory."

Coke's own quiet and repose were disturbed only once during his last years of retirement. When there was a rumor in 1631 that he was about to publish a book, Charles I, observing that Coke had become "too great an oracle amongst the people," ordered his house to be ransacked, and his books and papers were carried off. Coke had certainly become an oracle. Himself an Anglican, he had become a cherished hero of the Puritans. Even Ben Jonson and John Milton were writing verses to praise him. If Coke had sinned as a law officer of the Crown, it is important to remember that he was forgiven by his own generation. But his end was near. He died on September 3, 1634, at Stoke Poges, with this prayer upon his lips: "Thy will be done, thy kingdom come." He was buried in the church of Tittleshall in Norfolk. In his last illness he had achieved in a sense his greatest triumph. He was tenderly nursed by his wayward daughter, Frances, whom he had sacrificed at a time that must have seemed long ago.

The Glorious Revolution of 1688 finally curbed the king. It finally also established the supremacy of law in subjecting the king's officers to the common law. But, ironically, it disappointed Coke's fondest dream by establishing as the basic axiom of the English constitution the supremacy of Parliament. In every state, one of the three great powers of government, the executive, the legislative, and the judicial, must necessarily be supreme, or the state will fall into anarchy. In England the struggle had been between the courts and the Crown, but it was Parliament that finally won. The sovereignty of the British Parliament is expressed in the celebrated saying that it is so omnipotent that it can do everything except change a man into a woman. Coke himself recognized the triumph of Parliament when, as one of its leaders, he regretfully repudiated his dictum in *Dr. Bonham's Case.* "Of the power and jurisdiction of the Parliament," he declared, "for the making of Laws in proceeding by Bill, it is so transcendent and absolute, as it cannot be confined either for causes or persons within any bounds." The principle of the independence of the judge, for which Coke had so valiantly contended, was recognized in England by a provision of the Act of Settlement, which guaranteed the tenure of judges during their good behavior.

It is an obvious truth that men in all ages and climes have yearned for the supremacy of law. Certainly the quest for freedom is not a peculiar characteristic of the English spirit or a product of the genius of the common law. The ideas of great men, however, almost always have some strange vicissitudes. Since the French Revolution, continental European democracy had been taking over English libertarianism, including trial by jury—which has indeed become almost a universal institution—but it had been able to do so despite the fact that in theory it preserved the Byzantine tradition of the supremacy of the executive. This was done by creating special administrative courts, theoretically a part of the executive but actually independent of executive influence. The function of these courts was to guard the rights and liberties of the citizens, which were, by virtue of the dogma of the supremacy of the executive, beyond the cognizance of the ordinary courts, which administered only the civil law in cases involving controversies between individuals.

Coke's dream of judicial supremacy was realized in the wilderness of America, which had become the refuge of the Puritan fathers. Here ultimately developed a tendency to escape from the jurisdiction of the ordinary courts by creating more and more special administrative commissions to deal with new social problems arising from the concentration of wealth and the needs of the masses. It is enough to say here that in this new struggle Coke has become the sport of factions, and his fulminations against the extraordinary tribunals of Tudor and Stuart days, which were the bulwarks of royal tyranny, have become the gospel of those servants of corporate wealth and privilege who attack administrative commissions existing in a constitutional scheme in which the judicial rather than the executive power has triumphed.

The issues of Coke's time are still with us, even if in new forms, and the ordeal of Fascism has brought new questionings. The world that has fought for freedom and the supremacy of law grows more sophisticated and skeptical. There has long been a growing suspicion that the intoxication of libertarianism is not enough. The supremacy of law is truly a great ideal. It is right to defend the inviolability of "the law of the land." It is well to insist that every judge shall be secure in his tenure and that every official shall be responsible to every citizen for his wrongs. It is of supreme importance to cherish the individual civil liberties. But it is well to remember, too, that they have their limitations; that the impartiality of judges cannot be guaranteed merely by acts of tenure; that the supremacy of law only too often conceals the injustice of the individual rules of law; that the supremacy of law does not itself guarantee the good life, but only permits a continuation of the struggle to realize the good life. We should like to get done those things that we seem free to do but that always somehow elude our grasp. We have learned to our sorrow that civil liberty is not the same as economic liberty. We still struggle with "those two great pronouns, *meum* and *tuum*."

Sir William Blackstone

LAW AND POPULARIZATION

IF THERE IS ONE BOOK IN THE HISTORY OF THE LAW THAT IS KNOWN to every educated man, whether he be lawyer or layman, it is Sir William Blackstone's *Commentaries on the Laws of England*. It was the first attempt to popularize a mature legal system, and so successful was the attempt that the book became a universal best seller. It brought its fortunate author at least £14,000 in royalties, which in terms of modern purchasing power would amount to almost half a million dollars. The *Commentaries* adorned the shelves of every English gentleman's library in the eighteenth century, whether he actually read it or not, and copies were to be found even in the backwoods of America. For many generations it constituted the staple of legal education, and was the constant companion of every practicing lawyer, as well as the only standard reference work of the curious but bewildered layman.

The *Commentaries* constitutes the great classic of the common law, and Blackstone is its expositor. While he had neither a very original nor a creative mind, he had in their highest perfection the gifts of the popularizer. Such originality as he had lay in his conception of the law as a fit subject of popular instruction. When it is said, however, that he popularized English law, it must not be supposed that he wrote for the chimney sweep or the stable boy, or even for the coachman or the petty tradesman. His object was to explain English law to the lord, the squire, and the gentleman. He became a classic because he delineated the institutional scheme of the aristocratic oligarchy that ruled England in the eighteenth century. In gratitude, the gentry made him famous. The time was ripe for a sort of stocktaking of the common law, which had fulfilled the predestined lines of its evolution. The accomplishment of the Glorious Revolution of 1688 had ushered in an era of Tory complacency, which made it natural to admire and explain rather than to question and change. The first British Empire had been created, and all of England's chief rivals for colonies had been ingloriously defeated. The Commercial Revolution was completed, and, while the changes that were to lead to the Industrial Revolution were already under way, it still remained in the future. The steady growth of the spirit of commercial as well as scientific rationality made it seem particularly desirable that a knowledge of the law should be diffused at least among the ruling classes, while the very permanence of the common law seemed to augur well for the successful execution of such an enterprise.

In truth, the classic common law needed explanation. Swift was not indulging the latitude of the satirist when he said that the law was a maze of unintelligible pedantry, nor was Gibbon exaggerating when he observed that law was "a mysterious science and a profitable trade." The common law undoubtedly justified both observations. The very classicism of the common law betokened its complexity and esoteric character. It was now absolutely beyond the comprehension of the layman, and had become the highly prized and exclusive possession of a professional class. Although the common law had begun to be professionalized as early as the thirteenth century, it still remained for some time a subject of popular knowledge. As late as the fifteenth century, the better families sought to preserve at least some acquaintance, however casual, with the common law. In 1445, for instance, Agnes Paston, of the same family as Coke's first wife, wrote to her son Edmund: "I grete yow wel, and avyse yow to thynkk onis of the daie of youre fadris counseyle to lerne the lawe, for he seyde maine tymis that ho so ever schulde dwelle at Paston, schulde have nede to conne defende hym selfe." In the seventeenth century the common law had become so recondite a science that it was impossible even for the well-born and educated squire to "lerne the lawe."

The classical common law, like the classical Roman law, was a rich treasury of precedents, which had not yet been generalized into basic principles. These had to be extracted from the various forms of action and rescued from the toils of a system of pleading so baffling that a large percentage of cases was lost without any decision on the merits. The Englishman was, however, far worse off than the Roman. In Rome the professional class had always retained something of its early amateur character, and the law was taught in professional schools. The received Roman law of the Middle Ages was everywhere taught in the universities, including those in England, but not so the national common law. The insular common law was a subject of instruction only in the Inns of Court, where the practicing lawyers taught the next generation of lawyers, and that very badly. In the eighteenth century legal education had degenerated to such an extent that the student at the Inns of Court had to have a good stomach rather than a good mind. He had merely to keep a stated number of terms and to eat a prescribed number of dinners at each term, which came in all to sixty. If he decided really to practice law, he had to learn the tricks of the trade in the office of a practitioner, painfully copying deeds and pleadings and attending the sessions of the courts of the common law.

In this desperate situation Blackstone appeared almost as a *deus ex machina*. He came as a deliverer to lead the English squire out of the trackless wilderness of the common law. He was ideally suited by fortune, character, and temperament for the mission. Allowing for the accidents of human existence, his life and work fall into a consistent pattern. It is somehow rather amusing to think that the teacher of the common law, although he would still have been a teacher, very narrowly escaped the prospect of devoting his life to the teaching of the civil law. In fact, the *Commentaries on the Laws of England* owed a great deal in method and inspiration to the traditions of the civil law and to the example of the institutional treatises of the continental teachers of natural law, in which legal treatises had always played a greater role than decided cases. The great classic of the common law was really a civilian production. Thus did the civil law take sweet though belated revenge upon the one great country of Europe that had escaped a general reception of the Roman law.

William Blackstone was fortunate in the very misfortune of his birth. He was born not into the ruling oligarchy but into the family of a modest silk merchant of Cheapside, and he might have spent his life behind a counter if it had not been for the fact of his posthumous birth. There is no need to speculate whether this would have been a more useful life. There is no doubt, however, that it was better for him to have been born in Cheapside than in Mayfair. If he had been born into the charmed circle of governing families he might have become no more than a justice of the peace and spent his leisure in fox hunting rather than in writing, and he would have taken the social values of his class so much for granted that he would never have been moved to articulate enthusiasm. It is better, perhaps, for the popularizer not to be to the manner born but to be on the outside looking in.

It happened that early in the eighteenth century a gentleman by the name of Lovelace Bigg resided at Chilton Foliot in the county of Wiltshire, where he was the squire of the parish and the owner of the manor house. He had in all twelve children, of whom the third son, Thomas, went to London and became a physician. While there he made the acquaintance of one John Blackstone, an apothecary of Newgate Street, who also hailed from Wiltshire. It was not long before John Blackstone's son Charles and Dr. Thomas Bigg had become close friends—despite the fact that Charles was in trade and kept a small silk shop in Cheapside Street. Thomas Bigg's sister Mary made occasional visits to her brother's house in London, where one day she was introduced to Charles Blackstone. The silk merchant and the squire's daughter fell in love and were soon married. Of this romantic union, which had already been thrice blessed, William Blackstone was posthumously born on July 10, 1723.

Uncle Thomas stepped nobly into the breach and practically adopted the fatherless boy, taking care of his education and general welfare. "Billy" turned out to be a very studious boy, and his uncle was always bringing him books to read. When he was seven years of age, his uncle placed him in the Charterhouse School. At the age of twelve, William became more dependent than ever on his Uncle Thomas. His mother died and he was completely orphaned. The experience made him draw away from other boys and avoid their games and athletics. He became very shy and diffident and lived only in the world of books. He made an outstanding record at the Charterhouse School, becoming head of the school before he left at the age of fifteen. He delivered an oration commemorating its founder, and also won a prize medal for an oration on Milton.

The youthful Blackstone now entered Pembroke College, Oxford, which Dr. Johnson once called "a nest of singing birds" in tribute to the large number of poets and men of letters it produced. While at college Blackstone engaged in athletics no more than at the Charterhouse, although he did indulge in walking, which he enjoyed. He was simply not a good mixer. His diffidence made him look either proud and unapproachable or dull and sullen. The only consolation he could find was in his love of reading. As a boy he had liked Virgil but detested Cicero, probably because he was a lawyer. Even before entering

Oxford he had read all of Shakespeare's plays, on which later in life
he wrote critical notes which were published in an edition of the
bard's works. Of course, among essayists he admired Addison and
among poets Pope, who reigned supreme in this prosy age of the heroic
couplet. Blackstone, as we shall see, paid Pope the questionable homage
of imitation. In the eighteenth century, logic and mathematics were
also very much the vogue, and Blackstone loved both. His interest in
mathematics led him to study architecture, and before he was twenty
he had produced a treatise called "Elements of Architecture," which,
however, was never published.

Blackstone's ambitions, to be sure, may seem to have had nothing to
do with the rescue of the common law, but in fact they were vital. The
Commentaries could never have been written by a mere common lawyer
who had embraced the profession without regrets. He had to be a man
who had at least flirted with the muses but had become discouraged
too early. After all, Blackstone reasoned, he had to get on in the
world, and if he could not be a successful architect or poet or Shake-
spearean critic, he would have to enter one of the honorable professions. It would not do for a son of Cheapside merely to sulk and
nurse his spiritual wounds. At least lawyers, too, dealt with words. So
in the late fall of 1741, Blackstone, having gone through this period
of unhappy soul-searching and doubt, decided to become a lawyer, and,
while he still remained in attendance at Oxford, he entered the Middle
Temple. In taking what seemed the first step in leaving the world of
Oxford, which he loved, for the alien and uncongenial world of Westminster Hall, which he could not but have despised, he was moved to
write a poem in the heroic couplets of the time, which he entitled
"The Lawyer's Farewell to His Muse." He would have to justify his
stay in "the nest of singing birds." The disappointed poet about to
become the legal neophyte struck his lyre and in mournful accents
sang his woe. He compared himself to a wretch about to suffer the
unhappy fate of exile:

> As, by some tyrant's stern command,
> A wretch forsakes his native land,
> In foreign climes condemn'd to roam
> An endless exile from his home . . .

He would have to part from the "gay queen of fancy, and of art." He
would have to bid her "a long a last adieu," for

> The wrangling Courts, and stubborn law,
> To smoke, and crowds, and cities draw;
> There selfish Faction rules the day,
> And Pride and Avarice throng the way;
> Diseases taint the murky air,
> And midnight conflagrations glare . . .

There the joys of literature had no place:

> Shakespeare no more, thy silvan son,
> Nor all the art of Addison,
> Pope's heav'n-strung lyre, nor Waller's ease
> Nor Milton's mighty self must please:
> Instead of these, a formal band
> In furs and coifs around me stand,
> With sounds uncouth, and accents dry,
> That grate the soul of harmony.
> Each pedant sage unlocks his store
> Of mystic, dark, discordant lore;
> And points with tottering hand the ways
> That lead me to the thorny maze.

But stay! There was a compensation for him who stoically endured this "mystic, dark, discordant lore." In the "winding, close retreat" of Westminster Hall JUSTICE kept "the wond'ring world in awe":

> Oh! Let me pierce the secret shade,
> Where dwells the venerable maid!
> There humbly mark, with reverent awe,
> The guardian of Britannia's Law
> Unfold with joy her sacred page
> (The united boast of many an age,
> Where mix'd though uniform, appears
> The wisdom of a thousand years),
> In that pure spring the bottom view,
> Clear, deep, and regularly true,
> And other doctrines thence imbibe,
> That lurk within the sordid scribe;
> Observe how parts with parts unite
> In one harmonious rule of right;
> See countless wheels distinctly tend,
> By various laws, to one great end;
> While mighty Alfred's piercing soul
> Pervades, and regulates the whole.

Blackstone never quite lost that fair vision of ideal justice during the five years that he spent at the Middle Temple, although his worst premonitions of the "mystic dark, discordant lore" were amply fulfilled. He studied all the ancient worthies of the common law, including, of course, Littleton and *Coke upon Littleton*, which he thought "too much for Hercules." There were at least thoughts of distraction. He wrote a letter to an uncle, Seymour Richmond, to tell him that a young lady who was staying in the house where he roomed on Arundel Street was, despite her fortune, no rival to *Coke upon Littleton*, because, verily, she had "ye complexion also of a Jew." But, apart from this bit of persiflage, the same letter already gave a hint of the program of the future commentator. He explained what was wrong with the common law: it violated the profound sense of order that dominated the mind of the amateur architect. He wrote:

I have sometimes thought that ye Common Law, as it stood in Littleton's Days, resembled a regular Edifice: where ye Apartments were properly disposed, leading one into another without confusion; where every part was subservient to ye whole, all uniting in one beautiful Symmetry: & every Room had its distinct Office allotted to it. But as it is now, swoln, shrunk, curtailed, enlarged, altered & mangled by various & contradictory Statutes, &c; it resembles ye same Edifice, with many of its most useful parts pulled down, with preposterous Additions in Other Places, of different Materials & coarse Workmanship: according to ye Whim or Prejudice or private Convenience of ye Builders. By wch means the Communication of ye Parts is destroyed, & their Harmony quite Annihilated; & now it remains a huge, irregular Pile, with many noble Apartments, tho awkwardly put together, & some of them of no visible Use at present. But if one desires to know why they were built, to what End or Use, how they Communicated with ye rest, ye like; he must necessarily carry in his Head ye Model of ye old House, wch will be ye only Clew to guide him thro' this new Labyrinth.

There was still Oxford, God be praised! Two years after he was admitted into the Inner Temple he was elected into the Society of All Souls College, of which he was afterwards made a fellow. On June 12, 1745, at the age of twenty-two, the aspirant for the honors of the common law treacherously took a degree at Oxford as Bachelor of Civil Law. In spirit at least he remained a civilian and an Oxford don all his life. He was never so happy as when he was serving the college.

On November 28, 1746, however, he was called to the bar at the Middle Temple. He hunted all over London for a man of law who would give him employment and allow him to serve an apprenticeship in his chosen profession, but there was not a single one in the great city that would have him. He had perforce to practice by himself; but, alas, for years hardly a client knocked on his door. After seven years at the bar, which were years of endless waiting, he had argued only three cases. Men of affairs seemed to have no confidence in him. His voice, as well as his manner, lacked cordiality, and he did not inspire confidence. He had been an involuntary and embarrassed orator as a boy, and, when he entered a courtroom and beheld the gowned and bewigged judges on the bench, he must have invariably had an unnerving vision of ideal justice, for he would suffer an immediate attack of stage fright, and his mouth would become so dry that he could hardly speak. Perhaps his failure was also due to the fact that prospective clients instinctively felt that he was too honest. He once said: "I would rather starve than stoop to the low standards of some members of my profession." Thus did Blackstone fulfill the second condition of his success as a popularizer of the common law: he was a complete and abysmal failure as a practicing lawyer.

Fortunately, Blackstone was not the sort of person who burns his bridges behind him. He still had his fellowship at All Souls, and for the better part of seven years he puttered about at Oxford performing happily the manifold duties of a devoted don. He did all sorts of dull administrative jobs, which paid him a small stipend. He undertook, for instance, to put the college finances into order and to untangle the affairs of the University press. He even prepared a study of collateral consanguinity to help determine the right of admission to the college, which according to its charter depended on relationship to its founder. Absorbed in these occupations, he almost ceased to attend the courts. He added another small stipend to his income when, in the midst of this phase of his career as a don, he was appointed Recorder of Wallingford, a somnolent town in the county of Berkshire. This petty office, which came to him when it was resigned by his uncle, Seymour Richmond, was his only direct contact with the law in this unexciting period of his life.

Blackstone, however, lived the life of a busy practicing lawyer vicariously. He was fortunate enough to secure the friendship of William Murray, who was to become the Earl of Mansfield and Chief

Justice of the King's Bench, and in this capacity to earn the title of father of modern commercial law. Mansfield was a judicial reformer who succeeded in large measure not only in integrating the law merchant (which since medieval times had had an independent existence) into the body of the common law but also in infusing the common law itself with some degree of commercial rationality. He even attempted the innovation of abolishing the requirement of a "consideration" to support an informal contract. The common law did not recognize such a contract as binding unless some "good and valuable consideration" had passed, but in most cases this "consideration" had become a mere form, and Mansfield thought that it would better serve the purposes of commerce if it were abolished altogether. He reasoned that any promise that was given with the intention of contracting a binding obligation should be enforced. This idea, which had a civil-law origin, was, however, too revolutionary for the common lawyers. Mansfield failed, too, in his attempts to fuse the separate systems of law and equity. In all his strivings, he sought to give England not only a unified legal system but one that would meet the commercial needs of the times. He was the embodiment of the spirit of the Commercial Revolution and made a lasting impression not only on the commercial law of England but on that of all Europe.

The friendship of Blackstone and Mansfield was a union of opposites. Blackstone admired in his friend everything he himself lacked. William Murray was brilliant and vivacious, a good talker and a good mixer, toward whom men of affairs naturally gravitated. His social gifts were matched by his capacities, and he obtained an enormous practice at the bar. He came from Scotland but rapidly overcame the prejudice that in those days attached to the country of his origin. Dr. Johnson had Mansfield in mind when he made his famous quip that you can do a great deal with a Scotsman if you can only catch him young.

Murray attempted to introduce Blackstone to London society as well as to further his career. On one occasion Murray took his discouraged friend to a rather gala party at one of the Inns of Court. There Blackstone met and danced with a cruel charmer for whom he conceived an immediate infatuation. When she spurned the briefless barrister, he was for a long time inconsolable. It was the one really romantic adventure in Blackstone's life, but it hardly served to give him confidence in himself. He resumed his life at Oxford, determined not to expose himself again to the wiles and snares of the female of the species.

The year 1753 was the turning point of Blackstone's life. Mansfield then performed a rare service for Blackstone: he gave his friend some good advice after he had failed in an attempt to secure his advancement. The position of Regius Professor of Civil Law had fallen vacant at Oxford. It was subject to disposal by the Duke of Newcastle, the rather sorry Prime Minister of George II, and Mansfield made every conceivable effort to secure the post for Blackstone. He thought that he had succeeded and so informed his friend, who naturally was jubilant. The Duke of Newcastle wanted to make sure, however, that if any conflict arose between the government and the University the Regius Professor would support the government, and for this reason he summoned Blackstone to an interview. "I presume," said the Duke to the candidate, "in the event of any political agitation in the University, that your exertions may be relied on on behalf of the government." The candidate replied, however, rather irrelevantly: "Your Grace may be assured that I will discharge my duty of giving law lectures to the best of my poor ability." The Duke, however, had little interest in the law lectures per se, and he pressed the candidate further: "And your duty in the other branch, too?" Blackstone only bowed coldly. The next day the Duke announced the appointment of an ignorant political hack by the name of Dr. Jenner. Blackstone in the agony of his disappointment fell into a violent rage, but he could reasonably have expected no other result. He loved Oxford too much to have promised to betray it, and although he had not put this feeling into words, the Duke had readily surmised it from his manner. It was only another illustration of the honesty that had prevented Blackstone's success at the bar.

The advice that Murray now gave to his downhearted and bitterly disappointed friend was to forget the Duke of Newcastle and his Dr. Jenner and give a course of lectures at Oxford anyway. Since to attempt to lecture on the civil law would be to compete with a course already given at the University, which would be impossible, why not, said the shrewd Murray, lecture "on his own foundation" on the common law, which had never been taught at any English university? The novelty of this enterprise would be sensational enough to insure its success. For once good advice was taken. The arrangements with the

University authorities, who were not ungrateful for Blackstone's administrative labors, were rapidly made, and on June 23, 1753—a truly momentous day—a printed announcement of the proposed course of lectures on the laws of England was circulated at the University. The course was to be completed in one year, and the fee would be six guineas. The announcement thus explained the lecturer's purpose:

> This course is calculated not only for the Use of such Gentlemen of the University, as are more immediately designed for the Profession of the Common Law; but for such others also, as are desirous to be in some degree acquainted with the Constitution and Polity of their own Country.
>
> To this end it is proposed to lay down a general and comprehensive Plan of the Laws of England; to deduce their History; to enforce and illustrate the leading Rules and fundamental Principles; and to compare them with the Laws of Nature and of other Nations; without entering into practical Niceties; or the minute Distinctions of particular Cases.

The lectures appear to have met with considerable success, enough at least to encourage the lecturer to resume his attendance at the courts, in a renewed effort to secure practice, and to repeat the course the following year. It can hardly be said that Blackstone was an inspired lecturer. His own character was too phlegmatic to inspire his students with enthusiasm. One of his later students was the great law reformer, Jeremy Bentham, who recorded for posterity his opinion that Blackstone was a "formal, precise and affected lecturer—just what you would expect from the character of his writings—cold, reserved and wary, exhibiting a frigid pride."

James Clitherow, who was later to become Blackstone's brother-in-law, tells us that his lectures were crowded. They were attended, as Clitherow says, "by a very crowded class of young men of the first families, characters and hopes," and even by several students from colonial America. The need for the lectures was, however, so great that their success is not necessarily a tribute to the effectiveness of the lecturer. This much is apparent even if Bentham's opinion is discounted as prejudiced. Blackstone himself was reasonably well satisfied with the success of his lectures, for some five years later the son of the Cheapside silk merchant indulged in the self-encomium that his lectures "were favoured with the most diligent attendance, and pursued with the most unwearied application, by those of the noblest birth and most ample patrimony."

There is some doubt, nevertheless, that the lectures would necessarily have led to the *Commentaries*. But fortune was on Blackstone's side. On June 5, 1756, there died a gentleman by the name of Charles Viner who, although he had never been called to the bar, had been a student at the Middle Temple, and had devoted fifty years of his life to the compilation and publication of a collection of legal materials in twenty-three folio volumes, entitled *A General Abridgment of Law and Equity*. Viner himself was hardly much more than a hack, but he must have had a vision of more exciting vistas in popular education, for by his will be bequeathed to the University of Oxford the copyright of his *Abridgment* and other property to the value of £12,000, on condition that the University would establish a professorship of the laws of England. Blackstone was not mentioned by name in the will, but it has been asserted that Viner was moved to make his bequest by reason of the success of Blackstone's lectures, and that he actually desired that Blackstone should be the first incumbent of the new professorship. At any rate, the University authorities so interpreted his wishes, for on October 20, 1758, Blackstone was unanimously elected the first Vinerian Professor of the Laws of England. The appointment was for life or during good behavior, and Blackstone was to receive £200 a year for reading sixty lectures annually on the laws of England. Thus did the fortune of the hack make possible the elegance of the *Commentaries*.

On October 25, 1758, Blackstone gave his inaugural lecture as Vinerian Professor. It was later prefixed to the *Commentaries* as an "Introductory Discourse on the Study of the Law." It is not only an admirable discussion of the program of Blackstone's magnum opus but a most adroit and ingenious piece of salesmanship. It set out to convince every English gentleman that at least some knowledge of the laws of England was absolutely indispensable to him. It is true, conceded Blackstone, that the law had "generally been imputed (however unjustly) of a dry and unfruitful nature." But it could be made attractive, he insisted, by avoiding minute technicalities and sticking to broad general principles. Could the English gentleman afford to neglect that science which was to be "the guardian of his natural rights and the rule of his civil conduct"? No doubt still thinking with some asperity of Dr. Jenner, but exploiting also the sentiments of English patriotism, Blackstone declared that if an Englishman had to choose between ig-

norance of the civil law and ignorance of the common law, he had
"better be a stranger to the Roman than the English institutions."
True, the civil law was a great system, but "we must not carry our
veneration so far as to sacrifice our Alfred and Edward to the manes
of Theodosius and Justinian," unless, indeed, "we can also prefer the
despotic monarchy of Rome and Byzantium, for whose meridians the
former were calculated, to the free constitution of Britain, which the
latter are adapted to perpetuate."

How was the English gentleman to be made acquainted with the
fundamental principles of the common law? Blackstone would supply
him with only "a general map of the law," and would avoid, for instance,
"the subtle distinctions incident to landed property." He need not
concern himself with "the manual labor of copying the trash of an
office." He was assured that "that knowledge which is fit for a person
of birth or condition may be learned in a single year, without neglecting
his other improvements." Thus, education in the common law would
be a painless process. Even more important from the point of view of
the aristocracy, this education could be acquired without danger of
social contamination. At Oxford, unlike in the Inns of Court, "gentlemen may here associate with gentlemen of their own rank and degree."
Among persons of inferior rank Blackstone included "those of the
learned professions."

But if Blackstone was going to avoid technicalities, would the
learning the gentlemen acquired be of any real practical use to them?
They could not be their own lawyers, and if they became involved in
legal difficulties they would still have to employ counsel. Therefore,
the only practical use they could make of their legal education would
lie in their ability to keep some check upon those who represented
them in litigation. This may sound like an aspersion upon the honesty
of the members of the English bar, but it is precisely what Blackstone
had in mind. While he admitted that a thorough comprehension of the
minute distinctions of landed property would be impossible for "gentlemen of independent estates and fortune . . . yet still the understanding of a few leading principles, relating to estates and conveyancing,
may form some check and guard upon a gentleman's inferior agents, and
preserve him at least from very gross and notorious imposition."

Although Blackstone had aspired to be a poet, he did not accept the
dictum: "Give me the making of the songs of the people, and I care not

who makes their laws." He displayed his greatest ingenuity in explaining precisely why every man of substance from the greatest lord and squire to the meanest professional man should be interested in acquiring some knowledge of the laws of England. Even if he was not faced by the problem of keeping an eye on some rascally lawyer, he would find that it paid. The lord, the knight, the burgess who sat in Parliament, could surely profit by a knowledge of the common law. As Blackstone exclaimed: "And how unbecoming must it appear in a member of the legislature to vote for a new law, who is utterly ignorant of the old!" In the eighteenth century virtually the whole machinery of local government in England was in the hands of the country squire who as justice of the peace discharged numerous judicial as well as administrative functions. Surely the justice of the peace would find useful some acquaintance with the law of England. The existence of the glorious institution of trial by jury made more necessary than in any other commonwealth some acquaintance with the law. Blackstone apparently was not bothered by the fact that by the law of England the jury was the judge only of facts and not of the law. Indeed, he overlooked no possible means of persuasion. A physician, he conceded, would not have much use for legal knowledge, but even he might find himself in an emergency which might make it necessary for him to draw a will for an expiring patient. Blackstone topped off his adjurations by telling a favorite story of his about Servius Sulpicius, the celebrated Roman patrician and orator, who was so overcome with shame when Quintus Mucius Scaevola, the great oracle of the Roman law, upbraided him for his legal ignorance that he forthwith devoted himself to the study of the law, and with such proficiency "that he left behind him about an hundred and fourscore volumes."

If, when Blackstone was struggling for recognition, he ever had any doubts concerning the perfection of the British constitution, they disappeared entirely now that he had attained the dignity and security of the professor's chair. The son of the silk merchant of Cheapside was on his way to breaking into the charmed circle of the governing class of eighteenth-century England. Clients at last began to clamor for his services—if not as an eloquent advocate, at least as a learned consultant—and Blackstone began to resume attendance upon the courts. Within two years after he had become Vinerian Professor, he was doing so well that he was able to refuse the honor of an appointment as Chief Justice of the Court of Common Pleas of Ireland. The next year he obtained a patent of precedence in the courts and took silk. He was also elected a member of Parliament from Hindon, a pocket borough in Wiltshire near Salisbury. In politics he was, of course, an Old Whig, but the difference between an Old Whig and an Old Tory was hardly discernible.

While these honors were crowding upon him, Blackstone was engaged in courting Sarah Clitherow, daughter of James Clitherow, of Boston House, Middlesex. He was then approaching forty, almost a confirmed bachelor, but doubtless he felt that a wife would be a desirable adjunct now that he had attained a solid position in life. The courtship was leisurely on both sides: Blackstone had been wounded once, and as for the lady—well, she probably felt that a certain amount of hesitation would act as a desirable incentive. The couple were married on May 5, 1761, in an elaborate ceremony at St. Paul's, at which Mansfield was best man. They took a house in Lincoln's Inn Fields, London. Blackstone was also able to bestow upon his lady the use of a country estate he had already acquired. It was, of course, at Wallingford, where Blackstone was becoming quite the country squire. He called his country seat "Castle Priory." He appears to have led a contented if not an exciting life with Sarah, who bore him seven children. He doubtless put her on a pedestal, from which she must have found it hard to touch his deeper emotions or even to influence his daily life. In his *Commentaries,* Blackstone declared: "By marriage, the husband and wife are one person in law: that is, the very being or legal existence of the woman is suspended during the marriage, or at least is incorporated and consolidated into that of the husband." But if Blackstone believed that by the law of England husband and wife were one, he also doubtless believed that the husband should be *the* one.

In his effort to make his whole life a tribute to the ruling class, Blackstone developed all the habits and diseases of the English gentleman. He ate too much and exercised too little. He developed a fondness for port, to which he became quite addicted without actually drinking to excess. Had not Dr. Johnson said: "Claret is the liquor for boys, port for men; but he who aspires to be a hero must drink brandy." Needless to say, Blackstone did not aspire to heroism. His fondness for port and rich food inevitably made him suffer from gout and vertigo.

He became increasingly corpulent and irritable. By the time he was forty-seven, he had to use a magnifying glass to read small type. This nearsightedness made his countenance seem stern and forbidding, an impression that was accentuated by the fact that his left eyebrow would often become contracted in a nervous twitch.

Blackstone wrote his *Commentaries* in the years from 1765 to 1769, and they were published in four volumes. Their substance had been elaborated in almost a decade and a half of lecturing, and thus he only put into permanent written form the ideas and material he had long since communicated to the public. The immediate occasion for the preparation of the *Commentaries* was the fact that his lectures were being pirated. To protect this valuable property, the lecturer turned author. The public soon demonstrated how enormously valuable the property was by purchasing it in large quantities. In 1766, in order to hasten the completion of the *Commentaries,* as well as to secure more time for his ever increasing practice, Blackstone resigned the Vinerian professorship. It is said that he never sat down to work on the *Commentaries* without a bottle of port at his elbow. There is also a legend that, while writing the *Commentaries,* he was not infrequently disturbed by rowdy parties given by Oliver Goldsmith, who had just come into money by selling a play.

While still working on the *Commentaries,* in 1768, Blackstone was foolish enough to stand for Parliament again, and was returned from Westbury. It proved to be the most humiliating experience of his life and showed how dangerous it is for anyone who has written a book to dabble in politics. The notorious John Wilkes had been elected to the House of Commons in 1764, but he had been expelled for publishing No. 45 of the *North Briton.* In the winter of 1768–69, however, he was re-elected three times from Middlesex and expelled three times. In the course of a debate on the expulsions, Blackstone contended that prior expulsion was itself a ground for disqualification. Whereupon Grenville rose with a smile and read from Blackstone's *Commentaries* to prove from his own work that he was wrong. The author of the already famous work sat down in utmost confusion and was unable to say a word. Blackstone, who had never been a success as a public speaker or politician, retired from Parliament, saying that "amidst the rage of contending parties, a man of moderation must expect to meet with no quarter from any side." He proceeded to add prior expulsion as a ground for disqualification to the very next edition of the *Commentaries* but this proved to be even a worse mistake. The wits of the town began to drink toasts "To the *first* edition of Dr. Blackstone's *Commentaries*"! Blackstone was always particularly enraged when he was referred to as "doctor," because it reminded him of the days when he was an Oxford don and had no practice at the bar.

As a reward for his faithful support of the government in Parliament, as well as in recognition of the success of the *Commentaries,* in 1770 Blackstone was offered a judgeship of the Court of Common Pleas. Since this was the Court of Common Pleas of England rather than of Ireland, he hastened to accept. It was the achievement of the pinnacle of his life's ambition. It must have seemed wonderful, if not incredible, to him that a son of a silk merchant could become a judge of one of the three great courts of the common law. He sat on the bench of the Court of Common Pleas for almost a decade, but, while he was a competent judge, he left no particular mark on the history of the court.

During Christmas, 1779, Blackstone became ill with dropsy and "water on the chest." He recovered temporarily, but he had a relapse early in February, 1780, and soon fell into a stupor. He died at his house in Lincoln's Inn Fields on February 14, 1780, in his fifty-seventh year, survived by his wife and seven children. He was interred in the vault of St. Peter's Church at Wallingford, and his passing was not unnoticed. The following obituary appeared in the public prints the day following his death and, appropriately enough, it was in verse that the man was celebrated:

> Who rescu'd law from pedant phrase,
> Who clear'd the student's clouded eyes,
> And led him through the legal maze.

It was a just and perspicacious comment on the author of the *Commentaries.* Upon their appearance they had been greeted with almost universal acclaim. Even the few carping critics attacked only some of the views of the commentator rather than the merits of his work as a popular exposition of the common law. The most notable of these critics was Dr. Joseph Priestley, the famous Nonconformist minister and chemist, who spoke his mind concerning Blackstone's rather bigoted attitude towards dissenters. Horne Tooke, clergyman turned lawyer, said of the *Commentaries,* however: "It is a good gentleman's law book, clear but not deep." Everyone paid tribute to Blackstone's graceful and polished style. Even Jeremy Bentham shared the common opinion of the *Commentaries* as a literary masterpiece, although he disliked Blackstone intensely both as a teacher and a thinker. It has been said that Blackstone made Bentham a jurist "by virtue of sheer repulsion." Yet even Bentham himself praised the object of his disdain: "He it is, in short, who first of all institutional writers, has taught jurisprudence to speak the language of the scholar and the gentleman."

Blackstone succeeded admirably in his primary purpose, which was to give an intelligible description of the whole system of the common law. The *Commentaries* is divided into four books: the first is entitled "Of the Rights of Persons," the second "Of the Rights of Things," the third "Of Private Wrongs," and the fourth "Of Public Wrongs." Of the approximately two thousand pages of the *Commentaries,* about five hundred deal with the law of property, mostly real property which was held under innumerable forms of tenure; about four hundred deal with the criminal law; and about three hundred deal with the law of procedure. It is apparent from this distribution of space alone that even in the eighteenth century, and despite the marked progress of commercial enterprise, the common law was still primarily a land law and a system of maintaining the social order of the landowners. Blackstone devoted only about fifty pages to the commercial law of contract. The law of civil wrongs was still far more important than the law of civil obligations. Such an enormously important branch of law as the modern law of corporations was still in its infancy when Blackstone wrote, and it is treated in not more than twenty pages. This space is devoted chiefly to the joint-stock companies that had sprung into being in the seventeenth century, among which was the famous East India Company.

Blackstone's scheme of classification resembles that of the *Institutes* of Gaius, who like him was probably a lecturer turned author. The Roman law had its Gaius; the common law was bound to have its Blackstone. Both wrote in the classical period of a mature legal system, and classification is the most elementary requirement of any legal science. Blackstone, however, went far beyond even the classical Roman law; he followed in the footsteps of the seventeenth-century civilians who had embraced the gospel of natural law. He owed much to the great natural-law jurists like Grotius and Pufendorf. The latter had held the first professorship of natural law, even as Blackstone held the first chair of the common law. Blackstone did for the common law what the natural-law jurists had already done for the Romanized civil law. It will be recalled that their method was to extract from the historical excrescences and diverse technicalities of the Roman law the general principles which could be proclaimed as the irrefutable precepts of the law of nature. Even as Blackstone labored, a great contemporary French jurist was performing a somewhat similar service for French law. His name was Robert Joseph Pothier, and he worked at his task with such devotion, such singleness of purpose, and such obliviousness of the world around him that he came to be known as the lay saint of Orléans.

A mature legal system becomes capable of statement in the form of general legal principles. These have merely to be extracted from the accidental forms of procedure. It is the next step in legal science. Coke had restated the medieval common law, but only within the traditional procedural molds of writs and forms of action. Since his day even equity had become increasingly rigid and formalized. A restatement in terms of general principles had therefore become an urgent, if not desperate, necessity. The slight attention paid by Blackstone to the procedural minutiae of the common law was the most striking and valuable characteristic of his work. The *Commentaries* may be described as a grand quest for general legal principles. The common law was comparable to a disordered apartment, and it was to be swept of its cobwebs and restored to a habitable condition.

Blackstone represented the common law not only as the perfection of reason but as "a secondary law of nature," consisting of fixed and immutable principles. In one of his most revealing sentences he remarked that martial law was "in truth and reality no law" because it was built upon no settled principles. But every other branch of the law was full of legal principles, and Blackstone delighted to discover them and to demonstrate how beautifully consistent they were with each other. Legal principles were so important that, if they did not exist, it was necessary to invent them. The common law was full of precise maxims, and, if no other legal principles were available, the maxims themselves served as principles. Blackstone, living in the world of legal principles self-evident in their application to any state of facts, almost forgot the physical world. If the facts did not fit the principles, so much the worse for the facts. Blackstone was perfectly well aware that litigants, whose lawyers had advised them that the legal principles were on their side, had not infrequently been disappointed in their hopes of successfully asserting them, but he attributed this puzzling result not to any uncertainty of legal principle but to the unmanageability and recalcitrance of the facts to which the legal principles had to be applied. The law to Blackstone was a system of autonomous logic. Taking a few basic legal principles as the premises, one could derive all the other principles by a process of logical deduction. The very life of the law was logic, and the judge on the bench had to be only the master logician. With cold and relentless logic, he spoke the certain dooms of the law. The judge was thus merely a mouthpiece of the immemorial common law. A new decision was never more than an application of an old and familiar principle, which had existed from the beginning of time. Thus was the law "methodized" and explained and made to look like an exact science.

In this system of legal principles there was really little need for history. Blackstone was primarily interested in a dogmatic exposition of the common law as it existed in his own time. He had no taste for antiquarianism, and he was ill equipped to essay the role of historian. As Lord Ellenborough said, Blackstone was not a learned man, but one whom the necessity of writing the *Commentaries* had made learned. But writing for the layman, whom he wished to convince of the rationality of English law, he had to supply a reason for every rule, and sometimes the only reason he could discover was a historical one. He invented historical explanations with the same facility that he discovered legal principles, but his pretended history was not infrequently a flight of the imagination. In his historical "explanations" are to be discovered the inevitable howlers of the popularizer. The most ludicrous example is his explanation of why, when a whale was taken on the coast, the common law decreed that it should be deemed a royal fish and divided between the king and queen, the king to take the head and the tail to go to the queen. "The reason for this whimsical division," explained Blackstone, "was to furnish the Queen's wardrobe with whalebone." But it was Blackstone's explanation that was whimsical, for the whalebone is entirely in the head of the royal fish.

Writing for the layman, Blackstone also felt that, even though it was no part of his main enterprise, he should adorn his exposition of the common law with the trappings of legal theory and philosophy. He thus also discoursed somewhat on the nature of law in general and would sometimes compare the institutions of the common law with those of the Roman and civil law. These excursions were even more unfortunate than his attempts at historical divination. He defined municipal law as "a rule of civil conduct, prescribed by the supreme power in a state, commanding what is right and prohibiting what is wrong." But, if the supreme power could command, did it make any difference whether it was "right" or "wrong"? In either event, the command would have to be obeyed. Blackstone had a happy faculty of combining contradictory ideas. Yet his combinations were almost invariably useful in the conflicts of the world of law. A bad rule could always be attacked as morally wrong by one party in a legal dispute, while at the same time it could be defended by his opponent as the command of society which had to be obeyed despite its injustice. As a philosopher Blackstone achieved the feats of reconciling positive rules of English law with the precepts of natural law; the appeal to reason with the obscurantism of common sense; primitivism with traditionalism and the blessings of civilization; libertarianism with authoritarianism; Saxon simplicity, which he admired in contradistinction to Norman subtlety, with the awful complexities of the common law. A good style indeed covers a multitude of sins. Yet it would be unjust to blame Blackstone too much. Surely the contradictions of the popularizer are excused by the less obvious contradictions of the philosophers whom he popularizes.

While Blackstone's primary purpose was to give an intelligible account of English law, his secondary purpose was undoubtedly to write in praise of the laws of England. He wrote the song of songs that is English law. He created a cult of the common law, which is still flourishing. We hear much of "the genius of the common law" and "the spirit of our Constitution." He expresses great pride, of course, in the Glorious Revolution of 1688 and all its works. He also confuses the "rule of law" with the justice of rules of law. He calls the jury the "bulwark of northern liberty" and "the glory of the English law." The common law is not infrequently praised for overcoming the obstacles of its own creation. Even the delays of the common law are the price of social progress. A spirit of complacency pervades his pages, and a reverence for the landed gentry of his time, whom he regarded as "the most useful as well as considerable body of men in the nation." As for the king, writing in the age of George II, he could say, after explaining the maxim of the common law, that "the king can do no wrong": "The king, moreover is not only incapable of *doing* wrong, but even of *thinking* wrong; he can never mean to do an improper thing: in him is no folly or weakness."

The *Commentaries* celebrated English liberty, but Blackstone reserved his greatest praise for property. As Voltaire said, liberty and property were "the great national cry of the English." To be sure, liberty was dangerous, since it might easily encourage attacks on men of property; but, by equating liberty with the protection of existing rights, Blackstone cleverly avoided the necessity of extending the benefits of liberty to those who had no rights because they had no property. "So great, moreover," said Blackstone, "is the regard of the law for private property, that it will not authorize the least violation of it; no, not even for the general good of the whole community." He gave, however, a grudging assent to the taking of private property by eminent domain, provided reasonable compensation were made, and he held that taxation was not confiscation, only because it was based upon "consent in Parliament." There was no injustice in the game laws, only because there could be no vested rights in wild animals. Blackstone even held that an informer had a vested right to his reward. Thus, the king could not pardon an offense against a penal statute after the informer had brought the information. While property was founded in nature, the law, Blackstone pointed out, actually sometimes went beyond nature, as when it recognized rights of inheritance, for by nature a man ceased to exercise dominion over his property when he died. Blackstone justified property qualifications for the exercise of the right of suffrage as a means of saving the poor from themselves. If the poor had votes, they would be unable to resist the temptation of selling them to the highest bidder. Blackstone noted that the poor laws were imperfect in encouraging the "idle, dissolute and unemployed," but he blamed this state of affairs on the "fate that has generally attended most of our statute laws, where they have not the foundation of the common law to build on." He obviously much preferred the ancient common law to acts of Parliament, which might sometimes have disturbing effects.

Naturally, Blackstone perceived little need for any reform of the common law. He hardly needed to be reminded in the words of Horace Walpole that "there is a wide difference between correcting abuses and removing landmarks." If any reform of English law was at all necessary, said Blackstone, it could only be to eliminate "the little contrarieties which the practice of many centuries will necessarily create in any human system." Influenced by his friend Mansfield, he spoke kindly of the desirability of fusing law and equity but, after all, this would have been a change of form rather than of substance. He espoused practically no other reform of the civil law of any importance. He had, however, read Beccaria, and although he spoke of one of the provisions of the criminal law as "full of that tenderness and humanity to prisoners for which our English laws are justly famous," he did realize that there were some defects in the system of administering criminal justice. But it is to be doubted that he was more moved by feelings of humanity than by the intellectual conviction that the savagery of the criminal law was defeating its aim and endangering the respect which should be paid to all law, civil as well as criminal. Since juries were refusing to convict in cases in which the death penalty could be imposed for trivial offenses, Blackstone, in desiring to mitigate capital punishment, really wanted to make the criminal law more severe by making it more certain. In commenting on the law of domestic relations, Blackstone observed that, while the gentry no longer exercised the right to chastise their wives, "the lower rank of people" still did so out of their fondness for the old common law.

To read the *Commentaries* now is like visiting a museum of antiquities. But it became a classic precisely because its author reflected so well the social and economic as well as the intellectual currents of his time. Yet when Blackstone seems to be exhibiting most clearly the intellectual influences of the eighteenth century, he is perhaps only manifesting his legal classicism. In the eighteenth century "science" was certainly a respected if not a magic word, and Newton was its prophet. Rationalism was being made popular by John Locke. Nevertheless, Blackstone's emphasis upon logic and principle is also characteristic of the classical Roman law. They must have had their source, therefore, in the need for clarification and simplification common to the mature legal systems of both eras.

While the *Commentaries* soon ceased to be an exposition of existing English law, it was itself, despite Blackstone, responsible for ushering in the era of legal reform. For the first time the common law had been so clearly delineated and exposed to the public gaze that an irresistible pressure for reform was created. For all his conservatism, Blackstone had loosed a revolutionary force in attempting to bring the law out of the arcana of the lawyers and to submit it to the scrutiny of laymen. He was directly responsible, if only by way of "repulsion," for Jeremy Bentham, the greatest law reformer of all time. As an expositor of the classical common law, Blackstone is now of only historical importance. But as a popularizer of law, he is still a living force. Mankind still cries for deliverance from the lawyers.

Cesare Bonesana, Marchese di Beccaria

THE RISE AND DECLINE OF THE CRIMINAL LAW

IN THE SIXTEENTH AND SEVENTEENTH CENTURIES, THERE WERE emerging the classic features of the civil law of modern states. The law of property and contract occupied the apostles of natural law on the Continent, while in England the judges and the chancellors were giving final shape to the classical common law. A new public law had also come into existence in England in the course of the constitutional struggles between the courts, the Crown, and Parliament in the same centuries. But not even in the blessed isle, despite its tremendous exaltation of legality under the name of the supremacy of law, was there anything like a criminal law—if the limitation of power be regarded as the essense of law. The great jurists, as immemorially since Roman days, devoted their best energies and talents to the civil law, in which men's property was at stake, and left to the cultivation of insensitive and inferior intellects the problem of public prosecution, in which the very lives and honor of men were at stake. There were criminals and there were crimes, real and imaginary, for which men paid dearly, and there was, of course, a system of prosecution; but still it is no paradox to insist that there was no criminal law in the sense which men were to be taught the meaning of the term.

The man who perceived this fact most clearly and made the perception the basis of the system of criminal law which is still accepted by the modern world was a noble Italian youth, Cesare Bonesana, Marchese di Beccaria, who was endowed, appropriately enough, with an acute sensibility to suffering and an intellect capable of translating this feeling into a system of jurisprudence. Beccaria has been called the greatest of criminal-law reformers. But his remarkable achievement is not adequately evaluated in terms of criminal-law reform. He did not reform the criminal law: he created it. Moreover, he performed this feat when not yet twenty-seven years of age, and almost in spite of himself. Never was an innovator more disinclined to accept the challenge of destiny or more fearful of the risk he was taking. Few who know the conditions of the time would blame him.

Cesare Bonesana, the future Marquis of Beccaria, was born in the city of Milan on March 15, 1738, the scion of a family which numbered amongst its ancestors distinguished ecclesiastics, military men, and judges. Cesare was sent to be educated at the Jesuit College at Parma. The boy proved to be intelligent, but he was also of an extremely lethargic temperament, and he could find little in the Jesuit curriculum to hold his interest. He suffered indeed from boredom. He attempted to escape from the aridities of logic and philosophy into the world of classical literature, only to sink back into his habitual state of mental indifference. His intellectual powers were aroused for the first time only when he commenced the study of mathematics. Only then did he perceive the sway of pure reason, which fascinated him as it did so many others in the eighteenth century. But his love of mathematics paled in time, and left him disappointed and weary of spirit.

But there were then loose in the world that wonderful group of men who were to create the new world of the French Revolution. A man had to be lethargic indeed to resist the fascination of the French philosophers. Beccaria was approaching man's estate, and when he returned to Milan at the age of twenty-one, he happened to pick up a copy of Montesquieu's *Persian Letters*. The book excited him, and he embarked upon a course of reading in the Encyclopedist philosophers and other disciples of rationalism. He read with avidity Helvetius, D'Alembert, Voltaire, Buffon, Diderot, Condillac, Hume. He began to see the need for social reform and to be concerned with the happiness of mankind. Montesquieu and Helvetius especially exercised a strong influence over him. They suggested to him that man was a victim of his environment and that his misery was not entirely his own fault. For a while he even undertook to study law at Pavia, but his interest in it was purely philosophical and humanitarian.

The love affairs of great men are sometimes irrelevancies in evaluating the significance of their work in behalf of mankind. But the sensibility displayed by Beccaria when he fell in love argues a capacity for emotion which was indispensable in anyone who was to bring himself to attack the frightful penal system of eighteenth-century Europe. When he was twenty-two years old, Beccaria fell deeply and irrevocably in love with Teresa, the sixteen-year-old daughter of Lieutenant Colonel Domenico di Blasco, who, although he came of a noble family of Sicilian-Spanish origin, was not at the time very rich in worldly goods. Because of his impecunious state, the young lover's father, the Marchese Gian Saverio Beccaria Bonesana, was opposed to the match. In those days a father could apply to a magistrate for an order to imprison a rebellious son, and the irate and determined father secured one of these familial *lettres de cachet*. The son was forthwith incarcerated, but the place of confinement selected was, by special indulgence, his father's own house. There he remained a prisoner for three months, and his father moved heaven and earth to undermine his devotion to Teresa. He even called to his assistance the Marquis Stampa Soncino and the minister Kaunitz, but neither could shake the devotion and resolution of the young lover. But Teresa's father was not idle either, and he appealed to the Empress Maria Teresa herself, pointing out the nobility of his family and his readiness to provide a dowry of sorts for his daughter. At the end of three months, the young lover was released and hastened to marry his adored Teresa. The defeated and disconsolate father would have nothing to do with his daughter-in-law, but upon the intervention of Cerrati, a member of the Senate, he provided his son with some modest means. The father and son were finally reconciled as the result of the efforts of the latter's closest friend, Pietro Verri.

This Pietro Verri was the most important influence in the life and work of Beccaria. He was ten years older than his young friend, and he filled him with the courage and perseverance which he lacked. Pietro, too, came of an illustrious Milanese family. His father had destined him for the profession of the law, but he had preferred the study of literature and the writing of poetry. After fighting in the Austrian army, in which he distinguished himself for his bravery and achieved the rank of captain, he began to interest himself in economic problems. He became the moving spirit of a group of young men who were interested in social reform.

These young men were distressed by the numerous political, legal, and economic evils of Lombardy, which until lately had been under Spanish dominion. They therefore organized a society called the Accademia dei Pugni, the members of which met at the home of Pietro Verri. The members included, in addition to Pietro Verri and Beccaria, Alessandro Verri, the brother of Pietro, who held the office of Protector of Prisons and was thus able to give the members of the society first-hand accounts of the misery which he witnessed in the course of his duties. Another member who especially influenced Beccaria was Paolo Frisi, who was a mathematician and a corresponding member of the French Academy of Science. In their intercourse with each other the members took the names of illustrious Romans. Pietro Verri, for example, took the name of Lucius Cornelius Sulla; his brother Alessandro, that of Marcus Claudius Marcellus; and Beccaria was Titus Pomponius Atticus. Eventually, by June, 1764, the members of the society established a periodical called *Il Caffè*, which was an imitation of Addison's *Spectator*. It was published for some two years, until the society itself was dissolved as a result of dissensions among its members.

But in the meantime the society had already justified its existence by producing Beccaria's revolutionary essay, which he called *Dei Delitti e delle pene* (Of Crimes and Punishments). Becccaria was often bored by the discussions at the club, and tried the patience of his friends. The reform of the penal law was one of the objectives of the circle, and it was Pietro Verri's idea to assign this subject to Beccaria. Offhand it might have seemed that the choice was not a happy one. The criminal law supports the very foundations of the established order, and to attack its methods and principles required, in those days especially, a singular temerity. Italy was par excellence the land of ecclesiastical censorship and the home of the dread Inquisition. But Pietro Verri knew that his friend made up for his nervous disposition and timidity of temperament by his "eloquence and lively imagination." Indeed, as so frequently happens, the nervousness of his disposition was conditioned by the vividness of his imagination. Alessandro, as Protector of Prisons, was assigned to him as a guide through the hell of the Italian penal system, and he set to work in March, 1763. But Beccaria was by nature indolent, and he found writing an almost herculean task. He had to be constantly encouraged and assisted, but finally by January, 1764, the *Dei Delitti e delle pene* was completed, and the slender volume, which runs to less than two hundred pages, was published anonymously in Leghorn in July of the same year.

The anonymity of the publication reflected Beccaria's dread of the consequences. He, who loved nothing so much as a life of retirement and contemplation, had been called to end the greatest misery of his fellow men. But there was no point in abandoning the dictates of prudence, which included a due regard for his own safety. In the very pages of his essay on crimes and punishments he attempted to reassure himself: "I should have everything to fear, if tyrants were to read my book; but tyrants never read." Beccaria had great gifts of clarity and epigrammatic statement, but, as he explained later in a confidential letter to Abbé Morellet:

I must confess to you that in the course of my writing I had before my eyes the examples of Machiavelli, Galileo, Giannone. I heard the noise of chains, shaken by superstition and fanaticism, stifling the utterance of truth. The vision of this horrible spectacle obliged me to veil sometimes the light with clouds. I was desirous of defending truth without becoming her martyr. This idea of the necessity of obscurity has made me obscure sometimes without necessity.

But Beccaria's fears proved groundless. The chains of the Inquisition remained in their dungeons. Here and there a monk or a practicing criminalist denounced the work of Beccaria as that of a madman, impostor, and fool. But the illustrious men of Europe acclaimed the youthful author and his slender work. In fact, no one could believe that he was so young. As one commentator has said: "Never before did so small a book produce so great an effect." It went through three editions in Italy in the first six months after its publication. In the Kingdom of Naples it was, after due examination, published with the express approval of the censorial authorities. Even if tyrants did not read, they employed others who did. In his own Lombardy, Beccaria received the protection of Count Firmian, the liberal minister of Maria Teresa. As Beccaria himself wrote to Abbé Morellet: "Count Firmian protected my book, and it is to him that I owe my tranquillity." Elsewhere benevolent monarchs even proceeded to put some of Beccaria's precepts into practice. He was thus honored by Frederick of Prussia, Duke Leopold of Tuscany, and Catherine II of Russia. Catherine not only had his essay translated into Russian and inserted in her new code of laws, but invited its author to pay her a visit to assist in the work of legislation.

The essay *Of Crimes and Punishments* was translated into many European languages, but the most important one was French. The attention of Europe was fixed upon the French *philosophes,* who had initiated the impulses which had produced Beccaria's work and were to produce still greater movements of liberation. To be acclaimed and honored by them was to have achieved fame indeed. The Encyclopedists were swept with enthusiasm for Beccaria and his work. It was not only translated into French by Abbé Morellet, but it was annotated by Diderot, and the great Voltaire, upon whom the eyes of all Europe were fixed, even wrote a commentary upon it. The great mathematician D'Alembert declared when he read the *Dei Delitti*: "However small, the book will suffice to assure to its author an immortal name. What philosophy, what truth, what logic, what precision, and at the same time what sentiment and what humanity!"

The greatest triumph of Beccaria was achieved when in 1766 Abbé Morellet invited him, in the name of the Encyclopedist philosophers, to visit Paris. It proved also, however, the greatest ordeal of Beccaria's life. His behavior on this trip, which should have been a triumphal tour, verged on the comic and the absurd, and revealed further the extraordinary character of the man who had written the essay on crimes and punishments. It took the greatest persuasion to induce Beccaria to leave home, much as he appreciated the honor that had been bestowed upon him. His shy and retiring disposition made him shrink from the perils and excitements of the trip. But the chief reason for his unhappiness was that he would be separated from his Teresa.

Although he had then been married to her for six years and was already a father, he found the thought of the impending separation unbearable. When he left Milan for Paris on October 2, 1766, he sobbed as if his heart would break. On the first stage of the journey, which was planned to last the incredibly long period of six months, Alessandro Verri, who was accompanying Beccaria, was lighthearted and gay, as becomes one who would soon enjoy the delights of Paris, but Beccaria himself was still inconsolable. When only thirty miles from home he wrote: "I am continually oscillating between joy and hypochondria." He had nightmares in which he dreamed that his Teresa was ill and dying, and only the assurances of Alessandro Verri and the fear of becoming a laughingstock prevented him from returning at once.

Upon his arrival in Paris he was received in the house of the Baron d'Holbach, and introduced to D'Alembert, Helvetius, Diderot, Abbé Morellet, Malesherbes, Marmontel, Madame Necker, and other great figures of the day. Everyone made much of him. Yet he wrote to Teresa: "Remember that I love you tenderly, that I prefer my dear wife, my children, my family, my friends in Milan, and you chiefly, to the whole of Paris." Not many days passed before he wrote to Teresa again to ask her to spread the news that he was in such bad health that he would have to return. He even enclosed a fictitious letter setting forth the dire tidings, which he begged her to show to his friends in order to give an air of verisimilitude to the strategem. But Teresa was apparently not as distraught as her fond husband. She wrote to ask him to buy her some clothes and a certain face pomade. She, at least, was taking advantage of Paris. Beccaria was finally reunited with his Teresa, but the journey ruined his friendship with the Verris. Alessandro, jealous of the attentions that were showered upon his companion in Paris, fell out with him, and Beccaria upon his return fell out with Pietro, because he suspected that his friend had paid too much attention to his Teresa while he was suffering the torments of the damned in the French capital.

Beccaria was one of those men who have only one book in them—at least of any consequence. Indeed, it could not be otherwise with his temperament and philosophy. There was no longer Pietro Verri to inspire him and to prod him into distasteful industry. The invitation of Catherine II to come to Russia to assist her in the preparation of a penal code for her subjects was made shortly after his return from Paris, but after his harrowing experience the offer could not but be rejected. About a year later, however, Beccaria accepted an appointment as professor of political economy in the Palatinate school of Milan. He remained in this post for only two years, and took no steps himself to publish his lectures, which appeared only posthumously ten years after his death. The transition from penology to political economy may seem strange, but it has not been an unusual combination in modern times. After all, who better than the economist can understand the conditions that lead to crime and the measures necessary to prevent it? After his professorship in political economy, Beccaria was made a councillor of state and a magistrate, and from time to time he served on various commissions of inquiry. But while some penal reforms were made in his native Lombardy in his lifetime, they may be attributed more to the influence of his celebrated essay than to any great personal exertions on his part. The later part of his life was particularly solitary: he once even shunned a visit from the King of Naples. He was content to maintain his detachment from the scene of life, and to indulge his own private feelings and tastes. He seems to have adopted the philosophy of *carpe diem*, which he had urged in one of the productions of his adolescence. He continued to adore his Teresa with undiminished passion, but when she died on March 14, 1774, at the age of twenty-nine, he remarried in less than three weeks! Perhaps, after all, he was only a woman's man, who needed feminine society more than he needed any one woman. Beccaria lived on for more than twenty years, and died of apoplexy on November 28, 1794. There are now two statues to him in Milan, but little notice was taken of his death when it occurred.

There have been few figures in legal history as extraordinary as Beccaria. It must have been a truly dreadful penal system that could have aroused such a man as he. What were the cries of agony he heard amidst the clank of chains? What was "the horrible spectacle" he conjured in his vivid imagination? What did he see that made him shudder at man's inhumanity to man, when Alessandro Verri led him through the prisons of Milan? But what, on the other hand, accounted for the amazing success of the slender volume by an obscure Italian youth? What saved him from the martyrdom which he feared so much? The extraordinary character of Beccaria is matched by the extraordinary success of his book. That it should have come from Italy, the land of the Inquisition, is only less remarkable. After all, it was only natural that the earliest and most effective protest should have come from a country where penal conditions were among the worst. It was just, too, that a criminal law should be first created in the land where the modern civil law had been born. The needs of trade and commerce, which had nurtured the civil law, contributed to the monstrous penal system which eventually they were destined to destroy.

The penal system of continental Europe was an acute reaction to the period of club law which had prevailed in the Middle Ages. The degenerate system of composition, with its pecuniary penalties, was helpless to cope with an increasing amount of professional criminality, which consisted of various forms of theft and robbery and thus threatened the security of property. The irrationality of oaths, ordeals, and trial by battle in the far from primitive society of the Middle Ages made it difficult to suppress wrongdoing. Trial by battle in particular encouraged the lawlessness of the feudal lords. Habituated to the use of arms, they had nothing worse to fear when they burned, pillaged and robbed, than a form of trial in which they were only given an opportunity to display their professional skill. When the Lateran Council in 1215 in effect banned the use of ordeals by prohibiting the clergy from assisting in the rites, the immediate result was to add to the advantages of the knights, for those who could not fight were now left with practically no remedy. The good burghers and tradesmen, who had been brought into being by the revival of commerce, struggled against the prevailing anarchy within the walled fastnesses of their towns, and they could succeed only by laying aside even the pretense of humanity. But they were impeded in their efforts to extirpate theft, robbery, and violence by the narrowness of their jurisdictions and by the absence of any strong central power capable of coming to their assistance. The roads were bad, means of communication were difficult, and the professional brigands, who were constantly being recruited from the dregs of the population living in an indescribable state of squalor and misery, were able to ply their trades, if not with impunity, then with at least an even chance of success. But before long, as gunpowder came into use and it became possible to reduce the castles of the feudal lords to dust, the lords, who had discarded their useless armor and could thus be robbed as easily as the burghers when they ventured out on the perilous highways, began to cry loudly, too, for repressive laws. With all parties in interest united, the ferocity of the penal system was a foregone conclusion.

The penal system thus became a kind of state-organized lynch law, but far less merciful than a popular lynching. The criminal "law," if such it may be called, became increasingly arbitrary; a crime was simply an act which the judge deemed inimical to the interests of society; the reasoning of the judges was subtle and analogical; and indeed the whole criminal law was an ex post facto law; the opinion of a criminalist, who was recognized as an authority, was enough to send a man to his death; it is possible to doubt, in reading such criminalists of the time as Clarus and Farinaccius, that they were human. The judges, who often held their office by purchase, were extremely venal and devoid of any sense of justice as well as humanity, and death on the gibbet or some horrible form of mutilation was the punishment for an incredible number of the most trivial offenses. Benedict Carpzov, who was a judge in Saxony in the seventeenth century, the heyday of this penal system, imposed no less than twenty thousand capital sentences, and the only excuse his apologists have been able to find for him is that he lived in the dark period of the Thirty Years' War. Yet those who were done to death by the executioner were fortunate, for in the seventeenth century, as the result of slightly better notions of humanity, imprisonment, which in ancient and medieval times was rare except for purposes of detention, came into increasing use as a mode of punishment, and the prisons were cesspools of iniquity, depravity, disease, cruelty, and every other form of horror. No attempt was made to separate young from old, men from women, debtors from criminals, convicted criminals from accused persons awaiting trial, or to provide the rudiments of sanitation or decent food and bedding, and the prisons themselves became nurseries of crime and depredation.

It is a sufficient commentary upon the times to say that the conditions in Merrie England were only slightly better than on the Continent. It is true that English prisons were no less vile. It is also true that on the statute books there was an ill-digested mass of criminal legislation, and that in addition there were many common-law crimes, which made the whole penal system arbitrary and unpredictable. In the England of the thirteenth century there had been only a few felonies which entailed loss of life or limb and led to the confiscation of the offender's estate. But the criminal law, struggling against mounting professional criminality and inspired by the cupidity of the Crown, which waxed rich on fines and forfeitures levied on occasional malefactors, grew steadily more bloody. The crime of high treason proved particularly elastic. The Tudor criminal law, which was aimed, above all, at malefactors of high degree, marked the transition to savagery. During the thirty-eight years of the reign of Henry VIII, no less than seventy-two thousand executions took place. The dreaded Star Chamber, before it was abolished in 1641, had all but extirpated the quarreling and warring nobility, which threatened the peace of the Crown, and this, indeed, was its chief mission as an extraordinary tribunal existing apart from the traditional common-law courts. Yet before the Glorious Revolution there were only some fifty capital offenses. But as the professional criminals, who now attacked burgher and squire alike, multiplied, so too did the number of crimes punishable with death. In the reign of George II alone, sixty-three new ones were added. When Blackstone came to write his *Commentaries,* he estimated that there were one hundred and sixty crimes entailing the death penalty, and the number increased considerably in the next decade and a half. The penal law, morever, was a farrago of irrationality and whimsicality. To steal a horse was a capital crime, for instance; but to kill him was not. The penalty for picking a pocket to the value of twelvepence farthing, which was capital, was the same as for rape or murder. Among capital offenses were such crimes as felling a tree or associating a month with gypsies.

But if the English law of crime and punishment was no less ferocious than on the Continent, the system of prosecution was perhaps a bit more liberal to the accused. In contrast to the "inquisitorial" system of the Continent, with its public prosecutors, secret examinations, and torture, the English system of prosecution has been described as "accusatorial." The adjective denotes primarily the greater degree to which prosecution was left to private initiative. Except in the case of the felonies which directly interested the Crown, such as high treason, it was left to the subject to set in motion the machinery of prosecution. This archaic survival persisted, indeed, until late in the nineteenth century, when an Office of Public Prosecution was created. The English accusatorial system was bound to be less efficient, and hence less cruel, than the continental. Moreover, the procedure for bringing a criminal to trial was somewhat more elaborate in England. Since the close of the Middle Ages, it had been necessary in all cases of felony to secure an indictment by a grand jury, and this had to be followed by a trial before a petit jury—the "palladium of English liberty." But in the fifteenth and sixteenth centuries the accused was subjected to a preliminary secret examination before justices of the peace, the council, or the judges. The formal trial was, however, always public, and England was one of the few countries of Europe where torture was not normally employed in the examination of prisoners; even in the execution of sentences of death, it was confined to cases of high treason. Yet the advantages seemingly enjoyed by the accused were unfortunately largely nullified in practice. The judges, who held office at the pleasure of the Crown, at least until the period of the Glorious Revolution, were merely its servants, and in their zeal they strove to overcompensate for the lack of a public prosecutor in the English system. If mothers on the Continent frightened little children with the dread name of Carpzov, naughty English boys shuddered no less at the mention of the name of Bloody Jeffreys. There had to be an indictment, and any variance between the allegations of the indictment and the proof was fatal. But the accused was not allowed to see a copy of the indictment before the trial, and he was denied the right of counsel—in cases of treason until 1695, and in the case of the other felonies until as late as 1837. Although the Crown had the privilege of calling witnesses against the accused, it was denied to the helpless prisoner in the dock. As for the jury who tried him, they lived in fear of the king's judges, who in the post-medieval period not infrequently "amerced," that is, fined them for bringing in "false" verdicts. Under this system, a criminal trial rarely lasted more than a day, even when the charge was high treason, and before long the wretched prisoner found himself suffering the ignominies of the procession to Tyburn.

Ever since the sixteenth century at least, there had not been wanting some voices of protest against this or that barbarity of the penal system. Torture was condemned by Montaigne, who exclaimed that the man whom the judge had tortured in order not to put him to death if he was innocent died both innocent and tortured. The same sentiment was shared by other French men of letters, and even by some of the French legists. In the seventeenth century Christian Thomasius spoke out not only against torture but also against trials for witchcraft, and in the next century his views were supported by another leading apostle of natural law, Christian Wolff. In the eighteenth century Voltaire fought against some of the worst miscarriages of French criminal justice and dramatically exposed the evils of the times, especially in his celebrated defense of the Protestant Jean Calais. In England even Blackstone, who wrote contemporaneously with Beccaria and can hardly be regarded as a critic of the existing penal system, expressed himself against the denial of the right of counsel to prisoners whose lives were at stake, when such assistance was conceded in petty cases of civil trespass. Even earlier the conversational Dr. Samuel Johnson, who saw no need for abolishing the procession to Tyburn, which he held gratified the public at the same time that it supported the spirit of the criminal, had written a piece for *The Rambler,* in which he denounced "the periodical havock of our fellow beings" and pointed out one of the basic contradictions of the contemporary penal system. "To equal robbery with murder is to reduce murder to robbery; to confound in common minds the gradations of iniquity, and to incite the commission of a greater crime to prevent the detection of a less."

Such sentiments were an indication of a shift in public opinion, which was far more important than the utterance of occasional protests by individual philosophers, no matter how celebrated. Violence finally bred not more violence, but a guarded mercy. The change may be perceived most clearly in England, where the jury system afforded a means of registering popular opinion. While in the eighteenth century criminal prosecution had to struggle everywhere with an unwillingness of parties to stir up the public authorities and of witnesses to give testimony, in England it had to contend also with the disinclination of juries to convict. Juries resorted, for instance, to such stratagems as finding twenty golden guineas stolen by a thief to be worth only thirty-nine shillings. Wretches were thus less frequently hanged that jurymen might dine, and the penal system began to be reformed before the government took official action.

Apart from the naturalness of any revolt against protracted and excessive inhumanity, the causes of the revolution in penology were in the main the same that led to the greater revolution in economics, politics, and religion. Protestantism put an emphasis upon individual responsibility and the value of the individual human life. Men began to see that to live justly was no less important in this life than in the hereafter, and that they could live so only with some measure of security of person as well as of property. A wave of humanitarianism thus accompanied the wave of evangelicalism. The middle class, seeking to establish its power against the feudal nobility, shouted so many huzzas for liberty that it began to doubt the utility of savage and repressive laws. Tradesmen are not by nature bloodthirsty—only by necessity— and when they came to be the dominant factor in political life, and roads and police systems improved, they were ready to relent. Confiscations and the frequent levy of fines and forfeitures were alien to the spirit of the emerging capitalist economy, while the mass of heterogeneous criminal legislation would in time become a positive menace; for in bold capitalistic enterprise the line between the lawful and the unlawful is sometimes rather hazy. Laissez-faire economics also favored a greater resort to imprisonment as a penalty: when there was so much emphasis upon individual freedom, the deprivation of freedom was bound to recommend itself more frequently as a punishment. The desirability of populating the colonies in the New World also led, particularly in England, the greatest colonial power, to the frequent commutation of sentences of death into transportation beyond the seas.

Beccaria was the prophet of the new penal humanitarianism and, because conditions at length were favorable, he became a prophet with great honor in every country. While others had attacked this or that phase of the penal system, he was the first to examine its basic postulates and to develop in complete outline the basic principles of a new penal system. The brevity of his book on crimes and punishments was one of the secrets of its enormous success. A learned criminologist would have written a treatise full of technical details, which would have bored even the most sympathetic readers. But Beccaria fortunately stuck to the fundamentals, and he had the great gift of being able to set them forth in eloquent and aphoristic language. The moral principles he developed appear to have all the finality and certainty of mathematical axioms. The youthful philosopher had not studied mathematics in vain, and it was almost inevitable that he should come to be admired by celebrated mathematicians. The essay on crimes and punishments is virtually a form of "political arithmetic," to use Beccaria's own phrase, and he declares that the problems of punishment must be solved with "geometrical precision."

Beccaria himself was not unconscious of the sources, material and spiritual, of the Enlightenment. He appealed to "that tender emotion in which sensible minds sympathize with him who pleads the cause of humanity." He noted that commerce was animated by the knowledge of philosophical truth, and how in the preceding centuries "from the lap of luxury and effeminacy have sprung the most tender virtues, humanity, benevolence, and toleration of human errors." He observed, too, that the use of printing made it possible for the public to become the guardian of the laws. He was no less familiar with the new moral philosophy. He accepted the new revelation of the obligations of the Social Contract, and made them the basis of his penology. He had picked up somewhere also the pseudo-mathematical formula of utilitarianism, that the object of government is to promote "the greatest happiness of the greatest number," a formula that Jeremy Bentham was soon to make even more famous.

When men made the Social Contract, argued Beccaria, they surrendered no more of their liberty than was necessary to preserve the tranquillity of society. They did not grant an unlimited right to punish. The purpose of punishment was not vindictive, but deterrent, and its only justification was to prevent the commission of like offenses. The certainty of punishment was more important than its severity, and cruel and barbarous penalties were unnecessary. There was to be a "fixed proportion between crimes and punishments," measured by the extent of the injury done to society. Since human beings are rational and calculating creatures, they will ordinarily refrain from the commission of acts which can only become a source of pain and suffering to them greater than the profit they would derive from the commission of such acts. Crimes and punishments were therefore to be written down in a code which every man might read. Nothing was more fallacious than to appeal to the "spirit" of the laws. The judge was to be a mere assessor who imposed the specified penalty for the proven crime. "In every criminal cause," declared Beccaria, "the judge should reason syllogistically. The *major* should be the general law; the *minor* the conformity of the action, or its opposition to the laws; the *conclusion* liberty or punishment." Since the right to punish existed at all only when there was clear and convincing proof of guilt, the innocent could not be subjected to torture, which was itself a punishment. Secret examinations were objectionable because they afforded no reliable proof of guilt, and the rights of the accused could be adequately protected only in a public trial, which, moreover, was necessary if the administration of the penal law was to have its deterrent effect. In his discussion of specific crimes and punishments, Beccaria reveals even more clearly the premises of the new age. To him the major crimes are not lese majesty or heresy, but "crimes which are destructive of the security of individuals." The major penalties for him are fines and imprisonment. He was indeed the first to urge the entire abolition of capital punishment.

The principles of Beccaria did a good deal to transform the spirit of criminal-law administration even before the French Revolution. In all the chief countries of Europe reformers sprang up to urge the embodiment of these principles in legislation. Among the greatest of these were Jeremy Bentham and Sir Samuel Romilly, who struggled to secure an amelioration of the particularly barbarous English criminal law, but their efforts were long in vain because of the spirit of reaction that was inspired among English statesmen by the events of the French Revolution. On the other hand, in France, after the Revolution, penal reform was one of the first problems that occupied the Constituent Assembly, and the leaders of the Revolution, who were enamored of all things English, which they valued above their true worth, hastened to graft upon the French system of prosecution the English grand and petit jury, the chief features of the English system. Among the reforms was, of course, the abolition of torture and of secrecy of trials; but while a project for a penal code was also considered, its execution, due to the embroilment of France with the whole of Europe, had to be postponed until quieter days.

In the meantime, the ideas of Beccaria suggested to Anselm von Feuerbach, a Bavarian criminal-law reformer, a great slogan which was to dominate the whole movement for penal codification. The slogan was expressed still in Latin—*nullum crimen, nulla poena sine lege*—but when translated, the indebtedness of Feuerbach to Beccaria is readily perceived. It means, "No crime, no punishment, without a law." The slogan was fully realized for the first time in the French Code of Criminal Procedure of 1808 and the Penal Code of 1810, which have remained the classical models of all subsequent penal legislation. In these codes, which were the first examples of juristic art in the realm of criminal law, the philosophy of Beccaria triumphed completely.

In the classical codes of criminal procedure, a person accused of crime has almost as many advantages as the state. He is presumed to be innocent until proved guilty, and he may not be compelled to testify against himself. He has the right to employ counsel and to confront and cross-examine the witnesses of the state; he has the right to a prompt and public trial; he has also, almost everywhere except in the case of petty offenses, a right to a trial before a jury, which, having been introduced into the civil-law countries, has become an all but universal institution. Indeed, a prisoner now has a right to two trials: in the countries of both the common and the civil law he is given a preliminary hearing before some examining or committing magistrate, and then, if the state presents prima facie evidence of his guilt, a formal trial takes place. In France something of the secrecy of the old pre-Revolutionary procedure has been retained in the preliminary examination before the *juge d'instruction*, as the examining magistrate is called; but in the countries of the common law, prisoners are sometimes examined secretly by the police under conditions of duress, a procedure known as the application of the "third degree." On the other hand, in the process of institutional exchange, the countries of the common law have also taken over the institution of the public prosecutor, who in England is called the Director of Public Prosecutions and in the United States the District Attorney, so that the prisoner everywhere has to contend with a better machinery for the detection and prosecution of crime.

The classical penal codes themselves have been voluminous, but they are neatly arranged and well indexed. They are divided usually into "general" parts and "special" parts. The general parts set forth the doctrines applicable to all crimes—the rules of complicity, attempts, and intent in the commission of crimes. The special parts describe in detail the individual crimes, which moreover are organized into neat categories, such as crimes against the state, property, persons, public safety, public morals. Crimes are further divided into classes, which are determined by the gravity of the crime. In most common-law countries there is still a distinction between "felonies" and "misdemeanors," but since felonies no longer invariably entail death and confiscation, the distinction merely expresses varying degrees of moral disapproval. The continental codes, on the other hand, have a tripartite division of offenses, which are characterized as crimes, delicts, and contraventions, depending on the gravity of the offenses and the jurisdiction of the tribunals which may try them. England is today the only major country in which the whole penal law has not been codified; but, for all practical intents and purposes, the modern statutes which have revised the common law relating to the major offenses are codes in everything but name.

Yet, despite the more enlightened character of the modern criminal law, there is still a stupendous amount of criminality in even the most civilized countries. Doubtless it is not so great as in the eighteenth century, but it is open to question whether the improvement is due to the principles of the classical penology rather than to the growth of modern police systems, the magic of modern means of communication, the resources of modern science in detecting and pursuing criminals, and the improvement in standards of living. There is a universal realization that there is something wrong with the criminal law but little agreement about the proper measures to be taken. An endless number of crime commissions have been created, and almost every year some changes are made in this or that detail of the codes of criminal procedure, or penal codes, without altering their basic postulates. The system of Beccaria still rules in the criminal courts, though it has been all but discarded in the criminological laboratories and seminars. There is, indeed, a new criminological gospel loose in the world, which has revealed the absurdities of the classical penology.

Of course, Beccaria was right in demanding an end to the cruelties and barbarities of the penal system of his day—to arbitrariness, savage and mutilating punishments, torture, secret examination, and the denial of opportunities for defense. But the penological system which he constructed to justify these reforms rested upon a series of fantastic assumptions. As is so frequently true in the course of legal history, a series of attractive but gross fictions was invented to support reforms which in the main had empirical and practical justifications. In fact, the progress of penology was to demonstrate that the *theory* of the savage old criminalists was sounder than the theory of Beccaria. Where they had gone astray was in their horrible practices. And the particular weakness of the Beccarian system lay more in its theory of the substantive law of crimes and punishments than in its theory of criminal procedure.

The common law of tort had a great stock figure in the "reasonable" man. It was, indeed, a complex of rules for reasonable men. Beccaria invented the calculating man as the stock figure of the criminal law, but he was far less a reality than even the reasonable man. It is the rare criminal indeed who, before embarking on his crime, studies the penal code in order to determine the possible consequences to himself. If he does, it is only to get a suggestion of a crime to commit! It is a rarer criminal, even, who can master the penal code, and nineteenth-century criminal law had to solve the dilemma by indulging the secondary fiction that every man is presumed to know the law. Perhaps there is to be traced in this theory, too, the ideological influence of the new forms of business enterprise and of the economic theories engendered by them. But the criminal does not, like the capitalist entrepreneur, calculate profit and loss, assess the risk of his venture, and study the price of his crime. In view of the great intellectual ferment of the Enlightenment, it is really ironic to think that one of its apostles could conceive a no more original idea than to apply to the penal law the same technique which, at least since the age of Hammurabi, had been employed in the civil law in order to assure the security of property, that is, resort to the written word. It was easy enough on the basis of past experience to insert a list of punishable acts in the penal code. But what of the enterprising criminal who invented a new form of crime? Moreover, only a man who lived in the age of reason, and who was himself in love with mathematics, could have thought that it was possible to work out a rough proportionality between crime and punishment in terms of purely external and accidental factors. Is the burglar who breaks into a house through a window *always and invariably* more dangerous to society than the one who fortunately finds the door open? Is the thief who steals only fifty dollars *always and invariably* less dangerous to society than the thief who has stolen five hundred dollars? Is the killer who has slain once with premeditation, as, for instance, the husband who takes the life of a wife who has become a hopeless invalid, *always and invariably* more dangerous to society than the heedless bravado who kills a number of times in the heat of passion? As for the forms of punishments themselves, are fines and imprisonment always more humane than the death penalty when inflicted in a merciful manner? Many a criminal who has been sentenced to life imprisonment in even a model prison would have cursed Beccaria if he had known his name. Indeed, the domination of imprisonment in the classical penal system was only a new form of inhumanity. Fines obviously give an advantage to the rich. But, again, both fines and imprisonment had a great attraction in the economy of the new world. Fines may be calculated in the coin of the realm and imprisonment by the days of the calendar, and the criminal could be made to pay his debt to society in terms of the price system.

The absurdities of the Beccarian system were discovered first by the public prosecutors who had to cope with criminals. The judge is the great figure of the civil law, but in the penal law he plays second fiddle to the public prosecutor. Prosecutors everywhere escaped from the artificiality of the definitions of the classical penal codes by entering into a bargaining process with the criminal. They sometimes dismissed prosecutions altogether; at other times they accepted lesser pleas in order to secure a conviction. As the penal code grew in bulk, the penal law became arbitrary in its administration. The public prosecutor treated the penal code not as a series of commandments, every one of which was to be obeyed, but as a miscellaneous assortment of textual weapons, from which he could select those that were suited to his purpose, and whether he would proceed against a particular malefactor was not infrequently determined by political as well as personal considerations. The caprice or malevolence of the public prosecutor was less dangerous than in past centuries only because the savage punishments were gone. As a matter of fact, the safety of the individual rested as much upon the fact that public opinion had become more enlightened and humane as upon the limitations of the penal codes.

The experience of practice was reinforced by the speculations of modern sociology and psychiatry. The whole theory of moral responsibility, which was the very centrum of the Beccarian system, was attacked from both angles. Socialist theory in particular insisted upon the environmental factors, particularly malnutrition and poverty, in the causation of crime. Beccaria himself had called attention to the contradiction of "punishing by the laws the crimes which the laws have occasioned," but he had in mind the barbarity of the laws themselves rather than the influence of economic conditions. The relation between poverty and crime was undeniable, but it was not a solution of the whole problem. After all, not all the poverty-stricken were in jail. The school of Lombroso said that the criminal, like the poet, was born, not made. But it was equally obvious that not all the feeble-minded were in jail, or yet in hospitals for the mentally ill. Modern psychiatry concentrated upon personality traits in studying crime causation.

Thus was born the positivist school of modern criminology, as it is called, which has discarded altogether the classical conceptions of crime and punishment. It rejects the very conception of punishment, for which it substitutes that of social dangerousness and treatment. It is primarily interested not in the crime, which it regards only as a symptom, but in the criminal. It holds that the attempt to commit a crime may justify as long a course of treatment as a completed crime, and that it is impossible to determine in advance how long a period of confinement will be necessary. With cold scientific logic it insists, on the other hand, that the criminal who is incapable of reformation shall be painlessly exterminated. To carry out its program, it has urged and secured the widespread adoption of such measures as the indeterminate sentence and probation and parole, which permit within bounds the earlier discharge of promising offenders and the longer segregation and incarceration of repeated and dangerous offenders. Indeed, the more radical of the positivists insist that the only function of the criminal trial presided over by a judge should be to determine guilt, while treatment should be left entirely to psychiatrists, criminologists, and social workers. But not even the most optimistic of the positivists would maintain that successful treatment is always possible under the conditions of modern society. Probation and parole have largely modified the Beccarian system, but only on the paper of the statute books. The great twin measures of positivism have been defeated by political influence in their administration and by inadequacy of personnel, but, above all, by the contradictions of the social and economic system. To treat the criminal as a sick man, it is necessary to give him medical and economic advantages, which seem to penalize rectitude and put a premium upon crime.

These very contradictions of contemporary society explain, however, why the fictions of Beccaria still rule in the criminal courts, at least in countries which still maintain political democracy; they reveal also the sources of the strength of the Beccarian system. It is a wonderful system of make-believe, absurd in the world of science, but it cannot be abandoned in the world of modern political society. It is the political factor, which in the history of law has always prevailed over scientific considerations, that still counsels the preservation of the forms of the criminal law. Who in the contemporary world of greed and hate and clash of interests and classes would accept the scientific objectivity of the positivist criminologist? Tomorrow his "treatment" might be indistinguishable from that of the criminalists of old. In the history of law, Beccaria has gone down as the great criminal-law reformer. We are only now beginning to realize that perhaps his true significance is as a champion of freedom, for the penal codes have value only as guarantees of civil liberty.

Jeremy Bentham

THE VANITY OF LAW REFORM

IN DIFFERENT WAYS BOTH BLACKSTONE AND BECCARIA WERE IN-
voluntary law reformers. The most determined law reformer of all time,
however, was undoubtedly Jeremy Bentham. One of his disciples spoke
without exaggeration when he said that "the age of law reform and the
age of Jeremy Bentham are one and the same." Alfred Venn Dicey, the
celebrated modern expositor of the British constitution, once said that
"the history of legal reform in England in the nineteenth century is
the story of the shadow cast by one man, Bentham." But Sir Henry
Maine, who had a more universal and historical outlook, has gone even
further, and has said: "I do not know of a single law reform effected
since Bentham's day which cannot be traced to his influence." Bentham
was an Englishman, and his primary passion was the reform of the
common law. His significance is, however, not only European but
universal. Early in his career an admirer hailed him as the Newton
of legislation.

It was Sir Henry Maine, too, who said that Blackstone made
Bentham a jurist "by virtue of sheer repulsion." The epigram is, however, based upon the false assumption that it was the personality of the
commentator rather than the subject of his commentary against which
Bentham revolted. He regarded the common law as an Augean stable,
which, like Hercules, he was called upon to cleanse. Blackstone wrote
for a landed aristocracy that was already slipping, while Bentham
became the voice of a new class of industrialists that was beginning
to emerge. The commentator reflected to some extent the influence
of the Commercial Revolution, while the reformer anticipated the whole
legal and political program of the Industrial Revolution. Even as
Blackstone wrote, the Enclosure Acts had destroyed the English
peasantry as a class and had turned them into factory fodder. The age

of the machine was already in the offing, and before long the new science had ushered it in.

The intellectual stage was set when Bentham came upon the scene. The Newton of science had prepared the way for the Newton of legislation by stating the physical law of universal attraction. Hume had developed a philosophy and psychology based upon experience. The new psychological law of the association of ideas revealed that ideas came together in the mind as men did in the market. Adam Smith then proclaimed the gospel of free competition in *The Wealth of Nations*. Jeremy Bentham now proceeded to found the philosophy of utilitarianism as the justification of the needed legal and political reforms. Institutions were to be judged by their utility, and whether they were to be regarded as useful was to depend solely upon their capacity to produce a balance of happiness. Men, who acted from egoistic motives, responded only to the promptings of pleasure and pain. In their pursuit of pleasure, to be sure, individuals might injure each other, but to restrain the excesses of egoism, there was the legislator who would step in to prevent the commission of any wrongful act by threatening the infliction of a pain somewhat greater than the anticipated pleasure. By this means there would be secured an artificial identification of the interests of individuals in society. Such was the aim of the positive science of legislation.

The "positive" science of legislation championed by Bentham stood, however, in strange contrast to the "natural" science of economics, in which the interests of men were reconciled according to the spontaneous laws of exchange. The economics of laissez faire taught precisely that the intervention of the legislature was unnecessary in economic activity, and Bentham wholly accepted this doctrine. The legislation with which he concerned himself operated in the traditional spheres of civil and criminal law. Even then the scope of its interference with the natural laws of economic activity was really minimal. The civil law was dominated by the principle of freedom of contract which permitted entrepreneurs to make their own bargains. The whole force of legislation therefore would be felt in the criminal law, which merely protected the property men had gained by their bargains. The calculus of pleasure and pain held sway particularly in the field of criminal law, which was Bentham's chief interest during the greater part of his life. It is significant that in the field of civil law his greatest interest was to be civil procedure, which meant that he was to deal primarily with the machinery of enforcing those rights, which nobody who mattered really questioned. It was only late in life that Bentham began to interest himself in political questions or in questions of constitutional law.

The basic contradiction of Bentham's philosophy made him an eccentric and paradoxical figure. In English legal history Bentham occupies the position of the scandalous reformer who has become respectable. English lawyers still like to maintain the absurd belief that Bentham was an ignoramus in matters of English legal history, but even they admit the beneficent character of his reforms. He was certainly as great a satirist as Swift. He had a scurrilous wit, and he said the most dreadful things. Could anything be worse than his gibe, "Whether it is a question of a saucepan or a kingdom, is not the top the scum?" Yet actually Bentham was always respectable. He was a profound believer in the existing scheme of property relationships, and for the greater part of his life he was even contented with the political structure of the British government. He wanted to reform the law, but it was a matter of indifference to him whether the form of government was a constitutional monarchy, a republic, or a benevolent despotism. He made fun of the gentry who toasted the "Matchless Constitution," and thus rallied around waste, depredation, oppression, and corruption. Yet he believed that the good points of the British constitution far outweighed its bad ones. He once admitted that when he began his career as a reformer he "never suspected that the people in power were against reform" but supposed that "they only wanted to know what was good in order to embrace it." Although he lost this Socratic faith, he always remained a strange mixture of shrewdness and naïveté. He had, indeed, the optimism as well as the naïveté characteristic of the new economic philosophy of laissez faire. His conservatism was perhaps best exemplified in his aversion to the whole philosophy of the Social Contract and natural rights with all its revolutionary implications. Jeremy Bentham resolved not to meddle with economic laws. He would be a law reformer. The honor which he ultimately achieved in this role was alone sufficient to convince him that even law reform was respectable.

Although Bentham, as the founder of utilitarianism, which is a system of philosophy, could well claim the title of philosopher, he is better described as a legislative inventor. He despised all metaphysics and distrusted all abstractions. For him philosophy was only the theo-

retical basis of some concrete reform. What Bentham wished to found
was a science of legislation, and to do so he needed some general
formula. Machines were judged by their utility. Why should not social
institutions be judged by the same standard? Bentham was ultimately
to become far more absorbed in the machinery by which law was enforced than in the law itself. The legal devices he invented were
designed to have the beautiful functional simplicity and efficiency of
the machine. As a legislative inventor, it did not matter to Bentham
whether he devised a code for his own or for some foreign country. He
actually held himself out as ready to legislate for any country on earth
that should seek his services. If he were living today, he would doubtless have advertised. In fact, his inventions were to include scientific
as well as legal devices: for instance, a "frigidarium" to preserve fruits
and vegetables, and a mechanical monitor of order in the House of
Commons.

An inventor tends to achieve a reputation for eccentricity, and in
the case of Bentham this reputation was enhanced by the paradoxical
character of his thought, as well as by the extravagant poses of his old
age, when he had become an almost mythical figure. He seemed to exist
almost apart from his age, when in fact he was its most sensitive representative and responded most readily and unerringly to its stimulating
influences. The legal philosopher of industrialism was bound to seem
a strange figure to the pre-industrial age in which he began his career,
and the impression still survives. It is therefore particularly important
to realize that Bentham's personal life was not fundamentally abnormal.
The inventor of the "felicific calculus" suffered the pleasures and the
pains of the common lot of humanity, and was a product of the environment in which he lived. When his behavior did become fantastic, it
was only a defense mechanism against the hostile curiosity of his duller
contemporaries.

Bentham was a descendant of a bourgeois English family, the type
from which the industrialists of the next generation were to be recruited. His great-grandfather was a prosperous pawnbroker in the
reign of Charles II, and his grandfather was a flourishing attorney.
His own father, Jeremiah Bentham, also an attorney and clerk to the
Worshipful Company of Scriveners, increased the family patrimony
considerably by shrewd moneylending and dabbling in real estate.
Jeremiah Bentham had all the conventional middle-class ideas and
aspirations, and yet when his parents proposed to marry him to a girl

with a jointure of £10,000, he refused and married instead Alicia Grove, whom he had met at Buckholt Acres, a public place of entertainment. His parents regarded the match as a *mésalliance,* although the bride was the daughter of a prosperous tradesman of Andover. Two sons were born of this union, which occurred in 1744. Jeremy came into the world in Red Lion Street, Houndsditch, on February 15, 1748, and remained an only child for nine years, when his brother, Samuel, arrived to complete the family.

Jeremy Bentham went through the usual course of education for a child of his station in life—Westminster School, Queens College, Oxford, and Lincoln's Inn. Jeremiah Bentham was sure that his son would immortalize the family name by achieving the distinction of sitting on the woolsack, no less. And it must be admitted that there was good reason for his hopes. Jeremy was clearly a child prodigy. He was breeched at the age of three, and was known to his father's friends as "the little philosopher" at the age of five. He acquired Latin and Greek, music and French, with hardly any effort at all. He was, however, a shy, delicate, and sensitive child whose body was as small and weak as his mind was strong and quick. In fact, until he was sixteen he was hardly much taller than a dwarf. He hated athletics as much as he loved books.

Unfortunately for his personal happiness, the precocious and sensitive child was handled by everyone in such a way that he was bound to become a *révolté.* In Westminster School, which he entered at the age of seven, the fagging system still prevailed, and it was properly described by Bentham in later years as "a wretched despotism." Oxford was somewhat better but the unathletic and retiring boy of twelve was an object of both curiosity and sport among his fellows. One of them, Goodyear St. John, who was to become a parson, loved to hold Jeremy upside down by his legs.

The home environment did not make up for the trials of school. The servants loved to tease and frighten Jeremy with dreadful stories of ghosts, to such an extent that even late in life he could not rid himself entirely of the fear of phantoms. There were, to be sure, the brief but delightful pleasures of visiting his two grandmothers—Grandmother Grove, at Browning Hill near Redding, and Grandmother Bentham at Barking in Essex. Jeremy was also greatly attached to his mother, but she died before he was quite eleven. In a way this disaster proved to be not without benefit for the boy. Before he had left Oxford his father had remarried a "smart and sprightly lady" by the name of Mrs. Abbott, the widow of a fellow of Balliol, who already had two children. In view of this marriage, Jeremiah Bentham decided that it would be best to set up his eldest son in quarters of his own. He provided him on this occasion with two small estates which would yield him an income of about £103 a year.

Jeremy Bentham really hated his father, who had all the worst characteristics of the bourgeois and who certainly never understood his son. He could never resist the temptation of showing him off in company and lecturing him in private on the importance of worldly success. He was always talking of the necessity for "push." Everything was to be done by "pushing." "Pushing" was the one thing needful. And so on *ad nauseam*. Jeremiah Bentham was always giving his son what would have been good advice for somebody else. Doubtless he intended only to impart to his offspring the benefits of his own experience, but the most common type of pavement in hell is made of parents' good intentions. Jeremiah Bentham could be extravagant on rare occasions, but as a rule he was penny-wise and pound-foolish. He furnished his precocious son with inferior tutors to save a few shillings, and never supplied him with enough money for decent clothes. Indeed, in his undergraduate days Jeremy presented a decidedly shabby if not ragged appearance. When he was sixteen, however, his father, in a generous mood, took him on a grand tour of England and France in order to finish off his education.

Life always has its pleasures and its pains. The gloomy religion of Jeremy Bentham's own day, although it promised the bliss of heaven, emphasized the terrors of hell. In after years, he himself compared Westminster to "hell," and Browning Hill, where his maternal grandmother lived, to "paradise." The contrast of pleasure and pain was, however, peculiarly emphasized for him by a beloved mother and a hated father. His disposition was naturally cheerful, and he shunned somber and frightening objects as if they were ghosts. Shortly after coming of age, he read Oliver Goldsmith's *Deserted Village,* but it repelled him. "I liked nothing gloomy," he explained in later years. As for poetry in general, it was one of his blind spots. He loved music and the theater, flowers and animals, particularly cats, and all inanimate nature, but of verse he thought purely in terms of utility: doggerel might be useful in remembering some fact.

Bentham once described himself as "the feeblest of all feeble boys."

For such a boy there could be only the pleasures of the mind, and he read avidly—history, biography, and romance. When he was seven his French tutor La Combe, to his great delight, introduced him to fairy tales and Fénelon's *Telemachus,* which he came to regard as "the foundation stone" of his whole character, because he detected in it the first glimmering of the principle of utility. At the age of ten he already had read Locke and Mandeville, and when he entered Oxford two years later, he was apparently so captivated by the philosophy of rationalism that he had to struggle with his conscience before he could bring himself to sign the Thirty-nine Articles. In the following years he read Hartley, Beccaria, and Montesquieu, but it was to Hume, Priestley, and Helvetius that he traced the genesis of the principle of utility. He found it imperfectly formulated in Hume, but when he happened upon it in Priestley's *Essay on Government,* he exclaimed, in an inward ecstasy, "Eureka!" like Archimedes of old. When he read the *de l'Esprit* of Helvetius the next year, he discovered his true vocation. In giving the etymology of the word "genius," Helvetius explained that it was identical with inventiveness or productiveness. This led the young Bentham to ask: "Have I a genius for anything? What can I produce? What of all earthly pursuits is the most important?" In Helvetius he also found the answer. It was, "Legislation." The legislator was both moralist and educator and, almost like a god, molded men's lives. "And have I genius for legislation?" Bentham next asked himself, and he gave himself the answer, fearfully and tremblingly: "Yes!" When he was thirty Bentham declared: "What Bacon was to the physical world, Helvetius was to the moral." The moral world had theretofore had its Bacon, but its Newton was yet to come.

The youthful jurist at Lincoln's Inn was not only deeply immersed in the literature of the Enlightenment but was also conducting experiments in science. While at Oxford, he had persuaded his reluctant father to let him take a course in science. Now, in his chambers in Lincoln's Inn, he was conducting experiments in chemistry in a closet laboratory which he had himself fitted up. A musty smell from the tomes of Bracton, Littleton, and Coke might have been expected to emanate from chambers in Lincoln's Inn, but on occasion they stank to high heaven, for among Bentham's experiments was the evaporation of urine in order to obtain phosphorus. Although he maintained an interest in science all his life, Bentham never became a physical scientist himself. He lived the life of a scientist vicariously through his younger brother,

Samuel, whose education he practically took over. He made of him a
fine naval architect and inventor, and the relation between the brothers
always remained warm and intimate. In his young manhood Samuel
was Jeremy's chief confidant, and they maintained a lively correspondence. In their letters Jeremiah Bentham was always referred to
irreverently as "Q.S.P.," the initials of Queen's Square Place, the name
of the paternal residence. On one occasion Jeremy wrote to tell Samuel
that his father had extracted the promise of a visit but added: "O
Lord! if it be possible take this cup from me." Jeremy advised his
younger brother about everything, including the topic of women, and
he spoke with some authority since he had himself had some experiences with women of easy virtue. "Whatever they take patiently," he
advised Samuel, "do thou a little more. In general they will sooner for-
give thee too much than too little."

Despite his absorption in philosophy and science and the pleasures
of life, Bentham found time to read also in what he described in his
maturity as "the legal trash of the seventeenth century," upon which he
could then look down "from the heights of utility." The prodigy had to
wait to come of age to be admitted to the bar, but, as might be expected,
he had no ambition to gratify his father by striving to become Lord
Chancellor. Quite apart from everything else, the mere fact that his
father was a lawyer was enough to alienate him from the profession. But
practice was farthest from the thoughts of the young man who had already decided that he had a genius for "legislation." In litigation he beheld all the evil features of what he called "the Demon of Chicane."
When his father considerately put him in the way of a client, a friend by
the name of Chamberlain Clarke, who had brought an equity suit involving about £50, the young advocate advised the prospective client to dis-
continue the action, because the costs alone would be almost half the
amount at stake. This advice was sound, but not of the kind to encourage litigious clients to come knocking on his door.

It only remained for Jeremy to secure the parental consent to retire
from active practice and to devote himself to reform. Jeremiah Bentham
was profoundly shocked and bewildered, but what could he do? His
own flesh and blood was filled with a love of innovation. He was obviously a lost child. He had done everything humanly possible to make
him into a gentleman, yet he desired only to embark upon this mad
career. It was not only exasperating, it was incomprehensible. He had
never observed any signs of political radicalism in his son, who followed

strictly the Tory party line. Why, as a boy of twelve he had written a poem mourning the passing of George II! Submitted to Dr. Johnson, it had been pronounced "a very pretty performance for a young man," although the young man in later years himself described it as "a mediocre performance on a trumpery subject written by a miserable child." Jeremy had witnessed with satisfaction the coronation of George III, and a few years later he had approved the prosecution of that troublemaker John Wilkes. In fact, he had been present upon this instructive occasion in the King's Bench, where a student's seat had been secured for him at no little expense by his hopeful father. Unfortunately, however, a few years later, Jeremy was also present in the King's Bench when Wilkes's sentence of outlawry was reversed by Lord Mansfield. The youth was fascinated by the grace and eloquence of the great judge, who was something of an innovator himself, and his first composition as a reformer was written to repel the unjust attack upon his "living idol," whose house he had taken to haunting so that he might catch a glimpse of the judge's benevolent countenance.

Jeremy Bentham was now free to live upon his pittance of £103 a year, and to devote himself to the unselfish cause of law reform. The supreme apostle of the philosophy of pleasure and pain never came to know the pleasures and pains of matrimony. All his life long he remained a bachelor. But it has been discovered in recent years that he did experience a rather passionate love affair, which all but wrecked his career as a reformer. He fell in love with Mary Dunkly, a pretty pauper who was not quite eighteen. He met her at the home of his friend John Lind, who advised him to marry the girl and support her by his pen. This idea did not appeal at all to Bentham, who sought instead his father's consent to the match. Not only was the parental blessing not forthcoming, but Jeremiah Bentham threatened to disinherit his fatuous son. The son pleaded, but the father remained adamant. Law reform was a youthful folly that might be outlived, but marriage was an irrevocable step. In the end, law reform proved stronger than a penniless love in the calculus of pleasure and pain, and Jeremy Bentham not only gave up Mary Dunkly but in his misery yielded momentarily to cynicism and fell in with his father's plans to marry and resume the practice of law. Jeremiah Bentham had his eye on a Miss Stretton, a wealthy heiress, who lived with her mother in the country. Q.S.P., Jeremy reported to Samuel, actually took a house at Fetcham to be near them, but Jeremy did not prove a very ardent suitor, or the lady's mother, as the suitor himself put it, may have "smelt a rat." The whole scheme had to be abandoned, and Jeremy Bentham was saved for the cause of law reform. Such perils as these had led him to record this noble sentiment in his commonplace book for 1774–75:

Oh, Britain! Oh, my country! The object of my waking and my sleeping thoughts! Whose love is my first labour and greatest joy—passing the love of woman—thou shalt bear me witness against these misruling men. I cannot buy, nor will I ever sell my countrymen. My pretensions to their favour are founded not on promises but on past endeavours— not on having defended the popular side of a question for fat fees, but on the sacrifice of years of the prime of life—from the first dawnings of reflection to the present hour—to the neglect of the graces which adorn a private station; deaf to the calls of present interest and to all the temptations of a lucrative profession.

The career of Bentham as a law reformer seemed to begin logically enough. He attacked Dr. Blackstone. He had attended his lectures at Oxford as a youth of fifteen, but for all his immaturity he clearly perceived the implications of his teacher's philosophy. He admired his elegance but intensely disliked his ideas. He confided to his commonplace book the thought that Blackstone carried "the disingenuousness of the hireling advocate into the chair of the professor," and he added for good measure: "He is the dupe of every prejudice and the abettor of every abuse. No sound principles can be expected from that writer whose first object is to defend a system." He was shrewd enough to perceive that "upon the translation of the lawyer's dog-Latin scriptures into a sort of English, the darkness was but the more visible." Above all, Bentham wished to be the prophet of the Law as It Ought to Be. He therefore had to dispose of the oracle of the Law as It Is.

Yet the idea of publishing an attack on Blackstone was not Bentham's but that of his first intimate friend, John Lind. It only proves that the Lord has many instruments at hand to work His will. Lind was an ex-clergyman, who had sought his fortune in Poland and returned to England as the unofficial minister of the King of Poland. The friendship between Bentham and Lind rested upon their mutual admiration of Lord Mansfield. Bentham was to exhibit a remarkable capacity for attracting friends and disciples all his life. They followed each other in an endless procession, and they were the best proof that

Bentham was neither solitary nor an eccentric and that the work he did not only needed to be done but was inevitable.

John Lind sent the manuscript of his attack on Blackstone to Bentham for criticism. The critic did not like the work at all, and thought that the best constructive criticism would be to rewrite the effort of his friend. This was to prove characteristic of Bentham: he never attacked an abuse without also outlining the remedy. When Lind was presented with the *fait accompli,* he generously retired from the field. Bentham called his work *A Comment on the Commentaries,* but this was not published in its entirety until recent years. The part that Bentham decided to publish anonymously in 1776 was entitled *A Fragment on Government,* and it consisted of an exposition of the fallacies of Locke's Social-Contract theories and of the defects of the British constitution, which Bentham did not regard as quite perfect. The work of the unknown author caused a great sensation and was variously attributed to the leading legal figures of the day, including Lord Mansfield. Jeremiah Bentham, however, shared the secret of the book's authorship and, as usual, he could not resist the temptation to boast. To his great surprise, his son Jeremy was beginning to amount to something. As soon as it became known that the *Fragment* was the work of a youthful and unknown author, public interest in it virtually ceased.

Jeremiah Bentham had, nevertheless, done his son a good turn. There was one man who took note of the talents of the youthful author, and he was none other than the extremely wealthy, powerful, and brilliant Lord Shelburne, later to become Marquis of Lansdowne. Lord Shelburne was a Tory democrat, a patron of Priestley and Price, a friend of Franklin and the French *philosophes.* He was on the side of the American colonies, and even kept his head during the French Revolution. He was one of the few Englishmen of his time who understood the rising importance of the middle class and the significance of the revolutionary movement. He once even remarked: "I have long thought that *the people* have but one cause throughout the world—it is *sovereigns* who have different interests." He was, in fact, much more radical politically than Bentham. He believed not only in legal but in parliamentary reform.

Lord Shelburne thought that Bentham would prove valuable as a political pamphleteer, and one day some years later he made a sudden appearance at his chambers in Lincoln's Inn to invite him to come to Bowood Castle. The youthful author of the *Fragment on Government* was then in a state of profound discouragement and depression. He had been working on his most important theoretical work, *An Introduction to the Principles of Morals and Legislation,* and while he had had it printed, he could not bring himself to publish it. Now the unexpected visit of the noble lord, as well as his all but incredible invitation, gave him new confidence in himself. With a characteristic middle-class feeling of gratitude, he declared in later years in speaking of Lord Shelburne: "He raised me from the bottomless pit of humiliation. He made me feel I was something." On August 16, 1781, a memorable day in his life, Bentham set out for Bowood. Shortly after his arrival, he had a rather casual but disillusioning conversation with Lord Shelburne in the candle room. "Mr. Bentham," said Lord Shelburne, candles in hand, "what is it you can do for me?" Very much surprised, Bentham replied: "Nothing at all, my lord, nothing that I know of; I never said I could. I am like the Prophet Balaam: the word that God putteth into my mouth, that alone can I ever speak." Lord Shelburne doubtless took this reply as a declaration of political independence, but he was wise enough, nevertheless, to retain Bentham's friendship. The relation remained very cordial for at least ten years. But once when Bentham asked something of Lord Shelburne, the latter took the occasion to refuse. The Newton of legislation had a momentary impulse to be a legislator in fact, and had asked his noble friend to get him a seat in Parliament.

Bentham's first visit to Bowood, which lasted many weeks, was not only exciting but important in the development of his career. He was made much of by his host and Lady Shelburne, who played musical duets with him, and the experience flattered that egoism in him which he believed to be the sole spring of human nature. Lord Shelburne insisted that he read to the ladies at tea paragraphs from his new work, the *Introduction to the Principles of Morals and Legislation.* Even at Bowood, Bentham insisted on doing a daily stint, and his only complaint was that he had to dress twice daily. Bentham also felt some further flutterings of the heart. He was on the point of falling in love with Caroline Vernon, Lady Shelburne's sister, when she departed. He was then smitten by Caroline Fox, Lady Shelburne's niece, who was then hardly fourteen! When past fifty, and again when a very old man, he made her offers of marriage, which were rejected on each occasion.

The last time he wrote wistfully: "I am more lively than when you presented me with the flowers in the green lane," and then went on to report that in Spanish America he had been hailed "Legislator del Mundo" and petitioned for a code of laws.

Only one event threatened to disturb the serenity of Bentham's days at Bowood. When his incredulous father learned of his son's visit, he tried to crash the castle gates. He wrote to inform Jeremy that he and his wife were going to take the waters at Bath, and his son, forgetting that the road to Bath passed very near Bowood, mentioned his father's plans to Lord Shelburne, who kindly suggested that the couple interrupt their journey by stopping at the castle. Jeremy Bentham was quite panic-stricken at the thought of Jeremiah Bentham at Bowood. "Your Lordship is very good," he told Lord Shelburne, "but he is full as well where he is," and to his brother Samuel he wrote: "What a pretty scene would have been exhibited had I suffer'd my Lord to send for them! What a mixture of hectoring and puffing, and self-complacency and cringing and self-ostentation and forced civility."

Bowood was the great country house of the period, and Bentham was to meet many distinguished men there. On his first visit he met William Pitt and his brother, Lord Chatham, as well as Lord Camden, Chief Justice of the Common Pleas, and John Dunning, the famous leader of the King's Bench bar, who were, however, not impressed when Lord Shelburne submitted the *Introduction* to them for their perusal. They snubbed the young author, and their indifference was not calculated to increase his respect for the Law as It Is. At Bowood, Bentham also met Sir Samuel Romilly, who was to do so much to champion his ideas on criminal-law reform in Parliament, and Joseph Townsend, who was to write the most important treatise of the century on the poor law. By far his most valuable encounter at Bowood, however, was the Swiss pastor, Étienne Dumont, who became his humble disciple, the editor, adapter, and reviser of his work, which was sometimes published in French before it appeared in English. The most notable example of such prior foreign publication is Bentham's *Traités de legislation*. Dumont also became Mirabeau's secretary, and supplied the latter with material for his speeches from the private treasury of Bentham's writings. Toward the end of his life Bentham fell out with Dumont, but his place was promptly taken by John Bowring, the city merchant and apostle of free trade, who edited and published his collected works. There was probably never a writer who needed editors more than Bentham. He wrote profusely but sometimes chaotically. He found it difficult to keep his mind on one subject. Always the practical reformer, he was ready to abandon a work in progress for some topic of more immediate interest. For somewhat similar reasons, he often postponed the publication of a work for many years. Sometimes, however, the delay was due to fear of prosecution for criminal libel.

From 1785 to 1788 the scene of Bentham's activities shifts from England to Russia, which in comparison with his own country seemed to him from afar an enlightened land. His brother Samuel had gone to seek his fortune there in 1779, and had become the superintendent of Prince Potemkin's vast projects, which included the building of a Black Sea fleet, for use against the Turks, and the establishment of a new colony at which the latest methods in agriculture and industry should help bridge the tremendous gap between feudalism and the Industrial Revolution. Samuel wrote to ask his brother to secure for him needed books and supplies as well as a clever dairy manager and two dairymaids. Jeremy Bentham, dreaming of being a legislator, thought that Catherine the Great, that benevolent despot, would lend an ear to his ideas of law reform, and decided that he himself would accompany the dairy help. He set forth in August, 1785, and traveled by way of Paris, Lyons, Nice, Genoa, Smyrna, Constantinople, Bulgaria, and Poland. It proved to be a trying as well as an arduous journey. On the way from Smyrna to Constantinople, the ship almost foundered; the clever dairy manager seduced one of the dairymaids and carried on with her in a very distressing and acrimonious manner; on the last stage of the journey through Bulgaria, Bentham suffered from the sins of omission and commission of a drunken janizary who answered to the name of Ahmet. When he arrived at Crichoff in the Ukraine, which was his brother's headquarters, Samuel was away on a tour of inspection with Prince Potemkin. It did not take long for Jeremy to discover that the model colony was practically a madhouse, and that Russia itself was a most unpromising land for a legislator who believed in the principle of utility. Although he had come to Russia in the hope of obtaining an interview with Catherine, he did not even bother to see her when she passed through Crichoff about a year after his arrival. He had obviously come to the conclusion that Russia was not Utopia.

But the stay in Russia was not entirely time wasted. Word reached Bentham that Pitt was contemplating the enactment of legislation that would have reduced the legal rate of interest from 5 to 4 per cent. Although Adam Smith, whom Bentham regarded as inspired, had not denounced the existing law limiting interest, Bentham wrote his *Defence of Usury*. It was in the form of a series of letters addressed to George Wilson, who was then his most important friend. Wilson was a practicing lawyer, but he was not inimical to reform, and he was an important influence in Bentham's life during his early years. Wilson's chief complaint was that his friend did not possess even "a common degree of steadiness." If only he would stick to one project, and keep from pursuing "small game"! The letters on usury might not have been published if Jeremiah Bentham had not intervened. They made quite a stir when they appeared, and even Adam Smith complimented the work as "one of a superior man." The doctrine that Bentham espoused was that "interest, as love and religion, and so many other pretty things, should be free."

When Bentham returned to England, he settled down at a farmhouse near Hendon. It is from this period that his intimacy with Romilly dates. Bentham declared that they were attracted to each other by a mutual "love for pussies." Bentham lived an obscure existence, "seeing nobody, reading nothing and writing books which nobody reads," or at least so his friend Romilly said. There is evidence, however, that Bentham during these years harbored a truly magnificent pipe dream. Despite his disillusionment with Catherine, he still had not lost all faith in the benevolent despots. Even a Charlemagne, he reasoned, would be lost "in the labyrinth of jurisprudence," but not if he had a Bentham to guide him. He would draft a great code, a Pannomion, which should be promulgated in all enlightened lands with the opening of the new century. In the meantime, he would publish his *Introduction to the Principles of Morals and Legislation*, the theoretical foundation of his work of codification. In 1789 as much of the edition printed in 1780 as had not been devoured by the rats was released to the world but, alas, it attracted very little attention. Perhaps it was because the storm of the French Revolution had broken.

It was not the end of the century, and the universal code was not complete. But the French Constituent Assembly, which was doubtless ignorant of proper methods of legislative procedure, seemed to Bentham to present an unparalleled opportunity. He proceeded to prepare a tract which should give the Assembly the benefit of British parliamentary experience. Hearing, also, that the Assembly was contemplating the creation of a new judicial establishment, he proceeded to sketch a scheme of judicial organization, including even some features which he himself regarded as too radical, such as the popular election of judges. He developed now most of the basic ideas on civil procedure which he was to champion in later years. Indeed, it was the Revolution in France that first set him to thinking seriously along procedural lines. On August 26, 1792, the Constituent Assembly, influenced by his friend Brissot, included Bentham in the list of those upon whom it was conferring the honorary title of French citizen—a list that included Washington, Paine, Priestley, Wilberforce, and Mackintosh. In accepting the honor, Bentham banteringly testified to his own political conservatism. He observed that he was willing to become a French citizen in Paris provided he could remain an English citizen in London, and to become a republican in Paris provided he could remain a royalist in London. As the excesses of the Revolution mounted, he became increasingly alarmed. He regarded the proposed confiscation of the goods of the Church as a threat to the security of all property, and he had to be dissuaded by his friend Romilly from forming an association to counteract republican propaganda. Bentham's fear of the Revolution was at least partly responsible for his estrangement from Lord Shelburne. The Declaration of the Rights of Man and the Citizen, regarded as "the *ne plus ultra* of metaphysics," filled him with impatience. Yet, by a curious irony, his disciple Dumont had felt compelled to take an important part in its drafting, although he shared Bentham's attitude. Dumont indeed characterized the famous document as puerile.

In the two decades following the French Revolution, Bentham made most of his outstanding contributions to reform. He had at last achieved financial independence and could work without fear of his father. Jeremiah Bentham had died early in 1792, and by his will had divided his property equitably between his two sons. In addition to the estate at Queen's Square Place, Westminster, which included a cottage where the blind Milton had written *Paradise Lost,* Jeremy received property yielding an income of about £600 a year. But, while Jeremy Bentham himself did not abandon the cause of law reform, the governing circles in England apparently had more pressing problems. Although his fame was spreading to "that large place called *abroad*," as he himself put it, he remained largely a prophet without honor in his own country. In darkest Russia, feudal Spain, and distant Latin America, he was probably better known than in England. An English Protestant missionary in Spain arrested as a Carlist spy was released with apologies by the Alcalde of Corcuvion when the latter discovered that the prisoner was a countryman of the "grand Baintham." In Latin America, Bentham's ideas were accepted or suppressed in accordance with the fortunes of perpetual revolution. In America, Aaron Burr proposed to make Bentham legislator of Mexico when Burr should become emperor. But when his friend Romilly entered Parliament in 1808 to secure the adoption of Bentham's program of criminal-law reform, he suffered complete and abysmal failure. The hostility in England to Bentham's ideas is usually attributed to the spirit of reaction that prevailed there after the French Revolution, but it is doubtful that his schemes of reform, which were often in advance of the needs of the times, would have made rapid progress in England even in the absence of the great upheaval. While the Industrial Revolution had begun in England, the greater triumphs of the machine age and industrial capitalism were still to come.

Some of Bentham's most brilliant pamphlets on law reform were written in the 1790's. They included the *Draught of a Plan for a Judicial Establishment in France,* already mentioned; *Truth v. Ashurst,* a sardonic attack on the glorification of the common law, inspired by the extraordinary complacency of the charge made to the Grand Jury of Middlesex on the nineteenth of November, 1792, by Sir William Ashurst, judge of the King's Bench; *A Protest against Law Taxes,* exposing the evils of the high cost of justice; *Supply without Burthen,* a proposal to reduce taxes by extending the law of escheat to apply to the more remote cases of collateral inheritance; and finally two pamphlets on the poor law inspired by Pitt's scheme to supply each deserving pauper with a cow. The prophet of industrialism was naturally hostile to such a proposal. Bentham was a philanthropist, but he did not believe in coddling the poor, and he opposed the increasing relaxation of the labor test. He believed that no able-bodied pauper should receive aid except in exchange for labor, and consequently urged the adoption of industry-houses, where they would be put to work under a public contractor.

The industry-house was derived from the Panopticon scheme, the ruling passion of Bentham's life and his greatest preoccupation from 1792 to 1813. The Panopticon, or "inspection-house," was conceived by Bentham with the aid of his brother Samuel during his visit to Russia. John Howard, the humanitarian, had exposed the horrible conditions

in the prisons. Therefore it was for Jeremy Bentham, the practical inventor and reformer, to devise a model prison. The Panopticon was to be
a circular building, in which the prisoners' cells were to be arranged in
concentric circles and in such a way that each prisoner's cell would
be visible from the governor's lodge in the center. The governor would
be able at all times to view each prisoner's cell, but he himself would
remain unseen, and thus there would be begotten in the prisoners'
minds "the sentiment of an invisible omniscience." The governor would
reform the prisoners by teaching them profitable trades, and they would
share in the profits of their labor. The management of the Panopticon
was to be based upon what Bentham called the "interest-and-duty-
junction-prescribing principle." In other words, the governor would
manage the prison in accordance with the terms of a public contract,
which would make his profits depend on his success in rehabilitating
the prisoners.

When Burke was shown an architectural model of the Panopticon,
he exclaimed: "Yes, there's the keeper—the spider in his web." Certainly, while the Panopticon was to be operated on the most enlightened
penological principles of the time, its architectural plan was such that
it would have added to the misery of imprisonment the terror of the
perpetual deprivation of privacy. Bentham, too, in the first flush of
Adam Smith's new economic revelation, was prepared to make even
public punishment a source of private profit. Parliament in 1794
actually enacted legislation authorizing the scheme of contract management, as well as the purchase of a site. The negotiations for the contemplated site collapsed, however, and Bentham himself then arranged
to purchase a site of the value of more than £12,000. Indeed, his
expenditures in the promotion of the Panopticon mounted so rapidly
that by 1798 he was reduced to penury, and, compelled to shut up his
house, he was driven to live with his brother. Worn out by parliamentary committees and ministers, poor Bentham was, as William
Wilberforce, the crusader against slavery, put it, "dying of sickness of
hope deferred." Wilberforce also testified that he had seen "the tears
run down the cheeks of that strong-minded man." In 1812 the government finally rejected the Panopticon scheme, but in the following year
it granted Bentham £23,000 as a recompense for his labors and expenditures. This amount actually tripled the income Bentham had previously enjoyed. Even law reform paid! Bentham himself observed

bitterly that he had been "condemned to join the Baal Peor of blood-suckers."

The tribulations of the Panopticon scheme filled Bentham with a smoldering resentment against George III and his ministers in particular and the British aristocracy in general, and were undoubtedly an important factor in turning him in his old age towards political liberalism and parliamentary reform. The transition was marked by his acquisition in 1808 of the most important of his disciples, James Mill, the son of a village cobbler, who was to become the historian of British India and the champion of parliamentary reform. At the age of sixty, Bentham was to most of his countrymen the crank of the Panopticon scheme rather than the philosopher of utilitarianism. The "push" of Mill brought him into prominence as a political as well as a legal reformer. As Halévy puts it in his *Growth of Philosophic Radicalism,* "Bentham gave Mill a doctrine, and Mill gave Bentham a school." Bentham had already boasted with pardonable pride of the possession of something of a school, but certainly Mill enlarged it and made it a force in practical politics. Bentham was now the theorist of the political movement that was actively promoted by Francis Place, the remarkable tailor of Charing Cross; William Cobbett, the pamphleteer; Sir William Burdett, the parliamentary orator; and Major Cartwright, the popular propagandist.

Yet Bentham's conversion to political radicalism was slow and cautious. He did not at first accept the principle of universal suffrage, although he did so in the end, together with the whole program of political reform. From the principle of utilitarianism Bentham now deduced "a pure representative democracy" based on "secrecy, universality, equality, and annuality of suffrage." This contemplated not only universal suffrage but a legislature consisting of a single chamber and annual parliaments. This was the way to "maximize happiness," and, since this was now the great objective, Bentham preferred to speak of "the greatest happiness principle" rather than "the principle of utility." It expressed better the objective of political utilitarianism, which was obviously "the greatest happiness of the greatest number."

Bentham's political ideas were embodied in his grandiose *Constitutional Code for the Use of All Nations Professing Liberal Opinions,* the chief labor of his old age, apart from his great work, *The Rationale of Judicial Evidence.* In his old age Bentham was busy also with various codification proposals. He offered a Pannomion, or complete code of laws, to such diverse personalities as the Emperor Alexander I of Russia and James Madison, President of the United States of America. He also addressed a general codification proposal to all nations professing liberal opinions, and accompanied the offer with universal testimonials to his ability as a legislator.

As an old man, Jeremy Bentham seems to have cultivated deliberately those eccentric arts which have tended to obscure his role as the juristic prophet of industrialism. After the parliamentary indemnity had made him a wealthy man again, he rented Ford Abbey in Devonshire, where he lived surrounded by his friends and disciples. Everyone was greatly amused by the contrast between the sumptuous feudal abbey and the ideas of its tenant. However, due to the loss of £8000 which he had invested in a Devonshire marble mine owned by a crazy inventor, Bentham, after four years, had to give up his tenancy of Ford Abbey and remove to Queen's Square Place, where he lived during the remainder of his life. The place became known as "the Hermitage," and Bentham himself as "the hermit."

From the Hermitage, Bentham almost never ventured. It has been said that he was as certain to be at home as Robinson Crusoe on his island. He had no need to go out into the world, which was now knocking on *his* door. But an invitation to the Hermitage was difficult to get, for Bentham refused to exhibit himself to curiosity-mongers. When Madame de Staël applied to Dumont for an introduction, she said: "Tell Bentham that I will see nobody till I have seen him." But Bentham only remarked: "Sorry for it, for then she will never see anybody."

The Hermitage was fitted up to suit the tastes of its master. It was heated by steam coils, one of which ran under Bentham's writing seat. Every living room in the house was fitted up with a piano. Bentham encouraged mice to play in his study, although it caused trouble with his cats. Despite his age, he worked regularly every day, assisted by his secretaries, whom he referred to always as his "reprobates," and sustained by conversation with his friends and disciples at the dining table. The old master's conversation, however, was often of a blasphemous character. His name for the Bible was the "Jugg Book" (derived from "juggernaut"). For exercise he walked in the flowery gardens of the Hermitage at a pace between a run and a trot. Every day the old philosopher could be seen taking his queer walks, wearing a som-

brero-like hat and carrying his stick, affectionately named "Dapple." His
long and flowing white hair waved in the wind around his bare neck.
He was dressed in a brown Quaker-cut coat and light brown cassimere
breeches, and white worsted stockings were drawn over the knees of
the breeches. In appearance he resembled Benjamin Franklin, but he
looked even more benign and cheerful. Bentham himself referred to his
walks as his "ante-jentacular" and "post-prandial perambulations," and
as his "ante-prandial circumgyrations." All his life long, although he
could write a very pungent king's English, he loved to employ outlandish words and to invent still more outlandish ones. Some of his
coinages were happy, and have become part of the legal language—for
instance, the terms "codification" and "international law." In his old
age, however, his passion for exactness so dominated him that he became
as obscure and unintelligible as any lawyer speaking the worst of legal
jargon.

Bentham described himself in his last days as "a comical old fellow."
Although he was losing the possession of his faculties, he did not desist
from work. Down to the very end he was, as he put it, "codifying like
any dragon." When he died on June 6, 1832, his last thought was to
"minimize pain" in his friends and servants, and so he sent them away
from his bedside. His death occurred only one day before the Reform
Bill of 1832 received the royal assent. By his will he left his body to
science, and Southward Smith, one of his friends, delivered his funeral
oration while his body lay on the dissecting table. Today his skeleton
hangs in the Anatomical Museum of University College, London,
which had been founded by his friends and disciples in 1828 as a center
of utilitarian learning.

While he lived, Jeremy Bentham had loosed upon his generation
of lawyers and politicians a steady torrent of castigating words. Books
and pamphlets carried them to every country within the orbit of European civilization. Yet, like all reformers, Bentham had but a few leading ideas, at which he hammered again and again, and it is necessary
to have only the merest acquaintance with these ideas to perceive their
relation to the pattern of the Industrial Revolution. This is as true of his
utilitarianism as it is of his general philosophy of law and particular
ideas of legal reform. The very form of his thought reflects the new
economic philosophy. Pleasure and pain may be equated with profit
and loss in "the commerce of happiness." Bentham himself once said:
"Money is the instrument of measuring the quantity of pain and pleas-

ure." The ideas of pleasure and pain are associated in the market of the mind. Egoism is the basic axiom of the legal system even as it is of the economic system. The individualistic rationalism of capitalism is to be supreme also in the realm of law. The new spirit of business enterprise had made itself felt even in the ethic of Protestantism. It was inevitable that the secular legal system should also be co-ordinated. As for the contradiction between the legal and economic spheres of activity represented by the principle of laissez faire, presumably everybody was too busy making money to worry about this.

The basic assumption of Bentham was that social science was as possible as physical science, and that the basic postulate of such a science must be the principle of utility. Whenever he could, he sought to clothe his propositions in the language of science, and his passion for inventing abstruse Latin and Greek polysyllables was related to the same endeavor. Of course, the law was to be a social science based upon general principles of utility. Now the law, as Blackstone had demonstrated, had general principles, but Bentham perceived that these were not scientific but purely technical principles, which were the product of tradition rather than dictates of utility. Moreover, the law was administered by persons who had not the slightest interest in scientific truth and were totally ignorant of scientific methods of investigation. "In virtue of his office," observed Bentham contemptuously, "every judge, every law-officer is supposed and pronounced to be profoundly versed in the science of the law." For tradition per se Bentham had no respect, holding that "the antiquity of a law is no reason." In general, he believed that it is from "the folly not the wisdom of our ancestors that we have much to learn."

The best friends of the traditional common law could hardly contend that it was based solely on principles of utility. Some of its principles, to be sure, had utility, but it was purely coincidental. The growth of the common law—indeed the growth of all legal systems—was dominated far less by considerations of efficiency than by motives of political and economic strategy. The judicial organization of the common law was primarily the result of a conflict for jurisdiction that had been waged between the king's courts and the local courts. "Do they consider," asked Bentham, "what it was for, that circuits were set a-going?" And he thus answered his own question: "It was to enable the great tyrant to swallow up the little ones." In this process the interest of the subject was a secondary consideration. In the struggle between the king

and his subjects, it had, on the other hand, again become necessary
to abandon utilitarian efficiency in order to preserve some liberty to
the individual. It had thus become customary to counterbalance the
effects of evil laws with procedural devices and personal guarantees of
civil liberty. To manipulate such an irrational system the services of
a professional class had become necessary, and the profit they derived
from their services tended to make the legal system still more irrational.
The profit motive led them to prefer their own happiness to the happiness of the greatest number.

If law was to be a science, it was necessary, therefore, to undermine
the common faith in the traditional guardians and expounders of the
common law, namely the judges and the lawyers. To the fulfillment of
this task Bentham devoted all his gifts of satire and invective. Lawyers
and judges were leagued together in a perpetual conspiracy, and Bentham in season and out conjured up "the Demon of Chicane," even as
the family servants had conjured up spirits in his childhood. The frauds
and chicaneries of "Judge & Co." constituted one of his constant
themes. Lawyers were "harpies of the law," "hirelings of the law,"
and even "purchaseable male prostitutes." "It is as impossible," he said,
"for a lawyer to wish men out of litigation, as for a physician to wish
them in health." It was foolish to expect any interest in reform on the
part of a lawyer. "Would you have the husbandman," he asked, "turn
up his nose at the rottenness of the manure that is giving fertility to
his fields?" The judges only co-operated with the lawyers in preserving
the rottenness of the system. To elevate a practicing lawyer to the
bench, declared Bentham, was "as expedient as putting a procuress at
the head of a girls' school." Nobody has ever had a more acute understanding of the role of the profit motive in the activities of the legal
profession. The pursuit of profit was all right for merchants and manufacturers, but laissez faire was not for lawyers. No doubt Bentham
thought that legal superstitions were not proper objects of exchange.

Bentham's spleen did not extend merely to the machinations of the
judges but to their official daily output, which was judge-made law.
There had been, of course, legislation in the history of the common
law, but it was of secondary importance in comparison with the judge-
made law. The common law was embodied in judicial decisions, and
acts of Parliament were only dissonances in the harmony of the system.
So Blackstone had taught. But to Bentham, judicial decisions, which
were not available to the layman, and which he could hardly have un-

derstood if they had been available, were only the products of a secret manufactory operated for their own benefit by "Judge & Co." He described judicial decisions as "the sort of piece-goods called *law*, and *that* of the goodness that cloth would be, if spun out of cobwebs." Or again, varying the metaphor, he called judicial decisions "dog law."

It is the judges [he explained] that make the common law. Do you know how they make it? Just as a man makes laws for his dog. When your dog does anything you want to break him of, you wait till he does it, and then beat him for it. This is the way you make laws for your dog: and this is the way the judges make law for you and me. They won't tell a man beforehand what it is he *should not do*—they won't so much as allow of his being told: they lie by till he has done something which they say he *should not have done*, and then they hang him for it.

Precedent is not the Benthamite form of law. The only proper source of law is legislation. The legislator is the only possible regulator of the system of utility. He is an omnipotent god whose existence is demanded by the basic postulate of the felicific calculus, and if he does not exist it is necessary to invent him. Men in society must obviously know in advance the consequences that will be attached to certain actions, and the legislator must make the necessary calculations and announce his results in the form of laws. Law is the command of the state, but the legislator is its voice. A scientific conception of law necessarily implies a philosophy of *positive* law. It is obscurantism to speak of customary law, a slow and mysterious growth in the womb of history, or of natural law, which is discoverable by human reason but has not been created by it. It is only in positive law that there can be perceived a conscious process of adopting means to ends.

For any other conceptions of jurisprudence, Bentham had the utmost contempt: they were only systems of metaphysics. He defined jurisprudence as the art of being methodically ignorant of what everybody knows. Since Bentham regarded rights as the creatures of the law, it was inevitable that he should have no use for the Social Contract. Men were bound by the laws prescribed by a determinate sovereign whether or not they had agreed in advance to be bound by them. The present generation had certainly not participated in the Social Contract, and if it was bound by it at all, it could only be by virtue of its utility. The idea of the Social Contract was therefore only an unnecessary detour to the principle of utility. Declarations of the rights of man were idle compositions, since men had no natural rights which they could have surrendered in making the mythical Social Contract. "Natural rights," he said, "is simple nonsense; natural and imprescriptible rights, rhetorical nonsense—nonsense upon stilts." There was equally no room for huzzas for liberty in Bentham's philosophy of law. Since the legislator was omnipotent, there could be only such liberties as were expressly allowed by positive law. The very conception of law was a negation of liberty, and it plays only a very minor role in the gospel of utility.

Too much the practical reformer himself to be interested in working his conceptions of positive law into a formal system, Bentham left the task to a disciple, John Austin, who founded the "analytical" school of jurisprudence that remained dominant at least through the nineteenth century. It conceived of law as a command of the sovereign state, enforced by its organized sanctions. Austin, after he had left the army to devote himself to the study of law, lived next door to Bentham in Queen's Square Place in the declining years of the master. Some have pretended to see in Austin's military background a natural explanation of a philosophy of law which identified law exclusively with the state and force.

While Bentham left to a disciple the creation of a formal system of jurisprudence, he did not rest content with outlining the theory of positive legislation. The theory could be translated into reality only by revising the whole of the existing system of law in such a way that it would conform to the principles of utility. It is to the systematic restatement of every single branch of law that Bentham applied the term "codification," and from the Herculean character of this task he never shrank. There had, of course, been codes before Bentham, but he was the first to demand the *complete* code. He himself pointed out that "of all the codes which legislators have considered as complete, there is not one that is so." The individual was not left to discover the requirements of utility with no more than the aid of his own common sense. The omniscient legislator was to present him with a utilitarian Bible. The codebook is the Benthamite translation of the Vulgate. The law is to be taken away from the lawyers and given to the common man, even as the Bible had been made the possession of every Protestant. Bentham was really the Luther of the law. Naturally, the codebook would have to be written in clear, precise, and simple language if it was to be consulted by the common man in the management of his daily affairs. "Citizen," asks the legislator, who, of course, is Jeremy Bentham, "what is your condition? Are you a father? Open the chapter 'Of Fathers.' Are you an agriculturist? Consult the chapter 'Of Agriculturists.' " The general part of the code was to be employed as a textbook in the public schools and to be read in the churches, while its particular parts were upon the appropriate occasions to be called to the attention of those who would be affected by them; for instance, the law of domestic relations would be called to the attention of bride and bridegroom as soon as they were married. The code was also to be accompanied by a running commentary, giving the reasons for each provision. This would not only increase the educational value of the code and serve as an aid to interpretation, but would also prevent the inclusion of bad laws because no good reasons could be given for them. Such was the program intended to end the "uncognoscibility" of the common law.

Bentham's philosophy of positive law was natural enough as part of the program of a new social class. Unwritten law, embodying custom and tradition, preserved the rights and privileges of the landed aristocracy. The triumph of the emerging industrial plutocracy and its ally the middle class could be assured only by legislation. It was always the task of the legislature to create anew. The legislature in Bentham's mind was the British Parliament, the stronghold of the middle class. But, while legislation was inevitable, the passion for codification was an idiosyncrasy of Bentham's. Unlike continental countries, England already had a unified and national legal system which, so far as the ordinary rules of property and contract were concerned, was entirely adequate to the pre-industrial capitalism of the era in which Bentham wrote. On the other hand, Bentham's aversion to natural law was extremely shrewd. Even while the American and French Revolutions were creating a new class in the name of natural law, he perceived the danger to that class from this unsettling doctrine when its own program should be accomplished. Once natural law had been translated into positive law, the idea had to be discredited so that it would not prove a source of embarrassment to the actual holders of power. In fact, the theory of utility performed for the English law of property and contract the same function that the theory of natural law had fulfilled on the Continent in putting the Roman law into more modern dress. Utility was only a less metaphysical slogan.

Both the penal- and civil-law theories of Bentham were basically uncreative. His system of penal law rested upon the Beccarian idea of the quantitative proportionality between crimes and punishments. It was based more rigorously upon the principle of utility, and was infinitely richer in detail, as well as less sentimental. Bentham's central dogma is that "the evil of the punishment exceed the profit of the offence," and he spoke of the "value" of the punishment, which he regarded as a "counter-crime." Punishment fulfills its purpose by virtue of the principle of the association of ideas—of the ideas of pleasure and pain. While his scheme of punishments relied principally upon imprisonment, it included also a sublimated *lex talionis,* consisting of various supplementary symbolic penalties, such as compelling prisoners to wear clothes emblematic of their crimes. "The great art," said Bentham, "consists in augmenting the apparent punishment without augmenting the real punishment." The methods for rehabilitating prisoners urged by Bentham were based upon a rather mechanical psychology, but his suggestions were so elaborate and so rich that they approach the best conceptions of modern penology. It would have been a model prison indeed if Bentham had been its warden! He had the merit also of emphasizing the importance of rehabilitating not only the criminal but also his victim. "Punishment," observed Bentham, "which, if it goes beyond the limit of necessity, is a pure evil, has been scattered with a prodigal hand. Satisfaction, which is purely a good, has been dealt out with a grudging parsimony." This emphasis upon pecuniary satisfaction is typical of the spirit of the new economy. A reaction against the mores of the fox-hunting aristocracy is manifest also in Bentham's advocacy of punishment for cruelty to animals. The whole of his penal program was, of course, justified by the plea of economy. It would prove cheaper, he urged, than more sanguinary methods. Humanity paid dividends.

Bentham's theory of civil law was significantly even less original. Its basic theory of "expectation" was derived from Hume. In the psychological scheme of pleasure and pain, it was of the first importance that expectations should not be disappointed. The right of property must rest upon existing expectations, because security, the chief aim of the civil law, which Bentham accepted as an axiom, would otherwise be impossible. The civil law was also intended to promote subsistence, abundance, and equality of property, but it could do nothing directly to realize the first two of these ends, and could only attempt to lessen inequality. "When security and inequality are in opposition,"

Bentham declared, "there should be no hesitation: equality should give way." Security and equality might, however, be reconciled by removing obstacles to the free circulation of wealth, and by redistributing wealth when expectations were less likely to be disappointed, as, for instance, by limiting the freedom of testation. In fact, Bentham expressly said that the instincts of the jurists with respect to property were right. He accepted their results but not their reasoning or nomenclature. He preferred, for instance, to speak of "investitive" or "collative" events rather than of "titles." Similarly, he accepted the principles of freedom and sanctity of contracts. But while the jurists spoke of the binding character of promises as such, he emphasized the considerations of utility that demonstrated that promises when made should be kept. In Bentham's conception of obligations, "service" is the basis for enforcing promises. Obligation, which is painful, is an evil, but it is balanced by the pleasure of having an expected "service" fulfilled.

In his attack upon the procedure of the common law, Bentham, however, appears in all his glory as a law reformer. Indeed, he invented the very distinction between "substantive" and "adjective" law. In his conceptions of procedure there was no truckling to the jurists. Bentham, the inventor, attacked with gusto the obsolete machinery of justice, which was rapidly becoming an impossible anachronism in the industrial age. It was procedure, above all, that was dominated by non-utilitarian ideas of political expediency. Every species of technicality and delay was justified by the supposed necessity of preserving "liberty." It was a theory that had for its support the great name of Montesquieu. But what "liberty" was this, asked Bentham, "unless it be liberty in rulers to oppress subjects, and in lawyers to plunder suitors." The judicial forms were not the shields of liberty but of depredation and corruption. They were the source of the profit of "Judge & Co." The monstrous costs of legal proceedings were "taxes on justice"—the most unexpected and calamitous of all taxes. All this, Bentham pointed out, was in the teeth of Magna Charta: *We will deny justice,* says King John; *we will sell justice to no man.* This was the wicked King John. How does the good King George? He denies it to ninety-nine men out of a hundred, and sells it to the hundredth." To use his own words, Bentham was "bold enough to insinuate that fifty pounds may be too high a price to pay for five shillings, or four hundred miles too far to go for it."

Bentham believed that it was only when there were bad laws that there could be any justification for avenues of procedural escape. It was more logical to reform the laws themselves than to preserve cumbersome procedures. His procedural ideal, therefore, was not liberty but efficiency. The ideal procedure would be simple and inexpensive. It would be the procedure employed by the father of a family in investigating disputes among its members—a procedure shorn of technicalities, forms, and delays. This procedure would be so superlatively simple that litigants would need no lawyers. "Every man his own lawyer," was one of Bentham's leading slogans. So radical was this procedural point of view that it amounted virtually to the abolition of procedure. In the Benthamite system of procedure, the gospel of laissez faire came into its own, and so, too, did the fundamental law of capitalism. In effect Bentham said: Do not waste money in procedural luxuries; money is the basis of capitalist accumulation.

Bentham naturally devoted himself to the exposure of existing procedural abuses, and demanded their abolition. Thus he attacked the exaction of fees, judicial delays, meaningless oaths, special pleading, and exclusionary rules of evidence. The last two items were perhaps the leading ones on the Benthamite calendar. Since issues of fact were tried before the jury, it was supposed to be highly necessary that the issues to be submitted to them should be framed in such a precise and simple manner that they could be disposed of by the response of the jury's verdict. Before there could be a trial, therefore, the lawyers had to exchange lengthy pleadings—"a sort of written correspondence between two attorneys," as Bentham himself described the system. The supreme puzzle for the lawyers was to decide when a "general denial" would suffice and when a special plea by way of affirmative defense would be necessary. The "declaration" of the plaintiff had to be followed by the "plea" of the defendant, but the process of pleading did not usually end there. The "plea" might be followed by a "replication," the "replication" by a "rejoinder," the "rejoinder" by a "rebutter," and the "rebutter" by a "surrebutter." The system became so complex that even the lawyers were baffled, and cases were frequently decided on questions of pleading rather than on the merits. The common-law system of evidence, which was also supposed to be justified by the danger of confusing the jury, as well as by the need to protect the liberty of the individual, was no less irrational. It was a vast system of exclusionary rules, of which the chief was the "hearsay" rule, and the effect of the operation of the whole system was to keep out a great deal of evidence that was logically probative. Bentham aimed his shafts particularly at the more rigid rules, such as those that excluded the testimony of the parties themselves and made it impossible for husbands and wives to testify against each other. These rules furnished increasing opportunities for fraud in the daily mercantile relationships of a growing middle class.

Bentham paid comparatively little attention to the reform of criminal procedure. There had never been so much opportunity for profit in criminal as in civil practice, and therefore there were fewer abuses. Nevertheless, Bentham assailed the most celebrated institutions of the common law, the jury and the process of indictment by grand jury, but, on the other hand, demanded the institution of a public prosecutor, as on the Continent. Contemplating the day when there would be a perfect penal code, he also urged the abrogation of the traditional privileges of the accused, such as the privilege against self-incrimination and the rule against double jeopardy. He even favored the legalizing of secret informations. Bentham did not believe that these changes would lead to a restoration of torture and the Inquisition, for he believed that the publicity of the criminial trial would be a sufficient safeguard. Publicity he proclaimed to be the very soul of justice. "It is the keenest spur to exertion, and the surest of all guards against impropriety. It keeps the judge himself, while trying, under trial."

Bentham's scheme of judicial organization was a completely logical revolt against historical accident. It had been the practice in England to "cut courts out of one another with metaphysical shears." There had thus appeared courts for different kinds of cases, and even different courts for various stages of the same type of case. The dualism of law and equity was, of course, an absurd anomaly, and Bentham never tired of pointing to the reproach of the common law inherent in the very concept of equity. "The ruffian thief," he said, "is common law; the hypocrite thief is equity." Bentham's *bête noire* was Lord Eldon, the last architect of the classical system of equity, whose endless procrastinations in deciding cases in the Court of Chancery had become a public scandal. Bentham compared Eldon to Bloody Jeffreys, but to the latter's advantage: it was worse to perish of the law's delays than to suffer sudden death. It was absurd, also, that all the courts should be concentrated at Westminster, so that litigants had to go hundreds of miles to secure justice. Moreover, the fragmentation of jurisdiction prevented the arrival of the happy day when every man should be his own lawyer. No matter how simple the procedure, the layman would be stumped at the very outset by the necessity of knowing which court to choose. Therefore Bentham proposed "a system of local judicature, distributing justice upon the spot in all its branches," and in each locality there was to be but one court. "How happy the suitor," exclaimed Bentham, "where there is but one court, *the* court! The simplest of all clowns would not mistake his way to it." The court would be departmentalized like a well-organized factory. It was to be open at all hours of the day and night. "Justice only to sleep when injustice sleeps also," said Bentham. Each court was to be held by a single judge.

Since constitutional law dealt with the machinery of government, it was for Bentham a branch of "adjective" law. Although he was working out a constitutional Pannomion, or universal body of constitutional law, it was really a disguised version of the British constitution, with a broadened base of representation and with such modifications as were attributable to the increasing eccentricity of an aging philosopher. Thus, the "new" constitutional scheme contemplated the omnipotence of the legislature and the cabinet system. While the principle of the division of powers was rejected, and there was to be, of course, no Bill of Rights or Declaration of Rights, checks were provided upon the abuse of ministerial and official discretion. These were based on the idea that it was best to "minimize confidence" in the governors. While the Prime Minister would appoint the ministers, the Minister of Justice was to be an exception. He was to be popularly elected, because he would have the appointment of the judges. In order that "official aptitudes" might be "maximized," and expense "minimized," appointees for office were to be permitted to bid against each other for the available posts, which would go to the lowest bidder, namely, the one who offered to work for the least pay! Thus was a new oligarchic plutocracy to be substituted for the ancient aristocracy, and the creators of the Industrial Revolution put into the seats of government. In championing a single chamber, Bentham was far in advance of the times, but his idea was ultimately realized when the House of Lords was shorn of all real legislative power. Bentham believed that the British constitution was the best in the world, except for the American, which, however, he really never understood. It is interesting to note also that the utilitarians as a group did not offer the program of political equality in the belief that it would abolish economic inequality. Since everyone had freedom in the economic market, he should have freedom in the political market. Nevertheless, in the bargaining process in the political market, inequalities of fortune would tend to assert themselves. Bentham would never have adhered to the cause of political radicalism if it had been really radical. While he was working on the *Constitutional Code,* he also wrote a pamphlet called *Radicalism Not Dangerous.*

Apart from penal and procedural reforms, Bentham has been commonly credited with parliamentary reform, municipal reform, poor-law reform, the abolition of imprisonment for debt, the repeal of religious tests for office, the institution of national systems of education and public health, the idea of a permanent civil service, old-age pensions, the inauguration of a Register of Births, Marriages, and Deaths, the taking of the census, the establishment of a Register of Deeds, including the reform of land laws, as well as the extension of the idea of savings banks, and the introduction of cheap postage and postal money orders. A dragon of a codifier, with an intense interest in words, he also made important contributions to the study of semantics.

It would take temerity to dispute Bentham's title to be considered the greatest law reformer of all time. Undoubtedly, he left a rich heritage of ideas. It was a Frenchman who paid him the most graceful compliment. "Robbed by all the world," remarked Talleyrand, "he yet remains rich." He was, however, so much a product of his own times that it is difficult to say whether he is really responsible for a particular reform or a new institution. Perhaps the greatest tribute it is possible to pay him is to say that there would have been Benthamism if Bentham had never lived. It is customary to enumerate all the Benthamite ideas that have actually been translated into legislation. An equally long list, however, could be made of those of his ideas that have been rejected as extravagant or have achieved only partial institutional embodiment. A few examples should suffice to show that this was as true in England as on the Continent.

The reform of the penal law was perhaps the leading objective of Bentham's program. It was finally deprived of its sanguinary character not by Romilly, who was Bentham's disciple, but by Robert Peel, who was a member of a Tory Cabinet. But this was accomplished by a series of "consolidated" statutes rather than by the enactment of a complete penal code. The whole system of common-law pleading was cast into limbo and procedure was greatly simplified, but not to the point where every Englishman could be his own lawyer. The law of evidence was reformed but, while the disqualification for interest attacked by Bentham was removed, it remained as before an exclusionary system. Except for the introduction of a public prosecutor, the system of criminal prosecution remained basically unchanged. Yet, while the jury was not abolished, its use in both civil and criminal cases was greatly reduced. The public realized that since the perfect Benthamite system of laws had not been brought into existence, it was safer to maintain the traditional guarantees in criminal procedure. The Judicature Acts of 1873–75 finally reorganized the English judicial system by fusing law and equity and consolidating all the existing courts into one High Court of Justice, but the new court, while it possessed plenary jurisdiction, still sat at Westminster and during the day only. It would, moreover, have been a foolish litigant who resorted to the High Court without a lawyer. Bentham was undoubtedly least prophetic in his estimate of the future of the legal profession. Apparently he did not foresee that, with the growth of finance capitalism and the appearance of giant corporations and cartels, the substantive law itself would become so complex that even with the most simplified system of procedure, lawyers would become more necessary than ever. It may be, however, that his attack was only strategic: he may have intended only to frighten the lawyers to make them loosen their grip on procedure.

It is even clearer that the changes in public law made after Bentham's death were inevitable. The system of rotten and pocket boroughs was a historical anachronism that could not survive in England after the redistribution of wealth between classes and the shift of population between localities. As for municipal reform, centralization of administration was inevitable in a democratized England where the political power of the aristocracy had been broken. It was only by removing local administration from its grasp that its privileges could be undermined. Even if offices were not legally knocked down to the lowest bidder, the industrial plutocracy was bound to get a grip on the government.

The great passion of Bentham was for codification, and complete and systematic codes are today a commonplace not only in civil- but in common-law countries. It is impossible to doubt Bentham's influence upon this universal process of codification. Yet codes had been demanded by continental jurists in the seventeenth century, and in the eighteenth century by the French *philosophes* in the name of democratic simplification. Bentham's dream of codification was realized after the Revolution in France, which created the Code Napoleon. Promulgated in 1804, this historic civil code, which was so nicely adapted to the needs of the middle-class state that it has been called the *Code bourgeois,* was imitated in all Latin countries and became the basis of a new European common law. The only important European country that remained without a civil code until the end of the century was Germany, which then created the *Deutsches Bügerliches Gesetzbuch,* which was in turn imitated in countries as diverse and remote as Turkey, Brazil, and Japan. But while the codes were demanded in European countries after the French Revolution in the name of democratic simplicity, the real purpose they fulfilled had little to do with this Benthamite aim. Codification became a European movement because of the urgent need for national unity, which required also legal unity. Since legal unity did not exist in France, which still was divided into regions of Roman law and customary law, it was accomplished in the name of codification. The French civil code was soon followed by codes of civil and criminal procedure as well as by a penal code. At least so far as criminal procedure was concerned, the French paid no attention to Bentham's criticisms. He could not surmount the influence of the *philosophes,* who had delivered themselves of panegyrics on the subject of the English jury and other phases of English procedure, which the French legislators now proceeded to graft upon their own inquisitorial stock.

It is really amazing that Bentham with his mastery of semantics should have relied so much on codification as the guarantee of justice. He believed that codes could be made so scientific and precise that they would be proof against the arts of the jurists. The adoption of codes did not, of course, prevent the growth of new precedent, and interpretation still reigned supreme. As not infrequently happens, the mountain had labored and brought forth a mouse. It had produced an idea that was basically, for all its improvements, at least as old as Hammurabi. Nobody, however, seems inclined to admit the real purpose that inspires the greatest works of codification, which is always to effect some program of social, political, or economic reform.

There have been increasing doubts, too, concerning the desirability of accepting utilitarianism as a fitting basis of a science of society. It seems as dubious as the slogan of natural law. The institutions of man should, to be sure, be justified by their utility, but is the egoism of individuals its proper measure? Can a society really exist in which individuals are left free to pursue their own selfish interests? Can the greatest good of the greatest number be promoted by identifying private interest with the interest of society itself? Is society merely a sum of individuals? Is not the constant intervention of the state necessary to remove the effects of economic inequality? Does not the felicific calculus itself rest upon a series of fictions? Can pleasure and pain really be measured and compared? Bentham himself did not maintain that this could be done exactly, but then does the theory really have any scientific value?

But to ask such questions is to pass beyond the world and faith of Bentham. It was for the following generations, which experienced the full effects of the Industrial Revolution and were faced with the paradox of poverty amidst plenty, to work out a new program. There were increasing attacks upon property in the name of socialization. The more moderate reformers demanded even the socialization of private law, and created a host of administrative agencies, which played no part in the Benthamite legal scheme, to cope with the problems of the machine age. The new faith was still in legislation, but this was to be "social legislation," which should in itself attempt to effect a redistribution of property. The rallying cry was "social reform" rather than "law reform." Still more radical reformers, however, proclaimed the futility of gradual socialization and demanded socialism. They insisted that law by its very nature was incapable of dealing satisfactorily with economic problems that involved the interests of groups and classes. The individual was the only possible juristic unit; the juristic person was always fated to be an individual. Law was bound to be atomic, individualistic, and equalitarian. It was no mere accident that the greatest law reformer of all time was a supreme conservative. Bentham's absorption in procedural reform was symptomatic as well as prophetic. Law reform was always bound to be procedural reform—the invention of more and more administrative machinery capable of redistributing wealth in theory, but subject to all sorts of compromises in practice. Moreover, Bentham's ideal of procedural efficiency, although natural enough to every inventor, could never be completely realized in practice, because the law was dominated by considerations of political power. Indeed, the law was often deliberately made inefficient. Only too often, when one cog in the judicial machinery was made "efficient," it was only because the reform was needed to compensate for some horrible inefficiency in another part of the system. The net result was rarely real efficiency of operation. In the conduct of civil litigation, "efficiency" meant only that judgment would be rendered for the plaintiff as expeditiously as possible. It did not mean necessarily that the judgment would be collected or enforced—the real test of efficiency.

The radical reformers who doubted whether economic planning was compatible with forms of legal regulation could employ Bentham's own satire in ridiculing the opposition to his own schemes of reform: the "Procrastinator's Argument" ("Wait a little, this is not the time") and the "Snail's Pace Argument" ("One thing at a time! Not so fast! Slow and sure!"). As the radicals turned away from the Benthamite faith, the vanity of law reform became the slogan of more thoroughgoing reform.

John Marshall

THE ORDEAL OF CONSTITUTIONALISM

JOHN MARSHALL IS THE GREATEST NAME IN THE HISTORY OF American law, and one of the dominant figures in the patristic period of American history. All the other figures in the early history of American law are insignificant in comparison with him. As long as the Federal Constitution, which Marshall hoped would prove immortal, remains the basic governing charter of the American people, he will always be connected with the existence of the legal institution known as "judicial review." John Marshall and the institution of judicial review must be regarded as one and inseparable. As the demiurge of judicial review, he almost stands for American law itself.

It is quite universally agreed that the institution of judicial review is America's unique contribution to the art of government. This extraordinary legal invention has, indeed, been known simply as "the American doctrine," and has constituted that feature of the Federal Constitution which has been most admired by foreigners, despite the fact that many Americans themselves have been more restrained in their enthusiasm. As James Bryce once said, "No feature of the government of the United States has awakened so much curiosity in the European mind, caused so much discussion, received so much admiration and been more frequently misunderstood than the duties assigned to the Supreme Court, and the functions which it discharges in guarding the Ark of the Constitution."

Judicial review seems deceptively simple, but it is actually one of the most baffling of legal devices. It has sometimes been described as the exercise of a "veto" power over legislation, but such a characterization is wholly inaccurate. When a law is enacted, it is not submitted to the Supreme Court of the United States with the request that it determine its constitutional validity. This would constitute the Supreme

Court a third house of the American Federal legislature. It would be, in other words, a constitutional Council of Revision. But the Supreme Court is part of the judicial rather than the legislative machinery of the Federal government. It is an ordinary court, which adjudicates not only momentous constitutional controversies but suits between private individuals which revolve around questions of *meum* and *tuum*. The constitutional validity of legislation, as well as of executive acts, is decided only as an incident of litigation between individual litigants asserting specific rights. In the terminology of the constitutional lawyers, there must be a "case" or "controversy" before the Court before it will undertake to say that constitutional rights have been violated. Sometimes such a pronouncement will not be made until decades have elapsed since the enactment of the legislation which is challenged. Constitutional decisions depend upon the accidents of litigation. The process of constitutional interpretation is thus made to seem like an integral part of the ordinary legal process, supposedly controlled by precedent and standards of judicial objectivity and propriety, although actually constitutional questions usually raise explosive political issues. It is, moreover, a basic characteristic of the American doctrine of judicial review as it exists today that once a constitutional question has been decided by the courts, the decision is binding on all the departments of the Government. The Supreme Court of the United States is thus the final arbiter on all questions of constitutionality.

The institution of judicial review has English as well as European roots, but it is basically an American invention derived from American necessities. As an invention it is as distinctly American as the steamboat, the cotton gin, or the conveyer belt. It redeemed, moreover, the basic unoriginality of American law. The colonists, as Englishmen, had brought over with them the English common law, which they adopted with such modifications as were suited to their own conditions. They rejected by and large the English forms of land tenure and the incredibly harsh English criminal law, but they retained the civil elements of the common law, as well as its fundamental forms of civil and criminal procedure. In the American colonies, American lawyers often went to the Inns of Court for their education, and they made Blackstone as popular in America as in England. The extraordinary cultural phenomenon of "reception" was thus also manifested on the virgin American continent. Even as the peoples of medieval Europe had received Roman law, the people of America received the English common law.

It may seem remarkable that the royal common law should have survived in Revolutionary America but it must not be forgotten that the
Founding Fathers rapidly sloughed off their revolutionary fervor—a
circumstance that was in itself responsible for the success of judicial
review.

After the Revolution, the lawyers, who virtually dominated not only
the courts but all branches of American government, set themselves to
eliminating as many as possible of the indigenous qualities of American
law. In imitation of Blackstone, Chancellor James Kent of New York,
who administered English equity even in the backwoods of New York,
piously published his *Commentaries on American Law*. Another notable
figure in the early history of American law was Joseph Story, who sat
on the bench of the Supreme Court of the United States with John
Marshall, but who was even more important as a teacher and writer.
Story published a long series of texts, in which he restated the English
common law as it was adapted to American conditions.

If the crowning triumph of the English common law was the doctrine of the "rule of law," that of American law was the "absolute reign
of law," which is the way the institution of judicial review has been
characterized. Few will deny the aptness of the characterization. After
all, what did the "rule of law" in England amount to? It only subjected
the executive to the law. Coke, perhaps, had dreamed in his earlier
years of making the courts of the common law supreme over Parliament
as well as the king, but it was not the English judiciary but Parliament
that emerged triumphant from the English constitutional struggles. In
America, the revolutionary land of the free, however, the judiciary,
which in all lands had always been the most conservative branch of
government, was victorious not only over the executive but over the
legislative branch of government. The "American doctrine" is thus
the doctrine of judicial supremacy. Today it is hardly necessary to
explain this to a middle-aged American laborer who knows that the
"nine old men" who constitute the Supreme Court of the United
States once vetoed the attempt of an American state legislature to
interfere with his "freedom" to work as long as his employer pleased. If
judicial review is judicial supremacy, then it is certainly "the absolute
reign of law." There have even been some wealthy and conservative
lawyers who have thought and said that the American Revolution was
fought to realize Coke's dream of the supremacy of law.

The foreign influences in securing the establishment of judicial review were many. There was first the medieval idea of the supremacy of law. Then there was the complex of sentiments bound up with the English conception of the rule of law and the cult of the common law itself, which made it seem the quintessence of reason and the very embodiment of the law of nature. If there was a law which even the English king must respect, then surely there must be a law which could not be touched by the mere backwoods members of an American legislature. The English idea of "fundamental law" helped, too. There was the tradition of Magna Charta and the English Bill of Rights which Parliament could, but really would not dare, touch. In theory Parliament was omnipotent, but it would cease to be so in fact if it laid violent hands upon these sacred documents of the new middle class. There was also the fact that the American colonial legislatures were subordinate legislative organs. The Judicial Committee of the Privy Council in England had on occasion taken jurisdiction to review acts of the colonial assemblies, which, when they conflicted with the provisions of the colonial charters, were disallowed.

Of the ideologies of the Continent, the most potent was one born in the fertile brain of the Frenchman Montesquieu, the great political theorist among the eighteenth-century *philosophes*. This was the doctrine of the separation of powers, a product of the mechanistic philosophy of the age that worshiped at the shrine of the goddess of reason. It presupposed the desirability of an equilibrium of governmental powers. By analysis, all powers of government could be shown to be executive, legislative, or judicial, but in the practice of all countries they had long been hopelessly jumbled. To separate these powers and to assign to them their proper spheres was the task of the political theorist. When this was accomplished, the rights of the individual would be properly safeguarded. Such was the gospel according to Montesquieu. The Founding Fathers set out to create equal and co-ordinate departments of government, and apparently they decided that this objective could be accomplished only by leaving it to the judiciary to determine when each department had exceeded its proper sphere. The French themselves, after their own Revolution, decided that the separation of powers required the supremacy of the executive power. The English had long since apparently determined that the separation of powers, which Blackstone pretended to find in the confused and archaic English Constitution, should be realized through the legislative power. Thus, remarkable to relate, the same doctrine had led in America to the supremacy of the judiciary, in France to the supremacy of the executive, and in England to the supremacy of the legislature. In fact, of course, the doctrine of the separation of powers harbored an inherent fallacy. No such governmental equilibrium could ever be achieved, for in every state, unless anarchy was to prevail, there had to be some organ of government that would act as the regulator producing the state of equilibrium; but that meant inevitably that this power would be supreme, and if there was a supreme power, there could be no equilibrium.

The Founding Fathers were, however, practical men, and, while they were not unconscious of their English heritage and were not unacquainted with the French political philosophy, they responded more immediately to the impact of their own environment. This led them to create a form of government which, if it did not require judicial review as a matter of inexorable logic, at least originated an irresistible pressure for the institution. First of all they created not only a new form of government but a new form of law—the written constitution. They converted the idea of a number of fundamental laws into the idea of the one fundamental law. The distinction between a "written" and an "unwritten" constitution is now familiar enough, but it was a great novelty in the eighteenth century. The English constitution is and was then the classic example of an unwritten constitution. Although part of it was embodied in written legislation, it was unwritten in the sense that it had never been written down at one time as a complete scheme of government. It embodied a distribution of governmental powers, but it was not the result of a single creative act, but of tradition, which is always a slow and imperceptible growth. Every state in existence had had the same sort of unwritten constitution, whether it was a primitive gerontocracy or a highly organized state like Rome. Both the Greeks and the Romans knew the conception of an "unconstitutional" law, but they did not recognize that one kind of law could have a superior formal validity over another. But not only did the formal written constitution, which was supposed to embody a complete system of government, make it seem easier to determine which laws were unconstitutional, it also established spheres which were to be entirely removed beyond the competency of any governmental power, whether executive, legislative, or judicial. This was done affirmatively by granting certain positive rights to the individual by means of Bills of Rights, and negatively by forbidding the legislature to legislate on certain subjects altogether. Thus did the written constitution embody the theory of the governmental void, as well as the existence of governmental limitations. Under this constitutional scheme, it seemed natural for the courts to be selected as the agency for determining when the "inferior" law of the legislature was inconsistent with the "higher" law of the constitution.

This constitutionalism was, however, more a product of the spirit of the frontier than of the English conception of the rule of law. The more cultivated propertied classes of the colonial towns may have thought of liberty in the same way as the British Tories, both domestic and foreign, but the masses of the people thought of liberty in terms of the wild and undisciplined environment of the backwoods. To the frontiersman government seemed an evil that was not even necessary. The territorial extent of the Union that was finally achieved made direct democracy, moreover, an impossibility, and the framers of the Federal Constitution united in desiring a government of constitutional limitations, of checks and balances. In the scheme of representative government that actually emerged, it was conceived that the people had legislated once and for all when, in the Constitutional Convention, they had expressed their will by adopting the Constitution. The legislature, which had been created by the Constitution, then had only a delegated and limited authority. While it would have been absurd for the people to set limits to their own authority, surely the agents must be called to account when they had exceeded theirs? Thus the American legislatures were not sovereign but subordinate organs, whose function was only to carry out the terms of the constitutional compact—the American form of the Social Contract. Finally, there was the fact that the Constitution adopted by the thirteen colonies created a Federal Union. Federalism made necessary the existence of some form of machinery for determining at least when the states were invading the preserves of the Federal government. If the legislation of the states was to be beyond review, the result would have been anarchy rather than Federal union. This review did not necessarily have to be judicial. It could have been entrusted to a legislative or executive committee as well as to a court.

The greatest of all the pressures for judicial review, however, was not so much political as economic. While capitalism has thrived in countries that have had written constitutions but have not known the institution of judicial review (and it is thus apparent again that it was not inevitable), some form of review of legislative acts was necessary to protect pre-industrial American capitalism from the threats inherent in leveling state legislation. A vast new continent lay open to exploitation, and the merchant capitalists, the sires of the robber industrial barons of later decades, needed an institutional mechanism that would bar any attempts to curb their fierce energies. Having enlisted the support of the masses to rid themselves of their British masters, they became Tories themselves, and looked about for a way of frustrating the popular will. They were bent not only on establishing a national government but also on keeping in check any disruptive tendencies of the state governments. They were conservatives as well as Federalists, and they put their trust in the courts and not in the legislatures. Until a few decades ago, such a halo surrounded each of the Founding Fathers that it was considered impious to attribute economic motives to them. Yet the whole story of judicial review may perhaps be summed up by describing it as a legal device for safeguarding the interests of the wealthy and the privileged, which was sold to the American people in the fair name of nationalism.

John Marshall was the man of destiny selected by the Federalists to bring about the triumph of their principles, and he succeeded in laying the foundations of judicial supremacy. His whole career takes its significance from the opportunities of his time, for he did not himself create the ideas which he espoused and implemented. He lived through the whole patristic period and far beyond it, and thus personally participated in the movement of ideas and forces from which judicial review emerged as an established institution. It seems somewhat strange that he was a Virginian, in view of Virginia's later championship of states' rights and leadership in the Confederacy, but most of the great Virginians among the Founding Fathers first took the lead in putting across the Federal Constitution. The planter aristocracy turned away only later from the Frankenstein monster—the Federal Union—which they had helped to create, but John Marshall had never been a planter aristocrat to the manner born.

There have been three John Marshalls in American history. While he was living and shaping the course of American constitutional development through epochal decisions, he was a bugaboo to a large part of the electorate, which regarded with suspicion Federalism and all its works. After the triumph of the Federal Union was assured by the Civil War, he became hallowed as one of its great saviors and the prophet of nationalism. He became, indeed, the patron saint of the ensuing period of Constitution-worship. But, as the ordeals of constitutionalism in more recent times brought about a critical analysis of the patristic period and the drafting of the Constitution, there was a reaction against any estimate of Marshall in terms of simple nationalism. The reality is undoubtedly far more complicated. It is bound up with the motives of Marshall's nationalism and the intricacies of judicial review as an institution.

John Marshall came into the world on September 24, 1755, on the Virginia frontier. The site of the settlement in which he was born is now part of Fauquier County, but it was then known as Germantown. The birth of Marshall occurred only eleven weeks after Braddock's defeat, an event which taught the colonists that British troops were not invincible. On the maternal side Marshall was descended from the Randolph and Isham families, who were of the English gentry. Jefferson's mother and Marshall's grandmother were first cousins. John Marshall stemmed from far more humble stock on his father's side. His grandfather was known as "John Marshall of the forest," and was a man of the soil and the wild frontier. The father of John Marshall was Thomas Marshall, who gave the family its start on the road to fortune. This frontiersman married Mary Keith, daughter of Mary Isham Randolph. Fifteen children, of whom John Marshall was the eldest, were born of this union.

Thomas Marshall, whom his eldest son grew to admire as the embodiment of all the frontier virtues, was fortunate enough to become George Washington's assistant in surveying Lord Fairfax's vast estate, a large part of which John Marshall was to acquire. Thomas Marshall profited from his acquaintance with Washington, whom he idolized. He began moving in from the frontier, first from the ancestral home to a small abode which was no longer a log cabin but a frame house, situated in "The Hollow" in Goose Creek in the Blue Ridge, and thence to Oak Hill which, although in the same region, was quite a mansion for those days. He had entered politics, and before long he was a member of the House of Burgesses from his county, Sheriff of Fauquier County, Clerk of Dunmore County, and principal vestryman of Leeds Parish, which embraced Fauquier County. As a member of the House of Burgesses, Thomas Marshall participated in the first pitched legislative battle between the tidewater political machine, controlled by the planter aristocracy, and the upcountry, and helped to defeat the machine on the issue of a loan-office bill. The tidewater was doubtful about supporting resistance to the Stamp Act, but Thomas Marshall voted with Patrick Henry when he cried: "If *this* be treason, make the most of it."

When John Marshall had grown to manhood, he was over six feet tall, lanky and loose-jointed. He had a dark complexion, faintly tinged with red, and his forehead was straight and low. Strong, thick, raven-black hair covered his head. His eyes have always been described as particularly remarkable. They are said to have been "dark to blackness" and very "intense," fixing the beholder in an imperious gaze. It is also a fact, however, that John Marshall loved laughter and fun and joked at every opportunity. The imperiousness of his gaze may therefore be exaggerated—a part of his legend. Certainly he never dressed in the role of the master-Federalist. Throughout his life, even at the pinnacle of his career, he always dressed shabbily and looked ungainly. In appearance it is said he resembled Abraham Lincoln a good deal, but appearances have always been deceiving.

Since the youth of Marshall was spent on the frontier, where illiteracy was common, his opportunities for acquiring formal education were scarce. He was largely a self-educated man, although there were a few interludes of formal education. His father's library contained a small number of volumes, which he read eagerly. As a boy he was delighted with Pope's *Essay on Man,* which is said to have taught him the wisdom as well as the necessity for order. There he read: "One truth is clear, whatever is, is right." When Blackstone's *Commentaries* were published in America, in 1772, one of the subscribers was Thomas Marshall. His eldest son not only obtained from it his knowledge of the common law but undoubtedly took to heart its great moral lesson, the sacredness of property. The instinct of the frontiersman was thus reinforced by the mature judgment of the cultivated man of the world. John Marshall's formal legal education was obtained while the Revolutionary War was still in progress. For six weeks he attended the law lectures of George Wythe at William and Mary College, but he was at the time a lovesick swain whose mind must have been elsewhere. The scantiness of Marshall's legal education was to be reflected in his decisions. He did not pretend to profound legal learning and rarely cited cases. As a lawyer he argued his own cases on principles of logic rather than authority, and when he became Chief Justice of the Supreme Court, he found his freedom from legal precedents, the cant of the profession, a positive advantage. The manipulation of judicial review, which was a judicial disguise of a political process, required political abilities rather than a mastery of legal technicalities.

The experience of John Marshall in the Revolutionary War, during which he was able to observe the jealousy and mutual suspicion of the states, is supposed to have taught him the value of nationalism. Certainly these were factors which almost caused the failure of the American cause. Doubtless he took the lesson to heart. He himself said of his feelings in this trying period: "I was confirmed in the habit of considering America as my country, and Congress as my government." But the ragged continentals who were the soldiers of the Revolution apparently made no such lasting impression, for ultimately he was to align himself with the men of property who were bent on frustrating their yearnings for "the blessings of prosperity."

Both John Marshall and his father served in the Revolutionary War. The father crossed the Delaware with Washington, but his son missed the boat because of a promotion. He suffered with Washington, however, at Valley Forge and was one of the heroes of Brandywine and Germantown. He returned to Virginia while the war was still going on, because the term of enlistment of his regiment had expired, but the new command for which he was waiting never materialized and therefore he never went back to the front. It was then that the young captain studied law at William and Mary and obtained his license to practice. He also launched the romance that led to his marriage.

When Captain John Marshall came to Yorktown to visit his father, who happened to be stationed there at the time, he aroused great expectations. He was a hero returned from the wars. The young ladies of Yorktown gave a ball to which all the young officers were invited, but the gallant young captain excited the interest especially of the Ambler family. Jacquelin Ambler, the father, had been one of the richest men of Yorktown, but while he himself had fallen on less prosperous days, other members of the Ambler family were still extremely wealthy. When Captain Marshall appeared at the ball as badly clothed as usual, the older Ambler daughters, who had expected a dashing figure, were greatly disappointed. The captain's ingratiating qualities soon removed the bad first impression, but then it was too late. The very youngest daughter of the family, Mary Ambler, who at the time of the ball was only fourteen years old, had set her cap for him, as she expressly avowed, and John Marshall was captivated. After a courtship of three years, he married the object of his adoration. The thought that his connection with the Ambler family would be advantageous may very well have crossed John Marshall's mind. The father of the bride was Treasurer of Virginia and one of the most popular and influential men in the Old Dominion. He had won his own bride, Rebecca Burwell, against the ardent competition of Thomas Jefferson, which was no slight feat. It may possibly have been one of the factors that made the jilted suitor dislike John Marshall so much, quite apart from their differences of political opinion.

Marshall settled with his young bride of seventeen in Richmond, where her family lived. Soon after, however, Mary, whom her husband always called his "dearest Polly," became a chronic invalid. She suffered from a nervous indisposition, which seems at times to have affected her mind and made her always incapable of attending to the most ordinary household duties. It is said that Marshall was one of those men who put women on a pedestal and that he treated his invalid wife with an unselfish devotion and a tenderness that were constant and unremitting. As in the case of anyone who is put on a pedestal, we have no very clear picture of her character from Marshall's pen or her own. Whenever Marshall was away from home, he would write regularly to his "dearest Polly," but it was usually about his own experiences, and the letter almost invariably included a reference to the fact that he had not yet heard from her. His "dearest Polly" apparently never answered the anxious and tender husband's letters, although he was always protesting that he would gladly forego all the enchantments and experiences of his journeys to sit with her by the fireside. Marshall had ten children with her, of whom four died in infancy, with all the woe and tribulation attendant upon such events. It is difficult to believe that the relationship between John Marshall and his "dearest Polly" was mutually as idyllic as it is pictured. Even conceding John Marshall's enormous powers of idealization and his undoubted devotion to his wife, which led him to take care of her household duties even after he was Chief Justice, the marriage can hardly be regarded as "happy" by any usual standards. It is, moreover, not unreasonable to suppose that this misfortune of his private life affected John Marshall's public career. The pursuit of gain in his chosen profession may well have become for him especially the whole of life. Thus were strengthened the instincts of the stern man of property, the arch-conservative who became the arch-Federalist on the bench.

In the patristic period of America, government, too, was in the hands of lawyers. John Marshall rapidly fulfilled this condition of a public career. Within a few years, he became the leading lawyer of Richmond, which was then only a small, muddy town, but Richmond grew rapidly, and so did Marshall's success. The men of the frontier were not repelled by the carelessness of his dress, and his capacity for jollity brought him many friends. Marshall became Grand Master of the Masonic Order in Richmond, a leading member of the Barbecue Club and giver of "lawyers' dinners," a not infrequent card player at Farmicola's Tavern, and an assiduous quoit player. There is a story that an old planter who came to Richmond to obtain the best lawyer in town refused to employ Marshall because he had turned out to be the man whom he had seen walking down the street eating from a bag of cherries, but the planter changed his mind after he had heard the despised lawyer arguing someone else's case in court. Marshall did not become any more pretentious in appearance after he became Chief Justice. The purchaser of a turkey, who did not know who he was, once offered him a small coin to carry the bird home for him, and the Chief Justice with his love of fun accepted, walking stolidly behind his employer. The kind of lawyer Marshall was did not need much of a law library, but he purchased a number of volumes soon after he opened an office. Among them was a set of the works of Nicholas Machiavelli.

Marshall did not have the sort of practice that called for a mastery of histrionics. He possessed eloquence, but its effectiveness depended primarily upon the seeming cogency of his reasoning. He was almost exclusively a property lawyer, and questions of property consumed his best energies. In his first important case, in 1786, he defended the validity of the title to the Fairfax estate, with which the fortune of the Marshall family seems to have been peculiarly bound up. The father surveyed the Fairfax estate, the son defended the title, and seven or eight years later acquired the remainder of the estate himself in conjunction with his brother, James M. Marshall, his brother-in-law, Rawleigh Colston, and General Henry Lee, then Governor of Virginia, all of whom had formed a syndicate for the purpose. The purchase price was £14,000 in British money, a great sum in those days, but the advance of the money was undertaken by Robert Morris, the Pennsylvania speculator and financier, who was reputed to be the second richest man of the time and whose daughter Hester was married to John Marshall's brother. The early decades of the American Republic were a period of enormous land speculation in which almost every prominent figure of the period engaged. The interest of the speculators, whether Northerners or Southerners, was entirely financial and quite distinct from that of the planters, whose wealth depended on the utilization of the soil. The ownership of the Fairfax estate is a leitmotiv of John Marshall's career, and it is a far more revealing guide to his conduct in both public and private life than any vision of nationalism. It dominated his attitude as a judge and a politician and determined his responses to calls of public duty.

The public career of Marshall began with his election in 1782 to the Virginia House of Delegates in which he sat intermittently until the adoption of the Federal Constitution. The influence of his family connections is shown by the fact that despite his youth and inexperience he was elected a member of the Council of State, which shared executive functions with the Governor. A curious aspect of Marshall's career in state politics is that he was constantly re-elected to legislative office by a constituency in which a majority of the people must have been overwhelmingly opposed to his strongly conservative and nationalist views. The seeming paradox is perhaps explained by Virginia's freehold qualification for suffrage and by the practice of voting by open rather than by secret ballot—a method which must have made many of the voters afraid to reveal their true sentiments towards a great man of property. During his service in the state legislature in this period, Marshall displayed indifference to religious questions, but he stood firmly, although in vain, for the payment of British debts. He also revealed a greater degree of friendliness towards the Indians than was usual in the families of frontiersmen. With his calmer and more practical vision, he no doubt perceived that the settler had more to gain from peaceful relations with the Indian tribes than from violence, which only led to bloodshed and the destruction of property. It has been commonly assumed that the habitual lack of dignity and the boisterousness of the Virginia House of Delegates filled him with a disgust for legislative action and with a determination to create curbs against its excesses. The truth is that there were few men who loved boisterousness more than Marshall. He would have been delighted if the House of Delegates had voted for the payment of British debts even in a hilarious manner.

The first contact of Marshall with national affairs was in the State Constitutional Convention of 1788, of which he was a member. The Founding Fathers, meeting at Philadelphia to revise the Articles of Confederation, had discarded that unworkable instrument altogether and, with a revolutionary heedlessness of legality, had submitted the fateful document they had drafted to state constitutional conventions. The Articles of Confederation had provided that they should be altered only by the Congress of the United States with the unanimous consent of the *legislatures* of the thirteen states. The manipulation by which the ratification of the new Federal Constitution was secured verged closely upon chicanery and fraud, but the men of property were determined at all costs to secure the adherence of Virginia, whose consent was particularly crucial because of the wealth and influence of the Old Dominion. Marshall spoke in the Virginia Constitutional Convention on the judiciary article of the Constitution, and it is particularly interesting to note his declaration that, if Congress were "to make a law not warranted by any of the powers enumerated, it would be considered by the judges as an infringement of the Constitution which they were to guard. They would not consider such a law as coming under their jurisdiction. They would declare it void." Upon this occasion Marshall also declared that his ideal was "a well-regulated democracy," which was the ideal of the Founding Fathers, who were seeking means to curb any threats to property. Marshall himself admitted that the people who had elected him and John Randolph were against the ratification of the Constitution, but they voted for it nevertheless. Perhaps three-quarters of the people of Virginia were against ratification, but they could not stop the Federalist juggernaut.

Marshall became the Federalist party leader in Virginia after the adoption of the Constitution. In the two decades during which the Federalists controlled the national government, he was practically the personal agent of Washington in Virginia. In the continuing controversy over states' rights, the Republicans found a resourceful leader in Jefferson, who before long began to pay his compliments to John Marshall. He called him "hypocritical and cunning," and observed that "his lax, lounging manners" were only "the mask of Republicanism." The line of cleavage between Federalists and Republicans was perfectly clear. The mercantile and financial interests who had brought about the adoption of the Constitution were now ardent nationalists in favor of a liberal interpretation of the new charter of government, while the debtor and agricultural interests, who had opposed ratification of the Constitution, were now champions of states' rights and strict constructionists. The latter were also against the assumption of state debts and payment of the British, and they rioted against the imposition of the whisky tax. The same alignment of interests was apparent in foreign politics. The Federalists, but not the Republicans, shuddered at the French Revolution and the native Jacobin Clubs, and voted ostensibly to stay neutral in the conflict between Great Britain and France while they actually assisted the British cause by concluding the inglorious Jay Treaty of 1794. The Federalists themselves had virtually become British Tories and were ready to overlook British depredations upon American commerce.

While Marshall during this period was a power in Virginia politics, he was not a national figure, and no one would have then predicted his future destiny. But in 1798, by virtue of his management of the famous diplomatic negotiations with France known to history as the "X. Y. Z. mission," he became a great national hero. With Charles Cotesworth Pinckney and Elbridge Gerry, he sailed for Paris in 1797 to attempt to settle the differences between the two nations; but when he was met with a request by Talleyrand's agents for a forced "loan" and the payment of bribes to the members of the Directory, he very properly remained adamant and steadfast in his refusal. Marshall diverted himself during these weary months by taking in the Paris theater and by writing long letters to his "dearest Polly" in much the same vein as Beccaria's during his stay in the same gay capital. Marshall and Pinckney finally sailed for home, leaving Gerry, who was in favor of meeting the French demands, behind them. The dispatches they had sent home in the meantime had revealed the facts of the attempted extortion and stirred the whole country to furious indignation. When Marshall and Pinckney arrived in Philadelphia, they were received as great national heroes. Never have the American people been so disposed to reward a diplomatic failure. A dinner was given to the two members of the mission, at which the famous toast was drunk: "Millions for defense but not one cent for tribute." The experience not only made Marshall a national hero but may well have taught him a valuable lesson in popular psychology, namely, how easily men of all classes and parties succumbed to appeals based on the rhetoric of patriotism and the national interest.

It is particularly instructive to consider Marshall's reason for accepting a place on the X. Y. Z. mission. Until this time he had steadfastly refused to accept every offer to serve the national Government, over whose welfare he was presumably so much concerned, because it would have interfered with his practice and meant a loss of income. But the emoluments of the members of the mission were to be three times the amount of his annual income as a lawyer, and he accepted because the money would enable him to meet an installment on the purchase price of the Fairfax estate. Although the mission had lasted less than a year, he received almost $20,000. His expenses had not exceeded $5000. No wonder he had exclaimed that the appointment was a "God-send."

Upon Washington's insistent urging, Marshall became a candidate for Congress in the crucial campaign of 1798–99, following the enactment of the hated Alien and Sedition Acts, which were perhaps the chief political cause of the Federalist downfall. Despite the fact that the Blackstonian libertarianism of Marshall, as well as the maneuverings of the campaign, led Marshall to promise to vote for their repeal, he won the election by the extremely slender majority of 108. The X. Y. Z. affair had provided the Federalists with a temporary breathing spell only, and the handwriting was upon the wall. President Adams was having trouble recruiting members for his obviously short-lived Cabinet, and in the spring of 1800 he offered the post of Secretary of State to John Marshall, who accepted after a good deal of hesitation. He showed greater alacrity when, on January 20, 1801, he was nominated to the additional office of Chief Justice of the Supreme Court. He held both offices during the final weeks of the Adams administration.

The so-called Revolution of 1800 swept the Federalists out of power and installed Jefferson in office, together with all the works of Republicanism. But meanwhile the Federalists had prepared themselves for the impending catastrophe by passing the Judiciary Act of 1801 and by filling the expanded national judiciary with reliable Federalists. As Jefferson put it: "The Federalists have retired into the judiciary as a stronghold . . . and from that battery all the works of Republicanism are to be beaten down and erased."

The Federal Constitution had vested the national judicial power in a Supreme Court of the United States, and such inferior Federal courts as Congress should create. The Supreme Court was to have original jurisdiction in a limited number of cases in which foreign diplomatic officers or states might be involved, and appellate jurisdiction in all other cases arising under the laws, treaties, and Constitution of the United States. The Judiciary Act of 1789 had created Federal district courts, as courts of first instance, as well as circuit courts, and had fixed the appellate jurisdiction of the Supreme Court, which was made to include the duty of hearing cases on circuit by way of intermediate appeal from the district courts. Thus, while there were circuit courts, there were no separate circuit-court judges. Under this system, the six judges of the Supreme Court rode circuit in pairs, sitting with the district court to constitute the circuit court. The unavoidable necessity of constant traveling undoubtedly made very arduous the life of a justice of the Supreme Court of the United States. As Gouverneur Morris put it, one of his primary qualifications had to be "less the learning of a judge than the agility of a post boy." The Federalist Judiciary Act of 1801 therefore sought to relieve the Supreme Court justices of circuit riding by creating new circuit courts and judgeships. This may even have been a desirable reform, although it was somewhat doubtful that the new circuit judges would have enough to do to keep them busy. The main purpose, however, was to fill the new posts with Federalists, and they were appointed by the President and confirmed by the expiring Senate until the last hours of the Adams administration. Such was the origin of the "midnight" appointments of which historians speak.

With great popular acclaim, the Republicans hastened to undo the work of the designing Federalists. The Federal judges had fed the fury of the common people by undertaking to punish English common-law crimes, by browbeating juries, and by delivering political homilies from the bench. In 1802 the Judiciary Act of 1801 was repealed, with the result that the Judiciary Act of 1789 was restored. This re-establishment of the judicial *status quo*, however, was preceded by the most protracted and searching debate on the judicial power under the Constitution in American congressional history—so much so that it has been known as the Great Judiciary Debate of 1802. The members of the Senate and House vied with each other in eloquence and argument, particularly in canvassing the question whether under the Constitution the power of judicial review was entrusted to the Supreme Court of the United States. Strangely enough, the sacred document of 1789 contained no language expressly conferring such a power upon the Court. The only language in the Constitution upon which the power of judicial review could possibly be based was the declaration that the laws, treaties, and Constitution of the United States should be "the supreme law of the land." The Constitutional Convention at Philadelphia had considered only a proposal to make the President and justices of the Supreme Court members of a Council of Revision with power to annul acts of Congress. The wisdom of an inclusive power of judicial control of legislative acts had been debated only collaterally. The idea, however, as must be apparent, was in the air. The theory of judicial review had been set forth in No. 78 of *The Federalist,* written by Alexander Hamilton, the master mind of the Federalists. There were state cases in which state judges had apparently undertaken to review the constitutionality of state legislative acts, and these cases were discussed in the Judiciary Debate of 1802. Indeed, the birth of the institution of judicial review hovered like an impending doom in the whole course of the debate, and some of the speakers expressly warned that John Marshall, now Chief Justice of the Supreme Court, intended to declare unconstitutional the projected repeal of the Judiciary Act of 1801. For this reason, Congress not only voted to repeal the act but to suspend the session of the Supreme Court for fourteen months!

Marshall and the Federalists were certainly laying their plans. Marshall sought to persuade the associate justices of the Supreme Court to join him in challenging the constitutionality of the repeal of the Judiciary Act of 1801 by refusing to resume the duty of circuit riding, but the courage of his brethren was not equal to the occasion. The stage, however, was set for another maneuver, which had been begun even while the Great Judiciary Debate was in progress. Among the "midnight" appointments were seventeen commissions as justice of the peace, which had been duly sealed by John Marshall himself as Secretary of State but which for some reason remained on his desk undelivered. James Madison, the new Secretary of State, refused to deliver them after the close of the Adams administration. Thirteen of the appointees took no action, apparently regarding the office of justice of the peace as too petty to justify the expense of litigation. However, four of the appointees—William Marbury and three others— determined to invoke the original jurisdiction of the Supreme Court to secure a writ of mandamus to compel Madison to deliver their commissions. The writ of mandamus was the usual legal remedy to compel executive officers to perform ministerial acts.

Thus arose the case of *Marbury* v. *Madison,* the most famous case in American judicial annals. It might be supposed that John Marshall, who as Secretary of State had been responsible for the failure to deliver the commissions, would refuse to sit on the case because of his personal connection with it. Nevertheless, with characteristic boldness and determination, he proceeded to seize the opportunity that either had been made or had arisen. He feared perhaps that constitutional opportunity knocked but once. He held, first, that mandamus was unquestionably the proper remedy; second, that the Supreme Court undoubtedly had jurisdiction under the express provision of Section 13 of the Judiciary Act of 1789, which gave the Court the power to issue the writ of mandamus "in cases warranted by the principles and usages of law to . . . persons holding office under the authority of the United States"; but, third, that the Supreme Court could not exercise the jurisdiction which had been conferred upon it because Section 13 of the Judiciary Act of 1789 was unconstitutional, for the Constitution itself vested "original," as distinguished from "appellate," jurisdiction in the Supreme Court only in cases "affecting ambassadors, other public ministers, and those in which a state shall be a party." Thus, while the application before the Supreme Court was denied, an Act of Congress, the supreme legislative body of the nation, had been pronounced unconstitutional and void. The *coup d'état* had occurred, and the first step in establishing the sovereignty of the judicial power had been taken.

The soundness of the decision has long been questioned. Despite Marshall's reputation for logical argument, the decision rests upon unsound reasoning, and certainly his learning was not such that there could be any confidence in his history. The logic of the argument was borrowed from Alexander Hamilton and the speakers in the Judiciary Debate of 1802, but it was not compelling. It was basically the argument that, under a written constitution creating equal and co-ordinate departments of government, there must be some organ for determining the sphere of each, and that this organ must necessarily be the judicial department, for otherwise the Constitution would cease to be "the supreme law of the land." But obviously, as John Randolph had said in the Judiciary Debate of 1802: "The power which has the right of passing, without appeal, on the validity of your laws, is your sovereign," and there would no longer be equal and co-ordinate powers of government. The judgment of the Supreme Court, rather than the Constitution, would be "the supreme law of the land." In modern times some countries have adopted written constitutions, but they have refused to accept judicial review. The Federalists depended on the "logic" of their position only because they feared to admit frankly that they wished to have a means of keeping legislatures in check in order to assure the maintenance of sound conservative principles. Marshall himself did not cite the state cases in which judicial review had been applied, nor did he probably know what the Founding Fathers themselves had said in the Constitutional Convention, because its journal was not published until a good many years later. Indeed, although Marshall had spoken in favor of judicial review in the Virginia ratifying convention, he had in 1796, when appearing as a lawyer on behalf of Virginia debtors who were resisting the payment of British debts, argued against the existence of any power of judicial review! He contended that "the judicial authority can have no right to question the validity of a law, unless such jurisdiction is expressly given by the Constitution." Apparently the lawyer, who had not yet given hostages to fortune and cast his lot irrevocably with the creditor interests, could employ an argument, the logic of which as a judge he regarded as entirely fallacious.

The historical argument has always revolved around the "intentions" of the Founding Fathers, and the opponents of judicial review have always cried "usurpation." The fact is that *some* of the Founding Fathers favored judicial review, but they did not express any such intention in the Constitution. At best the intention of a group of men composing a legislative body is difficult to establish. The Founding Fathers might have intended to create state judicial review, but not Federal judicial review, or they might have intended to give the judicial department power to determine questions of its own jurisdiction without giving it the power to determine the jurisdiction of the legislative and executive departments—the very crux of judicial supremacy. In any event, at this late date it is hopeless to cry "usurpation."

John Marshall, in fact, decided only that the judiciary could determine the nature and extent of its own powers, but his argument assumed that the judiciary would also determine the nature and extent of the powers of the other departments, and would become the final arbiter of the Constitution. Indeed, he might have avoided the whole issue of constitutionality by holding that Section 13 of the Judiciary Act was intended only to confer power to issue mandamus in those cases in which the Supreme Court undoubtedly had jurisdiction. Mandamus may be not only an independent but an auxiliary remedy by which courts give effect to the jurisdiction which they otherwise possess. The Supreme Court had issued writs of mandamus before *Marbury* v. *Madison* and, despite the decision, has continued to do so ever since in aid of both its original and appellate jurisdiction. It was also extremely doubtful that Congress could not enlarge the scope of the original jurisdiction of the Supreme Court beyond the cases expressly provided for in the Constitution. In holding unconstitutional Section 13 of the Judiciary

Act of 1789, Marshall voided a provision of an act that had been drafted when he was a senator by Oliver Ellsworth, his predecessor as Chief Justice of the Supreme Court.

It has been customary to emphasize the judicial "statesmanship" of Marshall in handling the case of *Marbury* v. *Madison*. It is admitted that his reasoning was not original but that he grasped the proffered opportunity with boldness and imagination. The maneuver was unquestionably clever. He had so managed the situation that he was able to proclaim the power of judicial review without taking any affirmative action. If he had actually granted the relief which Marbury sought, the mandate of the Court would undoubtedly have been disregarded. Marshall certainly did not lack boldness, but the decision was actually self-denying and therefore did not need enforcement. The boldness of Marshall lay in his obiter dictum, which proclaimed the doctrine of judicial review, rather than in his decision, which provided no relief. In assessing the degree of Marshall's boldness, however, it must be remembered, too, that his contemporaries were more aroused by the issue of the freedom of the executive from judicial interference than by the question of judicial review. The denial of the writ of mandamus seemed to them, therefore, a signal victory. In any event, the judicial "statesmanship" and "boldness" of Marshall's decision are necessarily incompatible. Certainly it would not today be regarded as part of judicial statesmanship for a judge to go looking for trouble by indulging in obiter dictum.

That master politician, Thomas Jefferson, was not deceived by Marshall's cunning. He remained quiet for some months only because the suddenness of the Louisiana Purchase thrust more pressing problems upon him, and the approaching national election made him careful in dealing with the Federalists, who were full of open threats of secession. The timing of the decision was thus unfortunate from the Republican point of view. The party, however, had no one to blame but itself, for had it not postponed the session of the Supreme Court for fourteen months? Luck was, as usual, on John Marshall's side. As soon as the election was over, however, the Republicans felt justified by Marshall's *coup d'état* in completing the work that had been begun with the repeal of the Judiciary Act of 1801. They undertook to remove such Federalist judges as were making themselves particularly obnoxious. Under the Constitution, Federal judges held office during good behavior but there was available the political process of impeachment. This campaign got under way with the successful impeachment of John Pickering, the demented New Hampshire district judge. Next on the little Republican list was Samuel Chase, Associate Justice of the Supreme Court, and it was undoubtedly the intention, if the impeachment of Chase were successful, to proceed against John Marshall himself. For the one and only time in his life John Marshall became frightened. The hurler of judicial thunderbolts became so alarmed that in a private letter he declared it would be better for Congress to be given the power to reverse unpopular judicial decisions than to remove the judges who made them. Fortunately for John Marshall and the cause of judicial rectitude, the impeachment proceedings against Chase ended in acquittal, and the projected unseating of the Chief Justice himself had to be abandoned.

Marshall was now left with some peace of mind to proceed to the completion of a biography of George Washington—an enterprise which he had launched at the instigation of Bushrod Washington while the Great Judiciary Debate was still raging. Marshall thought that the biography of the father of the country, based upon the documents and correspondence turned over to him by his nephew, would prove a gold mine and enable him to liquidate further the indebtedness arising from the purchase of the Fairfax estate. His abilities as a political prognosticator may be judged from the fact that he thought that the attempt to repeal the Judiciary Act of 1801 would fail and that, relieved of circuit duties, he would have plenty of free time in which to push the biography to rapid completion. The biography itself proved a failure. It was, as one discerning critic put it, "the history of North America instead of the life of an individual." The Republicans stigmatized it as "a five-volumed libel." Parson Weems, who curiously was the principal sales agent for the work, was still left in undisputed possession of the field. The chief interest of the Washington biography is the light it throws upon the opinions of the biographer himself. John Marshall was accused by Thomas Jefferson of hypocrisy, but the charge is not well founded. At least, in the biography of Washington he developed the theme that the political divisions of the country were at bottom economic.

Marshall was not left for long to pursue the quiet avocation of authorship. He became involved in that strange episode in American history—the trial of Aaron Burr for treason. The trial, over which he presided in 1807, became as much a contest between Jefferson and

Marshall as a contest between the prosecution and the defense. So much passion prevailed on both sides, so inflamed was opinion in the whole country, that it would be unfair to judge of Marshall's conduct during the trial by normal standards. Actually, the decision which he made on the point of law involved in the case was not unwholesome, for he held that under the American Constitution the English law of constructive treason could not prevail, and that the crime of treason could consist only of an overt act of levying war. Nevertheless, his conduct during the trial was unquestionably partisan in favor of Burr, and it has been stigmatized as the one serious blot upon his judicial career. He excluded a great deal, if not most, of the important and relevant testimony, and permitted counsel to engage in invectives against the administration. He actually issued a *subpoena duces tecum* to Jefferson, commanding the President to appear in court and bring with him papers which were alleged to be needed as evidence. Worst of all, he attended a dinner given by Burr's chief counsel, who was also his neighbor, at which Burr himself was one of the guests. Whether Marshall knew that Burr would be present is uncertain, but the fact remains that he made no move to leave when he discovered Burr to be present. To arrive at a decision in favor of Burr on the law of treason, he had to disregard an earlier decision of his own to the contrary.

It is particularly necessary to understand Marshall's attitude toward the War of 1812 in order to evaluate the dominating motive of those decisions by which, during the following decade, he welded the nation into unity and supplied the national government with powers adequate to the discharge of its functions. The war demonstrated that the spirit of nationalism no longer moved the Federalists, whose stronghold was the North, but the people of the West and South, whose champion and mouthpiece was Henry Clay. It was a war for national expansion, bitterly opposed by the Federalists in Congress, all but three of whom voted against it. Like all other leading Federalists, John Marshall, supposedly the supreme nationalist, was entirely out of sympathy with the national movement that led to the War of 1812, and actively opposed the prosecution of the war. One can, to be sure, be a nationalist without being an expansionist, but such moderation rarely exists. Furthermore, one can be a nationalist without frustrating, as Marshall did, the only social legislation of the states which existed in his time. Nationalism is only a political principle, and all too easily yields to the pressure of economic interest. The Northern states, for all their Federalist principles, preached nullification with no less vehemence than the Southern states.

The great national issues of the period following the War of 1812 were slavery, with which was bound up the question of national expansion; free trade, which involved the issue of the tariff to protect Northern manufacturers; and the establishment of a national bank, upon which depended financial stability. Marshall had an opportunity to express himself directly with respect to only one of these issues. The content of his nationalism was entirely negative, and consisted exclusively of curbing the states on the ground that they were interfering with powers exclusively entrusted by the Constitution to the national government. Social legislation, interfering with contractual relationships, emanated, during the period of Marshall's hegemony, exclusively from the states, and the only affirmative congressional legislation seeking to exercise a national power was the legislation creating a national bank. Yet this rested only upon the implied power of Congress: it could be only one of those "necessary and proper" powers incidental to the carrying out of the express powers of Congress under the Constitution. The doctrine of implied powers was developed by Marshall with a limitless sweep, but it was applied only to sustain the creation of the second United States Bank. For the rest, Marshall's nationalism was expressed in resisting state encroachments by means of two of the clauses contained in the Constitution. One was the "contract clause," which forbade any state to impair "the obligation of contracts," and the other was the "commerce clause," which gave to Congress the power to regulate interstate and foreign commerce. The "contract clause," particularly, was the blunderbuss which John Marshall employed with deadly effect in laying low state enactments threatening the security of property. In these cases he had certainly the *general* interest of all men of property in protecting the obligations of contracts. The impartiality of judges is, however, customarily not questioned, because they make the precedents upon which their own rights depend.

The case that is primarily associated with Marshall's interpretation of the "contract clause" is the *Dartmouth College Case.* It is far more instructive, however, to begin with *Fletcher* v. *Peck,* decided by Marshall in 1810, because it shows even more clearly the influence of Marshall's personal interests. This is the case that involved that saturnalia of corruption known as the Yazoo land frauds. In 1795 the Georgia legislature, which had been corrupted almost to the last man, had granted to four land companies for half a million dollars a vast tract of fertile land now comprising most of the states of Alabama and Mississippi—land which was soon to be made still more valuable by Eli Whitney's invention of the cotton gin. When the extent of the fraud became known, a wave of furious indignation swept the state and the nation, and the next Georgia legislature proceeded to repeal the grant of its predecessor. The land speculators appealed to the Supreme Court on the ground that the repealing act impaired the obligations of their contracts. This was done by means of an obviously feigned controversy between a fictitious purchaser and seller of a tract of the Yazoo land.

Although it has been the theory of judicial review that the Supreme Court must pass on constitutional questions only in the course of adjudicating the rights of private parties in genuine controversies, it is a fact that precisely the most explosive cases in the history of judicial review have been trumped-up controversies manipulated for no other purpose than to secure legal decisions for the purpose of making political capital. Indeed, in this particular instance, the decision could not possibly restore the Yazoo land to the speculators, for prior to the commencement of the litigation Georgia had ceded its interest in the lands to the United States, which was immune from suit without its consent. John Quincy Adams noted in his diary that Chief Justice Marshall had indicated "the reluctance of the Court to decide the case at all, as it appeared manifestly made up for getting the Court's judgment on all points." In discussing another case, Marshall wrote to Story that "as I am not fond of butting against a wall in sport, I escaped on the construction of the act." These remarks would seem to suggest that Marshall knew how to escape constitutional questions when he really wished to do so, and that he knowingly violated this canon of proper judicial action.

Marshall, however, proceeded to decide the Yazoo case. He held without hesitation that the Georgia legislature could not undo the mischief it had wrought, because this would impair the obligation of a contract. Actually the obligation-of-contracts clause had been aimed at the paper-money evil that was rife at the time of the adoption of the Constitution. A legislative land grant was not really a commercial contract. A grant is an executed contract and the obligation-of-contracts clause had been designed to protect unperformed contracts. Most of the land speculators, including the parties before the Court, moreover, could hardly have been innocent purchasers, and the Georgia legislature had offered to refund the purchase price, which was mostly unexpended. As a matter of fact, the State of Georgia really had no right to grant the Yazoo lands, because they belonged to the Indians. Since John Marshall ignored all these circumstances, it is fair to surmise that as one of the holders of the title to the Fairfax estate, which rested upon the shaky foundation of a pre-Revolutionary British grant, he was vitally interested in establishing a precedent for the security of titles. Never has the righteous principle of the sanctity of contracts been proclaimed in so malodorous a case.

Within a few years the title to the Fairfax estate became directly involved in a case before the Supreme Court of the United States. Marshall, of course, could not participate in the decision of the case. But, in the meantime, that bright Bostonian, Joseph Story, had become a friend as well as an associate of the Chief Justice, whose opinions he well knew. Story was nominally a Northern Republican, but he had completely embraced the Federalist faith. Before his elevation to the bench and devotion to scholarship, he had acted as a lobbyist for the New England speculators who, following Marshall's decision, succeeded in securing an appropriation from Congress in settlement of the Yazoo land claims. Story may be regarded as the alter ego of John Marshall. Story supplied the legal learning which Marshall lacked, but he came completely under the latter's domination with respect to all questions of constitutional interpretation. There is, indeed, a legend that Marshall was in the habit of saying to Story: "That, Story, is the law; now you find the precedents." Story now wrote the opinion of the Supreme Court of the United States, from which only Justice Johnson dissented, upholding the validity of the Fairfax title. Many years later, Story was indiscreet enough to remark in a letter to George Ticknor apropos the decision that Marshall "concurred in every word of it."

At the single term of the Supreme Court which was held in February, 1819, John Marshall delivered three of his most epochal opinions. In *Sturges* v. *Crowninshield,* he held that a state insolvency law, enacted for the relief of bankrupt debtors, impaired the obligations of contracts even when applied to future debts. In the *Dartmouth College Case,* he held that the state legislature was impairing the obligation of contracts when it passed an act modifying the provisions of the college charter, which had been granted by the British Crown, and finally in *M'Culloch* v. *Maryland* he held that the creation of the second United

States Bank was within the legitimate powers conferred on the Federal government, and that the bank could not constitutionally be taxed by the states.

The *Dartmouth College Case* is especially interesting. The college was the victim of a feud that had arisen between the Federalists and Republicans, and the modification of its charter by the New Hampshire legislature was mixed up with issues of state politics. Daniel Webster, the supreme orator and showman, knew well how to capitalize on alma mater sentiment, as well as how to exploit political feeling. He came to a point in his argument before the Supreme Court at which he exclaimed with tears in his eyes: "It is, Sir, as I have said, a small college. And yet, there are those who love it." He broke down and could not continue, and the tears welled also in the eyes of John Marshall sitting on the bench. Yet Webster had so little faith in winning on the contract clause that he relied principally on fundamental principles of government which, while they were nowhere mentioned in the Constitution, were supposed nevertheless to prohibit the divesting of vested rights. Moreover, when the argument was concluded, Marshall had to announce that the Court was divided and that the case would have to be continued. The college then proceeded to move heaven and earth. James Kent, the American Blackstone, spoke to Justice Johnson when the latter visited him at Albany. Webster, who was on terms of cordial intimacy with Joseph Story, sent him four copies of his argument for distribution among his brethren. Governor William Plumer of New Hampshire even appointed Story a member of the Board of Trustees of the new university; but, although the judge declined, he was compromised in the eyes of both sides. In the end the desired decision was forthcoming. It seems to have to do only with college charters, but actually the decision itself was a new charter of business enterprise. The corporation was coming into its own as the preferred means of organizing capital; steamship companies, railroad companies, turnpike companies, were being formed, and they, too, were receiving charters from state legislatures. Was a charter—which was a grant of privileges to a public corporation—indeed a "contract"? Where was the necessary "consideration" for such a contract? A contract could not be purchased from any government. In England, Parliament had power not only to alter but to revoke a charter. Was the New Hampshire legislature to be powerless to regulate in the interest of the commonweal the creature of a royal grant? Marshall himself admitted that "the preservation of rights of this description was not particularly in the view of the framers of the Constitution, when the clause under consideration was introduced into that instrument." After all, the New Hampshire legislature had not attempted to confiscate the property of the college. It had merely sought to change the form of its organization. John Marshall brushed aside such considerations, because he perceived that the fate of all corporations was involved. "The law of this case," he said, "is the law of all."

The case of *M'Culloch* v. *Maryland* is Marshall's leading exposition of the doctrine of implied powers. It is virtually certain that the Chief Justice wrote most of the opinion in the *Bank Case* at Richmond months before he had heard the argument of counsel in the case. After all, he is reported to have once said: "The acme of judicial distinction means the ability to look a lawyer straight in the eyes for two hours and not hear a damned word he says." John Marshall had made up his mind long before, and now in the *Bank Case* he delivered himself of some of his most celebrated dicta. He neatly rephrased Alexander Hamilton on implied powers: "Let the end be legitimate," he said, "and all the means which are appropriate . . . which are not prohibited . . . are constitutional." Even more happily he exclaimed that "it is a *constitution* we are expounding." Marshall meant to imply in this dictum that a constitution, which is necessarily couched in broad and general phrases, should be construed liberally and in a statesmanlike manner. But it is nevertheless also true that in the amplitude of constitutional phrases the judicial fancy may roam free. The states, after all, had constitutions too. As was said by Spencer Roane, next to Jefferson the most implacable enemy of John Marshall: "That man must be a deplorable idiot who does not see that there is no difference between an unlimited grant of power and a grant limited in its terms but accompanied with unlimited means of carrying it into execution." On the more immediate question of the constitutional right of the state of Maryland to tax the Bank, Marshall frightened every man of property in the country when he proclaimed that "the power to tax involves the power to destroy." Here, however, he was only borrowing a phrase Webster had used in the argument. It was the decision in the *Bank Case* that led Jefferson to make his famous remark: "The judiciary of the United States is the subtle corps of sappers and miners constantly working under ground to undermine the foundations of our confederated fabric."

In a sense, the most eloquent and enduring of Marshall's decisions, although no less unpopular, was made in the case of *Cohens* v. *Virginia,* decided in 1821. His assertion of the appellate power of the Supreme Court over the judgments of state courts, which brought into question the supremacy of the Federal Constitution, treaties, or laws, was essential to the functioning of a successful Federalism. The power to review the judgments of state courts had been conferred upon the Court by Section 25 of the Judiciary Act of 1789, but the states had long asserted that they were as capable as the Federal courts of enforcing Federal law, and that this provision of the Judiciary Act was unconstitutional. Joseph Story had indeed already decided the question in one of the cases involving the Fairfax title. But no constitutional doctrine could really be considered established until it had had the imprimatur of John Marshall! The occasion for the decision was as trivial and unreal as that which had led to *Marbury* v. *Madison.* Congress had authorized the District of Columbia to conduct a lottery. Two lottery peddlers had sold some of the lottery tickets in Virginia, where the sale of such tickets was prohibited, and had been arrested and fined $100. They appealed to the Supreme Court, alleging the supremacy of the Federal law. Actually, Marshall upheld the conviction on the ground that Congress intended the lottery to be a local affair, but not until he had first sustained the appellate jurisdiction of the Supreme Court and expounded the supremacy of Federal law in the most sweeping terms. It was not so much a judicial opinion as a state paper. It was justified not by its legal logic but by the necessities of Federalism. It revealed, moreover, Marshall's dream of immortality. It was not a dream of personal immortality, for he was not an intensely religious man. He dreamed of the immortality of the Constitution— "framed for ages to come."

These decisions of Marshall hardly met with universal acclaim. He was subjected to such virulent attack in the *Bank Case* that he himself wrote articles in defense of his decision which he published anonymously. It can be regarded as only dubious judicial etiquette for a judge to turn anonymous pamphleteer in an attempt to justify his own decision. The only really popular decision Marshall ever made was in the case of *Gibbons* v. *Ogden,* decided in 1824. After the invention of the steamboat, New York State had granted to Fulton and Livingston a monopoly of operating in the waters of the state, and other states had followed suit. Clearly, such monopolies would have dealt death blows to the freedom of interstate commerce, the regulation of which had been expressly confided to the national government. In declaring these monopolies unconstitutional, Marshall was unquestionably on sound ground. Yet even here he is confused in his treatment of the far more difficult question whether the states had concurrent power to enact legislation affecting interstate commerce in the absence of any Federal regulation. This was to be the crucial issue of the future. It was decided ultimately in favor of state power, but Marshall himself hinted that he would regard the failure of Congress to regulate as regulation itself. "There is great force in this argument," he said, "and the Court is not satisfied that it has been refuted." In the meantime, the people were grateful that commerce had been kept free. The readiness with which they responded to the only genuine instance of Federalism, which did not directly involve the process of riveting conservative economic views into the Constitution, is as revealing as it is significant.

All of John Marshall's constitutional decisions have certain well-marked general characteristics, which illuminate the workings of his mind and judicial art. He denied the creativeness of his own activity. He always represented himself as a mere mechanical mouthpiece of the law. He therefore had no choice but to follow its commands. He generally declared that the consideration of any question of constitutionality posed a dreadful dilemma for the Court, but it was a dilemma from which it must not shrink when the answer was plain and unmistakable. He was always talking about what "the American people" or simply "the people" had ordained in establishing the Constitution, although in fact only a small minority of the American people had participated in its drafting and ratification. He commonly assumed what he really had to prove. A favorite expression of his was to say, especially when he got into difficulties: "It can require no argument to prove . . ." His logic was as irresistible as that of any proposition in Euclid, but only when his major premise was granted. He often mentioned specific clauses of the Constitution, but he was really expounding a political philosophy which could not be proved from the Constitution itself.

The Supreme Court of the United States during this period had become known as "Marshall's Court." The Chief Justice exercised an extraordinary ascendancy over his colleagues, aided no doubt by the fact that they all lived together in one boardinghouse. The truth is that even the Republican judges had succumbed to Federalist principles. The best example of this is Joseph Story, who was a Republican only in false face. Before Marshall became Chief Justice, it had been the practice of the judges of the Supreme Court to deliver separate opinions in each case. Marshall instituted a change in this practice, so that the judge who delivered an opinion spoke for the whole Court unless there were dissents. From the point of view of judicial technique, the change helped to establish Marshall's ascendancy, as well as to strengthen the position of the Court. It enabled him to speak magisterially for a court rather than merely in his own person, and it made it more difficult for his enemies to attack him.

The beginning of the end of Marshall's domination came with the election of Andrew Jackson in 1828. The previous year there had been rumblings of revolt among his own colleagues, and he found himself twice in the role of a lonely dissenter. Jackson was, if not a more bitter, a more effective antagonist than Jefferson in the campaign against judicial review. He held the view, like Lincoln after him, that each of the three great government departments, the executive, the legislative, and the judicial departments, had the right to determine the constitutionality of its own acts. He filled the Supreme Court with justices of his own political faith, and the hold of the Federalists upon the Court was broken. In 1832 Marshall even suffered the mortification of having a mandate of the Supreme Court openly flouted by the State of Georgia, which had set herself to dispossess and destroy the Cherokee Indians. When Marshall in the case of *Worcester* v. *Georgia* properly held that jurisdiction over the Indians had been confided exclusively to the Federal government, Jackson refused to take any step to give effect to the decision. It is reported that he said: "John Marshall has made his decision: *now let him enforce it.*"

If there had ever been any genuine liberalism in the political philosophy of John Marshall, it disappeared in his last years. He displayed his rock-ribbed conservatism most clearly when he participated in the Virginia Convention of 1829–30, which met to revise the constitution of his native state. The mere fact that he allowed himself to be persuaded to participate in the Convention despite his duties as a judge indicates the importance he attached to the occasion. He fought in the Convention to maintain the most oligarchical political system that ever existed in any American state. He even voted to retain the freehold principle of suffrage, but had to content himself with a less rigid property qualification.

The last years of Marshall were very unhappy and even full of despair. He not only suffered the ignominy of judicial defeat and political disillusionment, but his health failed and he suffered extreme physical pain. On December 25, 1831, his "dearest Polly" died, and the bereaved husband was inconsolable. The day before she died she had hung about his neck a locket containing a wisp of her hair, and for the remainder of his life John Marshall never parted with it night or day. On the first anniversary of his wife's death, Joseph Story found the Chief Justice in tears. Reminded by his wife's death of his own mortality, John Marshall made his will, disposing of his bank and rail-road stock and his immense landholdings. One provision of the will indicates the vanity of the man. He left a thousand acres each to such of his grandsons as should be named John. The colossus of judicial review presided over the Supreme Court of the United States for the last time on January 12, 1835. He died in the evening of July 6, 1835, in Philadelphia, the city of the Constitution, where he had gone for medical treatment, and his body was sent by coasting vessel to Richmond for burial.

In his declining years John Marshall began to lose hope of solving the bitter political disputes of his time by judicial decision, and even began to despair of the future of the Union. He wrote to Story: "The Union has been preserved thus far by miracles. I fear they cannot continue." It is just as well that he did not have to witness the greatest ordeal of constitutionalism, which was the Civil War. It took this bloody and destructive conflict to establish American nationalism upon a firm foundation. It was, indeed, the exercise of the power of judicial review in the Dred Scott decision, which denied the power of Congress to exclude slavery from the territories, that precipitated the Civil War. The author of that decision was Roger Brooke Taney, who succeeded Marshall as Chief Justice of the United States. Significantly Taney, the "pliant tool" of Jackson, has been subjected to the same rationalizing process as Marshall himself. Excepting his one "fatal error," this Southerner and slavocrat is pictured as a champion of a progressive democracy, which he is supposed to have inaugurated by upholding the power of the states. He is credited with the invention of the magic conception of the "police power," in the name of which state legislation intended to promote public health, safety, or morals may be upheld despite inhibitions of constitutions. He thus laid the foundation for undoing most of those extreme doctrines of John Marshall that would have made any legislative regulation impossible. Nevertheless, the dominating motive of Taney was not a vision of state democracy but the desire to preserve the system of slavery. In the case of John Marshall, the good that he did, which was nationalism, lived after him. Most of the evil that he did was interred with his bones, but this did not prevent the even greater evils that were committed in the course of the subsequent history of judicial review. Yet undoubtedly the aura of sanctity with which he surrounded property and contract still remains as the most powerful emanation of the Marshall legend. In estimating Marshall's place in history, it must not be forgotten that the supremacy of the nation could have been affirmed without voiding state legislation that was not beyond a doubt unconstitutional. The conflict between the states may not have been as "irrepressible" as we have become accustomed to think, and if so some of John Marshall's applications of the doctrine of judicial review must perhaps share part of the blame for the holocaust.

The fame of Marshall has proved enduring. He was the beneficiary of the victory of Northern arms, and nothing succeeds like success. Yet precise estimates of his character and doctrines will always differ. Curiously, perhaps the minimum estimate of Marshall and his work has been expressed by the greatest judge who has sat on the bench of the Supreme Court of the United States since his time. Justice Oliver Wendell Holmes, who achieved that objectivity towards the process of judicial review which Marshall lacked, observed on the hundredth anniversary of the day on which Marshall took his seat as Chief Justice: "I should feel a greater doubt whether, after Hamilton and the Constitution itself, Marshall's work proved more than a strong intellect, a good style, personal ascendancy in his court, courage, justice and the convictions of his party."

It is not any more difficult to perceive Marshall's faults than it is to comprehend his virtues. The faults were perhaps inevitable, considering the nature of the institution of judicial review which he manipulated in the formative period of its history. If he not infrequently compromised the integrity of the judicial function, it may well be that it was because judicial review, if it was to succeed, could have operated in no other way at the time when the fate of the infant Federal Union was at stake. The Federal Constitution created governmental vacuums, but it is a law of physics that nature abhors a vacuum. John Marshall could hardly have failed to fill the vacuums with Federalist principles, even as the Jacksonian democracy later filled them with the principles of states' rights. It is only a seeming paradox that a judge should have been one of the great figures of the patristic period, and that his greatness as a judge should depend upon his capacities as a politician. Judicial "statesmanship" is called for on the bench primarily in the manipulation of judicial review, and a knowledge of political history is necessary to an understanding of constitutional decisions. Moreover, politics is never practiced for the sake of politics. While nationalism is the romantic *décor* of judicial review, conservatism readily becomes its essence.

It was to be expected, too, that Marshall would habitually indulge in extremes of doctrine. In his constitutional palette, the only colors were black and white. He thought only in terms of power and lack of power. It seemed to him that to concede that the states might possess legitimate power might result in the complete destruction of the Federal government. "The power to tax is the power to destroy" is an axiom characteristic of his thought. But Justice Holmes once revealed its fallacy when he observed: "The power to tax is not the power to destroy while this Court sits," and he was undoubtedly pointing to the chief weakness of Marshall's reasoning when he added: "In those days it was not recognized as it is today that most of the distinctions of the law are distinctions of degree." Most of Marshall's basic doctrines, except the doctrine of judicial review itself, have been so qualified that they no longer express existing constitutional law. It has been said of *Marbury* v. *Madison* that nothing survives of the case "except its influence," and the same is true in greater or less degree of his other epoch-making decisions. Yet in reproaching Marshall for dealing in absolutes, it is easy to fall into anachronism. Such was the feebleness of Federal power that it seemed to call for the application of absolutes. The refinements of constitutional doctrine are a luxury of a Federalism triumphant and secure.

Indeed, the shape of judicial review today is a post-Civil War creation. Marshall employed it, with one exception, exclusively against state legislation, and the only act of Congress which he held unconstitutional dealt with the powers of the judiciary, which might more readily claim the right to determine the extent of its own jurisdiction. The substantive scope of judicial review was, however, immeasurably expanded as a result of the Civil War. Even as Marshall seized upon the obligation-of-contracts clause the post-Civil War generation of constitutionalists grasped the opportunity offered by a still more generous phrase, which changed greatly the physiognomy of judicial review, although it did not alter the basic lines of its evolution as laid down by John Marshall himself.

Little is now heard of the obligations of contracts. The master constitutional slogan is now "due process." The change in the constitutional balance of power after the Civil War was expressed by the Fourteenth Amendment. It subordinated the states to the national government, but to protect the civil rights of the emancipated Negro slaves it also provided that no state should "deprive any person of due process of law, nor deny to any person within its jurisdiction the equal protection of the laws." The term "due process" had a long history connected with Magna Charta, and the identical due-process clause had been contained in the Fifth Amendment to the Federal Constitution, but as a limitation upon the Federal government only. It had never been understood, however, as more than a procedural requirement intended to assure that no man would be deprived of his rights or condemned, except after an opportunity to be heard and according to some provision of law. After first rejecting such an interpretation, Marshall's successors finally held in the 1880's that due process was also a substantive requirement that state legislative acts should be "reasonable." They held, besides, that a corporation was a "person" within the meaning of the Fourteenth Amendment and entitled to its protection. The new concept of due process was applied also in the interpretation of the Fifth Amendment, and thus became the master "test" of Federal as well as state legislation. Any law disliked by a majority of the Supreme Court judges was without "due process," and so limitless was the sweep of the concept that the equal-protection clause became a needless luxury. Under the banner of due process, industrial and finance capitalism were to march to their greatest triumphs, while liberals and progressives were left merely to rail at five-to-four decisions, and the "nine old men."

It may seem strange that judicial review has survived the ordeal of the Civil War and all the political and economic vicissitudes of the American Republic before and since. The "nine old men" have frequently moved the nation to anger, but never to the point of ridding itself of judicial supremacy. Liberals have only hoped and prayed for "better" judges, who would not misconstrue but put new life into the sacred document of 1789. The tolerance even of liberals is, however, not inexplicable. Judicial review is still inextricably intertwined with Federalism, and there is a general fear that to tamper with the institution will rend the "confederated fabric." The Supreme Court, moreover, seems to afford a valuable means of protecting the civil liberties which are guaranteed by the Bill of Rights, and in recent years the Court has protected such liberties with a commendable degree of firmness.

The trouble lies, indeed, not so much in judicial review as in the amplitude of the constitutional phrases upon which it operates. Well, then, could not the treacherous phrases be removed from the fundamental law, or redefined? Perhaps, and yet there never has been a more necessary and precise-looking clause than the commerce clause, with which perfect wonders of judicial legerdemain have been accomplished. In fact, the secret of the functioning of judicial review lies not in itself but in the whole system of checks and balances of which it is a part. Certainly when it was first devised, there had never been a supposedly democratic system that was so nicely calculated to frustrate the popular will. It may seem easy to get rid of the effect of unpopular constitutional decisions by amending the Constitution. The people, after being protected by the judiciary, have on occasion proceeded to sanction by constitutional amendment the very encroachment against which they have been protected. The process of amending the Constitution is very cumbersome and rigid, and the recall of the decisions of the nine men, whether old or middle-aged, can hardly be undertaken as an everyday constitutional enterprise.

The institution of judicial review has long acted as the shock absorber of the whole American governmental system. It has become the habit of the American people to blame most of their troubles upon the incorrigible nine. Their ability to absorb an almost endless amount of abuse and vilification itself testifies to the beauty of judicial review as a legal disguise of a political process. In the course of judicial review, the most crucial and momentous issues of public policy, upon the enlightened and objective decision of which the welfare of the whole nation depends, are subjected to the traditional process of judicial arbitrament by which are decided the petty everyday controversies of private individuals in which society itself is supposed to have no immediate stake. It seems a great, if not an ultimate, conquest for the realm of law and the peaceable ordering of social relationships that even governments should be subjected to the hallowed judicial process by which the rights of individuals are determined. It may seem that only expediency will guide a legislature in fixing the limits of permissible constitutional action. It is so disarming to pretend that a court, enjoying all the guarantees of independence and impartiality, will be less tempted to drive a coach and four through the Constitution. The interests of society, however, can hardly be presented adequately in the forms of private litigation. When John Doe is pitted against the United States, Uncle Sam must necessarily seem a bully. Social forces must be strangled in the intricate meshes of legal technique. Law is a web of precedents, but legislation is always an effort to break the web and escape. The law is a verbal art, which is dominated by logic rather than by social purpose, by precedent rather than by free decision. When social issues are decided on legal grounds, it is not so easy to demonstrate with unanswerable finality that the judges have departed from the letter of the Constitution, and when supposedly "liberal" judges make illiberal decisions, the average citizen becomes sadly confused. It is plain that the ideal of "a government of laws, not men" has proved vain, but the oracles of the Constitution continue to escape the popular wrath. The very conditions of the judicial process which make it possible for them to frustrate the popular will enable them to escape retribution. They are saved by the veneration which is accorded to the acts of judges, who are supposed to speak the impartial dooms of the law. It is the tradition to believe that even when the individual judge has erred, the integrity of the law itself remains. The historian of the future may well record that the absolute reign of law was the last great delusion of a nation that put its faith in legalism.

Rudolf von Jhering

LAW AS A MEANS TO AN END

THE PIONEER OF THE BASIC MODERN TRENDS IN JURISPRUDENCE WAS a German, Rudolf von Jhering. He might appropriately be called the Mark Twain of German jurisprudence. Gifted with a rare sardonic humor, he led the revolt against philosophical abstraction and conceptualism in German jurisprudence and the glorification of logic as a juristic method, which enabled the jurists to disguise the law as a system of legal mathematics. It so happened that this attack upon logical method in the law hit the basic evil of all nineteenth-century jurisprudence. The controversy raged about logic, but the real issue was a new social gospel whose acceptance was being prevented by false logic. Socialism was in the air, but the jurists remained oblivious even of the need for social legislation which would bring about a socialization of the civil law. They simply persisted in applying logically the basic postulates of the individualist philosophy which had become established with the rise of capitalism.

Jhering has been called the German Bentham, but the comparison is not apt, for Jhering's creed was a social utilitarianism. He did not share Bentham's passion for codification, taking little or no interest in the drafting of the German civil code, which took place during his lifetime. Jhering was interested in function rather than in formal definition. It seems strange that a social struggle should have been carried on in terms of a controversy over the place of logic in juristic method, but controversy in jurisprudence is always oblique. The first revival of commerce raised the issue of the reception of the Roman law, because that system of law was far more advanced than Germanic law; the rise of capitalism was tied up with the movement for natural law, which afforded a means of rationalizing the Roman law; and it was to be expected that the demand for far-reaching social changes should lead to bitter discontent with a juristic method that was employed to give the basic institutions of the existing order an appearance of eternal and unalterable truth. Logic had always been the chief tool of jurisprudence from Gaius to Blackstone. It served well enough in periods of relative tranquillity when there was no need to question the premises which underlay the logical deductions of the jurists. Logic, however, was bound to become the chief focus of attack in an age of rapid transition and change.

The nineteenth century, which was a period of great scientific inventiveness, was paradoxically a period of comparative stagnation in the field of the civil law. The jurists were content with the rationalization of the basic legal principles of property and contract, which had been accomplished in the name of "equity" in the countries of the common law and in the name of "natural law" in the countries of the civil law. Such legal inventiveness as was manifested in the nineteenth century was in procedural law and in the amelioration of the criminal law. Bentham, although a great procedural inventor, believed in the fundamental verities of Adam Smith, and therefore had no violent quarrel with the substantive principles of the common law. The movement for codification, which he stimulated, produced its greatest accomplishment in France, when Napoleon caused to be drafted one civil code for all the provinces of France; but this Code Napoleon merely restated the precepts of natural law and the principles of customary law as they had been worked out by the great French legists of the sixteenth and seventeenth centuries. In the United States there had been produced the one great original procedural invention, the device of judicial review, which was revolutionary in form but not in effect, and actually retarded the development of the substantive law. With a judicial oligarchy in control of legislation, the basic dogmas of property and contract remained unaltered far longer than elsewhere, and the philosophy of laissez faire had become the touchstone of the Constitution.

It is a rather singular irony that the juridical revolution should have occurred in Germany, which began the nineteenth century with the most backward legal system among the countries of western Europe. The Industrial Revolution did not come to Germany until after the middle of the century, but the juridical revolution occurred earlier there than in England, the United States, or France. History later repeated itself when Socialism was first realized in Russia, the land of the czars. In Germany the causes of the juridical revolution were the same as those of the Industrial Revolution, namely, political unification and the application of the very latest science. Germany thus had the advantage of the latest juridical machinery, even as it had the advantage of the latest industrial machinery. All the juristic discoveries of the nineteenth century seem to have been "Made in Germany." But it is no exaggeration to say that through most of the nineteenth century Germany could boast the greatest jurists and the worst legal system of any country in Europe. Such men as Karl Friedrich von Savigny and Theodor Mommsen, the great Romanists, and Bernhard Windscheid, the master of the pandects, as well as Otto von Gierke, Karl Friedrich Eichhorn, Georg Ludwig von Maurer, and Rudolf Sohm, the leading Germanists, who indefatigably investigated the origins of Germanic law, all achieved international reputations. But these jurists were interested only in legal history or the philosophy of law. They paid little or no attention to the needs of practical jurisprudence, which they left entirely in the not too capable hands of the practitioners. Since political unification is the first prerequisite of any effectively functioning legal system, the task of the jurists would perhaps have been hopeless. They sought fame, therefore, in purely scientific labors.

The scientific cultivation of jurisprudence, in the historical as well as the philosophical fields, is a characteristic of the maturity of law. The arts of jurisprudence are not cultivated by people in primitive or archaic civilizations; there are no jurists; and the needs of practice are all-absorbing and sufficient. The first phase of juridical philosophy had been represented by speculations concerning natural law in ancient Greece and Rome as well as in the Europe of the sixteenth and seventeenth centuries. But it was in the nineteenth century that philosophies of law were elaborated in all their infinite variety. Juristic philosophy even became an independent branch of philosophy. The connection between the maturity of law and the development of the philosophy of law is manifest particularly in England, precisely because England has never been the home of abstract philosophy. Yet in the first half of the nineteenth century the English produced a juristic philosopher in the person of John Austin, the founder of the so-called analytical school of jurisprudence, who attempted to separate the law from moral philosophy and to found a positive science of law based upon the precepts of the existing system of English law. In Austin is manifest the beatitude of the common law; analytical jurisprudence is simply the rationalization of the established order, which is considered eminently satisfactory.

Austin studied legal philosophy in Germany but this flirtation with German jurisprudence had apparently done him no harm.

But during the same period in Germany there reigned triumphant the "historical" school of jurisprudence founded by that German aristocrat, Karl Friedrich von Savigny. The very fact that he had deigned to enter upon an academic career as a teacher of Roman law was regarded as an act of unparalleled grace. Savigny conducted monumental researches into the history of Roman law, but even in this activity he had an unfortunate effect upon practice, for he tended to elevate the ancient Roman law as the "pure" law above the law of the pandects, the *usus modernus pandectarum,* the modified Roman law which had actually obtained in the German states since the general reception of Roman law in the fifteenth century. But far more mischievous in its effect was the philosophy of history which was espoused by Savigny and which became the accepted doctrine of the historical school. Representing the political reaction in Germany, which had so firmly entrenched absolutism in all the Germanies that it could not be broken even by the revolution of 1848, Savigny taught that a nation's law, like its language and other cultural attributes, was an unconscious emanation of the *Volksgeist,* the "genius" of its people. Customary law was therefore law par excellence—the chief source of law. For this reason, Savigny opposed codification for Germany and in a celebrated pamphlet, *Vom Beruf unserer Zeit für Gesetzgebung und Rechtswissenschaft* (On the Vocation of Our Times for Legislation and Jurisprudence), denounced the creators of the Code Napoleon as "miserable dilettanti." He thus opposed not only the revolutionary doctrine of natural law but positive legislation. It might be supposed that he would have been nonplused by the fact that the *Volksgeist* in Germany had manifested itself in the reception of the alien Roman law, but he simply invented the fiction that in mature systems of jurisprudence the learned jurists act as the representatives of the *Volksgeist.* In fact, however, the historical school could not reconcile the contradiction between the reception and the theory that the origin of law was to be found in the folk-spirit. Karl Marx once gibed that Savigny had become so absorbed in the sources of the law that he was oblivious of the main stream.

The "historical" school was misnamed, for it was really a philosophical school. The reaction to the historical school, which began even during Savigny's ascendancy, did not give a more realistic basis to German jurisprudence. The opposing school, correctly called the "philosophical" school, took its inspiration from Hegel, who had a profound belief in absolute monarchy. Hegel regarded the state as the embodiment of freedom and reason, but the state was represented by the monarch. He perceived in law the evolution of the idea of freedom, and in the freedom of the will the essence of individual freedom. Apparently he was not bothered very much by the obvious facts that the German states at least were not the embodiments of liberty, and that the science of the law had always been overshadowed by restraint. In Germany, the fact that it was nonsense was not usually regarded as a legitimate objection to a philosophy. As Heinrich Heine said, Britain ruled the seas, France ruled the land, and Germany ruled the clouds. Hegel's emphasis upon the freedom of the individual led to a "will jurisprudence." The jurists, instead of considering social and practical requirements, thought in terms of individual intention and the realization of the individual will in the construction of legal transactions, and in terms of legal powers rather than legal duties. In both the mature Roman law and the common law, lawyers also made much of "intention," but they never carried the business to quite the same degree of absurdity. The "civil" law, which is often called private law, is always the preserve of the individual, but "will jurisprudence" reflected as never before the freedom of contract which the jurists had made omnipotent.

In addition to the adherents of Savigny and Hegel, there were the "Germanists," whose master was Otto von Gierke. The Germanists really believed in the *Volksgeist,* and were hardly, if at all, outdone by the Romanists in the ardors of historical research, but they were alienated by Savigny's predilection for the pure Roman law and his slighting of the Germanic elements in practice, which really represented whatever adaptations had been made to current needs. The Germanists undoubtedly conducted valuable researches into the origins of German law, but their efforts to re-establish the quainter and more Gothic legal elements of the German past were only another phase of romanticism. The mature Roman law was, of course, a far better basis for a modern jurisprudence than the medieval *Saxenspiegel* or the *Schwabenspiegel,* the two great monuments of archaic German law. But the question was not whether either Romanistic or Germanistic elements were to be preferred but whether given legal institutions met contemporary needs. The endless squabbles between the Romanists and the Germanists were an important factor in postponing the adoption of a German civil code.

The condition of German jurisprudence had been aggravated not only by its contact with German philosophy since the days of Immanuel Kant but by the habits and traditions of German university life. The undue emphasis upon academic rank, which could be achieved only by contributions to scholarship, led to an endless production of doctoral dissertations and treatises, whose ostensible purpose was the increase of juristic knowledge but whose actual purpose was academic advancement. The passages in the *corpus iuris* of Justinian had been the subjects of learned commentaries for centuries, and originality could rarely, if ever, be achieved except by absurdity. Moreover, unlike the case in England and America, the bar and the judiciary were rigidly separated bodies, and the fructification of scholarship by men with experience in practice rarely occurred. Until about the middle of the nineteenth century, the medieval practice of submitting questions of law to a member of the university faculties had not disappeared, but such submissions were usually only another opportunity for the academic airing of a favorite juristic theory. The atmosphere, social and political, of the typical German university town, usually located in a provincial center, was, too, not calculated to stimulate bold and independent thinking.

Rudolf von Jhering was not an iconoclast born. Although he had the right temperament, it did not reveal itself publicly in the first two decades of his career. Born at Aurich in East Friesland on August 22, 1818, he came of a family that boasted a long line of jurists and civil servants. His great-great-grandfather was Hermann Conring, one of the few German realists who had pioneered in economics as well as political science, and who had left his mark in ridiculing the Holy Roman Empire. Jhering had the conventional education of his time. He left the Gymnasium at the age of eighteen and studied at Heidelberg, Munich, Göttingen, and Berlin. His intention at first was to enter the civil service, but the government of his native town in its infinite wisdom refused him a post because his brother was already in the civil service. Saved for jurisprudence, he thereupon entered upon the teaching of Roman law. The first five years of his academic career were spent successively at Basel, Rostock, and Kiel, but it was not until he reached Giessen in 1852 that he settled down for more than a decade and a half of teaching, and the composition of the work which he then believed would be his magnum opus, the *Geist des römischen Rechts auf den verschiedenen Stufen seiner Entwicklung* (The Spirit of the Roman Law in the Various Stages of Its Development), which appeared in four volumes from 1852 to 1865 and was translated into the principal European languages.

But, before his academic and literary career began, Jhering had suffered a loss which left a saddening influence upon his life. On April 3, 1849, the very day of her wedding anniversary, Jhering's wife gave birth to a boy. But on April 12, although everything had been going well, she suddenly died while trying to sit up in bed. "The poetry of life," said Jhering in a letter to the advocate Frohlich in Schleswig, who was to be his next father-in-law, "is gone." Thereafter there was only hard work and dedication to the spirit of the Roman law. Jhering was to be married twice again, and to have four sons and a daughter, but he proved at times a difficult and irritable husband. Although he depended a great deal on feminine companionship and had a great many friends among women, "the poetry was gone."

Jhering was a jurist, but he had an artistic temperament and a vivid North German imagination. The German poet and dramatist Friedrich Hebbel had been a friend of his youth, and Jhering himself had even dreamed of leaving his mark on literature. He had tried his hand at writing a comic novel, which had been praised by his admiring friend but not published. He once confessed to a juristic friend that even while he was working on the *Geist* he had to struggle against the temptation to write a play. Such a project was never really begun and, punning, Jhering explained that he resolved that it should not be said of him that he had given up the *Geist* in his lifetime. Yet the artist in him made him sweat over every sentence of his book, polishing and repolishing. The *Geist* was certainly a triumph of literary craftsmanship.

Jhering, however, was not only the literary artist but the accomplished musician. An adagio of Beethoven could make the tears run down his cheeks. He was a good enough pianist to give a concert, and he actually did once when the expected performer failed to make his appearance at Giessen, where Jhering was very active in promoting the musical life of the town. He was a person of great enthusiasm with a keen zest for the sensual pleasures of life, although he suffered at times from extreme depression. He loved nature, particularly mountain scenery. He had traveled a good deal in Switzerland and Italy, but he once rejected a call to teach in Holland because all it had was canals. He was also an indefatigable gardener, and a connoisseur of good food and drink.

Jhering prided himself particularly on his taste in wine. On one of his journeys he found a cask of what he deemed to be an exceptionally fine wine, but it proved to be too large to go through his cellar door. Not at all disturbed, he had the basement wall opened up to get the cask into the house. Jhering's reputation as a connoisseur of wine brought many wine salesmen to his house, but he had effective methods of getting rid of them. He would pretend to be deaf and behave as if he thought the salesman was a prospective student who wished to register for his course in Roman law, or he would inquire of the salesman whether he could sell him some adulterated wine, because that was the only kind his friends appreciated, and when the salesman admitted that perhaps he could supply such wine, Jhering would have him thrown out of the house. His friends retaliated once when Jhering's cellar was flooded: they spoke meaningfully of the water that had thus been introduced into his wine.

In his early days at Giessen there was little in the life and labors of Jhering that betrayed the philosophy of his later years. In a sense an adherent of the historical school, he criticized the theories of Savigny but without striking a true note of revolt. He rejected the narrow nationalism of Savigny, and emphasized the universal character of the later Roman law. He declared that the historical school debased legal science to the plane of territorial jurisprudence and made the scientific boundaries coincide in jurisprudence with the political. He perceived in the Reception the working of a process of international legal exchange. "To prevent reception from without and to condemn the organism to development" from within outwards "is to kill it," he said. "That sort of development begins with the corpse." He appreciated the contradiction between the reception of Roman law and the workings of the folk-spirit, and pointed to the "singular irony of scientific fate that a thought that should have brought death to the Roman law was invoked to save its life." Ostensibly a historian of Roman law, he was really bent on a search for its permanent usable elements. He even formulated a slogan to express this objective: "Through the Roman law, but beyond and above it."

Such, too, was the purpose and philosophy of the *Geist*. It was to be a study, as much anthropological as legal, first, of the specifically national ideas which were revealed in the oldest Roman law, the *ius civile,* which was the exclusive possession of Romans, and, then, of the career of Roman jurisprudence as a universal system, when it had become the *ius gentium,* the law of Roman and foreigner alike. Although he published no less than four volumes of the *Geist,* Jhering never got beyond the analysis of the general characteristics of the specific Roman system, which was pushed only to the point of completing the discussion of the general conception of a right in Roman law. Jhering in these days spoke of the "higher" or "productive" jurisprudence as the cause to which he had devoted his life. But in attempting to rediscover the "spirit" of the Roman law in the various shapes of its development, he was as much a dogmatist as Savigny. He was attempting by a process of mere introspection and psychological interpretation to develop the peculiar nature of Roman legal concepts and ideas. In Roman law he discovered the conceptions of liberty and equality as national concepts, and in the methodology of the Roman jurists he perceived a unique contribution to the science of law. If he had known more English law, he would have discovered the folly of this enterprise much sooner than he did, for the same values were to be discovered in the history of the common law at an analogous level of development. The "spirit" of the common law was in fact the same as the "spirit" of the Roman law. Characteristic ideas and institutions are to be discovered in primitive, archaic, and mature law, but they are determined not by national elements but by social and economic needs that are pretty much universal in the same phase of the historical evolution of a legal system.

If Jhering's labors on the *Geist* did not suggest the rebel, neither did his public or his private life. The good professor lectured to his classes on the Roman law during the day and went home at night to a good dinner. Occasionally he played a game of whist with cronies who were as often men of science as men of law, for he was much interested in the new Darwinian hypothesis. There was not much excitement in the provincial town of Giessen, which Jhering described in one of his letters as a pestiferous hole. Indeed, the first stirrings of revolt are discernible only in Jhering's letters.

Many of the leading jurists of the day were his friends. The two great friends of his early life were Karl Friedrich von Gerber, who shared his early passion for "productive" jurisprudence and helped him to found a legal periodical to advance the cause, and Bernhard Windscheid, the master of the pandects. When these friendships cooled in later life, they were more than replaced by an extraordinarily tender devotion for Oskar Bülow, who was engaged in promoting a scientific legal procedure based upon concepts of public purpose rather than of individual convenience.

Even the letters of the Giessen period reveal some of the pangs of Jhering's artistic temperament—doubts of the value of his own labors, intimations of the wasteland of German jurisprudence, humorous touches of despair. Writing to Gerber, he once observed: "There prevailed not so long ago in the natural sciences a method of investigation that bore the strongest resemblance to present methods in jurisprudence —the study of nature from the pages of Ulpian and Paulus." Occasionally he expressed a positive distaste for everything that even smacked of jurisprudence. He rejoiced that in Windscheid he had found a friend "who does not regard every word of a Roman jurist as gospel." "My life," he once confided to him, "is a rather unvarying and monotonous idyll that is bound up with the sections of Puchta's compendium on the pandects; the only change is that every day is devoted to different sections." Jhering used Puchta's book as a text and had even dedicated the first volume of his *Geist* to Savigny's pathetic disciple. A year later he also confessed that "there lives in my consciousness a demoniac force that cannot be satisfied with the quietude of conventional life, that yearns for adventures and extravagances of all sorts." With humorous despair, he observed that the *Geist* was "a book for educated laymen (for which reason many uneducated jurists do not read it)." Jhering must have felt particularly neglected when he once complained bitterly that the correspondence of scholars was inspired only by books, and that it was necessary to write a whole volume to get a single letter.

There were other signs that all was not well in the soul of the professor, that he was getting ready to kick over the traces. There is one letter in particular that makes it manifest that the humorous extravagance of Jhering could not be suppressed much longer and that the heedless satirist would soon emerge into the open. In a letter to Gerber, dated May 3, 1858, Jhering described the matriculation of the young Princes Ludwig and Heinrich at the University of Giessen in a manner that would have caused his expulsion for all time from its academic precincts if it had been made public at the time. He described four scenes in a crescendo of irreverent merriment. *Scene 1*: The princes are greeted at the railroad station by the rector of the university, who is deaf, and there occur all the contretemps of misunderstanding inherent in such a situation. *Scene 2:* The princes take a ride through the woods but, taking a forbidden road, they get lost and have to be rescued. *Scene 3:* The greeting of the princes by a deputation of their loyal subjects the next day. *Scene 4:* The reception for the princes in the home of the rector. Scene 4 is particularly hilarious. It seems that the rector had many children and, to avoid the dangers that might result from their deviltry, a chamber had been specially prepared for the reception and locked up pending the arrival of the great day. But, as the princes approached the house, the rector in his agitation fell down the stairs. Even worse, it developed that the rector's wife had hidden the key to the reception chamber so carefully that she could not find it. The somewhat bruised rector therefore had to lead the princes to the unprepared living room. When the rector's mother-in-law observed the approach of the princes, she hid herself, in her terror, behind the sofa. When she could stand her cramped position no longer, she burst forth and darted out of the room.

Jhering's break with the historical school and his abandonment of conceptual jurisprudence began about 1860 on the eve of the German struggle for national unification. A decade later he was an open and avowed champion of a new juristic method. The forces that produced the new Germany made it possible for him to develop the natural bent of his temperament, but the transition was cautious and slow. The sober professor could not become the satirist overnight. His interest in politics had never been strong. There is no evidence that he had participated in the events of 1848 or that he had been moved by the revolutionary fervor of this stirring year, although he was then a young man of thirty. He was active in the Schleswig-Holstein agitation, but he was aroused less by the justice of the cause than by the fact that his wife's relatives came from the duchy. Much as his heart might swell with patriotism, he disliked military training and maneuvers. His love of tomfoolery got the better of him, and he dressed Azor, his dog, in a military uniform and drilled him daily in the military art to the great delight of his children. Unfortunately the dog one day escaped out of doors in all his military splendor, and his academic master had to leave hurriedly on a vacation.

The war of 1866 against Austria at first distressed Jhering greatly. The basic tenet of his later philosophy was that law was a method of reconciling conflicting interests rather than a process of determining abstract rights, and the conflict with Austria was an object lesson in the importance of interests. He wrote at the time to his friend Windscheid: "What a conflict between the feeling of right and of interests. My feeling of right aligns me on the side of Austria. I condemn the criminal sport of Bismarck that plays with everything that can be called justice and truth. And yet I shudder at the thought that justice may triumph!" But the professor of jurisprudence rapidly overcame his scruples when right was overcome by might. He became an ardent admirer of Bismarck for the rest of his long life. "I bow," he said, "before the genius of a Bismarck who has delivered a masterstroke of political combination and energy unique in history. . . . I would not have believed nine weeks ago that I would be writing a dithyramb about Bismarck."

Immediately after the war with Austria, Jhering actually made an attempt to enter politics. He stood as a candidate for the parliament of the North German Confederation from East Friesland. He lost by only a few votes, but he seems to have taken his defeat very cheerfully. Perhaps he was defeated because during the campaign he wrote a humorous self-portrait in which he boasted of the legitimacy of his birth and gave his religion as "Romanist." Jhering must have been thinking of this election when in his old age he said: "An ideal election procedure would not only count the votes but weigh them."

At this time there were also deep disturbances in Jhering's own life. Quite apart from the fact that the political struggle was upsetting his accustomed ways of thinking, he was estranged from some of his friends. In September, 1867, he also lost his second wife, who had long been ailing. The familiar surroundings of Giessen became particularly hateful. Fortunately, at this time he received a call to the great University of Vienna. It was an indication of the degree to which his fame had spread. He spent only four years in the Austrian capital, but they were almost too stimulating and exciting. He wrote to his young friend Oskar Bülow shortly after his arrival: "Life in Vienna is consuming!" Here he found the social life he had missed in provincial Giessen. Vienna satisfied his deep craving for feminine companionship and music. He married again. He played the role of the celebrated professor, lecturing to classes of several hundred. Among his students were no less than three princes, including the Russian Prince Leo Gallitzin, who called his teacher the Prometheus who had brought the light of jurisprudence to mankind. In Vienna, Jhering lived also through the brief but stirring days of the Franco-Prussian War. He allowed his son Hermann to enlist in the German forces despite the embarrassment it would cause him. He fought the war vicariously through his friend Oskar Bülow, who was actually participating in it as a captain in the German army. He wrote him extraordinarily tender and tremulous letters. When he heard of the fall of Paris, his juristic work seemed suddenly to become trivial and absurd, and he spoke of it as "juristic twiddling." He bowed down before the idol Bismarck with more profound reverence than ever.

Everyone was amazed when Jhering announced in 1872 that he had accepted a call to Göttingen and would shortly leave Vienna. It seemed incredible that he should desire to exchange the social and professional allurements of the great capital for a town not much less provincial than Giessen. But it was precisely because of the distractions of Vienna that Jhering fled. They were interfering with his work, and the call of his work was the more insistent. He had already begun to expose the absurdities of conceptual jurisprudence, but he also wanted to develop a more positive juristic gospel of his own. Vienna had stimulated him and increased the fertility of his ideas, but to get them on paper he needed the quiet of Göttingen, and to Göttingen he retired to spend the last two decades of his life. He acquired a spacious house with a beautiful garden, and he was ready at last to commence a new lifework. Before he had left Vienna, the Emperor had made Jhering a "Von" by conferring upon him the knightly Cross of the Order of Leopold. With humorous self-abnegation, he had accepted the honor on the theory that it might be useful to his children and later descendants.

Jhering's attack on the vagaries of conceptual jurisprudence began with a series of six "Confidential Letters," which were published anonymously from 1860 to 1866 in a German legal periodical. Of all his writings they are the most reminiscent of Mark Twain. Their anonymity doubtless explains the completeness with which Jhering yielded to his penchant for hilarious satire. He did everything possible to make it difficult to detect the secret of their authorship. Thus he even made himself the butt of his own satire. He complained that a series of letters had never before been devoted to jurisprudence. The only belletristic endeavors in jurisprudence had been books devoted to the "spirit" of this or that system of jurisprudence. There had been "spirits" of Roman law and of Prussian law, and he expected the publication of a spirit of

Hessian law, and the like. He had dedicated his *Geist* to Puchta, the faithful disciple of Savigny. Puchta now became his *bête noire,* even as Blackstone had been Bentham's. He gave a slight hint of his identity, but it was rather vague. It consisted merely of an anecdote of a ravenous guest who appeared at a castle masquerade and proceeded to devour an endless quantity of food. When finally he was unmasked he turned out to be one of the castle guard.

Fifty years before his time, pretended Jhering, "civilistic construction" had been unknown. But now a civilist and construction were as inseparable as a lady and crinoline. By a process of interpretation, concepts were derived from juristic texts. The concept, the civilistic homunculus, mating with his like, became productive and begot children. The jurists analyzed the nature of obligations, and the more complex variety of obligations in the Roman law gave them more headaches than the theologians derived from the concept of the Trinity. Between various types of obligations there was supposed to be all the difference between animals on two and four legs, although the distinctions were of no practical importance. The jurists debated, for instance, whether an obligation was to be conceived as a right *to* an action, *in* an action, or *over* an action. They dwelt especially upon the mysteries of juristic personality. Succession to property was defined as a right to the personality of the dead—the juristic version of the reincarnation of souls and juristic proof of the immortality of the soul. The juristic personality was no more received by the grave than the soul. Again, construe the juristic nature of theater-going, and you will discover that the ticket entitles you to enter the theater only as a representative of an abstract juristic personality. By way of reaction to juristic personality, one jurist had, however, conceived of freedom as the right of property in the human body. Freedom of speech would thus be a derivative of the individual's right of property in his means of speech—the freedom of the tongue. When you scratched yourself, you only exercised a property right.

The second of the "Confidential Letters" dealt especially with the concept of *hereditas,* or heirship, in Roman law, which presented great complexities because the Roman heir was regarded as a universal successor who inherited not only the property but the personality of the deceased. Jhering felt that unless he solved this riddle he would be cast into the abyss, like one who could not solve the riddle of the sphynx. Jhering pretended that he woke in a cold sweat in the middle of the night feeling that he had grasped the nature of *hereditas*. When the doctors were called in, they diagnosed his condition as a case of brain fever, never suspecting that it was actually a case of juristic delirium. When he finally read one history of the Roman law of inheritance, he felt like a man who had thrown away a lottery ticket that had won.

The third and fourth letters were primarily devoted to the divorce between theory and practice, which had become a prime characteristic of Jhering's generation. He pictured the theoreticians as the makers of the sword of justice, which they had sharpened so finely that it could split hairs, and developed the theme that, while a barber did not go to a razor maker as a preliminary to learning the art of barbering, a practicing lawyer was required to undergo a period of training with theoreticians. He gave humorous examples of the differences in approach between theoretical and practical jurisprudence, but none perhaps was so amusing as the discussion of the case of the peasant who was forcefully evicted by a rascally neighbor after he had taken possession of his absent brother's property. He lost the lawsuit, although he had clearly been in possession, because he could not prove that in holding the property he had had the requisite *animus domini,* the intention of exercising dominion, as required by Savigny's theory of possession.

The fifth letter was an imaginary address on a juristic museum of objective and subjective law, and the sixth and final letter commented on the frightful flood of juristic literature which was produced by the *Privatdocenten* who aspired to become professors. It was the rule in Roman law that only those could inherit who had children, that is, *liberi.* Punning on the Latin word, Jhering remarked: "The significance possessed in Rome by bodily fruitfulness is possessed among us by spiritual fruitfulness; without *liberi* no inheritance was the rule there, without *libri* no professorship is the rule here." Jhering suggested the advisability of giving professors the *ius scribendi,* which would entitle them to professorships if they published no books.

Jhering's most elaborate satire of constructive jurisprudence is his fantasy, *The Heaven of Juristic Concepts.* Although composed in his declining years, it represented a return to the mood of the "Confidential Letters." He imagined that he had died and gone to the heaven of juristic concepts. The theoretical jurists had a heaven separate and apart from the heaven of the practical jurists. The sun still shone in the heaven of the practitioners, and it even had an atmosphere, but the heaven of juristic concepts was a cold, dark void in space. The sun was the source of all life, but the concepts could not endure contact with life, for they existed for themselves alone. Moreover, the eyes of the theoretical jurists, like those of the owl of Minerva, were accustomed to the dark. In the heaven of juristic concepts are personified all the riddles of constructive jurisprudence. To make certain that he was free of earthly atmosphere, Jhering had to undergo a quarantine before entering the heaven of juristic concepts. There he found Puchta, who had been the first to enter. Savigny, who had never quite understood the art of construction, had had difficulty in securing admittance but had finally succeeded on the strength of his work on the theory of possession and his *Vocation of Our Times for Legislation and Jurisprudence.* Accompanied by a guide, Jhering made a tour of the heaven of juristic concepts, and discovered all sorts of marvelous machines and contrivances—a hairsplitting machine capable of splitting a hair into 999,999 accurate parts; a climbing pole so smooth that a ray of the sun could slide down it surmounted by three mastheads, where juristic problems were placed that had to be brought down; a construction apparatus and a dialectic-hydraulic interpretation press with two pumps for infiltration and elimination; an excavation machine for digging deep into questions of law; and, finally, a giddy wall that rose to an immense height. Then Jhering and his guide toured the Academy of Legal History, where legal formulas and texts were restored and where sources were not only traced but invented, and the Hall of Concepts, which they entered not through a door but by butting their heads through the wall. In the Cerebrarium of the Hall of Concepts they found an anatomical-pathological cabinet of concepts. In the laboratory of the Cerebrarium was fashioned the brain-substance of the theoretical jurists, distinguished by the *mons idealis*—which enabled them to disregard practical consequences and to treat jurisprudence as a system of legal mathematics. It was impossible really to exhaust all the strange phenomena which existed in the heaven of juristic concepts, but Jhering awoke at last to find himself back on earth.

Jhering's first public attack on conceptual jurisprudence was his little book *Der Kampf ums Recht* (The Struggle for Law), which had its origin in a lecture he delivered to the bar association in Vienna, but it caused a tremendous stir. Published in 1872, it was translated into every European language, and even into Japanese. Paradoxical in form and content, almost as continuously epigrammatic as Oscar Wilde, it created furious discussion and controversy. To the more obtuse of Jhering's critics, it seemed to have been written merely in praise of litigiousness. The story has even been circulated that *The Struggle for Law* was inspired by Jhering's loss of no less than three suits involving his landlord in Giessen. It has also been surmised that the book's philosophy was a reaction against the famed *Gemütlichkeit* of the Viennese character. But presumably every philosophy has a personal background. Actually the *Kampf* was a bridge between Jhering's two major works and two major periods of activity. It was an attack on the historical school at the same time that it anticipated Jhering's future theory that the law was not a system of abstract rights but a method of reconciling conflicting interests.

The basic idea of the *Kampf* was that the origin of law is to be found in social struggles. The concept of struggle is in law what the concept of labor is in political economy. "The end of the law is peace," proclaimed Jhering, but he added:

The life of the law is a struggle—a struggle of nations, of the state power, of classes, of individuals. . . . The means to that end is war. . . . Peace without strife, and enjoyment without work, belong to the days of Paradise. . . . For the law is Saturn devouring his own children. The law can renew its youth only by breaking with its own past. . . . The birth of law like that of men has been uniformly attended by the violent throes of childbirth. . . . A principle of law won without toil is on the level with the children brought by the stork: what the stork has brought the fox or the vulture can take away again.

But if the life of the law is a struggle, it can endure only if the individual is ever ready and vigilant to defend his rights. He must not be materialistically minded and think only of the profit and loss in litigation. He must think of the sacred rights of personality and the welfare of society, for these will depend upon the extent to which legal rights are asserted and observed. Most persuasively Jhering urges every individual to the struggle for law.

Property is but the periphery of my person extended to things . . . the battle for one's legal rights is the poetry of character. . . . If I were called upon to pass judgment upon the practical importance of the two principles: 'Do no injustice,' and: 'Suffer no injustice,' I would say that the first rule was 'Suffer no injustice,' and the second: 'Do none!'. . . . Every man is a born battler for the law in the interest of society. . . .

The battler for constitutional law and the law of nations is none other than the battler for private law. . . . What is sowed in private law is reaped in public law and the law of nations. . . . Every despotism has begun with attacks on private law, with the violation of the legal rights of the individual.

Jhering undoubtedly also said much that merely glorified the litigious individual. He praised the traveling Englishman who would not allow himself to be cheated even of a shilling. "I recollect," he also wrote, "having heard of a judge who, when the amount of the object in litigation was small, in order to be relieved of the burden of the trial, offered to pay the plaintiff out of his own pocket, and who was greatly offended when the offer was refused." But nothing in the *Kampf* aroused so much controversy as Jhering's eloquent defense of Shylock, and his denunciation of those machinations by which he was cheated of his pound of flesh. Shylock was right to say: "I crave the law." It was absurd to cheat him by sophistry of a legal right which was admitted to be his.

The concept of the law as a social struggle was, of course, the direct antithesis of the philosophy of the historical school, and the *Kampf* contains in passing some of Jhering's best barbs against its exponents, as, for instance, when he observed that in the theory of the historical school the Roman law of debtor slavery grew in the same way as "the grammatical rule that *cum* governs the ablative." However, the polemic against the historical school was incidental; Jhering was, rather, outlining a positive new philosophy that would supersede it. Those who saw in the *Kampf* only the glorification of litigiousness were significantly the reactionaries who wondered where all this talk about the rights of personality would lead. Doubtless to law reform! In czarist Russia, the *Kampf* became indeed a sort of revolutionary handbook. But here and there even the bourgeois thrilled to Jhering's eloquent insistence upon the rights of personality. Actually Jhering did not summon every individual to perpetual litigiousness. He contemplated only that every individual would defend the basic moral conditions of his existence. Thus, the officer would defend his honor, the peasant his land, the merchant his credit. In a sense Jhering merely reaffirmed Aaron Burr's famous dictum that law is that which is boldly asserted and plausibly maintained.

The essence of Jhering's final philosophy of law was expressed in *Der Zweck im Recht,* the first volume of which appeared in 1877. This

magnum opus of his later years has been translated into English under
the title *Law as a Means to an End*. Jurisprudence itself has been only
a succession of slogans, and the English title is perhaps a better slogan
than the German original. The impulse of the book derived, of course,
from the unhealthy state of German jurisprudence, but Jhering was
the typical German professor, at least to the extent of evolving his
extremely practical theory from a purely philosophical conception. He
prided himself indeed on being something of a philosopher, although
the professional German philosophers have never conceded the validity
of his claim.

Jhering's fundamental philosophy is based upon a theory of psychological causation. The physical world was entirely subject to the laws
of cause and effect. In the animal world some actions were wholly
automatic and involuntary. *Homo sapiens* in the discharge of his natural
functions was subject to the same law as the animal kingdom, but the
operations of his mind were not involuntary. On the contrary, they
were always guided by some concept of purpose. But, said Jhering,
"You might as well hope to move a loaded wagon from its place by
means of a lecture on the theory of motion as the human will by means
of the categorical imperative. . . . The real force which moves the
human will is interest." Thus, "interest is an indispensable condition of
every action," and "purpose is the creator of the entire law." Since
human life and social life are synonymous, the entire scheme of the
law may be stated in the proposition: "I exist for myself, the world
exists for me, I exist for the world."

The law was not a system of delimiting abstract rights but a system
of reconciling conflicting interests. Legal concepts had within themselves no productive power, and they were not in themselves eternal.
The jurists must cease acting as if the legislators themselves must
respect the juristic concept. One legal principle could not be derived
from another by a process of logical deduction. The idea of analysis and
combination of legal principles, which jurisprudence had borrowed from
mathematics, was a false dogma. The world of legal concepts was not
self-contained. Society would not wait for the jurist to "construe" its
needs. Facts must not be stretched upon the procrustean bed of legal
concepts. Legal principles could not be extended merely by a process
of analogy; they did not contain in themselves the correct solutions for
every legal controversy. A case could not, for instance, be decided merely
by determining whether a particular transaction fell into the category

of "contract," "sale," or "lease." The judge was not an automaton who pronounced his judgments merely on the basis of pre-established legal principles. Justice itself was only a changing idea of proportionality. Constructive jurisprudence was barren and bankrupt, and must be replaced by a system of social mechanics.

Man was an egoist, but he was capable of altruism. The levers which society employed to overcome his egoism were reward and coercion. "Law," Jhering said, "is not the highest thing in the world, not an end in itself, but it is merely a means to an end, the final end being the existence of society." He saw "law evolving as the politics of force," as "the intelligent policy of power," "as the union of the intelligent and farsighted against the nearsighted." He realized that "public spirit within the system of egoism is a phenomenon just as strange as a flower on a bare rock," and it is for this reason doubtless that he placed the chief emphasis on coercion. But coercion was redeemed by the fact that "the right to coerce forms the absolute monopoly of the state." "Individual, association, state—such is," said Jhering, "the historical stepladder of social purposes."

The *Zweck* is devoted mostly to a discussion of the chief ends that should be served by law. Jhering saw the world of plenty that was already coming into existence. "A poor man today," he said, "is served for a few pennies by more people in all parts of the earth than Croesus could conjure up if he had wished to enjoy all his treasure chambers." But, while he had a good deal of sympathy with socialism, which he expressed in a midnight tête à tête with his son Hermann, the philosophy he preached was not outright socialism but, rather, "the socialization of law," a slogan that has been as powerful in modern jurisprudence as the slogan "law as a means to an end" itself. In Germany, social reforms were introduced by the Emperor Wilhelm himself upon the advice of Jhering's idol Bismarck, and Jhering even saw nothing incongruous between socialism and monarchy. He described the Manchester economic and political philosophy of preventing the interference of one individual with the freedom of another as a method of preventing the wild beasts in the zoo from tearing each other to pieces. He was eloquent in his denunciation of the abuses of capitalism.

Unlimited freedom of trade [he said] is a license for extortion, a letter of marque for robbers and pirates with the right of holding up all who fall into their hands—woe to the victim! That the wolves cry for freedom is easy to understand. But when the sheep, as has often been the case in this question, join in the cry, they only show thereby that they are sheep.

He also declared: "In my eyes there is no error more serious than the idea that a contract as such, as long as its content is not illegal or immoral, has a just claim upon the protection of the law." The evils of modern corporate enterprise were already apparent enough to arouse him to vehement protest. "Under the eyes of our lawgivers," he observed, "the joint stock companies have been transformed into organized agencies of robbery and deceit . . . whose secret history covers more baseness, dishonor, villainy than many a penitentiary, except that the thieves, robbers and swindlers instead of lying in irons are bedded in gold." Nobody realized better than he the emptiness of legal equality. "Equality," he said, "may be as much as anything else equality of misery." He was also unique among German jurists of the time in his concern over civil liberties and constitutional limitations. As a German, he found the American ideas of judicial review alien to him, but he did preach a doctrine of "auto-limitation" in the relation of the state to the individual, which was later to be erected into a system by another German jurist, Georg Jellinek.

It is easy to probe the difficulties and limitations of Jhering's thought as a systematic philosopher, and there have been many critics of his ideas of purpose and interest. Jhering was a satirist, and, like all satirists, he took advantage of the traditional latitude and exaggerated the undoubted evils of his time. Logic does have a genuine place in juristic method, as in all the social sciences. The passion for "constructive jurisprudence" that was so characteristic of the German jurists had its origin in the need to systematize and unify the variations in the law of the pandects, and so to create a system of German common law which should be a fitting substitute for a German civil code, which was then still lacking. There are also undoubtedly some rules of law that are purely formal in character, and must therefore necessarily be arbitrary. Such rules may have a social purpose, but the same social purpose could as readily be served by some other legal rule.

Indeed, the fundamental difficulty of Jhering's philosophy is precisely that it provides no objective criteria for determining the purpose which the law is to serve or for selecting the interests which the law is to protect. Law was undoubtedly a means to an end—but what end? Who was to determine the end? The individual, the society, the personal ruler, the abstract state? When one end is assumed, is only a particular means to be allowed? In relation to the individual is egoism rather than altruism to be encouraged? When is the lever of reward superior to the lever of coercion? Jhering was always talking of the demands and needs of "life," and he tended to comprise in the law the whole of life. But the purposes of life are many and manifold, and Jhering provided no infallible guide through the maze of purposes. His thought was itself a struggle of contradictions between egoism and altruism, idealism and realism, Benthamism and social utilitarianism, individualism and socialism, nationalism and internationalism, lust for power and respect for law.

But the very fact that, unlike other German philosophers, Jhering never really built a system was the secret of his enormous influence. The relativism of his thought proved popular because it could serve to rally all the forces which were attacking the undoubted abuses of his age. Doubtless there had always been jurists who suspected that the law served some social purpose. The merit of Jhering was to put this thought at the very center of jurisprudence and to employ all the resources of his wit and satire to keep it there. His ridicule of eternal legal concepts was no mere side play of a juristic philosopher. It reflected the socialist attack on property and the complications of modern industry which were putting the classical concepts of property to the test. Friedrich Nietzsche, a kindred spirit, read the *Zweck* although his eyesight was failing, because he thought that Jhering was proclaiming new values. Jhering resembles Nietzsche in the variety of his disciples who exceeded the fervor of the master. He has been responsible in one way or another for all the modern schools of jurisprudence not only in Europe but in America.

In Germany, Jhering was responsible for the "free-law" school, which grew out of his attack on the formal and objective elements in the judicial process. If law was not created by a process of logical deduction, rules of law were themselves illusory and represented only a logical disguise of intuitive judgments. Why not, therefore, free the judge entirely from the trammels of the supposed rules of law and allow him to base his judgments freely on his social intuitions? Ernst Fuchs, who may perhaps be regarded as the leader of the free-law school, preached a sort of juridical *Kulturkampf* against "pandectology and cryptosociology," both of which terms he invented. Another disciple, Eugen Ehrlich, explored even more thoroughly than Jhering the place of logic in juristic method and issued a call for the creation of a "living law." While Jhering was not the primary influence in the field of modern criminology, his ideas were in harmony with its emphasis upon the criminal rather than his crime, and he undoubtedly helped to create the criminological school of Franz Liszt, the representative of positivism in Germany. Along more conventional lines, Jhering's insistence upon the jurisprudence of interests led to greater attention in Germany to business usages and to the case method of studying law. At the other extreme, he inspired even the Marxists, who made use of the jurisprudence of interests to point to the desirability of effectuating class interests. Jhering was like the sorcerer's apprentice who could not stop the magical process which he had initiated.

In France, Jhering's influence was impeded by his idolatry of Bismarck and his justification of the Franco-Prussian War. French jurists were accustomed to speak of German jurists in general, and such jurists as Jhering in particular, as *"jurisconsultes brutaux,"* and to characterize their works as *"brigandages juridiques."* Yet, despite the fact that he was regarded as an apostle of imperialism and power politics, it is easy to perceive the relation of his thought to such a modern French juristic theory as the theory of the "institution" and "concrete order."

It was certainly no accident that Jhering also exercised so much influence on the other side of the Atlantic in America. There were strong similarities between legal conditions in Germany and in the United States. Germany was revolting against the reception of the Roman law and was struggling to adapt it to the needs of a unified state. America, a Federal union, was still in the toils of adapting the English common law to the needs of a democratic and increasingly industrialized nation. Germany had to overcome the extravagances of the historical school, while America was still the home of the seventeenth- and eighteenth-century philosophy of natural rights thinly disguised as constitutionalism. There was thus a certain affinity between Karl Friedrich von Savigny and John Marshall and his judicial successors. America, too, was suffering from the tyranny of legal concepts. Constitutional problems involved vast social, political, and economic interests, but the method of reconciling them was to ignore realities and to solve the problems in terms of abstract constitutional concepts such as "freedom of contract," "due process," and "interstate commerce," by a process of pseudological analysis. The revolt which was ultimately led by Justices Holmes and Brandeis owed much to the thought of

Jhering. In fact, the title of Brandeis' book, *Other People's Money*, is a phrase which is to be found in *Law as a Means to an End*. Jhering's observations on freedom of contract and the evils of corporations had, too, an obvious bearing on the American constitutional scene.

The gradual emergence of a new constitutionalism was accompanied by the rise of an American school of sociological jurisprudence, of which Jhering may justly claim to be at least the godfather. The first leader of this sociological school, Dean Roscoe Pound of Harvard, spoke of the "law in action" in contrast to the "law in books," of the law as a method of "social engineering," and of "the effective limits of legal action." He even wrote a book, called *The Spirit of the Common Law*, in an effort to discover the essential characteristics of the Anglo-American legal tradition. But, unlike Jhering, Dean Pound never freed himself of his preoccupation with legal concepts and techniques; and as his ideas grew increasingly conservative, a critical spirit swept American legal philosophy, and a "realist" school was born. The "realists" did not always agree among themselves, but generally speaking they were much closer to Jhering's later thought than was Dean Pound. They had the same skeptical attitude towards the efficacy of legal rules and concepts, and placed the same emphasis upon purposeful legal activity of the judge and the jurist and upon the administrative element in the American legal system. The whole modern American growth of administrative agencies, such as boards and commissions, from the Interstate Commerce Commission to the National Labor Relations Board, owes much to Jhering's gospel of purpose and interest. The influence of American constitutionalism had retarded the growth of administrative agencies, but they are a commonplace now in a highly industrialized America. Unlike the traditional courts, they exist to accomplish some particular social purpose or to correct some particular social abuse, but they are designed to fulfill their tasks without observing all the techniques and procedures of the conventional legal system. It is significant that one of the most brilliant of the realists, Jerome Frank, was chairman of the Securities and Exchange Commission before he became a judge of a United States Circuit Court.

Jhering himself was not unaware of his influence in foreign lands. In a letter written on November 11, 1881, to his friend Oskar Bülow, he noted the acclaim his *Zweck* had received in North America, and on another occasion, in mentioning an honorary membership conferred upon him by the faculty of the University of Kasan, he remarked that his fame had apparently penetrated even to the Arctic. But he undoubtedly regarded as the greatest honor of his old age a visit which he was invited to pay to his idol Bismarck. He considered that he had already been privileged enough when Bismarck graciously accepted an honorary degree from the University faculty. But his joy knew no bounds when, during his visit to Bismarck, the latter addressed him as "colleague." The satirist was certainly dormant when, in writing to Bismarck on September 15, 1888, he even attributed his legal ideas to him, and remarked that he had only carried out in jurisprudence the ideas expressed by his idol in politics.

On the second day of the Christmas season, Jhering always wrote a letter of condolence to the wife of his friend Julius Glaser. Since he had been ailing for some years, he wondered in the letter of 1891 whether he would be alive to write the following year. While he was in the midst of planning a trip to the Berchtesgaden region, he died suddenly on September 17, 1892, in his seventy-fourth year. Shortly before his death he had celebrated his fiftieth *Doktor-Jubiläum*. There is no definite knowledge of the nature of the heaven to which Jhering gained admittance upon his death. It could hardly have been, however, the heaven of juristic concepts.

Oliver Wendell Holmes

LAW AND THE FUTURE

MANKIND HAS THE UNFORTUNATE HABIT OF DWELLING UPON the significance of the careers of great men only upon the hundredth anniversaries of their birth or death, a habit particularly unfortunate in the case of Justice Holmes. True, he hardly suffered from obscurity or neglect during his long life. He was past sixty when he was appointed an associate justice of the Supreme Court of the United States, and when past ninety he was still a member of the Court. Great age itself inspires respect, but the longevity of a really great man becomes the occasion for universal tribute, and the birthdays of the aged justice were observed with marks of affection and respect. "Many men," he had himself said while yet in middle age, "especially as they grow older resent attempts to push analysis beyond consecrated phrases, or to formulate anew. Such attempts disturb the intellectual rest for which we long. Our ideal is repose, perhaps because our destiny is effort, just as the eyes see green after gazing at the sun." But he had proved himself the great exception to the rule.

Despite the adulation, however, it is very much to be doubted that the moral of his career, particularly important for a war-torn world, was commonly understood. This moral is not, of course, to be found in the mere fact that Holmes was himself an active participant in one of the great wars of history. Bent on the pursuit of wisdom, the undergraduate Holmes was on his way from the Athenaeum, one of Boston's libraries, with a copy of Hobbes's *Leviathan* in his hands, when he received a summons to the colors. The war between the states had been unleashed. Back went the *Leviathan* unread to the library and off to the war went the young Holmes with his regiment, the Twentieth Massachusetts Volunteers, in which he held a commission as lieutenant. He was wounded three times in the course of the war: in the breast at Ball's Bluff, October 21, 1861; in the neck at Antietam, September 17,

1862; and in the foot at Marye's Hill, Fredericksburg, May 3, 1863. The young officer, however, did not allow himself to be lionized, nor did he pose as a hero. In after life, too, he did not like to talk about his war experiences. Not being a pacifist, he did not question the right of the state to ask him to give his life, and he once even said: "I think that the sacredness of human life is a purely municipal ideal of no validity outside the jurisdiction." He simply took no pride in his own soldiering.

Yet the Civil War itself and his narrow escape from death, especially at Ball's Bluff, have a great deal to do with the essential significance of Holmes today. If there is ever to be peace among men, a world federation modeled in some degree upon the Federal Union, which the Civil War came so close to disrupting, must become a reality. This will be possible only if rules of law can be substituted for the rule of force and an international tribunal created to which even great states will consent to submit their disputes. Obviously, the success of such an international jurisdiction must depend upon the degree of objectivity which the judges bring to the task. They must be prepared to exorcise, in addition to the demons of personal and class selfishness, bias in favor of their own nations. They must be prepared to uphold the powers of an international legislature against the claims of their own countries. Now, of all the judges who ever sat upon the bench of the Supreme Court of the United States, the tribunal of the world's first great Federal Union, Justice Holmes displayed the judicial virtue of objectivity in its purest form, and this despite every temptation to the contrary derived from his personal prejudices and class affiliations. It may be that his narrow escape from death at Ball's Bluff strengthened his perception of the vanities of existence, than which nothing is more calculated to suppress pride of opinion.

As a judge Holmes coped with the problems of Federalism which had been aggravated as well as solved by the addition of the Fourteenth Amendment to the Constitution of the United States. These were purely American problems, and for his success in handling them Holmes was duly honored as a prophet in his own country. The universal acclaim which was his portion, however, testified to some more profound, if inarticulate, instinct of the common man, which made him perceive the wider significance of Justice Holmes's work. This was simply that the future of Federalism was somehow bound up with the future of law itself in the national as well as the international sphere. The miracle of Justice Holmes was all the more astounding because, if there was one country of the world where the objectivity of judges was attacked more than anywhere else, it was in the United States of America.

The United States not only lived under the rule of law but could boast the more dubious glories of "the absolute reign of law," as American constitutionalism has been happily called. In other countries judges could nullify legislation only to a limited extent by the process of mis-interpretation and the manipulation of procedure, but in the land of the free the wide amplitude of constitutional phrases, particularly in the period since the Civil War, imposed no other limit than the judges' own sense of self-restraint. A holocaust of social legislation began, which continued through the New Nationalism of Theodore Roosevelt and the New Freedom of Woodrow Wilson, to achieve its climax under the New Deal of Franklin Roosevelt. State social legislation was held again and again to contravene the due-process clause, but when the Federal government moved against the same evils, the commerce clause, the good old blunderbuss of John Marshall, was held to be too narrow to justify its interference. Thus was created the "twilight zone," in which government was impotent. More and more embittered were the cries that arose against the "nine old men," who came to be widely regarded as the bondsmen of the men of property. As the judges patiently labored in the arid wastes of American constitutionalism to make bricks without straw, the people prayed with increasing fervor for a deliverer.

They found him, as sometimes happens, in the seats of the mighty. His name was Oliver Wendell Holmes, and while his extraordinarily long career was connected chiefly with American constitutionalism, his fame spread rapidly throughout the world. In the science of the law, "Justice Holmes" became a name to conjure with. "There is Holmes," an admirer said, "and there are all the other judges." He has been hailed as the greatest American judge since John Marshall, but it would be a mistake to confine his significance to the dialectics of American judicial review. If he was universally revered, it could have been only because of some universal interest which men had in him. While they did not formulate this feeling in precise terms, it was derived from the preoccupation everywhere with the judicial process itself. It was simply more sharply focused in the controversies which raged about the Supreme Court of the United States.

Jurists had long fostered the delusion that law was a system of logical postulates. From existing rules and concepts were supposed to be derived the solutions of any controversies that might arise. But gradually it was coming to be recognized everywhere that the law was a scheme of social ends which involved the continuous balancing of conflicting interests. In this process the personality of the judge was of prime importance, and there began to be manifested a growing curiosity about all the elements of the judicial process. To be sure, there had always been some interest in the human qualities of the judge, but legal guarantees of judicial tenure and independence were considered sufficient to guard him against the temptation to depart from precedent and logic. Once these guarantees had been provided, however, it was assumed that the judge became a mechanical mouthpiece uttering the impartial dooms of the law. Sir William Blackstone, who lived after the Act of Settlement, which established judicial independence in England, regarded the judges as the mere oracles of the law. But the present more sophisticated generation, which thought of the law as a means to an end, questioned the mechanical theory of the nature of the judicial process despite all Acts of Settlement and guarantees of judicial tenure. It invented such skeptical epithets as "the phonographic theory of the judicial function," and "slot-machine justice," and applied them to the traditional views. It doubted that the demon of partiality could be exorcised in so simple a manner, and began as never before to search the judge's soul. Juristic theorists on the Continent, particularly those known as the apostles of "free law," and some of the American "realists," if for no other reason than that they were ready to leave so much to the creative activity of the judge, began as never before to probe the recesses of the judge's psyche. They wanted to know not only what judges were supposed to do but what judges did in fact. Indeed, judges themselves began to write books or to make speeches, which would have been all but unthinkable in past generations. They might well have been labeled "confessions." Such a book was Justice Cardozo's *Nature of the Judicial Process.*

The common man knew nothing of the controversies of the schools of law, and cared little for their disputes about the reality of rules of law. But he, too, was interested as never before in what judges did in fact, and no one can doubt that there was good reason for his concern. The law was no longer a private preserve of jurists endlessly refining the absorbing distinctions between *meum* and *tuum.* A movement for the socialization of private law, the creation of a host of administrative agencies in all of the leading industrial countries of the world, had immeasurably expanded the law's domain, until it could be said without exaggeration that it embraced almost the whole of life. The proliferation of the administrative agencies, which involved the creation of special new boards and commissions to deal with acute social and economic problems, represented in itself a flight from the judges of the traditional courts. But the immense bulk of social legislation was everywhere subject in greater or lesser degree to the scrutiny of the traditional courts, especially in the countries of the common law, which cherished the doctrine of the supremacy of law. The movement for social legislation was itself a compromise with socialism, and socialism itself had challenged the objectivity of the judicial process by bringing to the forefront the question of the possibility of orderly social change by means of the traditional processes of the law, which meant the adjustment not only of the relations of individuals but of the power of classes. The theory of communism, by asserting that law was simply the will of the ruling class and that law itself was destined to disappear in a classless society, raised not only the question of the objectivity of the judge but of the future of law itself as a mode of regulating social relations. There were still primitive societies in remote and backward corners of the world to remind civilized men that the career of the law had, after all, been brief, and that it might not prove eternal.

Perhaps it is not entirely a paradox that the era of skepticism, if not disillusionment, about the judicial process should have produced a judge who realized all that is best in the judicial function. As Holmes himself said of John Marshall: "A great man represents a great ganglion in the nerves of society, or, to vary the figure, a strategic point in the campaign of history, and part of his greatness consists of his being *there.*" In the last analysis, men were reassured by the objectivity of Justice Holmes, not only because his opportunities for partisanship were so great but because as a member of the Brahmin caste he should have been disposed to take advantage of them.

It is easy to plot the course of the lives of the judges who in the generation of Holmes had achieved the dizzy pinnacle of a seat on the Supreme Court of the United States. Before their elevation to this august tribunal, they had been either active politicians or busy and successful lawyers with great industrial corporations or railroads or public utilities as their clients. According to the traditional theory of judicial tenure, they were supposed to forget the hurly-burly of this existence and to remove themselves from the influence of their past associations as easily as they removed their sack suits when for the first time they donned the black judicial robes. But usually in their subsequent careers they only demonstrated what the weakness of human nature made almost inevitable, namely, that a man cannot change a lifetime of habits of partisanship by taking a judicial oath. The past is always an entangling alliance.

The background of Oliver Wendell Holmes was quite different. He had his roots deep in the "harmless, inoffensive, untitled aristocracy of New England," which his own father, the celebrated Dr. Oliver Wendell Holmes, the witty and crotchety Autocrat of the Breakfast Table, had dubbed "the Brahmin caste." Oliver Wendell Holmes, Junior, was born on March 8, 1841, in Boston, which his father had declared to be the hub of the solar system. The playful doctor wrote to a friend that his first-born was "a second edition of your old acquaintance, an o.w.h.," and he was to prove indeed a chip off the old block both in his longevity and in his philosophy of life. The doctor himself had studied law for a year at the Harvard Law School before he turned to medicine and, after contributing to medicine the discovery of the nature of puerperal fever, had given his best energies to literature and the lecture platform. The good doctor was not, of course, in revolt against the social values of his New England, but he was a satirist as well as a philosopher, from whom the little o.w.h. could not have helped but learn much. In particular, the doctor had become aware, perhaps in revolt against the tyrannies of Calvinism, of the darker aspects of human responsibility and life. It is said that in a way he even anticipated Freud, and there can be no doubt that he suspected the humbug of logic as a guide to existence. Had he not written of "the wonderful one-hoss shay, that was built in such a logical way, it ran a hundred years to a day"? A suspicion of logic was to prove one of the son's most valued characteristics as a judge.

The Holmes family hailed from Connecticut, but it had Boston connections. Among the more remote of these was Anne Bradstreet, the poet. Through the Wendell side of the family, Dr. Holmes was related to Wendell Phillips, the leader of the abolitionist movement, who was his cousin, and to the Richard Henry Danas, father and son, as well as to William Ellery Channing, the well-known divine. The heritage of Wendell Phillips was perhaps particularly important in making the young Holmes aware of the stirrings of reform and revolt in the New England past. The old New England had been interested in black slavery. Holmes was to concern himself with some of the effects of white wage slavery. It was, after all, only just that a son of the New England that had fought the Civil War to insure the triumph of capitalist enterprise, which had then found its bulwark in the Fourteenth Amendment, should become the voice of protest against the further frustration of social reform.

The young Holmes had all the advantages of the Puritan aristocracy. The family lived first on Montgomery Place for eighteen years, but later moved to the more fashionable Beacon Street. "We Americans live in tents," Dr. Holmes once humorously observed. The country home of the family was first at Pittsfield and later at Beverly Farms. The young Holmes attended Mr. Dixwell's Latin School in Boylston Place, Cambridge, where he finished his course in June, 1857, and entered Harvard. Sixteen years later he was to marry Fanny Dixwell, the daughter of the principal of the school. The marriage, which lasted almost sixty years, proved singularly happy, although it was never blessed with children. When Fanny Dixwell died in 1929, Holmes wrote to a friend: "For sixty years she made life poetry for me."

In his youth Holmes mingled with the Brahmin great. His father inducted him into the famous Saturday Club. Emerson in particular was his mentor. Holmes not only saw Emerson plain but discussed Plato with him. Emerson advised the young Holmes: "You should hold Plato at arm's length. Say to him: 'You have been pleasing the world for two thousand years; see whether you can please me.'" Thus encouraged, the young Holmes had the temerity a year later to write a critical essay on Plato, but when he showed it to Emerson, the latter observed: "Yes, you have done very well, but you haven't killed Plato. When you shoot at a king you must kill him."

As not infrequently happens, it is not the later profession of the great man that appeals to him in his youth. The young Holmes even tried his hand at etching, but philosophy was even closer to his heart. Although they later drifted apart, William James was a boon companion of Holmes in his young manhood. Their conversation was of a rather cosmic character, and in later years they still wrote to each other about their "dilapidated old friend, the Kosmos." It was in a letter to William James that Holmes expressed one of the profoundest conclusions of all philosophy, a conclusion in which is already implicit his later attitude as judge: "The great act of faith is when a man decides he is not God." There is an old Latin maxim, *inter arma silent leges* (the laws are silent amidst the clash of arms). As an old man, Holmes summed up his career up to this time by saying: "When I was twenty-one, I had taken my degree, received a commission and been wounded in battle." The war interrupted the studies of the young Holmes. His career in the law began after he was mustered out of the Union army and entered the Harvard Law School. But considering the sort of young man the aspirant was, the career could not have been embraced without many doubts and much hesitation, without soul-searching and regrets. Certainly etching was not for him, except possibly as a hobby, but there must have beckoned the alluring role of philosopher. His father had quit the law, and the law presented itself to the son as "a ragbag of details." But the young Holmes finally succeeded in persuading himself, as he put it epigrammatically in later years: "Every calling is great when greatly pursued." He succeeded finally, indeed, in wedding the two loves:

The law [he once declared eloquently in a speech] is the calling of thinkers . . . I say—and I say no longer without any doubt—that a man may live greatly in the law as well as elsewhere; that there as well as elsewhere his thought may find its unity in an infinite perspective; that there as well as elsewhere he may wreak himself upon life, may drink the bitter cup of heroism, may wear his heart out after the unattainable. All that life offers any man from which to start his thinking or his striving is a fact. And if this universe is one universe, if it is so far thinkable that you can pass in reason from one part of it to another, it does not matter very much what that fact is.

Holmes's concept of the law always remained grand. The law itself was "an anthropological document," which revealed the history of human culture. He once said that "the business of a law-school is not sufficiently described when you merely say that it is to teach law, or to make lawyers. It is to teach law in the grand manner, and to make great lawyers." To a man who held such ideas the practice of the law could not be a humdrum, pettifogging, money-grubbing business. He was admitted to the Massachusetts bar in 1867, and by 1873 had become a member of the Boston law firm of Shattuck, Holmes and Munroe. But he never had a very great practice or achieved any great forensic triumphs. It is significant that, although many stories were to cluster about the name of Holmes in later years, there are none of the type that are at once called to mind when Lincoln is mentioned. The formative years of Holmes as a lawyer were spent primarily in study and contemplation rather than in the hurly-burly of the law courts. He taught constitutional law at Harvard, lectured on the common law at the Lowell Institute, edited the *American Law Review,* and got out an edition of Kent's *Commentaries.*

The Lowell lectures eventually grew into a legal classic, and they were published in book form in 1881 under the title, *The Common Law.* Superficially regarded, the book may give the reader the impression that the interest of its author was in antiquarianism. It deals, indeed, with the origins of law, particularly the common law, with the history of tort, crime, property, and contract. But Holmes was no mere antiquarian; he had no love for historical antiquities for their own sake. "It is revolting," he once said in another place, "to have no better reason for a rule of law than that so it was laid down in the time of Henry IV. It is still more revolting if the grounds upon which it was laid down have vanished long since, and the rule simply persists from blind imitation of the past." Holmes was interested not in the rules but in the reasons behind the rules. Even in the ordinary civil and criminal law, which dealt only with the small concerns of individuals, he always sought for the reasons of public policy which had been responsible for the origin or survival of a particular legal rule or doctrine. He always asked what social end was served by them. Upon the very first page of *The Common Law,* in one of his most quoted passages, he set forth the basic tenet of his philosophy of legal history:

The life of the law has not been logic: it has been experience. The felt necessities of the time, the prevalent moral and political theories, intuitions of public policy, avowed or unconscious, even the prejudices which judges share with their fellow-men, have had a good deal more to do than the syllogism in determining the rules by which men should be governed. The law embodies the story of a nation's development through many centuries, and it cannot be dealt with as if it contained only the axioms and corollaries of a book of mathematics.

He saw the law always approaching and never reaching consistency of theory, because it was always in the process of growth. While its substance was likely to correspond with the dictates of convenience, its form and machinery depended very much upon its past. Borrowing a metaphor from the science of his father, he compared precedents which had survived although they had outlived their usefulness to the clavicle in the cat. He studied legal history because he believed that "history sets us free," yet with that humorous skepticism of his he could also see that ignorance of the past of a legal institution might sometimes have the same result. "Ignorance," he declared, "is the best of law reformers." Perhaps he had Jeremy Bentham in mind.

The philosopher of law, who always had an academic slant, looked at the complex of state imperatives known as law as a series of rules, which contained an endless number of "oughts" that were all equally valid and real. Holmes, looking at the law from the point of view of the realistic and hardheaded practical lawyer advising a client what he could safely do, came to the conclusion that rights and duties were "nothing but prophecies." He further enlarged upon the theme by saying: "If you want to know the law and nothing else, you must look at it as a bad man, who cares only for the material consequences which such knowledge enables him to predict, not as a good one, who finds his reasons for conduct, whether inside the law or outside of it, in the vaguer sanctions of conscience." He thus concluded in a celebrated sentence: "The prophecies of what the courts will do in fact, and nothing more pretentious, are what I mean by the law." This conception of a right as "the hypostasis of a prophecy" gained great currency and had much to do with the growth of American realism, which glorified the courts as virtually the only source of law and gave the laws of man a superficial resemblance to the laws of science.

When he formulated this conception of the law, Holmes was no longer "the young Holmes," but had become a judge of an important American tribunal, the Supreme Judicial Court of Massachusetts. The event occurred in the year 1882, when Holmes was past forty. He was offered the judgeship at the same time that he received an offer of a full professorship at the Harvard Law School. Harvard, it is said, never quite forgave him for preferring the bench to its quiet cloisters. Dr. Oliver Wendell Holmes, who was still very much alive, exclaimed characteristically when he heard of his son's appointment: "To *think* of it!—my little boy a Judge, and able to send me to jail if I don't behave myself." In a more dramatic vein, the little boy who had grown up said of his appointment to the Massachusetts bench: "It was a stroke of lightning which changed all the course of my life."

Justice Holmes, as we may now begin to call him, served on the

Massachusetts bench for two decades, and during the last three years of his tenure he was Chief Justice. He struggled with "the ragbag of details," with questions of "here and now," which, he said, occupied "nine hundred and ninety-nine thousandths of the ability of the world." He tried to persuade himself that, even in wrestling with the petty problems of litigants, he was coming to grips with the great mysteries of life. "The glory of lawyers," he said in a speech delivered in the middle of his career on the Massachusetts bench, "like that of men of science is more corporate than individual. Our labor is an endless organic process. The organism whose being is recorded and protected by the law is the undying body of society." In another speech he declared:

My keenest interest is excited not by what are called great questions, and great cases, but by little decisions which the common run of selectors would pass by because they did not deal with the Constitution, or a telephone company, yet which have in them the germ of some wider theory, and therefore of some profound institutional change in the very tissue of the law.

But we may guess also that he was still assailed by the doubts that had made him exclaim defiantly that "every calling is great when greatly pursued." For he confessed that when he once looked in his docket and found that he had expressed himself in only a thousand cases, he mused upon all the great questions he had missed. This was characteristic of Holmes. As he himself once said: "It is the merit of an ideal to be unattainable."

In his decisions as a Massachusetts judge are to be perceived clearly the quality of Justice Holmes as a writer and thinker and the basic lines of his later constitutional philosophy. Even in the little cases that "did not deal with the Constitution, or a telephone company," he got off striking sentences that were quoted and remembered. "A horsecar," he observed, for instance, in one decision, "cannot be handled like a rapier." And in another he said: "A trespasser is not *caput lupinum*." To the lawyer's eternal question, "But where will you draw the line?" he replied epigrammatically: "Most differences are merely differences of degree, when nicely analyzed." He expressed his philosophy as a judge also by observing in another case: "If it is a bad rule, there is no reason for making a bad exception to it." Stories, too, began to be told of the Justice's wit. When Chief Justice, he said apropos of long-winded lawyers that they should take a course in risqué French novels and so learn to speak by innuendo rather than at length.

Justice Holmes, who was the son of a famous man, was becoming famous in his own right. In 1902, Horace Gray, one of the associate justices of the Supreme Court of the United States, who hailed from Massachusetts, tendered his resignation to Theodore Roosevelt, whose thoughts at once turned to Holmes. It will be recalled that the Rough Rider had some rather refreshing views concerning the national judiciary. He knew that the personal opinions of a justice of the United States Supreme Court were of the first importance. He was to say some years later that a decision might depend upon "whether a Judge of the Supreme Court came down heads or tails." It seemed to him that Justice Holmes would support sound Republican principles and that he was "pro-labor," for he had dissented in cases in which his brethren on the Massachusetts bench had held unlawful not only secondary boycotts in interunion disputes but even peaceful picketing. It is rather instructive to consider in connection with these decisions that the Massachusetts Constitution declared that the judges of the state should be "as free, impartial and independent as the lot of humanity will admit." The lot of humanity had apparently not admitted a great deal. It took more than a constitutional provision to exorcise the devil of class interest.

Roosevelt finally sent the name of Holmes to the Senate, and he was duly confirmed. The *New York Evening Post* said editorially of the appointment in its issue of August 12, 1902, that Holmes "had been more of a 'literary feller' than one finds on the bench, and he has a strong tendency to be 'brilliant' rather than sound." Holmes himself railed privately at the thought that the chief point in his favor seemed to be that he had taken the labor side. There is probably nothing that could have hurt the pride of Justice Holmes more than this superficial judgment. He no doubt told himself that he was a philosopher and a judge, and that being pro-labor or anti-labor had nothing to do with his decisions. Indeed, it is ironic to think how wrong Roosevelt was about the character of Holmes, and how immediately he was disappointed in his appointee. If there was any law of the United States that was close to Roosevelt's heart it was the Sherman Act, but in the very first year of his tenure Justice Holmes dissented in the *Northern Securities Case*, in which the majority of the Court, holding that the Sherman Act was intended for the preservation of competition, ordered the dissolution of the railroad trust. The public in general, and Roosevelt in particular, at once had a sample of the gifts of the "literary feller." In his dissent he declared:

Great cases like hard cases make bad law. For great cases are called great, not by reason of their real importance in shaping the law of the future, but because of some accident of immediate overwhelming interest which appeals to the feelings and distorts the judgment. These immediate interests exercise a kind of hydraulic pressure which makes what previously was clear seem doubtful, and before which even well-settled principles of law will bend.

Thus did Justice Holmes serve notice that he intended to resist hydraulic pressure. But Roosevelt remarked that the Justice had no more backbone than a banana peel.

Thus began, too, the career of the man who has been called "the great dissenter"—great not by reason of the mere number of his dissenting opinions, which were not frequent, but great by virtue of the greatness of the thoughts which they embodied and the greatness of the issues which they involved. The generation that had gone in search of a just man, even as once Diogenes had gone in search of an honest man, fell in love with Justice Holmes, applauded his dissents, and revered the man. "Justice Holmes dissenting" became a familiar national catchword, and the Justice himself became the voice of the inarticulate millions whose hopes of social betterment were being regularly frustrated by the "nine old men." In a series of brilliant and unforgettable opinions, he protested against the majority's prejudiced reading of the Constitution.

The dissents of Justice Holmes fell into two main categories. First and foremost, of course, was the category of social legislation. He could see no insurmountable constitutional barriers against legislation regulating hours of labor, outlawing yellow-dog contracts and the injunction in labor disputes, or establishing minimum wage standards for women. But second, and perhaps no less important, was the category of civil liberty. Particularly in the period of antiradical hysteria which followed the First World War, he reaffirmed in moving and eloquent phrases the traditional liberties of freedom of speech and of the press. These dissents stemmed from the same personal philosophy by which he could find tolerance for even radical social legislation, and were indeed bound up with the attempt to achieve a better social order. The freedom to urge social changes was vital in a world of crisis, in a world of almost permanent emergency. If the assertion of Marxist theorists that there was no possibility of peaceful and orderly change was to be refuted, it could be done practically by giving object lessons in tolerance even for extremist views.

Justice Holmes, borrowing a phrase from the famous lawyer Rufus Choate, once said that one must know how "to strike the jugular." The aim of Holmes was always sure and unerring when it came to striking down one of the shibboleths of the reigning constitutional apologetics. His colleagues not infrequently accepted in theory the classic dictum of Marshall that "it is a *Constitution* we are expounding," but they almost invariably violated it in practice. To Holmes, however, it was a basic article of constitutional faith. At almost the very beginning of his career on the bench of the Supreme Court, he declared:

Considerable latitude must be allowed for differences of view as well as for possible peculiar conditions which this court can know but imperfectly, if at all. Otherwise a constitution, instead of embodying only relatively fundamental rules of right, as generally understood by all English-speaking communities, would become the partisan of a particular set of ethical or economical opinions, which by no means are held *semper ubique et ab omnibus.*

Justice Holmes illustrated his point by observing that "No court would declare a usury law unconstitutional, even if every member of it believed that Jeremy Bentham had said the last word on that subject." Not long thereafter he phrased the same thing in another way when speaking of the limitations of the judiciary. "Great constitutional provisions," he said, "must be administered with caution. Some play must be allowed for the joints of the machine, and it must be remembered that the legislatures are ultimate guardians of the liberties and welfare of the people in quite as great a degree as the courts." Holmes believed that "constitutional law, like other mortal contrivances, has to take some chances," and that the "great ordinances of the Constitution do not establish and divide fields of black and white. Even the more specific of them are found to terminate in a penumbra shading gradually from one extreme to the other."

The emphasis of Holmes, it is easy to see, was quite different from Marshall's. The latter, it is true, subscribed to the need for a flexible interpretation of the Constitution, but only to uphold the implied powers of Congress, not to permit the states to indulge in experiments. Marshall was close to the period of the framing of the Constitution, and he did not deal with economic and social conditions, which had altered profoundly in the course of time. Marshall was seeking to establish the power of the new Federal judiciary, while Holmes was concerned to restrain it within some measurable bounds. The whole trouble with the Constitution in Holmes's day was that it had become too flexible—so flexible that the conservative judges were permitted to read their own social and economic views into the sacred document. They could exclaim almost gleefully, "It *is* a Constitution we are expounding!" Holmes was unique in that he pleaded actually for the right of legislative experiment. "Legislation," he said, in one of his most celebrated dicta, "may begin where an evil begins." The thought of Marshall was preoccupied with constitutional clauses like the commerce and the obligation-of-contracts clauses, but the mind of Holmes was dominated by a right that was nowhere expressly mentioned in the Constitution—the right to experiment.

The Fourteenth Amendment was naturally the most frequent target of Justice Holmes's epigrams. The Supreme Court had made it the charter of laissez faire. It conceived the word "liberty" to mean liberty of contract, which it erected into a great dogma against every form of legislative interference with the economic laws which had been recognized as sound by men of property ever since the days of Adam Smith; it conceived of businesses as "property" in order to bring them within the scope of the due-process clause; it finally conceived of "the equal protection of the laws" as an interdiction of every form of legislation which attempted to alter the balance of class power, denouncing such attempts as class legislation. It thus sought to create a constitutional world in which the reigning plutocracy could rest secure, but in which the coming generations would be stultified at birth. The few piddling concessions the Court made to legislative power were only familiar examples of the exercise of the police power.

Justice Holmes created the rallying cries against these attitudes of the majority of the judges. "The Fourteenth Amendment," he declared ironically, when the Supreme Court invalidated a New York law prohibiting employment in bakeries for more than ten hours a day, "does not enact Mr. Herbert Spencer's *Social Statics*," and he added, "A constitution is not intended to embody a particular economic theory, whether of paternalism and the organic relation of the citizen to the state or of *laissez faire.*" In observing that "general propositions do not decide concrete cases," he suggested that the judges were reading their own views into the Constitution and usurping the functions of the legislators. "I recognize without hesitation," he said, "that judges do and must legislate, but they can do so only interstitially; they are confined from molar to molecular motions." Thus judicial legislation should operate only within a narrow scope. In declaring labor legislation to be necessary in order to establish "the equality of position between the parties in which liberty of contract begins," he punctured the dogma of liberty of contract. In another decision, he pointed out that contract "is merely an example of doing what you want to do, embodied in the word liberty. But pretty much all law consists in forbidding men to do some things they want to do, and contract is no more exempt from law than other acts." He chose the conception of a business as "property" to illustrate the "dangers of a delusive exactness" in the application of the Fourteenth Amendment.

By calling a business "property," [he said] you make it seem like land, and lead up to the conclusion that a statute cannot substantially cut down the advantages of ownership existing before the statute was passed. An established business no doubt may have pecuniary value and commonly is protected by law against various unjustified injuries. But you cannot give it definiteness of contour by calling it a thing.

It was in this case, involving an Arizona law prohibiting injunctions in labor disputes that he made another of his famous declarations. "There is nothing that I more deprecate," he said, "than the use of the Fourteenth Amendment beyond the absolute compulsion of its words to prevent the making of social experiments that an important part of the community desires, in the insulated chambers afforded by the several states." The police power he dismissed with his characteristic realism as one of the "apologetic phrases" of American constitutional law.

Justice Holmes's dissents in cases involving civil liberties are among the noblest of his utterances. They stand comparison with passages in Milton's *Areopagitica.* In his own phrase, he knew that "the object of art is to pull the trigger of an emotion." He could see in two pamphlets (protesting against the sending of American troops to Russia in 1917), for the publication of which a sentence of twenty years' imprisonment had been imposed under the Espionage Act, only "poor and puny anonymities to turn the color of legal litmus paper." It seemed to him "perfectly logical" to indulge in "persecution for the expression of opinions. . . . To allow opposition by speech seems to indicate that you think the speech impotent." But, he went on:

When men have realized that time has upset many fighting faiths, they may come to believe even more than they believe the very foundations of their own conduct that the ultimate good desired is better reached by free trade in ideas—that the best test of truth is the power of the thought to get itself accepted in the competition of the market, and that truth is the only ground upon which their wishes safely can be carried out. That at any rate is the theory of our Constitution. It is an experiment, as all life is an experiment.

Even more eloquent, perhaps, was the dissent of Justice Holmes from a judgment upholding a conviction under a New York Criminal Anarchy Act. In refusing to acknowledge the existence of any clear and present danger to the safety of the government in the publication of a left-wing socialist manifesto, he observed:

It is said that this manifesto was more than a theory, that it was an incitement. Every idea is an incitement. It offers itself for belief and if believed it is acted on unless some other belief outweighs it or some failure of energy stifles the movement at its birth. The only difference between the expression of an opinion and an incitement in the narrower sense is the speaker's enthusiasm for the result. Eloquence may set fire to reason. But whatever may be thought of the redundant discourse before us it had no chance of starting a present conflagration.

When a majority of the Supreme Court upheld the government in its revocation of the second-class mailing privilege of Victor Berger's newspaper, the *Milwaukee Leader*, Justice Holmes again dissented and said: "The United States may give up the Post Office when it sees fit, but while it carries it on the use of the mails is almost as much a part of free speech as the right to use our tongues."

The extent to which he is misunderstood is perhaps one of the tests of a great man. It is so easy for him to be all things to all men. In the case of Justice Holmes this misunderstanding took several forms. He was frequently regarded as a stanch liberal, and sometimes even as a wild-eyed radical. In view of the ringing nature of some of his dissents, it is easy to perceive how this misunderstanding arose. But it is particularly difficult to assess the liberalism of a judge, for the legal and political aspects of a question often have no common denominator;

liberalism is a political faith, while legal issues are enmeshed in principles and precedents; thus judges may decide against their personal in-
clinations and sympathies. In fact, Justice Holmes's own social and
economic philosophy was very conservative, especially in the earlier
phases of his career. It became more complex as he grew older, but he
never abandoned the eternal verities of Adam Smith. Not only did he
believe that the Sherman Act was based upon "economic ignorance
and incompetence," but he even doubted that the Interstate Commerce
Commission was a fit body to be entrusted with rate making. He spoke
admiringly of "the originality, the courage, the insight shown by the
great masters of combination," and described Ida Tarbell's *History of
the Standard Oil Company* as a "young woman's tale." He was fond
of saying that when he thought of economic problems, he proceeded
to omit all talk about ownership, and just considered "who eats the
wheat, wears the clothes, uses the railroads, and lives in the houses"—
which was hardly a solution of the problems brought about by the concentration of ownership. He had no use for social nostrums, and he
regarded both socialism and Karl Marx as humbugs. "The notion," he
once said, "that with socialized property we should have women free
and a piano for everybody seems to me an empty humbug." The
socialist argument never seemed to him to get "much farther than look
at the big house and the little one." Even for Brooks Adams, who was
not an orthodox Marxist and who was like himself a member of the
Brahmin aristocracy, he had an amused contempt. He thought that
Brooks Adams treated "the English Church as an accessory to a great
land-grabbing scheme, and the Christian Church in general as belonging to the time when men believed in magic." Even Charles Beard's
book, which did so much to debunk the prevailing Constitution
worship, for which he himself had little use, Holmes denominated "a
covert sneer" at the sacred document. Some of Justice Holmes's remarks
about life, law, and logic sound a lot bolder than they really are. It
must not be forgotten that he began his career as a legal historian, and
that the desire to sweep away historical survivals is not the same as
revolutionary activity.

Another partial misunderstanding of Justice Holmes is to be found
in the tendency to regard him as "a Yankee strayed from Olympus."
There was something of the Olympian in his view of life, but it must
not be supposed that he detached himself from the controversies of
his time or that he did not view them in a realistic light. It is difficult

for a true conservative to be one-hundred-percent Olympian. No one appreciated better the relationship of the Supreme Court of the United States to the contending social forces of his time. Speaking of the court in 1913, he remarked: "We are very quiet there, but it is the quiet of a storm center, as we all know." A pure Olympian could perhaps have defended civil liberties, but it took something of a realist to observe that while "eternal vigilance is the price of freedom . . . to the laboring men eternal hard work is the price of a living." The impression of the Olympianism of Justice Holmes is derived from his judicial utterances, which were cast in grand and noble language. But his everyday humanity is more apparent in his private letters. In his judicial decisions he spoke of "free trade in ideas" and "the power of the thought to get itself accepted in the competition of the market." But in his letters he referred to "the right of an anarchist (so-called) to talk drool in favor of the proletarian dictatorship."

But if Justice Holmes was not entirely the Olympian, freedom from the necessity to engage in bitter economic struggle and a lifetime of reading in the great classics had taught him the rare virtues of tolerance of other men's desires and opinions. His very remoteness from his own age made him tolerant of its foibles and passions. The temper of his mind was skeptical. "When I say that a thing is true," he would frequently remark, "I mean that I can't help believing it." But he respected also the "can't helps" of others and their attempts to translate them into legislation. In private life, skepticism consists of believing nothing. In the aspect of public life which involves the process of constitutional interpretation, skepticism consists of believing almost everything. The wide amplitude of constitutional phrases made him feel that "one who administers constitutional law should multiply his skepticisms." While he himself would have based legislation "upon regrets rather than hopes," others might have a more positive faith. After all, he was a son of Puritan New England, and if there was one well-marked characteristic of the Puritan, it was his eternal readiness to regulate the lives of others. It was an old Puritan idea that "legislation may begin where an evil begins."

Perhaps he himself held more aloof than other judges because, as a Brahmin aristocrat, he had not the slightest doubt of the survival of his class, despite all the programs embodied in social legislation. Perhaps he appreciated better the supremacy of economic over mere human laws. It is highly significant that he once said that the objection to class legislation is that it recoils upon the very class that has secured its enactment. The man who said that really had supreme confidence in the future of his own class. Judges could no more calm the storm in the center of which they sat than Canute could stop the waves. "Judges," he once said, "are apt to be naïf, simple-minded men, and they need something of Mephistopheles. We too need education in the obvious—to learn to transcend our own convictions and to leave room for much that we hold dear to be done away with short of revolution by the orderly change of law." A philosopher had become, if not a king, at least a Supreme Court judge.

But if Holmes was not a radical, he was all the more valuable to the liberal cause. After all, if his championship of social legislation had sprung from partisan motives, there would have been less reason for admiring and applauding him. He would not have been unique in the history of the judicial function. He might have been on the right side so far as liberals were concerned, but he would still have been taking sides. To realize this, it is only necessary to contrast him with Justice Brandeis, with whom, after the latter's appointment to the Supreme Court bench by Woodrow Wilson, he almost invariably became associated in dissent. "Justices Holmes and Brandeis dissenting" replaced "Justice Holmes dissenting." Yet one could hardly think of two men who had less in common, emotionally and intellectually. Indeed, they differed so profoundly that it is rather an ironic commentary on the human mind that they should almost always have arrived at the same conclusions. But the conservatives who moved heaven and earth to block Justice Brandeis's appointment were right from their own selfish point of view.

Justice Brandeis had fought "the curse of bigness" and the manipulation of other people's money, and he was an ardent champion of social legislation. He was as much a partisan as Justices Peckham, Butler, or Sutherland were partisans. He stood for human rights even as they stood for property rights. Justice Holmes himself once observed to his secretary when Brandeis left after a visit: "I'm afraid Brandeis has the crusading spirit. He talks like one of those upward and onward fellows." Nevertheless, there is good reason to think that Justice Brandeis was an important influence in Justice Holmes's intellectual life. Those great dissents of Holmes in which human liberty was reduced to a few simple syllogisms and sanctioned with a few well-chosen epigrams were not unconnected with Brandeis's statistics and economic facts, even though the latter could not get Holmes to read the dismal stuff. Yet Justice Brandeis never achieved the veneration and acclaim of his colleague, and the most important reason, quite apart from the fact that he wrote like an economist rather than a poet, was precisely that he lacked Holmes's judicial objectivity.

Justice Holmes captured the imagination of his contemporaries not only by virtue of the nobility of his philosophy but also by virtue of the colorfulness of his personality. Judges only too often are likely to behave like stuffed shirts, but Justice Holmes always made good copy. The son of the crotchety doctor who kept a rattlesnake in a cage at home, Justice Holmes was full of mild pranks and a sly humor and was never too greatly concerned over the conventionalities of the judicial office. He read not only Latin and Greek literature, but risqué French novels; not only Plato and Aristotle, but *Nize Baby* and *Gentlemen Prefer Blondes*. Yet he refused to read the daily newspapers, steadfastly maintaining that it was a waste of time! One of his favorite sayings was: "Life is like an artichoke. You pull out a day, only an hour or two is available for spiritual thoughts." He loved to watch jugglers, and he went to burlesque shows. At a particularly raw one he is said to have exclaimed to a stranger at his side: "Thank God that I am a man of such low tastes." Later in life he learned to ride a bicycle and debated with mock humorous gravity whether it was a seemly diversion for a judge. He had on his side the authority of the celebrated Dr. Johnson, who excluded from the amusements becoming to a judge only "chucking farthings in the piazza." Even when past sixty, Justice Holmes used to run to fires with his wife. There is a cycle of Holmes stories almost as rich as the Arthurian legend. It may well be that the Justice's love of amusement had a great deal to do with his tolerance of social experiments. By dismissing them as soon as possible from his mind, he was able to get back to his books and foibles.

In the home of Justice Holmes at 1700 I Street in Washington, D. C., which in time became a sort of national shrine, there hung beneath the chandelier in the well-stocked library a toy skeleton which Mrs. Holmes would sometimes agitate when twitting the Justice about his age. He was accustomed to say that he would resign from the bench only when work ceased to be fun but, as he wrote to a friend in 1924, "Time is like judicial legislation. It works interstitially—but from six months to six months it shows results." He resigned in 1932 and died in 1935. It is rather ironic to think that the bitterest cries arose against the "nine old men" in the decades when one of the noblest of old men sat upon the bench.

A conservative majority was still entrenched in the Supreme Court when the New Deal of Franklin Roosevelt was swept into power. As the Court killed the NRA and the AAA, it seemed as if the ferment injected into American constitutional law by Justice Holmes had been in vain. Indeed, it seemed that he had done more harm than good with his dissents, by filling the common man with hope and giving him the impression that he was not playing against loaded dice. The twilight zone of the Constitution seemed to spell the twilight of American civilization. But after the President's famous "horse and buggy" interview and his threat to pack the Supreme Court, the old men, in Mr. Dooley's famous phrase, began to follow the election returns and to uphold what only yesterday they had condemned. The death or resignation of some of the justices made it possible virtually to reconstitute the Court, and the constitutional doctrines of Justice Holmes, with their emphasis upon legislative autonomy, were no longer dissenting but prevailing opinions.

Justice Holmes was not only the greatest American judge but that almost mythological figure, the perfect constitutional censor. The perfect censor is, however, a contradiction in terms, for to fill the role is really to abdicate the function. Perfect constitutional censors would find some reason to justify almost any legislative act and, if judicial review was to serve the purpose for which it had been created, they would soon be replaced by less than perfect censors. The institution of unlimited judicial review itself remains as a source of future mischief. Whether American Federalism would ever have survived without it must always remain a speculative historical question.

Certainly American Federalism has been a success, but it has nevertheless been purchased at a price—a bloody civil war. The experience suggests that an international order purchased at such a price would be bought very dearly. A facile optimism would be even less justified with regard to the future of law, with which the more universal aspect of the career of Justice Holmes is bound up. Great as Oliver Wendell Holmes was as a man and a judge, he was not God, and it must not be forgotten that one judge does not make a bench any more than one swallow makes a summer.

At least the immediate future of law in a world that is still threatened by fascism, despite its defeat on the battlefield, is none too bright.

Fascism has denied that a society in which conflicting interests are permitted to work out their destinies can exist. The gospel of Holmes has no place in the philosophy of Hitlerism. Before Hitler was born, Holmes had said that the "tacit assumption of the solidarity of the interests of society is very common, but seems to me to be false." Indeed, the profound faith of Holmes in "the free trade of ideas" was only the most magnificent part of his faith in the system of free competition with its perpetual clash of interests.

Yet the gospel of law as a balancing of interests, which itself reflected the chaotic social struggle of the past decades, was responsible for the skepticisms and confusions of free law and realism and the dogmatisms of communism and fascism. If law were a scheme of reconciling interests in accordance with the dictates of some social end, it could best be administered by the enlightened judge, whose hands were no longer bound by rule and precedent. But to free the judge was impossible for the very reason that the interests which clashed were so violently opposed to each other. Such a scheme was possible only in a just society in which every man did not mistrust his neighbor and did not fear those who wielded political power. The system of free law, which went under the name of equity, had been possible only in an age of political absolutism; but it, too, had hardened into rule and precedent. Something of the same fate has overtaken the new administrative agencies, created in the flight from the traditional courts, which have tended to become bound by red tape (the name for administrative precedent). The attempt made in recent decades in the name of criminological positivism to achieve flexibility in the administration of the criminal law has been carried out for the most part only on paper. The contradictions of the philosophy of interests were only working themselves out in the structure of the legal order. Even the philosophy of Marxism found corroboration in its teachings. The Marxist conceded that the concern of the judge was with interests, but he asserted that they were class interests. Then came the fascist who, made aware of the conflict of interests, proceeded to eliminate them all.

The very recognition of the social ends of law paradoxically multiplied the doubts and increased the confusion. When the law was deemed to adjudicate only private interests, to decide between two individual litigants in a controversy in which society itself had no stake, it was possible to be tolerant of its failures, to believe in the reality of precedents, to respect the objectivity of the judge. But as soon as the tremendous stake of society itself in every legal controversy, private as well as public, was realized, many began to doubt that the law could stand the strain. The very intensity of the conflict of interests was bound to compromise, if not to prevent entirely, the true achievement of social ends and the socialization of law, which seemed to be so much desired, at least as an abstract goal.

In the atomic age, with its threat of the destruction of civilization, it seems more than ever that a way must be found to curb the irresponsible power of national states. World government seems to imply a system of world law rather than the freedom of action which now obtains in the Security Council of the United Nations. But law itself has worked successfully thus far only in curbing the conduct of individuals. Labor unions, great corporations, associations, federal states—in fact, any great aggregates of persons, power, or capital—have never been satisfactorily subjected to the rule of law. The first great legal discovery made by men was that the reign of law required the disassociation of the social atom. They succeeded in breaking up the clans, but they only substituted for them the omnipotent state. Of course, sovereign states, too, are composed of individuals, but as long as they have the backing of sovereign states the reign of law is still a dream of the future. Thus far, extended periods of peace have occurred only when one state became so powerful that it dominated all the rest. But the hegemony of no state has been maintained forever. A universal conquest would be possible only if the monopoly of atomic power could be preserved, but no weapon has remained a secret for long. Twentieth-century man with his rich cultural and economic heritage, is a particular unpromising victim of conquest and enslavement.

As a matter of fact, while the application of sanctions seems the most obvious characteristic of an effective system of law, early courts often had to rely upon the voluntary acceptance of their judgments, and even in this day the observance of rules of law by individuals is to a large extent voluntary. Thus far international law in its development has attempted to ape the course of evolution to be traced in municipal law. Attempts have been made to set up courts and increasingly to bring about the application of sanctions. The future may show that this has been a mistake and that world law can be established only upon a voluntaristic basis. It may be a hopeful circumstance that the Security Council of the United Nations is an administrative rather than a judicial body, whose procedure is flexible and whose decisions are not dictated by hard and fixed precedents. On the other hand, it may be that eventually the great powers will consent to accept certain limited, but nevertheless definite, constitutional limitations. This comfort may perhaps be drawn from the history of American Federalism, but no one may assume the mantle of prophecy except at his peril.

At least, as Justice Holmes himself has said: "This day marks the fact that all thought is social." Behind the threat of universal catastrophe, behind all the confusions of the competing faiths, there remains a central drive to deal with human relationships by some method more suitable to the age of science than the means of allaying the primitive blood-feud. To quote Justice Holmes for the last time: "For the rational study of the law, the black-letter man may be the man of the present, but the man of the future is the man of statistics and the master of economics." He might have added also the man of science. When a scientific method is introduced into the ordering of the relations of men in society, it will become a system of technological relationships rather than a scheme of variable and arbitrary rules and precedents. But if this happens, the law, at least as we know it today, will have disappeared, for it will have ceased to be purely normative: it may describe rather than prescribe conduct. There was no law in primitive societies, and there may be no law in the scientific society of the future in the sense in which we think of law today. For such a society to become a reality, humanity may have to do more than merely reconcile conflicting interests. It may have to solve the social and economic problems which create these conflicts. Whether this will prove possible by contemporary legal methods, whether socialization can be accomplished without violence and the rending of the fabric of society, must depend in large part upon the number of men who are like Holmes. If, as in the case of Federalism, the very crux of any world order may be the machinery for the distribution of power, the success of world government may depend upon men who believe in the value of social experiment and are capable of the supreme virtue of objectivity.

Index

and other interests, as preparation for the *Commentaries*, 191–2; flirtation with the muses, and composition of "The Lawyer's Farewell to His Muse," 192–3; decides to study law and enters the Middle Temple, 192, 194; compares common law to disordered edifice in letter to Seymour Richmond, 194; takes a degree at Oxford as Bachelor of Civil Law, 194; activities as Oxford don, 194, 195; called to the bar at the Middle Temple but fails at practice, 195; appointed Recorder of Wallingford, 195; leads life of practicing lawyer through friendship with Mansfield, 195–6; has romantic adventure at party at Inns of Court, 196; fails in attempt to secure appointment as Regius Professor of Civil Law at Oxford, 197; on advice of Mansfield determines to lecture at Oxford on the common law, 197; announcement of lectures, 198; popularity of lectures, 198–9; appointed first Vinerian Professor of the Laws of England as result of Charles Viner's bequest, 199; adroitness of inaugural lecture as professor, 199–201; revival of his practice, 201; refuses appointment as Chief Justice of the Court of Common Pleas of Ireland, 202; elected member of Parliament from Hindon, 202; marriage to Sarah Clitherow, and settlement at Wallingford as country squire, 202; develops habits and diseases of English gentlemen, 202–3; composes *Commentaries*, 203; elected to Parliament again from Westbury, 203; his opinion on prior expulsion in Wilkes controversy causes his humiliation and retirement from Parliament, 203–4; appointed judge of Court of Common Pleas, 204; service as judge, 204; death of, 204; obituary, 204; contemporary critics of, 204–5; description of his Commentaries, 205–10; as involuntary law reformer, 210–11
Blasco, Colonel Domenico di, 214
Blasco, Teresa, wife of Beccaria, 213–14, 217, 218–19

Blood-feud, in primitive societies, 4–6, 7; in Babylonia, 27; in Homeric Greece, 33; in England, 127; and objective of a world order, 355
Blood money, 6
Blood relationship, 6
Bloody Jeffreys, 222, 262
Blues and Greens, circus factions of Constantinople, 74, 76, 80, 81, 82
Bologna, law school of, 89
Bonham's Case, 181, 186
Boule, or Council of Four Hundred, in Athens, 40, 44
Bowood Castle, 244, 245
Bowring, John, disciple of Bentham, 245
Boxing match, as a primitive procedure, 6
Bracton, 167, 177, 239
Braddock's defeat, 276
Bradstreet, Anne, 336
Brahmin caste, 335, 336
Brandeis, Louis D., 328–9, 350–51
Brandywine, 278
Brasenose College, Oxford, 146
Bribery, of officials in Babylon, 21
Bride price, in Babylonia, 25
Brigandage, in Code of Hammurabi, 27
Brissot de Warrille, Jacques-Pierre, 248
British debts, payment of, 281, 282, 288
Britton, 167
Browning Hill, 237, 238
Bruce, Edward, Lord Kinlosse, 151–2
Bruce, Robert, 137
Bubonic plague, in Constantinople, 88
Buckingham, George Villiers, Duke of, 156, 179, 180, 184
Buckley, Justice Sir Henry Burton, and obituary of equity, 161
Buffalo police, of Plains Indians, 3
Buffon, George Louis Leclerc, 213
Builders, treatment of, in Code of Hammurabi, 27
Bülow, Oskar, 315, 317, 318, 329
Burdett, Sir William, 251
Burghley, William Cecil, Baron, 141, 149, 170
Burgh-on-Sands, 139
Burial charges, in Lagash, 18
Burke, Edmund, 167, 250

256, 306, 307, 308–10, 311, 315, 324, 327
Juristic concepts, 70, 71, 306, 319, 320–21, 324, 327, 328, 329, 330
Juristic literature, 311, 320
Juristic person, 71, 267
Juristic personality, 319
Jurists, Roman, 52–6, 60–61, 68–72, 79, 82–4, 109
Jury, 129, 130, 145, 159, 186, 201, 208, 210, 222, 223–4, 226, 227, 261, 262, 266, 285
Justice of the peace, 9, 133, 190, 201, 222, 286
Justice, origin of, 7
Justiciar, 142
Justin, birth, 73; departure for Constantinople, 73; enlistment in Imperial guard, 73; marriage to Euphemia, 73; adoption of Petrus Sabbatius Justinianus, 73–4; becomes Emperor of the East, 75; character of reign of, 76; death of, 77; legislates on impounding corpse of debtor, 86
Justin of Nassau, 95
Justinian, Emperor of the East, birth, 74; adoption by uncle Justin, 74; journey from Tauresium to Constantinople, 74; education of, 74; role in making Justin Emperor, 75; role in Byzantine Empire during life of Justin, 76; marriage to Theodora, 76; accession to throne, 77; resolves to restore glories of Roman Empire, 77; ecclesiastical policy of, 77; motives for undertaking restoration, 78; vanity of, 78; ministers and servants of, 78–9; conquests of, 79; resolves to restore Roman law, 79–80; interruption of project by Nika Sedition, 80; suppression of revolt, 81–2; role in codification of Roman law, 82–4; original legislation of, 86; Persian wars, and destruction of Gothic Kingdom by, 88; conspiracy against, 88; death of, 88; fate of codification of, 88–90; compared with Edward I, 117, 120, 126

Kant, Immanuel, 311
Kassites, and invasion of land of the Two Rivers, 28

Kaunitz, Wenzel Antoin, Prince von, 214
Keeper of the Great Seal, 141, 142, 144, 145, 148, 149, 171
Keith, Mary, 276
Kenilworth, 122
Kent, James, 295, 339
Kings, and customs, 7; as chief judges, 9; in Greece, 33; in Rome, 49, 50; and fashioning of legal systems, 116–17; in Blackstone's Commentaries, 209
King's Council, in England, proclaims peace of Edward I, in absence of king, 124; as reservoir of administrative energy, 128; and proceedings in local courts, 129; Chancellor as member of, 142; petitions to, 144; commitments to prison by, 174
King's peace, 117, 124, 134, 136, 144, 221
Kinship solidarity, 53
Kish, Sumerian city, 17, 18
Knightley, William and Winifred, 165
Kyrbeis, 32

Labeo, 55, 56
Labor, and the law, 342, 343
Labor, concept of, in political economy, compared with concept of struggle in law, 322
Labor contract, in Roman law, 69–70
Labor unions, 354
La Combe, French tutor of Jeremy Bentham, 239
Lagash, Sumerian city, 17
Laissez faire, 224, 234, 235, 254, 255, 261, 307, 345, 346
Lambertszoon, Jan, and escape of Grotius, 104
Land, as security for debt in Athens, 38–9
Land grants, 293, 294
Land law, in England, 129, 133, 134, 157, 200, 205, 264, 270
Land of the Two Rivers, 16, 33
Land ownership, in Athens, 34, 39, 44, 46
Land speculation, 280–81, 292–3
Land tenure, in Babylonia, 25
Larsam, rival of Babylon, 19, 22
Lateran Council of 1215, 219
Latin America, and fame of Jeremy Bentham, 245, 248, 249

382